Inequality and Growth in Modern China

UNU WORLD INSTITUTE FOR DEVELOPMENT ECONOMICS RESEARCH (UNU-WIDER) was established by the United Nations University as its first research and training centre and started work in Helsinki, Finland, in 1985. The purpose of the Institute is to undertake applied research and policy analysis on structural changes affecting developing and transitional economies, to provide a forum for the advocacy of policies leading to robust, equitable, and environmentally sustainable growth, and to promote capacity strengthening and training in the field of economic and social policymaking. Its work is carried out by staff researchers and visiting scholars in Helsinki and via networks of collaborating scholars and institutions around the world.

World Institute for Development Economics Research (UNU-WIDER)
Katajanokanlaituri 6 B, FIN-00160 Helsinki, Finland
www.wider.unu.edu

Inequality and Growth in Modern China

Edited by
Guanghua Wan

A study prepared for the World Institute for Developement Economics Research of the United Nations University (UNU-WIDER)

OXFORD
UNIVERSITY PRESS

Great Clarendon Street, Oxford OX2 6DP

Oxford University Press is a department of the University of Oxford.
It furthers the University's objective of excellence in research, scholarship,
and education by publishing worldwide in

Oxford New York

Auckland Cape Town Dar es Salaam Hong Kong Karachi
Kuala Lumpur Madrid Melbourne Mexico City Nairobi
New Delhi Shanghai Taipei Toronto

With offices in

Argentina Austria Brazil Chile Czech Republic France Greece
Guatemala Hungary Italy Japan Poland Portugal Singapore
South Korea Switzerland Thailand Turkey Ukraine Vietnam

Oxford is a registered trade mark of Oxford University Press
in the UK and in certain other countries

Published in the United States
by Oxford University Press Inc., New York

© United Nations University—World Institute for
Development Economics Research (UNU-WIDER) 2008

The moral rights of the authors have been asserted
Database right Oxford University Press (maker)

First published 2008

All rights reserved. No part of this publication may be reproduced,
stored in a retrieval system, or transmitted, in any form or by any means,
without the prior permission in writing of Oxford University Press,
or as expressly permitted by law, or under terms agreed with the appropriate
reprographics rights organization. Enquiries concerning reproduction
outside the scope of the above should be sent to the Rights Department,
Oxford University Press, at the address above

You must not circulate this book in any other binding or cover
and you must impose the same condition on any acquirer

British Library Cataloguing in Publication Data

Data available

Library of Congress Cataloging in Publication Data

Data available

Typeset by SPI Publisher Services, Pondicherry, India
Printed in Great Britain
on acid-free paper by
Biddles Ltd., King's Lynn, Norfolk

ISBN 978-0-19-953519-4

1 3 5 7 9 10 8 6 4 2

Foreword

Alongside its remarkable record of growth, China has experienced a dramatic rise in inequality in the period of reform since 1980. At present, every dimension of inequality matches or surpasses that in India and approaches the levels seen in Latin America where inequality has been notoriously high and may have adversely affected economic performance. Special concern has been directed at regional disparities and the rural–urban divide in China, which is perceived as undermining the social stability and legitimacy of the ruling communist party.

From an international perspective, rising inequality in China slows down poverty eradication and threatens the Millennium Development Goals. It has also contributed to sluggish domestic demand since the late 1990s, adding to the pressure to export, and hence increasing the likelihood of trade disputes with both developing and developed countries.

While there is a reasonable body of research on inequality in China, most published studies focus on measurement issues. Less attention has been given to the causes and consequences of rising inequality, which need to be understood before policy initiatives can be undertaken. This volume, arising from a UNU-WIDER project on Inequality and Poverty in China, aims to help fill these gaps in the literature. It contains a selection of chapters originally presented as papers at two project conferences, one in Beijing in April 2005 and the other in Helsinki in August 2005. Prominent economists including Justin Lin, Kai-Yuen Tsui, Shi Li, and Xiaolu Wang are among the contributors who examine topics such as the growth–inequality nexus, the applicability of the Kuznets hypothesis to China, the impact of development strategies on inequality, and the role of geographical factors, financial deepening, schooling, and innovation capabilities in driving the inequality trend in China.

The chapters in this collection employ data carefully assembled from a variety of sources and apply state of the art techniques to the analysis, ensuring that the main findings are reliable and robust. The volume will be viewed as a core reference by the growing number of academics, students, policymakers, and others interested in the level and trend of poverty and inequality in China.

Anthony Shorrocks
Director, UNU-WIDER, Helsinki

Acknowledgements

In December 2006 the *Journal of Comparative Economics* (vol. 34, no. 4) published symposium articles on 'Analyzing the Socioeconomic Consequences of Rising Inequality in China' guest edited by Guanghua Wan and Xiaobo Zhang. Chapter 1 in this present volume 'The Inequality–Growth Nexus in the Short and Long Run: Empirical Evidence from China' by Guanghua Wan, Ming Lu, and Zhao Chen, was included in the symposium (pp. 654–67) and UNU-WIDER and the authors kindly acknowledge the *Journal of Comparative Economics*, the Association of Comparative Economic Studies, and Elsevier Inc. for inclusion of the revised (after this volume reviewers' comments) paper.

The Review of Income and Wealth (series 53, no. 1, March 2007) comprised a special issue on 'Inequality and Poverty in China' guest edited by Guanghua Wan, and included the original version of Chapter 5: 'Forces Shaping China's Interprovincial Inequality' by Kai-yuen Tsui (pp. 60–92). UNU-WIDER and the author kindly acknowledge *The Review of Income and Wealth*, the International Association for Research in Income and Wealth, and Blackwell Publishing for inclusion of the revised (after this volume reviewers' comments) paper.

Special thanks to John Bonin, Bart van Ark, and Stephan Klasen for their ongoing support of research from UNU-WIDER and facilitating publication.

The editor would like to thank several anonymous referees for their detailed and timely reports, which were invaluable in shaping the book. I acknowledge the generous assistance given by Cai Fang and Xu Jin, the Institute of Population Studies of the Chinese Academy of Social Sciences, and Barbara Fagerman of UNU-WIDER in overseeing the project activities that took place in China. Adam Swallow of UNU-WIDER provided various assistance for which I am grateful. Thanks to Lorraine Telfer-Taivainen of UNU-WIDER for formatting and preparing the manuscript. Finally, I owe a great deal to Project Assistant, Janis Vehmaan-Kreula of UNU-WIDER, who provided tremendous help in running the China project.

UNU-WIDER gratefully acknowledges the financial contributions to the research programme by the governments of Denmark (Royal Ministry of Foreign Affairs), Finland (Ministry for Foreign Affairs), Norway (Royal Ministry of Foreign Affairs), Sweden (Swedish International Development Cooperation Agency—Sida), and the United Kingdom (Department for International Development).

Contents

Preface ix
List of Figures xvi
List of Tables xviii
List of Acronyms and Abbreviations xx
Notes on Contributors xxi

1. The Inequality–Growth Nexus in the Short and Long Run: Empirical Evidence from China
   Guanghua Wan, Ming Lu, and Zhao Chen   1

2. Income Inequality in China and its Influencing Factors
   Xiaolu Wang   18

3. Poverty Reduction in China: Trends and Causes
   Yin Zhang and Guanghua Wan   33

4. Development Strategies and Regional Income Disparities in China
   Justin Yifu Lin and Peilin Liu   56

5. Forces Shaping China's Interprovincial Inequality
   Kai-yuen Tsui   79

6. Financial Development, Growth, and Regional Disparity in Post-Reform China
   Zhicheng Liang   112

7. Spatial Convergence in China: 1952–99
   Patricio A. Aroca, Dong Guo, and Geoffrey J. D. Hewings   125

8. China's Regional Inequality in Innovation Capability: 1995–2004
   Peilei Fan and Guanghua Wan   144

9. Widening Gap of Educational Opportunity? A Study of the Changing Patterns of Educational Attainment in China
   Min-Dong Paul Lee   163

Contents

10. Poverty Accounting by Factor Components: With an Empirical Illustration Using Rural Chinese Data
    Guanghua Wan   184

Index   205

Preface

Guanghua Wan

P.1 Introduction

It is accepted that growth helps reduce poverty without a worsening distribution of income and that income inequality is positively correlated with poverty in the absence of economic growth (Bourguignon 2004). The real world, of course, does not operate that way. Typically, growth (negative or positive) and inequality changes (rising or declining) occur simultaneously, making it difficult to disentangle their separate effects on poverty. Moreover, the relationship between growth and inequality is complex. There exist many channels through which economic growth may affect income or welfare distribution. Meanwhile, future growth and poverty profile depend on the current level and dynamics of inequality. The well-known Kuznets hypothesis has been tested in countless cases, and yet no consensus has been reached regarding the impact of growth on inequality. On the other hand, a large literature has recently emerged which aims at explaining the mechanisms and consequences of changing inequality on growth (Banerjee and Duflo 2003). Again, no conclusion can be drawn so far. Clearly, much research, theoretical as well as empirical, is called for in order to better understand the poverty–growth–inequality (PGI) triangle. Such a lack of understanding on the triangle poses a challenge or dilemma to development strategists and policymakers: should growth or inequality be prioritized in the design and execution of economic policies?

Post-reform China serves as one of the best examples to illustrate the dilemma. Starting with the household production responsibility system in the rural areas, the Chinese economy has been experiencing near double digit growth over the past three decades. Such a remarkable growth record has helped to lift millions of farmers out of poverty, particularly in the 1980s and early 1990s. At the same time, however, inequality in terms of income or other welfare indicators has risen dramatically at the inter-person, inter-region, or inter-sector level (Wan 2007). The increasing inequality must have contributed to the recent slowdown in poverty reduction in rural areas and to

Preface

the emergence of urban poverty in China since the economy has maintained its growth rate throughout the post-reform period. Further, China's growth prospect seems to hinge on the inequality profile as the increased inequality is perceived to undermine China's social and political stability, which undoubtedly have repercussions for economic growth. Particularly worth mentioning is the huge urban–rural gap which narrowed down during 1979–85 and has since grown unabated. This gap, along with the coast–inland divide, are responsible for the sluggish domestic demand which is putting pressure on China's economic growth.

Clearly, analysing inequality and growth in the case of China is not only interesting as described above, but also important for a number of reasons. First, China's achievement in poverty reduction has been astonishing; the absolute poor, mostly living in rural areas, was cut down from 300 million in the early 1980s to 30 million at the turn of the millennium. This significantly altered the global poverty picture. Whether or not the Millennium Development Goals of the United Nations can be achieved depends, to a large extent, on the future progress in China's fight against poverty, which in turn is determined by income growth and inequality changes in both rural and urban China. Second, China's growth prospects and the inequality related domestic demand have profound implications for the US, EU, and other economies. To say the least, an expanded demand inside China will help to ease the tension over China's huge trade surplus and over the ever growing trade disputes. To increase the domestic demand, policy measures must be taken to reverse the rising trend in inequality. Finally, a better understanding of China's inequality and growth experiences, both successes and failures, may help international organizations and other national governments in tackling the poverty–growth–inequality (PGI) triangle.

It is thus not surprising that there exist many studies on the issues of growth, inequality, and, more recently, poverty in China. Most growth studies are concerned with sources and mechanisms of growth such as the impacts of reforms, FDI, total factor productivity, trade and so on. Regarding inequality, earlier research mostly focused on measurement of regional inequality. This is followed by inequality decompositions aiming at gauging the broad compositions of regional inequality. More recently, attention is being turned to analysing inequality at the disaggregated levels of counties, villages, households, and even individuals. Relative to the growth and inequality issues, less has been done on poverty, partly because poverty study requires household level data, which are rather limited for China.

Early research efforts certainly help enrich our understanding of the PGI triangle in China. However, the current literature tackles the triangle separately despite the fact that they are entangled together. For example, little is known about the short and long run impacts of rising inequality on China's growth (Chapter 1 in this volume). Also, the contributions of growth and

Preface

inequality to poverty or poverty changes are seldom examined (Chapter 3 in this volume). Even taking poverty, growth, and inequality individually, more research is needed. For example, the existing literature is silent on the root sources or causes of the rising inequality and the slowdown in poverty reductions in China. In particular, it is useful to quantify the relative contributions of relevant factors to inequality and poverty. As another example, inequality has been typically analysed in terms of income and consumption. But, education is at least as important as income in determining human well being in China.

It is against the above background that in 2004 the World Institute for Development Economics Research of the United Nations University (UNU-WIDER) launched the project on Inequality and Poverty in China. Two international conferences were held under this project: one in Beijing in April 2005 (co-hosted by the Institute of Population and Labour Economics, Chinese Academy of Social Sciences) and the other in Helsinki in August 2005. Some 40 papers written in English were selected from over 300 submissions and were presented at these conferences. This volume is part of the output of the project, which focuses on inequality, poverty, and growth in China. Issues addressed include regional/personal variation in incomes and other human well being indicators, the gap between the coastal regions (which have strongly benefited from the expansion of China's exports) and the interior regions, and the urban–rural disparity. Also examined are roles played by various factors in shaping the poverty–growth–inequality picture, including policy biases, resource endowment, location factors, financial development, and total factor productivity.

A distinctive feature of this collected volume is the use of alternative datasets; both aggregated (secondary) and household level (first-hand) data are used. Also, data from government sources (e.g. National Bureau of Statistics and Ministry of Agriculture), as well as research projects (e.g. the China Household Income Project, CHIP, and the China Household Nutrition Survey, CHNS) are employed by different contributors. Such diverse databases offer a more comprehensive picture on inequality and poverty in China, and to some extent, may help make research findings more robust. Nevertheless, some inconsistency is not unexpected with the use of different datasets.

P.2 Chapters in this Volume

The book starts with the chapter by Wan, Lu, and Chen, which tackles the inequality–growth interrelationship. This is the most fundamental relationship in the PGI triangle and represents one of the most controversial issues in the current growth literature. The authors introduce the polynomial inverse lag model in a system of equations framework so to enable analysing the impact of

Preface

growth on inequality, and vice versa. A particular innovation of the chapter lies in the simultaneous identification and measurement of these impacts in one unified framework and for any time horizon: short, medium, or long run. Fitting the model to aggregated province level panel data from China, it is found that inequality is harmful to growth no matter what time horizon is considered and that the growth–inequality relationship is non-linear. However, growth does not seem to affect inequality in China.

In the second chapter, which is complementary to the first one, Wang focuses on the impact of growth on inequality by directly testing the Kuznets hypothesis using Chinese data of 1996–2002. He attempts to address the question, 'What factors help to increase or reduce inequality?' Major findings from this study include (1) growth and inequality are positively correlated, predicting further rises in income inequality in China in the short and medium run—in other words, the Kuznets hypothesis is rejected in the case of China; (2) job creation and investment in infrastructure are crucial for bridging the urban–rural gap and for reducing inequality, especially in the rural areas; and (3) fiscal transfer seems to exert little or regressive effects on inequality, implying government policy failure and the need to develop the social security system in both urban and rural China.

What about the impacts of growth and inequality on poverty? The third chapter by Zhang and Wan introduces the newly developed Shapley value technique to disentangle the contributions to poverty changes made by income growth and income inequality, respectively. Relying on the popular Foster–Greer–Thorbecke measures, poverty and its changes are computed and decomposed under different datasets and alternative assumptions about poverty lines and equivalence scales. The analyses show that both income growth and favourable distributional changes can explain China's remarkable achievement in combating poverty in rural areas in the first half of the 1990s. However, in the second half of the 1990s, both rural and urban China suffered from rapidly rising inequality and stagnant income growth, leading to a slowdown in poverty reduction, and even to a reversal in the poverty trend.

The next four chapters deal with income inequality across regions in China. Lin and Liu, in Chapter 4, focus on the impact of China's development strategies on regional inequality. Development strategies are classified as comparative advantage defying (CAD) or comparative advantage following (CAF). They conclude that poor regions generally followed CAD by adopting capital intensive technologies while affluent regions followed CAF by emphasizing the development of labor intensive industries. Therefore, different development strategies are responsible for the increased disparities in China. The authors believe that China's accession to WTO has forced the adoption of the principle of comparative advantage as a guideline for the future development of the national economy. As a consequence, the trend of widening regional disparities will be abated.

Preface

The majority of studies on China's inequality focus on its level despite the fact that it is also useful to explain changes in the level of inequality. The latter is the focus of Chaper 5 by Tsui who proposes a framework under which a change in total inequality can be expressed as a sum of changes in spatial variations in the growth of total factor productivity (TFP) and in factor inputs. Applying this technique to China, it is found that the increase in regional inequality from the mid-1960s to the mid-1970s is mainly due to the contribution of TFP overwhelming that of physical capital. The opposite is true for the 1980s. The increase in the 1990s is mainly driven by the skewed distribution of investment in favour of the richer coastal provinces reinforced by the increasing contribution of TFP.

Just as growth strategy, TFP and factor inputs affect regional inequality, so does financial development. Liang, in Chapter 6, examines the impact of financial deepening on regional growth for coastal and inland regions, respectively. For coastal regions, financial deepening, particularly lending to the private sector, tends to facilitate economic growth. However, central bank lending to the provincial governments is found to be negatively correlated with economic growth, thus a decline in the level of government intervention in credit allocation may promote economic growth. For the inland regions, most financial indicators are insignificant in explaining growth. These results suggest that the weak finance–growth linkage in the less-developed regions had contributed to the coast–inland gap in China. Therefore, it is imperative to initiate policy measures to improve the efficiency of capital allocation and investments in inland areas.

Using the non-parametric methods of kernel density function and Markov chain analysis, the focus of Chapter 7, by Aroca, Guo, and Hewings, is on growth convergence for the period 1952–99, with a special emphasis on spatial interactions among the Chinese regions. The interactions are found to have grown since 1978 and become stronger since 1991. Beijing and Shanghai seem to have become the so-called 'hot spots'. In terms of the density function of per capita GDP, the year 1957 clearly saw a one-peak distribution with a long flat right tail. For 1978, there were several peaks in the tail. It exhibited a tendency to move towards the twin peaks shape in 1999. These imply that China's regional income distribution had moved from convergence to stratification and from stratification to polarization, confirming the new economic geography's prediction—a sharp polarization in the presence of high interregional transportation costs.

So far inequality has been explored in terms of income variables. The next two chapters deviate from the common practice by turning attention to regional inequalities in innovation capability and education. Obviously, both underlie income inequality. The contribution by Fan and Wan (Chapter 8) addresses two sets of research questions: first, what was the trend of China's regional inequality in innovation capability and how did it change from 1995 to 2004? Second, how much did the relevant factors contribute to the regional inequality in innovation

Preface

capability? Empirical results demonstrate that the east–central–west inequality has increased over time, whereas the inter-provincial inequality decreased from 1995 to 2000, but increased from 2000 to 2004. Utilizing a recently developed regression-based inequality decomposition technique, it is revealed that major factors driving the inequality trends are location, industrialization and urbanization, human capital, and openness (foreign direct investment). Also, unbalanced development in high-tech parks exerts a growing power in explaining innovation disparity in China.

In Chapter 9, Lee presents a picture on the distribution of educational attainment in China. He also tests the urban bias hypothesis. The study finds that rapid expansion of education in the last decade has benefited younger students and helped to eliminate gender bias against girls. However, school enrolment data show persistent and deteriorating regional inequality. Students from inland provinces suffer from lack of educational opportunity, and this becomes more pronounced as they progress to higher grades. Finally, a decomposition analysis indicates that the causes of inter-provincial educational inequality are quite complex and cannot simply be explained by the urban bias hypothesis.

The book ends with Chapter 10 by Wan who argues that in reality policymakers must face the vital and pragmatic question, 'What output or, more fundamentally, what factor growth or redistribution is more crucial for poverty eradication—physical capital, human capital, or other inputs?' Simply saying 'promoting growth' or 'reducing inequality' is far from sufficient. Towards answering these questions, Wan develops a procedure for attributing total poverty at a given point in time to components associated with income generating factors or resources. Another procedure is proposed to attribute a change in poverty to the growth and redistribution effects of individual income generating factors. These procedures are applied to a set of data from rural China, demonstrating that redistribution is more important than growth as a policy instrument in combating poverty.

P.3 Suggestions for Future Work

Limited space allows only a small selection of papers to be included here and many issues remain unexplored. First, there is an urgent need to study the impact of incomplete reforms on inequality and poverty. Sector segregation was rather minimal in pre-reform China in terms of wage structure. As wage setting has decentralized while monopoly power has developed in some sectors due to incomplete reform or lack of second generation reform, salary gaps across sectors have increased significantly. In earlier days, bank staff were highly paid. Now, those working in telecommunications or energy related sectors are being overremunerated. It would be important and interesting to analysis this kind of impact and its role in affecting poverty and inequality outcomes.

Second, the consequences of the rising inequality seem to have been overlooked by the research community. This is rather disappointing given the increasing coverage of inequality related incidents in the public media. For example, rural migrants are being blamed for crime increases in urban China. However, few realize that a main root cause of this is unacceptable levels of inequality between urban residents and immigrants in income and access to school, healthcare, and many other benefits. As another example, Chinese society is overwhelmingly shocked by two phenomena which are recently exposed to the public: student prostitution and student homicide. Both are known to grow out of relative deprivation and envy, but debates on these phenomena are seldom, if ever, placed in the context of inequality and poverty.

Third, the size of the middle-class in China is considered to be crucial for the stability of the country, and its dynamics may impinge on political reforms. Yet, analytical studies have not appeared which provide an assessment of the middle-class population, its composition, and relevant dynamics. Given the huge difference in political strength, it is necessary to examine rural and urban China separately, taking into account the urbanization process. Clearly, such work awaits nationwide household or individual data which are not publicly available.

Finally, it is imperative to evaluate policy recommendations or policy measures from research outputs in terms of feasibility and results. As one example, the campaign of 'west development' has been in full swing with tremendous inputs, financial or non-financial. However, its impact on regional inequality is yet to be properly analysed. Another example relates to the urban–rural gap. Despite the initiative of 'building a socialist new countryside', how to improve the living standard of the rural poor remains an open question. The *Hukou* or household registration system has been blamed for the persistent urban–rural gap. This, in fact, is not a minority view. However, it is not clear how eliminating this restriction would help close the urban–rural or regional gap. An obvious counter example is the persistent gap in India where such administrative restriction is not instituted.

References

Banerjee, A.V., and E. Duflo (2003). 'Inequality and Growth: What Can The Data Say?', *Journal of Economic Growth* 8: 267–99.

Bourguignon, F. (2004). 'The Poverty–Growth–Inequality Triangle', paper presented at the Indian Council for Research on International Economic Relations, New Delhi, 4 February.

Wan, G. H. (2007). 'Understanding Regional Poverty and Inequality Trends in China: Methodological and Empirical Issues', *Review of Income and Wealth* 53(1): 28–34.

List of Figures

1.1a	Impact of one unit increase in inequality on investment and education, instant and lagged marginal effects	11
1.1b	Impact of one unit increase in inequality on investment and education, cumulative effects	12
1.2	Inequality–growth nexus, instant and lagged effects and cumulative effects	13
2.1	Relationship between rural Gini coefficient and GDP per capita measured in RMB, provincial data, 1996–2002	23
2.2a	The two urban inequality curves	28
2.2b	The two rural inequality curves	28
2.2c	The two rural–urban inequality curves	28
3.1	Growth rates of real GDP per capita, rural and urban per capita income	42
4.1a	Coefficients of variation of GDP per capita and per worker	57
4.1b	Gini coefficients of GDP per capita and per worker	57
4.2	Per capita GDP and consumption expenditure in China's provinces in 1952	60
4.3	Per capita GDP in each province in 1978	61
5.1	Overall inter-provincial inequality	85
5.2	Trends in overall inter-provincial inequality based on official and adjusted data	86
5.3	Within region inequality	87
5.4	Between region inequality	88
5.5	Contributions to inter-provincial inequality	95
5.6	Overall between regional and within region contributions of capital	95
5.7	Total factor productivity (before deducting the effects of FDI and agglomerative effects)	96
5.8	Contribution of FDI	97
5.9	Contributions of agglomeration	98
5.10	Shares of secondary sectors in Liaoning and Guangdong	98
5.11	Contribution by quality adjusted labour	99

List of Figures

6.1	China's coastal–inland income disparity, 1985–2003	116
7.1	Moran's *I* for regional GDP per capita, China 1952–99	131
7.2	Moran scatterplot for regional GDP per capita, China 1957	132
7.3	Moran scatterplot for regional GDP per capita, China 1978	133
7.4	Moran scatterplot for regional GDP per capita, China 1999	134
7.5	Moran scatterplot map for regional GDP per capita, China 1999	135
7.6	Chinese empirical density, 1957, 1978, and 1999	136
7.7	Chinese empirical density conditioned by space, 1957, 1978, and 1999	138
7.8	Stochastic kernel for Chinese regions relative to the per capita GDP of the neighbouring provinces	140
7.9	Contour for Chinese regions relative to the neighbours' per capita GDP	140
8.1a	Innovation inequality at regional level, measured by total patents per capita	148
8.1b	Innovation inequality at regional level, measured by invention patents per capita	149
8.1c	Innovation inequality at regional level, measured by utility model patents per capita	149
8.1d	Innovation inequality at regional level, measured by design patents per capita	150
8.2a	Innovation inequality at provincial level, measured by total patents per capita	150
8.2b	Innovation inequality at provincial level, measured by invention patents per capita	151
8.2c	Innovation inequality at provincial level, measured by utility model patents per capita	151
8.2d	Innovation inequality at pronvincial level, measured by design patents per capita	152
9.1	Percentage of the population aged over 6 years who never attended school	166
9.2	Average provincial transition probability from grade 1 (1994) to grade 9 (2002)	172
9.3	Inter-cohort comparison of transition probability from elementary to junior highschool, between provinces, 1994–2002	174
9.4	Inter-cohort comparison of transition probability from grade 7 to grade 9, between provinces, 1995–2002	175
10.1	Shapley decomposition of poverty	189
10.2	Decomposing the endowment component of poverty	190
10.3	Decomposing poverty changes	193
10.4	Decomposing a marginal contribution	193

List of Tables

1.1	Estimation results	10
2.1	Estimates of the income inequality models (fixed effect)	24
2.2	Contribution of variables influencing inequality, 2002	29
2.A1	Estimation results	31
3.1a	Rural poverty levels and changes using RCRE data	46
3.1b	Rural poverty levels and changes using CHNS data	48
3.1c	Urban poverty levels and changes using CHNS data	50
3.2a	Decomposition and growth elasticity of poverty measures ($\theta = 1$)	51
3.2b	Decomposition and growth elasticity of poverty measures ($\theta = 0.8$)	52
3.2c	Decomposition and growth elasticity of poverty measures ($\theta = 0.5$)	53
4.1	Dataset for empirical analysis	70
4.2	Regression results	72
4.3	Regression results (including regional dummies)	73
4.4	Regression results (including Barro's structure impact variable and regional dummies)	74
5.1	Proportion of investment in fixed assets of state owned units by sources of funds (10,000 yuan)	81
5.2	Regression results from production function estimation	94
6.1	Descriptive statistics and correlation	119
6.2	Financial development and economic growth in China	121
7.1	Conditioned by space	139
8.1	Patents in China, 1995 and 2004	147
8.2	Summary of regression models, with initial 19 variables	155
8.3	Summary of regression models, with 14 variables	156
8.4	Robustness test	157
8.5a	Result of decomposition, 1995–2000	159
8.5b	Result of Decomposition, 2001–04	160
9.1	Transition probability from grade 1 to 9 among the cohort who entered primary school in 1994, by provinces	170

List of Tables

9.2	Decomposition results and population compositions in the sampled provinces	178
10.1	Estimated income generation function (dummy variables not included)	197
10.2	Effects of factor inequality on poverty level	199
10.3	Growth and inequality effects on poverty change from 2000 to 2001, by Factors	201

List of Acronyms and Abbreviations

ABC	Agricultural Bank of China
ADBC	Agricultural Development Bank of China
BOC	Bank of China
CAD	comparative advantage defying
CAF	comparative advantage following
CCB	China Construction Bank
CPI	consumer price index
DGP	data generating process
FDI	foreign direct investment
FGT	Foster–Greer–Thorbecke
GDP	gross domestic product
GE	generalized entropy
GMM	generalized method of moments
ICBC	Industrial and Commercial Bank of China
ICT	information and communication technology
LISA	local indicators of spatial association
MPS	material product system
NBS	National Bureau of Statistics
NERI	National Economic Research Institute (China)
PBC	People's Bank of China
PGI	poverty–growth–inequality
PIL	polynomial inverse lag
PRC	People's Republic of China
RCCs	rural credit co-operatives
RCFs	rural co-operative foundations
RPIs	retail price indices
SOE	state owned enterprise
TCI	technology choice index
TFP	total factor productivity
TVEs	township and village enterprises

Notes on Contributors

Patricio A. Aroca is Head of IDEAR at Universidad Católica del Norte, Antofagasta, Chile, and an affiliated research professor at REAL, University of Illinois at Urbana-Champaign. He works on input–output analysis, spatial econometrics, regional growth, and labour inter-regional migration. From 1997 to 2000 he was Dean, Faculty of Economics and Business, Universidad Católica del Norte and consultant for the World Bank, IADB, UNCTAD, and CELADE-ECLAC.

Zhao Chen is an associate professor of economics at the China Centre for Economic Studies (CCES), Fudan University, and Director of the Fudan Institute for Industrial Development Studies. His research interests include: urban and rural development, economic transition, and economics of information and organization. He also has co-authored publications on regional development and income distribution.

Peilei Fan is an assistant professor at the Urban and Regional Planning Program, Michigan State University, USA. She has a PhD in economic development and an MSc in electrical engineering and computer science, both from Massachusetts Institute of Technology (MIT), USA. Her research foci include: innovation policy, high-tech industrialization, and Asia's urbanization.

Dong Guo gained her PhD in urban and regional planning at the University of Illinois at Urbana-Champaign, where she worked at the Spatial Analysis Laboratory (SAL) and at the Regional Economics Application Laboratory (REAL) as a research assistant. Currently, she is a post-doctoral student at Université de Bourgogne, Dijon, France. Her interests are urban and regional economic analysis and applications of spatial analysis and spatial econometrics.

Geoffrey J. D. Hewings is Director of REAL, professor of geography and regional science, of economics, and of urban and regional planning. In 1996, he was made a University Scholar by the University of Illinois and in 2003 was awarded with the Doctor Honoris Causa by Université de Bourgogne, France, for his contribution to the field of input–output modelling. His major research interests are in the field of urban and regional economic analysis with a focus on the design, implementation, and application of regional economic models.

Notes on Contributors

Min-Dong Paul Lee is an assistant professor of management at the University of South Florida. He received his PhD in sociology from Cornell University. Before embarking on an academic career, he worked in the field of international development and corporate social responsibility. His research interests stem from his career experiences, and include corporate social responsibility, sociology of education, social inequality, and organizational behaviour.

Zhicheng Liang is a PhD candidate at CERDI, Université d'Auvergne, France. His major research fields include market oriented reforms in transitional countries, sources of economic growth, income distribution, finance and monetary economics, decentralization, and regional disparities.

Justin Yifu Lin is a professor of economics and the founding Director of the China Centre for Economic Research, Peking University, China. He has published numerous books and journal articles in the areas of economic and agricultural development, transitional economics, new institutional economics, and China's economic development, and has served in many international organizations and China's governmental departments as an adviser.

Peilin Liu is an associate research fellow at the Department of Development Strategy and Regional Economy, Development Research Centre of the State Council, China. He has published journal articles in economic growth, poverty, regional economy, and energy economics.

Ming Lu is an associate professor of economics at Fudan University, China, and Director of the Centre for China Development and Policy Studies. He is also a research fellow at the Employment and Social Security Research Centre (ESSRC) and the China Centre for Economic Studies (CCES), Fudan University. His recent research includes work on social economics and labour market, inequality, and economic development.

Kai-yuen Tsui is a professor of economics at the Chinese University of Hong Kong. His research interests focus on China's regional disparities, fiscal decentralization, and the evolution of China's system of administrative jurisdictions. He has also published theoretical papers on the measurement of inequality and poverty.

Guanghua Wan is a senior research fellow and project director at the World Institute for Development Economics Research (UNU-WIDER). Previously, he taught econometrics and development economics at the University of New England and the University of Sydney. An honorary professor of some leading universities in China and a prolific researcher with over 50 analytical papers in reputable refereed journals, he is a pioneer in developing the regression-based decomposition techniques for inequality and poverty accounting.

Notes on Contributors

Xiaolu Wang is Deputy Director of the National Economic Research Institute, China Reform Foundation. He has published more than 70 academic articles and book chapters, and several books. His research interests are economic growth, development, and income distribution in China.

Yin Zhang is a lecturer in economics at the School of Social Sciences, University of Dundee. Her research interests include economic development, applied macroeconomics, and applied econometrics.

1

The Inequality–Growth Nexus in the Short and Long Run: Empirical Evidence from China*

Guanghua Wan, Ming Lu, and Zhao Chen

1.1 Introduction

The literature on the relationship between inequality and growth is large and still growing. Yet, theoretical and empirical evidences are mixed (Banerjee and Duflo 2003, and references therein). Typically, cross-section regressions yield a negative relationship (Benabou 1996b), while the contrary is found using panel data models with fixed effect (Li and Zou 1998; Forbes 2000). In addition, Barro (2000) indicates that the relationship is non-significant when rich and poor countries are pooled together.

As asserted by Forbes (2000), the changes of sign in the inequality–growth relationship can be explained by the difference in the time horizon considered. She concludes that in the long run the relationship is negative while it is positive in the short or medium run. This assertion is supported by Banerjee and Duflo (2003). However, neither of these studies considers short, medium, and long run relationships in one unified framework. In fact, no previous attempts have been made to incorporate very short run effects into growth regressions.[1] Can this assertion or conclusion be used to reconcile the mixed empirical results? Answering this question is not only helpful in settling the intensive debate among academics, but also vital for policymakers. If the assertion is valid (i.e. the growth–inequality relationship switches signs over

---

* The authors are grateful to two anonymous referees for detailed and constructive comments. Ming Lu and Zhao Chen received financial support from the National Social Science Foundation of China and the New Century Scholar project funded by the Ministry of Education of China.

[1] By 'very short run' we mean instant impacts without any delay or with delay by one time period.

different time horizons), possibilities exist for inter-temporal tradeoffs of growth by manipulating income distributions. Under this circumstance, policymakers can strive to curtail inequality in order to gain in the long run at the cost of a slowdown in growth in the short run. Otherwise, a low (high) inequality must be maintained or targeted in order to achieve growth if the short, medium, or long run relationship is negative (positive).

The conventional approach to discovering the long run versus short run relationship is by averaging growth and relevant variables over different time horizons, and then estimating a growth regression model. For example, Forbes (2000) uses data averaged over a five-year interval in a growth regression and claims that this is a medium or short run relationship, which is found to be positive. Subsequently, she also reports results using ten-year averages, which indicate an insignificant relationship. On the basis of these, Forbes asserts that the short run positive relationship may not contradict the long run negative relationship. She seems to imply that if a longer time horizon, say 20 years, is considered for averaging data, the relationship may become negative. Meanwhile, Barro (2000) relies on averages over a ten-year interval to estimate long run relationships.

This practice of averaging is questionable on a number of grounds. First, no consensus exists regarding what time horizon constitutes or defines the short, medium, or long run concepts. For example, a five-year interval can be considered as short run by some and medium run by others. Further, if conflicting results are obtained with a 20-year and a 25-year averaging, can one attribute these to medium and long run differences? What happens if a five-year and a six-year averaging give rise to different results? It is important to note that if the true relationship does involve a change in sign at all, there must be a point where such a change occurs (say from period t to period $t+1$). In this case, one can state that the relationship is positive (or negative) over time horizon t periods and becomes negative (or positive) over time horizon $t+1$ periods. An appropriate analytical framework should enable identification of this turning point or possibly multiple turning points. In this regard, the conventional averaging procedure is problematic, if not inapplicable at all.

Second, averaging data is usually justified on the ground that it takes away business cycle effects on growth.[2] However, business cycles differ in length for the same economy over time and for different economies. They start and end at different time points for different economies as well. Simply applying one

---

[2] Another argument against using annual data is that they are subject to shocks and may cloud the underlying true relationship. This argument seems untenable given the inclusion of the disturbance term in any econometric equations, which could accommodate shocks and other errors. In passing, it is noted that Barro (2000) opts for using averaged data but for different reasons, namely unavailability of high frequency data for some variables and the inability of the existing theories in establishing very short run associations between growth and its determinants. Nevertheless, the inability should not prevent one from modelling empirical short run relationships. After all, the medium or long run relationships are built on the short run counterpart. The former do not exist without the latter.

time interval in averaging data, for one country over time or for different countries, may not help eliminate the cycle effects. In other words, taking averages is useful only when business cycles are properly identified. In this case, the cycles must be completely synchronized among different economies under consideration and they must be of precisely the same length over time. These are unlikely to be true even if difficulties in business cycle identification can be left aside.

Third, short, medium, and long run relationships between inequality and growth are different aspects of the same underlying economic or growth process, which corresponds to a particular data generating process (DGP). A DGP is exactly what an econometric model intends to capture or describe. When estimating different regressions, forced by arbitrarily chosen different time intervals for averaging data, one might model different DGPs rather than different aspects of the same DGP. From this perspective, the changes in sign may not reflect the difference between the long and short runs. It may be caused by the use of different averages and by other differences inherent in different regression models.

Fourth, as pointed out by Attanasio et al. (2000), annual data provide information that is lost when averaging. This averaging practice is particularly puzzling as paucity of data is often cited as a major hurdle in estimating growth regressions (Durlauf 2001). It can be easily ascertained that with a five-year or a ten-year averaging, 80 or 90 per cent of sample observations are lost. Finally, it is illogical to make short, medium, and long runs mutually exclusive as far as model specification is concerned. After all, these different runs correspond to different aspects of the same DGP and thus should be embedded in a common DGP or a common regression equation. In any case, it is desirable to develop a framework that allows for identification of the growth–inequality relationship over all possible time horizons. One can then discuss findings with a precise definition of time intervals. Under this circumstance, results from different studies can be compared even if data used are of different frequencies. For example, one does not have to stick to five-year averages in order to compare results with Forbes (2000).

The main purpose of this chapter is to introduce such a modelling framework that enables identification of the short, medium, and long run effects in one model. A second purpose is to extend the work of Barro (2000) and Lundberg and Squire (2003) by adding important equations and by combining the simultaneous model with the newly introduced framework. In particular, education is endogenized in this chapter. Although this can be justified intuitively, theoretically, and empirically, few previous studies have made such an attempt with the exception of Heerink (1994). Finally, we use annual data from within China to explore the inequality–growth nexus over different time horizons.

1.2 Theories on the Inequality–Growth Nexus and the Modelling Framework[3]

Several mechanisms are theorized to yield negative effects of inequality on growth. First, under imperfect capital market, a higher inequality means more individuals facing credit constraints. Consequently, they cannot carry out productive investments in physical or human capital (Galor and Zeira 1993; Fishman and Simhon 2002). These can take place in the short run or long run. Second, a worsening inequality generates a rise in the fertility rate among, and less investment in human capital of, the poor (de la Croix and Doepke 2004). This is most likely to happen in the long run. Third, a more unequal income distribution may cause weaker domestic demand that may slow down the economy, as has occurred in China since the late 1990s. This demand related impact is expected to prevail mostly in the short run. Fourth, a growing inequality increases redistributive tax pressures, which deters investment incentives thus growth (Alesina and Rodrik 1994; Persson and Tabellini 1994; Benabou 1996b). Finally, a worsening inequality may lead to a more unstable sociopolitical environment for economic activities (Benhabib and Rustichini 1996). The last two mechanisms require certain time duration for the effects to materialize.

On the other hand, Galor and Tsiddon (1997a, b) develop two theories, both predicting a positive inequality–growth relationship. In one model, the level of human capital is determined by home environment externality. When this externality is large a high level of inequality may be necessary for growth to take off in a less developed country. In a second model, major technical changes help enhance mobility and concentration of high ability workers in technologically advanced sectors, which will generate growth as well as higher inequality. Also, Benabou (1996a) shows that when human capitals of heterogeneous individuals are strongly complementary within localities, more inequality is inductive to growth, at least in the short run. In addition, a high or rising inequality prompts the middle-class to vote for changes in taxation rate. Both higher (Saint-Paul and Thierry 1993) and lower taxation rates (Li and Zou 1998) could promote economic growth. Finally, conventional wisdom states that high inequality implies more savings or more investment (Galor and Moav 2002). All these positive effects can materialize in the short or long run.

Clearly, these theories indicate that the overall impact of inequality on growth cannot be set a priori (Aghion et al. 1999). More pertinent to this chapter, the short and long run effects may well differ in magnitudes as well as in signs. As noted above, the very short run effect is so far overlooked, despite its existence and

---

[3] For a survey of literature on inequality and human development, see Thorbecke and Charumilind (2002). While human development, growth, and inequality are all interrelated, we focus on inequality and growth in this chapter. The absence of regional time series data on health and environment in China prevents us from considering these variables in our empirical model.

importance. Even medium and long run effects are not modeled appropriately in the empirical literature. It is important to point out that the existing theories implicitly or explicitly assume that inequality affects growth through its impacts on physical and human capital formation. This point will be taken up later in this chapter when our empirical model is specified.

To enable identification of the inequality effects over different time horizons, distributed lag models can be used. Among the alternative distributed lag structures, the polynomial inverse lag (PIL) of Mitchell and Speaker (1986) is preferred as it possesses two attractive features: its flexibility in uncovering the true lag structure and its easiness in estimation. The second feature is especially important as we will combine PIL with simultaneous equations.

Let Y denote growth and X denote inequality; then the PIL model can be written as:

$$Y_t = b + \sum_{i=0}^{\infty} w_i X_{t-i} + e_t \tag{1}$$

where

$$w_i = \sum_{j=2}^{n} \frac{a_j}{(i+1)^j}, \quad i = 0, \ldots, \infty \tag{2}$$

In the above model, w_i are the distributed lag weights, indicating the impacts of X on Y over the time interval i. The notation a_j represents the parameters to be estimated and n is the degree of polynomial. Substituting (2) into (1) and re-arranging yield:

$$\begin{aligned} Y_t &= b + \sum_{i=0}^{\infty} w_i X_{t-i} + e_t \\ &= b + \sum_{j=2}^{n} \sum_{i=0}^{m-1} \frac{a_j}{(i+1)^j} X_{t-i} + \underline{\sum_{j=2}^{n} \sum_{i=m}^{\infty} \frac{a_j}{(i+1)^j} X_{t-i}} + e_t \end{aligned} \tag{3}$$

The underlined term on the right-hand side of (3) becomes negligible for t greater than 8, thus can be omitted, as suggested by Mitchell and Speaker (1986). On the basis of (3), one can obtain the effects of X on Y over any time interval, such as five or eight years. The instant impact is given by $w_0 = \sum_{j=2}^{n} a_j$, the lagged impacts are given by $w_i (i = 1, 2, \ldots, \infty)$, and the cumulative impacts are given by $\sum_i w_i$, depending on how the short and

5

long runs are defined. In particular, we can use the infinite sum to indicate the very long run impact.

An expanded version of (3) with the underlined term omitted is:

$$Y_t = b + a_2[X_t + \frac{1}{2^2}X_{t-1} + \frac{1}{3^2}X_{t-2} + \ldots + \frac{1}{m^2}X_{t-m+1}]$$
$$+ a_3[X_t + \frac{1}{2^3}X_{t-1} + \frac{1}{3^3}X_{t-2} + \ldots + \frac{1}{m^3}X_{t-m+1}] \qquad (4)$$
$$+ \ldots + a_n[X_t + \frac{1}{2^n}X_{t-1} + \frac{1}{3^n}X_{t-2} + \ldots + \frac{1}{m^n}X_{t-m+1}] + e_t$$

The expressions in the square brackets are polynomial inverse lag (PIL) terms associated with different degrees of polynomial n.

One can set $m = 9$, add variables other than Xs in (4), and use the resultant regression to analyse the inequality–growth relationship. However, the issues of heterogeneity, measurement errors, and endogeneity have received considerable attention in the literature (Atkinson and Brandolini 2001; Durlauf et al. 2005). These must be addressed before empirical estimation. In particular, Banerjee and Duflo (2003) argue why cross-country data are deficient due to significant differences in cultural structure, political system, and financial institutions. While not claiming the absence of heterogeneity, this problem is less severe in this chapter because data from within China will be used. More importantly, China remains a socialist country with strong institutional, cultural, political, and even economic controls across regions. Despite so, some dummy variables will be incorporated into our empirical model to further address the heterogeneity issue.

Regarding measurement errors, this is largely related to the inequality variable, not or less applicable to other variables, as pointed out by Barro (2000). To be more precise, inequality data used in most cross-country regressions are calculated under different concepts of income (e.g. GDP, wage, disposable income, or expenditure), different income recipients (e.g. individual, household, or family), and different sampling procedures (e.g. proportional sampling, stratified sampling) or even different coverage of population (e.g. national, subnational, regional, or small-scale survey). In this chapter, the regional urban–rural income ratio will be used to measure inequality. The rural as well as urban income data are based on household surveys conducted by the National Bureau of Statistics (NBS) of China. Both the rural and urban surveys use the same sampling technique and cover the whole of China. Further, the income data are all collected at the household level and are consistent across different regions and over time. Therefore, we do not consider the measurement error as a major problem, at least insofar as variable definitions, population coverage, and sampling techniques are concerned. Using the urban–rural income ratio as an inequality indicator is justified on the ground that the urban–rural income gap constitutes over 70 per cent of the overall regional inequality (Kanbur and Zhang 2005; Wan 2007). And no regional inequality data are available to us. Wei and Wu (2001) adopt the same practice. Bourguignon and Morrison (1998) find that the urban–rural labour productivity ratio is highly correlated with overall inequality.

The endogeneity problem is resolved by specifying and estimating simultaneous systems of equations, not by relying on lagged variables and the GMM estimation technique in a single equation. Recall the brief review of various growth theories in section 1.2: the impact of inequality on growth is mainly channelled through its effects on physical and human capital formations.[4] Thus, it is necessary to include investment and education equations in the system. Consequently, we end up with a four-equation system after adding the usual growth and inequality equations. In contrast, Barro (2000) and Lundberg and Squire (2003) did not endogenize the human capital variable in their models. It is noted that estimating the inequality equation permits testing of the controversial Kuznets hypothesis.

Using INE_{PIL} to denote the inequality terms associated with PIL (INE_{PIL} = RHS of (4) excluding b), $incm$ to denote the income level lagged by one year, the systems of equations are specified as (detailed definitions of variables are provided in the Appendix):

$Incmgr = f_1(popgr, invt, edu, gov, cpi, trade, urbangr, private, incm, incmsq, central, west)$
$Invt = f_2(INE_{PIL}, gov, cpi, trade, urban, private, incm, incmsq, central, west)$
$Edu = f_3(INE_{PIL}, peduexp, urban, incm, incmsq, central, west)$
$Inequality = f_4(incmgr, trade, agrexp, urban, private, incm, incmsq, central, west)$

The first equation in the system explains per capita income growth (*incmgr*), which is determined by population growth (*popgr*) as a proxy of labour input, investment expressed as proportion of GDP (*invt*), and human capital defined as average years of schooling (*edu*). These are standard growth determinants. Following Clarke (1995) and Barro (2000), we add government expenditure as a ratio of GDP (*gov*) and inflation (*cpi*) to this equation. The former represents government interference in economic activities and the latter may capture macroeconomic conditions or business cycle effects. Also controlled are openness (*trade*), changes in urbanization (*urbangr*), and privatization (*private*) variables. The convergence literature appeals for the inclusion of the lagged income level (*incm*). Location dummy variables for central and western provinces (*central, west*) are used in this and all other equations to contain heterogeneity.

In specifying the investment function, the most relevant variable, besides inequality (*INE*), is lagged per capita income (*incm*) as a proxy of savings plus its square (*incmsq*). As with the growth equation, government interference (*gov*) and macroeconomic conditions (*cpi*) are important independent vari-

---

[4] Demand related impact of inequality must eventually work through capital and labour inputs.

ables. Little is necessary to justify the inclusions of openness, urbanization level (*urban*), and privatization in the investment model.

Although various growth theories indicate that inequality matters for human capital formation, few earlier attempts were made to include the education equation. It is well known that income (*incm*) is a determinant of education as schooling is costly in China. The income–education relationship may be non-linear, so we include a square term of income (*incmsq*) in the model. Also, education is likely to be affected by government spending on education, culture, and health (*peduexp*). Needless to say, more urbanized regions enjoy better education due to serious biases in education provision in China; thus the urbanization variable (*urban*) is relevant.

Leaving income growth and location dummy variables aside, five other variables are included in the inequality model. The Kuznets hypothesis dictates that the income variable and its square ought to be considered. Privatization is included as it is commonly perceived to be a cause of inequality in China. On the other hand, openness and urbanization are included as Wan et al. (2005) and Lu and Chen (2006), respectively, find that they contribute to regional inequality. Given that the inequality variable is defined as the urban–rural income ratio, government support to agriculture (*agrexp*) is expected to help narrow the urban–rural income gap.

1.3 Empirical Evidence from China

China represents a very interesting case for studying the inequality–growth relationship. Except the urban–rural disparity, pre-reform China was basically an egalitarian society. The low inequality was identified as a strain on economic growth. This is why Deng Xiaoping, at the onset of economic reforms, famously stated 'let some get rich first'. The reform period has seen remarkable growth. Although regional inequality and the urban–rural gap declined from the late 1970s to the mid-1980s, both increased rather dramatically since the mid-1980s (Wan 2007). China's growth is preceded by a fairly low initial inequality in the pre-reform period. From this perspective, the inequality–growth relationship seems to be negative. However, the Chinese experience depicts a positive correlation when pre- and post-reform periods are examined separately.

There is more. In early 2004, the Premier of China announced a growth target of 7 per cent, which is lower than any of the growth rates in China since economic reform began in 1978 (excluding the unusual period from 1989 to 1990). Such a move is unprecedented and represents a major policy shift to address, at least partly, the inequality problem in China. The high and rising inequality is perceived to hurt the national economy from the perspectives of slacking domestic demand and political instability. Directing resources to the rural sector and non-coastal regions is expected to slow down growth in the short run, but may help achieve sustainable growth in the long run. Clearly, policymakers in China, past and present, see both (short run) positive and (long run) negative effects of inequality on growth.

These observations appeal for a proper analytical study. Toward this end, data at the regional or provincial level for 1987–2001 are used to estimate the systems of equations outlined in section 1.2. Though desirable, earlier data are too incomplete to be useful. Excluding Taiwan, Hong Kong, and Macao, China has 31 provinces or regions, including four autonomous municipal cities. Hainan province was created in 1988 and is merged with Guangdong. Chongqing is the youngest region in China. Fortunately, data for Chongqing are available. Most data for Xizang (Tibet) are missing. Therefore, our sample consists of 29 regions. All observations in value terms are deflated by rural and urban consumer price indices (CPI), respectively. For details on data sources and data construction, see the Appendix.

The systems of equations are estimated with three-stage least squares after setting $m = 9$. To determine the degree of polynomial n, the general to specific approach is followed. This approach is also recommended by Mitchell and Speaker (1986). We started with $n = 6$, in which case high collinearity leads to automatic drops of some PIL terms by STATA. When n is reduced to 5, the PIL term in the investment equation is insignificant. Once this term is removed, all PIL terms are significant at the 10 per cent level. The estimation results are reported in Table 1.1.

The estimated models are of good quality with most parameters significantly different from zero. Notwithstanding that little can be said a priori about the signs of many estimates, the positive and significant impacts of physical and human capital investments, trade, urbanization, and privatization on growth are consistent with economic theory. Government expenditure is found to be detrimental to growth (when investment is held constant) but helpful in increasing investment. These are acceptable since this variable is included as a proxy for government intervention, particularly in bank lending. See Clarke (1995) and Partridge (1997). As far as the education equation is concerned, higher income is found to cause more human capital formation and urbanization is positively related to regional education level; both findings corroborate well with normal expectations.

One interesting finding relates to the income terms in the growth equation. It shows that growth does not depend on income levels in China, at any conventional level of statistical significance. This is different from Barro (2000), who shows that the growth–inequality relationship is conditional on the level of development: it is positive across developed economies and negative in the developing world. It is noted, however, that inequality does not enter the growth equation directly in our model. Another income related finding is that the Kuznets hypothesis is rejected. In contrast, a U-pattern is supported by the Chinese data, which is in line with Wan (2004).

Table 1.1: Estimation results

Right-hand side variables	Growth equation Coefficient	t-ratio	Investment equation Coefficient	t-ratio	Education equation Coefficient	t-ratio	Inequality equation Coefficient	t-ratio
PIL ($n=2$)			−0.285	−1.707*	0.137	1.930*		
PIL ($n=3$)			1.563	2.312**	−1.071	−1.818*		
PIL ($n=4$)			−1.351	−2.598***	2.287	1.716*		
PIL ($n=5$)					−1.351	−1.652*		
peduexp					0.0006	0.300		
agrexp							−0.041	3.727***
incmgr							−0.043	3.071***
popgr	−0.068	−1.015						
invt	1.58	7.215***						
edu	3.561	3.028***						
gov	−1.529	−6.141***	1.16	7.733***				
cpi	−0.442	−4.604***	0.262	3.011***				
urbangr	0.375	5.282***						
urban			−0.073	−1.352	0.042	8.400***	−0.013	4.333***
trade			−0.025	−1.136			0.007	7.000***
private			−0.416	−5.012***			−0.02	3.333***
incm	−53.468	−1.308	6.629	0.161	7.399	1.735*	−12.322	4.444***
incmsq	0.698	0.234	1.058	0.352	−0.476	−2.817	0.874	4.348***
central	7.956	3.716***	−5.48	−3.914***	0.282	2.541**	0.272	2.989***
west	−5.557	−2.621***	4.833	2.271**	−0.403	−2.385**	0.76	6.129***
constant	292.929	2.003**	−76.008	−0.524	−22.97	−1.581	46.571	4.782***

Note: ***, **, * significant at the 1, 5, and 10 per cent levels.
Source: Authors' calculation.

Some comments on the inequality equation are in order. As indicated by the coefficients of the location dummy variables, the urban–rural divide is more severe in western than in central regions, which in turn is more severe than in coastal regions. This is understandable as urban China is more equal across locations, while development in rural China is heavily reliant on geographic conditions. When everything else is the same, the rural west usually lags behind with the east leading. Also, Table 1.1 indicates that in addition to the variables of government support to agriculture and income growth, privatization helps reduce the urban–rural income gap. This is justified because township and village enterprises (TVEs) in China, a major component of the privatization index, represent an important driving force in narrowing down the urban–rural gap, although they may contribute to the growing inequality among rural regions (Wan and Zhu 2006: 71–86). Consistent with Wan et al. (2005), trade is an inequality increasing variable.

Now attention is turned to the crucial question, 'How does inequality affect growth?' Since the impact is channelled through investment and education, we first examine the relationship between inequality and these two factors. Referring to equation (1), the marginal effects of inequality are given by w_i. These are shown in Figure 1.1a. In particular, the instant impact is given by w_0, which is negative in the investment equation but positive in the education

Inequality–Growth Nexus

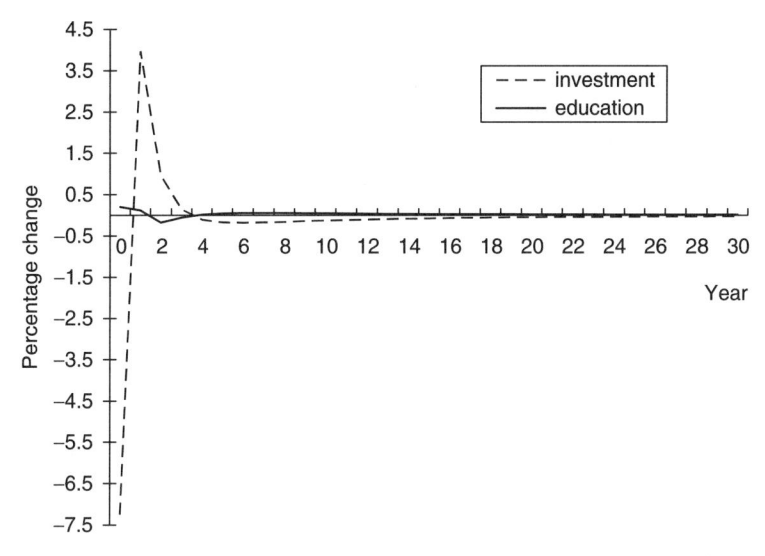

Figure 1.1a: Impact of one unit increase in inequality on investment (dashed line) and education (solid line), instant and lagged marginal effects

model. The impact of inequality on investment turns to be positive after one year and remains so for a number of years. It reverts to be negative after four years and reaches the negative peak in year six, before eventually converging to zero. On the other hand, inequality seems more beneficial to human capital formation over all time horizons except in years three and four. The positive effect reaches a peak in year seven and then converges to zero. This positive relationship between inequality and human capital corroborates well with the theories of Benabou (1996a) and Galor and Tsiddon (1997a, b).

It is also useful to sum w_i to obtain the cumulative effects over different time horizons. These are plotted in Figure 1.1b, which demonstrates that inequality is detrimental to investment no matter what time interval is considered. This is consistent with Alesina and Rodrik (1994), who demonstrate that high inequality may lead to political instability, which is detrimental to investment and growth. Also, China's capital market is rather underdeveloped. Consequently, higher inequality means more serious credit constraints and less productive investments (Galor and Zeira 1993; Fishman and Simhon 2002). Moreover, as mentioned earlier, a growing inequality increases redistributive tax pressures, which deters investment incentives (Alesina and Rodrik 1994; Persson and Tabellini 1994; Benabou 1996b). Finally, the negative inequality–investment relationship corroborates well with the fact that investment rate is low in inland regions where the urban–rural gap is large. In contrast, investment rate is high in coastal areas where the urban–rural gap is relatively smaller. Figure 1.1b also indicates that inequality helps promote accumulation

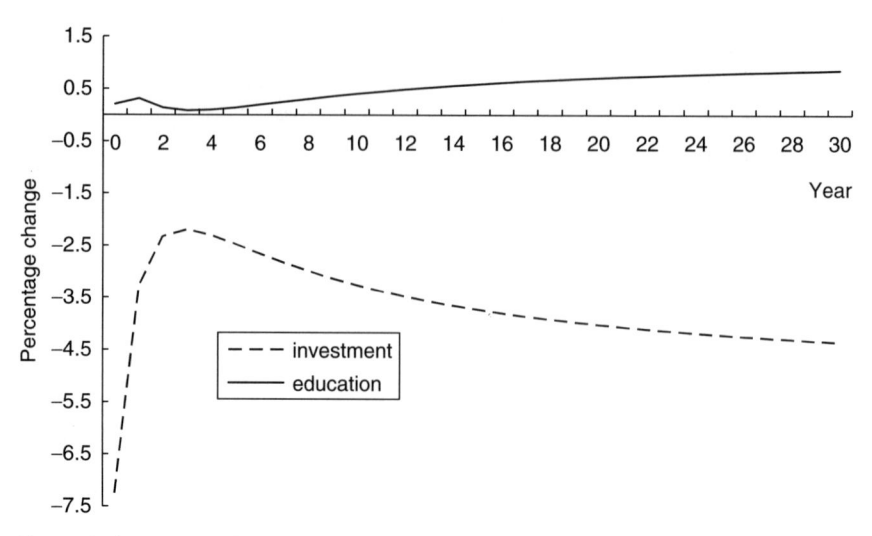

Figure 1.1b: Impact of one unit increase in inequality on investment (dashed line) and education (solid line), cumulative effects

of human capital, which may imply the validity of Simpson's (1990) inverted-U pattern between education and inequality in China. As is known, educational level in China has been on the rise and such a rise is accompanied by the increasing inequality. It is useful to point out that the education–inequality relationship is largely an empirical one as alternative theories exist, which predict opposite effects of inequality on education. Our modelling results support the proposition of Perotti (1992), who concludes that rising inequality enables the rich to obtain education first when the tuition fee is high relative to income. Mayer (2000) confirms the positive impact of inequality on college education in the USA. It has been widely publicized that education is exceedingly expensive in China, particularly for secondary and post-secondary studies. From this perspective, the positive impact of inequality on education is understandable.

Once the impacts of inequality on education and investment are identified, it is straightforward to simulate the inequality–growth relationship by allowing inequality to increase at a certain margin or percentage. Figure 1.2 shows the instant or lagged as well as cumulative impacts on growth when China's urban–rural income ratio is raised by 0.1 unit. The instant and lagged effects fast decrease to zero after an initially negative and then positive influences in the first four years. The cumulative line demonstrates a negative relationship between inequality and growth, and this relationship holds no matter what time horizon is considered. Most interestingly, the relationship is found to be nonlinear, a key point underlying the theory proposed by Banerjee and Duflo (2003).

Inequality–Growth Nexus

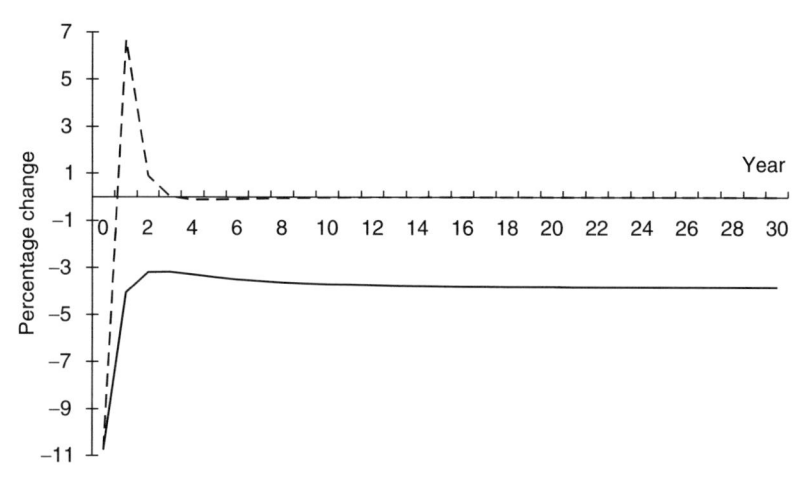

Figure 1.2: Inequality–growth nexus, instant and lagged effects (dashed line) and cumulative effects (solid line)

1.4 Summary

In this chapter we introduce the polynomial inverse lag (PIL) model in order to accommodate, within one unified framework, potentially differing impacts of inequality on growth over different time horizons. Applying simultaneous equations incorporating the PIL to data from one country, namely China, our results are expected to suffer less from the problems of heterogeneity, endogeneity, and measurement errors, commonly encountered in cross-country growth regressions.

Despite the seemingly positive correlation between growth and inequality in post-reform China, our empirical results unequivocally point to the negative effects of inequality on growths in the short, medium, and long run. The negative effects stem from the strong and negative influence of inequality on physical investment, which consistently overweigh the mostly positive impacts of inequality on human capital. The inequality–growth relationship is found to be non-linear, so are the inequality–investment and inequality–education relationships.

As with any other study, this chapter can be improved in many aspects such as data quality, model refinements, and better estimation techniques. One particular avenue for future research lies in the development of bootstrapping or other tools in order to attach statistical significance to the identified effects of inequality on growth. Another issue that is yet to be dealt with is the robustness test of our research findings. This could be difficult given the open-ended nature of growth theories (Brock and Durlauf 2001).

Appendix: Data

1. Unless indicated otherwise, data for the period 1987–98 are all from *Comprehensive Statistical Data and Materials for 50 Years of New China* (NBS 1999). Data for years 1999–2001, unless indicated otherwise, are from *China Statistical Yearbook, 2000, 2001* and *2002* (NBS various years).
2. *popgr* = population growth rate. Except for Hebei, Heilongjiang, and Gansu, 1999–2001 data of agricultural and non-agricultural population are from provincial statistical yearbooks. Population data of Hebei, Heilongjiang, and Gansu in 2000 are from *China Statistical Yearbook, 2001*. For these three regions, the 1999 population data are the averages of the neighboring two years, and the 2001 data are forecast based on data in 2000 and the growth rate during 1999–2000.
3. *incm* = per capita income lagged by one year. Regional income is the weighted average of urban and rural per capita incomes, with non-agricultural and agricultural population shares as weights. Both urban and rural incomes are deflated by regional urban and rural CPIs. For Shanghai, Beijing, and Tianjin, urban and rural CPIs are the same.
4. *incmsq* = *incm* squared.
5. *urgap* = urban–rural income gap. It is defined as urban–rural per capita income ratio.
6. *incmgr* = income growth rate. It is calculated on the basis of *incm*.
7. *invmtgdp* = investment/GDP ratio. It is computed as total fixed capital investment over GDP.
8. *edu* = education. *China Population Yearbooks* report regional population by education attainment as from 1987. Unfortunately, such data were not published for 1989, 1991, and 1992, and data for 1987 and 1988 are incomplete as illiterate population are not reported. Also, unlike data for other years, the 1994 data did not consider population below the age of 15. To estimate data for these years, we compute average years of schooling using data for the other years and then fit the model:

$$\ln(edu) = f(\cdot) + \mu$$

where *edu* is per capita years of schooling, $f(\cdot)$ is simply a linear function of time trend and regional dummies, and μ is the error term. This model is estimated by the GLS technique, allowing for heteroskedasticity in the panel data. The R^2 of the estimated equation is 0.966. Denoting the predicted value by ^, we have

$$\hat{edu} = \exp[\ln(\hat{edu})] \exp(0.5\hat{\sigma}^2)$$

where $\ln(\hat{edu})$ denotes the predicted values of $\ln(edu)$ and $\hat{\sigma}^2$ is the estimated variance of μ. Data for 1987–9, 1991, 1992, and 1994 are estimated by the above model.
9. *gov* = governmental consumption ratio, exclusive of expenditure on culture, education, science, and healthcare. Unlike in the existing literature we cannot exclude education and defense expenditures as these substatistics are not available at the regional/provincial level.
10. *trade* is computed as the trade/GDP ratio. Trade data are converted into RMB.

11. *cpi* are used to proxy inflation. CPIs of Qinghai are from provincial statistical yearbook.
12. *agrexp* = proportion of provincial fiscal expenditure on agriculture.
13. *peduexp* = per capita government expenditure on culture, education, science, and healthcare.
14. *private* = privatization, computed as the proportion of workers and staff in non-state-owned entities.
15. *urban* = urbanization, defined as the proportion of non-agricultural population in the total.
16. *urbangr* = growth rate of *urban*.
17. *center, west*: location dummies for central and western China, respectively. Consistent with most of the literature, central provinces refer to Shanxi, Inner Mongolia, Jilin, Heilongjiang, Anhui, Jiangxi, Henan, Hubei, Hunan, and Guangxi, and western provinces include Sichuan, Guizhou, Yunnan, Shaanxi, Gansu, Qinghai, Ningxia, Chongqing and Xinjiang.

References

Aghion, P., E. Caroli, and C. Garcia-Penalosa (1999). 'Inequality and Economic Growth: The Perspective of the New Growth Theories', *Journal of Economic Literature* 37(4): 1615–60.

Alesina, A., and D. Rodrik, (1994). 'Distributive Politics and Economic Growth', *Quarterly Journal of Economics* 109(2): 465–90.

Atkinson, A. B., and A. Brandolini (2001). 'Promise and Pitfalls in the Use of "Secondary" Datasets: Income Inequality in OECD Countries as a Case Study', *Journal of Economic Literature* 39(3): 771–99.

Attanasio, O. P., L. Picci, and A. Scorcu (2000). 'Saving, Growth and Investment: A Macroeconomic Analysis Using a Panel of Countries', *Review of Economics and Statistics* 82(2): 182–211.

Banerjee, A. V., and E. Duflo (2003). 'Inequality and Growth: What Can the Data Say?', *Journal of Economic Growth* 8: 267–99.

Barro, R. J. (2000). 'Inequality and Growth in a Panel of Countries', *Journal of Economic Growth* 5(1): 87–120.

Benabou, R. (1996a). 'Heterogeneity, Stratification, and Growth: Macroeconomic Implications of Community Structure and School Finance', *American Economic Review* 86(3): 584–609.

—— (1996b). 'Inequality and Growth', in B. S. Bernanke and J. J. Rotemberg (eds), *NBER Macroeconomics Manual*, MIT Press: Cambridge, MA.

Benhabib, J., and A. Rustichini (1996). 'Social Conflict and Growth', *Journal of Economic Growth* 1(1): 129–46.

Bourguignon, F., and C. Morrisson (1998). 'Inequality and Development: The Role of Dualism', *Journal of Development Economics* 57: 233–57.

Brock, W. A., and S. N. Durlauf (2001). 'Growth Empirics and Reality', *World Bank Economic Review* 15(2): 229–72.

Clarke, G. R. G. (1995). 'More Evidence on Income Distribution and Growth', *Journal of Development Economics* 47(2): 403–27.

De la Croix, D., and M. Doepke (2004). 'Inequality and Growth: Why Differential Fertility Matters', *American Economic Review* 93(4): 1091–113.

Durlauf, S. N. (2001). 'Manifesto for a Growth Econometrics', *Journal of Econometrics* 100: 65–9.

—— P. A. Johnson, and J. R. W. Temple (2005). 'Growth Econometrics', in P. Aghion, and S. N. Durlauf (eds), *Handbook of Economic Growth*, Elsevier North-Holland: Amsterdam.

Fishman, A., and A. Simhon (2002). 'The Division of Labour, Inequality and Growth', *Journal of Economic Growth* 7: 117–36.

Forbes, K. J. (2000). 'A Reassessment of the Relationship between Inequality and Growth', *American Economic Review* 90(4): 869–87.

Galor, O., and O. Moav (2002). 'From Physical to Human Capital Accumulation: Inequality in the Process of Development', Brown University Working Paper 99-27, Brown University: Providence, RI.

—— D. Tsiddon (1997a). 'The Distribution of Human Capital and Economic Growth', *Journal of Economic Growth* 2(1): 93–124.

—— —— (1997b). 'Technological Progress, Mobility, and Economic Growth', *American Economic Review* 87(3): 363–82.

—— J. Zeira (1993). 'Income Distribution and Macroeconomics', *Review of Economic Studies* 60: 35–52.

Heerink, N. (1994). *Population Growth, Income Distribution, and Economic Development: Theory, Methodology, and Empirical Results*, Springer: Berlin.

Kanbur, R., and X. Zhang (2005). 'Fifty Years of Regional Inequality in China: A Journey Through Central Planning, Reform and Openness', *Review of Development Economics* 9(1): 87–106.

Li, H., and H-F. Zou (1998). 'Income Inequality is Not Harmful for Growth: Theory and Evidence', *Review of Development Economics* 2(3): 318–34.

Lu, M., and Z. Chen, (2006). 'Urbanization, Urban-Biased Policies and Urban–Rural Inequality in China: 1987–2001', *Chinese Economy* 39(3): 42–63.

Lundberg, M., and L. Squire (2003). 'The Simultaneous Evolution of Growth and Inequality', *The Economic Journal* 113: 326–44.

Mayer, S. E. (2000). 'How Did the Increase in Economic Inequality Between 1970 and 1990 Affect American Children's Education Attainment?', unpublished manuscript, Joint Center for Poverty Research, University of Chicago: Chicago, IL.

Mitchell, D. W., and P. J. Speaker (1986). 'A Simple, Flexible Distributed Lag Technique: The Polynomial Inverse Lag', *Journal of Econometrics* 31: 329–40.

Partridge, M. D. (1997). 'Is Inequality Harmful for Growth? Comment', *American Economic Review* 87: 1019–32.

Perotti, R. (1992). 'Income Distribution, Politics and Growth', *American Economic Review* 82(2): 311–17.

Persson, T., and G. Tabellini (1994). 'Is Inequality Harmful for Growth? Theory and Evidence', *American Economic Review* 84: 600–21.

Saint-Paul, G., and V. Thierry (1993). 'Education, Democracy, and Growth', *Journal of Development Economics* 42(2): 399–407.

Simpson, M. (1990). 'Political Rights and Income Inequality: A Cross-National Test', *American Sociological Review* 55(5): 682–93.

Thorbecke, E., and C. Charumilind (2002). 'Economic Inequality and its Socioeconomic Impact', *World Development* 30(9): 1477–95.

Wan, G. (2004). 'Inequality and Economic Development in Transition Economies: Are Nonlinear Models Needed?', *World Economic Papers* 4: 1–13.

—— (2007). 'Understanding Regional Poverty and Inequality Trends in China: Methodological and Empirical Issues', *Review of Income and Wealth* 53(1): 28–34.

—— M. Lu, and C. Zhao (2005). 'Globalization and Regional Inequality in China', *Social Sciences in China* (3): 17–26.

—— Y. Zhu (2006). 'Town and Village Enterprises and Employment Generation in China', in B. Guha-Khasnobis and R. Kanbur (eds), *Informal Labour Markets and Development*, Palgrave Macmillan: New York.

Wei, S., and Y. Wu (2001). 'Globalization and Inequality: Evidence From Within China', *NBER Working Paper* 8611, National Bureau of Economic Research: Cambridge, MA.

2
Income Inequality in China and its Influencing Factors

Xiaolu Wang

2.1 Introduction

During China's economic reform, especially from the 1990s, income inequality between rural and urban areas, among regions, and between different social groups, increased rapidly. The Gini coefficient in China was 0.32 in 1980, dropped to 0.26 at the initial stage of economic reform of 1980–4, and then increased to 0.36 in 1990. It reached 0.45 in 2001 (WIID 2000; World Bank 2004). China is being transformed from an egalitarian society to a highly unequal country. According to the *World Development Report 2004*, China's Gini coefficient ranked, in an ascending order, eighty-fifth out of 120 economies (World Bank 2004). Next to China is a group of Latin American and Sub-Saharan African countries, many of which have been confronted with very high inequality as well as economic stagnation.

The deterioration of income distribution represents a serious challenge to social justice, as it can lead to social conflict and undermine economic growth (see Chapter 1 of this volume). Of the 35 countries with worse income distributions than China, 13 experienced negative GDP growth in 2002–3, constituting the majority of the 23 countries with negative growth.

Using province level panel data, this chapter attempts to answer the following questions: Is the Kuznets curve (Kuznets 1955) applicable in China? What factors are responsible for the widening income gap? What can be done to reduce income inequality? Relevant policy implications will thence be derived.

2.2 Literature Review and Hypotheses

Based on an analysis of historical data mainly from the USA, UK, and Germany, Kuznets (1955) puts forward the well-known inverted-U curve: income inequality

Inequality Determinants

tended to expand at an early stage of industrialization, and then to shrink as an economy grew. This has induced considerable debate in the last 50 years. Some economists suggest that a widening income inequality is a necessary cost for economic takeoff, whereas growth itself will eventually lead to reductions in inequality. This suggestion implies that efficiency automatically leads to equity. Conversely, other economists seriously challenge this suggestion on the basis of theoretical models or empirical studies.

According to Kuznets (1955), the later decline in income inequality is not unconditional. On the contrary, changes in income inequality are considered to be the result of a series of economic, political, social, and demographic conditions. He disagreed with the two contrary presumptions: (1) the 'later blooming' poor countries must follow the development path of the industrialized countries; (2) the poor countries face new problems totally irrelevant to the historical experiences of the industrialized countries. What is needed, instead, is a careful analysis of past and present circumstances. Kuznets also disagrees with the argument that developing countries should do nothing about the expanding income inequality. According to Kuznets (1955: 26) it is dangerous to argue that completely free markets, lack of penalties implicit in progressive taxation, and the like, are indispensable for the economic growth of the now underdeveloped countries.

Kuznets discussed the effects of a few factors on income inequality, particularly those of industrialization and urbanization. He concluded that under certain conditions migration from the agricultural to non-agricultural or urban sector can lead to larger inequality, but can reduce inequality afterwards. Changes in the saving rate, population growth pattern, and even political systems can also affect income inequality.

A considerable literature exists on testing the Kuznets hypothesis. Some early studies confirm the existence of the inverted-U curve (e.g. Paukert 1973; Ahluwalia 1976; Ahluwalia et al. 1976) while others find the opposite (e.g., Deininger and Squire 1996). Regarding the inequality–growth relationship, it is worth noting that some authors argue that serious inequality causes political and social instability and undermines investment and economic growth, as happened in Latin America and Sub-Saharan Africa (Galor and Zeira 1993; Alesina and Perotti 1996; Rodrik 1997). But, if inequality induced social conflict eventually leads to political reforms promoting democracy and income redistribution, the country may escape the inequality trap and economic stagnation (Acemoglu and Robinson 2002). More recently, the World Bank (2001, 2003, and 2004) argues that economic growth plays a crucial role in poverty reduction. But these reports can not identify a clear effect of growth on the reduction of inequality, although growth is found to be affected by severe inequality. It seems that growth is a necessary but not sufficient condition for reducing inequality. Based on a set of cross-country regressions, Bourguignon (2003: 17) concludes that the distributional effects of growth depend on the initial conditions prevailing in a country and that country specificity may also mean ample room for policy intervention in determining the distributional effects.

It is clear that the inequality–development relationship, as proposed by Kuznets, depends on an array of factors. Some play a prominent role at lower levels of economic development while others are more important at the later stages of development. The author of this chapter hypothesizes that there are four groups of factors that may exert effects on income inequality in China, and these hypotheses will be tested below.

The first group of factors relates to economic growth. It is commonly assumed that a tradeoff exists between economic efficiency and equity. When efficiency is the central concern, economic growth may be faster, but social equity may be compromised, and vice versa. On the other hand, economic growth usually brings about jobs which could raise the incomes of the poor and help alleviate poverty. The overall impact of growth on inequality is thus uncertain. This group of factors include economic growth rate, investment ratio (investment to GDP), level of FDI (as a proportion of GDP), trade dependence (ratio of import and export values to GDP), urbanization ratio (the share of urban population in total), labour migration ratio (the ratio of rural immigrant workers to urban employment), and registered urban unemployment rate.

With respect to urbanization and rural–urban migration, Kuznets points out that initial migration can cause enlargement of the low income groups in the cities, resulting in higher urban inequality without reducing rural inequality. Later on, however, the incomes of migrants or their next generation may rise, leading to reductions in urban inequality. Furthermore, as low income rural population decreases with massive migration, the urban–rural gap will narrow down. This effect may be more evident in China because rural labour surplus has been a serious problem. Urban unemployment rate reflects the growth of employment opportunities from the reverse direction.

The second group of factors relates to income redistribution and the social security system. Income redistribution can reduce inequality, but its effectiveness depends on the rationality and efficiency of the fiscal transfer and social security systems. In this study, the author focuses on the net transfer payment amongst provinces through the fiscal system (see Wang and Fan 2003, 2004). However, two issues should be noticed. First, net transfer payments may have played a role in reducing inter-regional income disparity other than reducing inequality within provinces, but this cannot be tested using the panel data model in the current study. Second, as shown in the literature, the current fiscal transfer system in China is not well designed and its function is not clearly defined. This might have undermined its effectiveness in reducing inequality (Wong 2005).

Other variables in the second group include the rates of coverage of the basic pension system, the basic medical insurance system and the unemployment insurance system which are operational in urban areas (most rural areas are not covered). These systems have been established in recent years, and their effectiveness still needs to be examined.

The third set of factors is the provision of infrastructure and other public goods. A large volume of literature stresses the effect of public education on reducing income inequality, because education can increase the stock of human capital within middle and low income groups and improve their employment and income earning ability. Public infrastructure, such as transport and telecommunication facilities, may also benefit this group by offering them more opportunities for employment and self-development. The variables being tested include average years of schooling, the density of highway and railroad network, and the telephone coverage rate.

The fourth group includes factors reflecting institutional arrangements. China, along with other transitional economies, has experienced privatization of public properties. In a market economy, private property is an important means for earning income. Consequently, privatization can lead to larger income inequality. However, there are also cases showing a reduction of income inequality arising from market development (World Bank 2003). The market oriented rural reforms in the early 1980s are responsible for the significant drop in the urban–rural income gap in China. Also, development of urban private sectors in more marketized areas in later periods did contribute to job creation and poverty reduction. By contrast, unemployment was observed as an important source of poverty and inequality in some less market oriented areas. To test the overall effect of marketization on income inequality, the marketization index of the National Economic Research Institute (NERI) (Fan, Wang, and Zhang 2001; Fan, Wang, and Zhu 2003, 2004) will be used.[1]

Inappropriate government intervention in the operations of enterprises, unjustified government levies, corruption, and similar institutional problems may affect income inequality. When political power is used in the allocation of resources without adequate monitoring, it induces rent-seeking behaviour and leads to unfair income distribution. Three variables are used to test for these effects: government intervention (using the proportion of time spent by entrepreneurs dealing with various government departments), enterprise non-tax burden (as a proportion of annual sales), and the 'grey income' index.[2] The

---

[1] The NERI index of marketization measure relative achievement in marketization of China's provinces in five fields, consisting of 23 indicators. The five fields are government–market relations, development of non-state enterprises, development of commodity markets, development of factor markets, and market intermediaries and legal environment for markets. A 0–10 score is assigned for each indicator.

[2] 'Grey incomes', not necessarily illegal, refer to incomes that recipients are unwilling to disclose. If derived from corruption or earned illegally, 'grey income' may widen income inequality. The author assumes that the latter is proportionally related to the former, and calculates this index in the following way: (1) take final private consumption from the provincial GDP account sheets as true resident consumption; (2) use the consumption expenditures from the

first two variables are collected from the NERI survey data, covering more than 3,000 enterprises, and the grey index are calculated from NBS data. All other data are from NBS (various years) unless otherwise indicated.

2.3 Does the Kuznets Curve Exist in China?

To carry out the analysis, the author uses panel data from 1996 to 2002 across 30 provinces (including four autonomous regions and four municipalities that are under direct central administration; Tibet is excluded due to shortage of data). There are many differences among different provinces. Yet, because of common history, cultural tradition, economic and political systems, policy environment, and reform experiences, they are expected to follow similar development path. The future of less developed provinces is expected to resemble the development status of today's advanced provinces. This makes the panel data analysis valid.

The Gini coefficient is used to measure inequality within urban and rural China, separately (the overall Gini is unavailable). To indicate the urban–rural income gap, the author uses the ratio of urban disposable income to net rural income, both on a per capita basis. Thus, at least three equations will be estimated to model income inequality in the urban areas, rural areas, and between urban and rural areas, respectively.

Two alternative functions are specified. Models 1a, 2a, and 3a (see below) include the provincial GDP per capita and its quadratic term as independent variables. This functional form allows for symmetrical increasing and decreasing segments of the Kuznets curve. However, the curve may well be non-symmetrical (see Deininger and Squire 1996 and Figure 2.1). To permit this possibility, the GDP variable is transformed into the logarithmic form and then included, along with its square, as the independent variables. This yields models 1b, 2b, and 3b (see below).

It is argued in the literature that a correct functional form should predict zero inequality when income is zero (Wan 2002). For this reason, the constant term should be excluded. However, given that the models are used to approximate real-world situation (zero income for everyone is virtually impossible in reality), it is more important to fit the models to the data as accurately as possible. The constant terms are, therefore, retained in the hope that they may help improve the goodness-of-fit.

Using notation *GINI* to denote Gini coefficient, *RUD* to denote urban–rural gap, subscript u to index urban China, r to index rural China, we have the following models:

NBS urban and rural household surveys and the provincial urban and rural population data to derive the reported resident consumption. The difference between the two consumption estimates, expressed as a percentage of the former, is defined as the 'grey income index'. A higher value of this index approximately implies more serious corruption in the relevant province.

Inequality Determinants

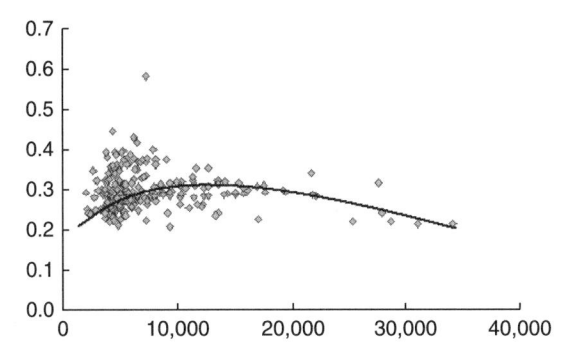

Figure 2.1: Relationship between rural Gini coefficient (on the Y-axis) and GDP per capita measured in RMB (on the X-axis), provincial data, 1996–2002

Source: Data from NBS (various years).

$$GINI_u = A_u + a_1 Y + a_2 Y^2 + v_u \tag{1a}$$

$$GINI_u = B_u + a_1 \ln Y + a_2 (\ln Y)^2 + w_u \tag{1b}$$

$$GINI_r = A_r + b_1 Y + b_2 Y^2 + v_r \tag{2a}$$

$$GINI_r = B_r + b_1 \ln Y + b_2 (\ln Y)^2 + w_r \tag{2b}$$

$$RUD = A_d + c_1 Y + c_2 Y^2 + v_d \tag{3a}$$

$$RUD = B_d + c_1 \ln Y + c_2 (\ln Y)^2 + w_d \tag{3b}$$

where Y is per capita GDP in 1996 constant price; A, B, a, b, and c are parameters to be estimated, and v and w denote the error terms. For easy reference, equations (1a), (2a), and (3a) will be referred to as linear models while (1b), (2b), and (3b) will be termed loglinear models.

The estimation results are tabulated in Table 2.1. It is clear that under the linear models, the coefficient estimates for GDP per capita are highly significant and positive and those for quadratic GDP per capita are negative and significant. These imply acceptance of the Kuznets hypothesis. Although some coefficients become insignificant under the loglinear models, they all have higher R^2s than their linear counterparts, and thus are preferred.

It is worth noting that all models predict increasing inequality in urban and rural China, and between urban and rural residents over a considerably long period. According to the preferred models, urban inequality would continue to increase in the very long term and will attain its maximum at GDP per capita of RMB two million. This is practically indifferent to a non-decreasing function.

Table 2.1: Estimates of the income inequality models (fixed effect)

	Model 1a	Model 1b	Model 2a	Model 2b	Model 3a	Model 3b
Dependent variable	$GINI_u$	$GINI_u$	$GINI_r$	$GINI_r$	RUD	RUD
Y	1.98E-3		2.39E-3		6.08E-5	
	(10.765**)		(6.273**)		(3.423**)	
Y^2	−3.52E-08		−5.67E-8		−6.71E-10	
	(−6.467**)		(−5.044**)		(−1.235)	
ln Y		27.878		85.225		−1.228
		(2.174*)		(3.067**)		(−1.053)
$(\ln Y)^2$		−0.9554		−4.210		0.0914
		(−1.325)		(−2.695**)		(1.376)
C	13.757	−144.942	16.126	−393.023	2.2632	6.378
	(13.161**)	(−2.543*)	(7.465**)	(−3.182**)	(23.39**)	(1.246)
R^2 (within)	0.4829	0.5460	0.1871	0.2154	0.1181	0.1236

Note: Numbers in parentheses are t-ratios; * significant at the 5% level; ** significant at the 1% level.
Source: Author's calculations.

Meanwhile, rural inequality would achieve its maximum at per capita GDP of RMB 25,000 in 1996 constant price, which is unlikely to be achieved before 2012. Interestingly the urban–rural gap would never decrease. To summarize the above results, further increase in income inequality in China is expected in the foreseeable future.

2.4 What Factors are Influential for Income Inequality?

In this section, the four groups of factors affecting income inequality, as discussed earlier, will be examined. A number of variables are added to earlier models in order to assess their effects on income inequality. Again, both the linear and loglinear models are considered. They are called extended linear and loglinear models. To economize on space, only extended loglinear models are shown below:

$$GINI_u = C_u + a_1 \ln Y + a_2 (\ln Y)^2 + a_3 YR + a_4 RI + a_5 RFI + a_6 OPEN \\ + a_7 URB + a_8 UEM + a_9 TRP + a_{10} RPES + a_{11} RUEM + a_{12} RMED \\ + a_{13} RWD + a_{14} HWD + a_{15} TEL + a_{16} ED + a_{17} MKT + + a_{18} LM \\ + a_{19} GI + a_{20} EB + a_{21} GY + e_u \quad (1d)$$

$$GINI_r = C_r + b_1 \ln Y + b_2 (\ln Y)^2 + b_3 YR + b_4 RI + b_5 RFI + b_6 OPEN \\ + b_7 URB + b_8 UEM + b_9 TRP + b_{10} RPES + b_{11} RUEM + b_{12} RMED \\ + b_{13} RWD + b_{14} HWD + b_{15} TEL + b_{16} ED + b_{17} MKT + b_{18} LM \\ + b_{19} GI + b_{20} EB + b_{21} GY + e_r \quad (2d)$$

Inequality Determinants

$$\begin{aligned}RUD = {} & C_d + c_1\ln Y + c_2(\ln Y)^2 + c_3 YR + c_4 RI + c_5 RFI + c_6 OPEN + c_7 URB \\ & + c_8 UEM + c_9 TRP + c_{10} RPES + c_{11} RUEM + c_{12} RMED + c_{13} RWD \\ & + c_{14} HWD + c_{15} TEL + c_{16} ED + c_{17} MKT + c_{18} LM + c_{19} GI + c_{20} EB \\ & + c_{21} GY + e_d\end{aligned} \quad (3d)$$

where C is a constant, YR is the GDP growth rate; RI is the investment ratio; RFI is the ratio of FDI in total investment; $OPEN$ is the ratio of imports and exports to GDP; URB is the urbanization ratio; UEM is the registered urban unemployment rate; TRP is the per capita net transfer payment; RPE, RUE, and RME are the coverage rates of the urban pension, unemployment insurance, and medical insurance systems, respectively; RWD and HWD are the railroad and highway network densities; TEL is the telephone coverage rate; ED is the average year of schooling of the population above 6 years of age; MKT is the marketization index; LM is the labour migration ratio; GI is a variable of government intervention; EB is non-tax burden of enterprises; GY is the grey income index; e is the error term.

Estimation results of the extended models are presented in Table 2.A1 in the Appendix. They indicate that the extended log-linear models have higher R^2s than their linear counterparts, and they have more estimates which are statistically significant. The Hausman test favours the fixed effect specification for models (1d) and (3d), but random effect specification for model (2d). Variables with very low t-ratios were dropped from the models and re-estimation is undertaken. The final results of the preferred models are shown as follows:

$$\begin{aligned}\hat{GINI}_u = {} & -346.17 + 72.94\ln Y - 3.731(\ln Y)^2 + 0.0514 RI + 0.0602 RFI \\ & + 0.0343 OPEN + 0.3345 UEM - 0.0041 TRP + 0.1249 RPES \\ & - 0.0311 RUEM + 0.0192 RMED + 1.802 ED - 0.6531 MKT \\ & + 2.003 EB + 0.0509 GY + \hat{e}_u\end{aligned} \quad (1d)$$

$$\begin{aligned}\hat{GINI}_r = {} & -161.21 + 41.28\ln Y - 2.166(\ln Y)^2 - 0.2327 YR - 0.1360 RFI \\ & + 0.0074 TRP - 0.0450 RWD + 0.2544 TEL - 0.5118 MKT + \hat{e}_r\end{aligned} \quad (2d)$$

$$\begin{aligned}RUD = {} & -30.64 + 7.839 Y - 0.4597(\ln Y)^2 - 0.0053 YR + 0.0093 OPEN \\ & + 0.0002 TRP + 0.0035 RMED - 0.0035 RWD - 0.0085 HWD \\ & + 0.0403 TEL - 0.0658 ED + \hat{e}_d\end{aligned} \quad (3d)$$

Both the urban and urban–rural inequality models (1d) and (3d) show relatively high explanatory power; their within R^2s are between 0.6 and 0.7. The overall R^2 of the rural inequality model (equation (2d) with random effect) is 0.43. Per capita GDP and its quadratic term are significant in all three models.

What about the impact of growth factors on urban inequality? In model (1d), the investment ratio (RI), FDI ratio (RFI) and trade dependence ($OPEN$) all have positive coefficient estimates with t-ratios above 1, although insignificant. The insignificance of *RFI* and *OPEN* is likely due to their multicollinearity with ln*Y* (correlation coefficients are 0.656 and 0.746, respectively). They are also correlated with *Y* (correlation coefficients are 0.622 and 0.748, respectively). These multicollinearities may be responsible for the insignificance of *Y* in equation (1c). Trade dependence has a positive and significant impact on urban–rural gap, possibly due to its positive effect on urban incomes but less effect on rural incomes. Not surprisingly, urban unemployment rate is positively related to urban Gini coefficient, confirming that unemployment is one of the causes of inequality.

The effects of economic growth rate (*YR*) on rural inequality and the urban–rural income gap are negative, and significant in the rural inequality model. This is because high economic growth generates employment, thus helps transfer rural labour to non-agricultural sectors, which may lead to poverty reduction in rural China. The urbanization ratio and labour migration ratio are dropped from the models because of their low, although negative, *t*-ratios.

Regarding the second group of factors—transfer payments and social security systems—the fiscal transfer payment is found to have a negative impact on urban Gini coefficient, but positive one on rural Gini and the urban–rural income gap, all significant at the 1 or 5 per cent levels. Thus, the transfer payment system was effective in urban China only. It is known that some transfer payments in rural China were used to encourage local investment and supplement wage expenditure of the local public sector, thus they did not help the poor.

The objective of the social security system is to reduce inequality. However, only the unemployment insurance scheme is shown to have a negative effect on the urban Gini, confirming the importance of unemployment as an inequality determinant. Surprisingly, both the pension and medical insurance systems have positive and significant effects on the urban inequality, suggesting that the urban middle and high income groups may benefit more from these systems than the low income groups. According to the results of an unpublished NERI survey undertaken in 2005, the average reimbursement from the medical insurance system is higher for urban middle and high income groups than for low income groups. The same is true in terms of reimbursement ratio out of per capita medical expenditure. In other words, the coverage is lower for the poor. This indicates existence of obstacles in extending the coverage to the poor within the current system. In addition, these systems are absent in most rural areas, and thus only urban residents can benefit. This explains why the medicare system has a positive effect on urban–rural inequality.

As to the third group of factors—public goods and infrastructures—the average year of schooling exerts a positive and significant impact on urban Gini. Its estimate for the urban–rural inequality is negative, but insignificant. These results echo the fact that education opportunities are unequally distributed among different social groups, and the poor are disadvantaged in this regard. Turning to transport and telecommunication facilities, both the railroad and highway densities have negative estimates; the former on the rural

Inequality Determinants

Gini coefficient and the latter on the urban–rural income gap, both are significant at the 10 per cent level. These results suggest that the development of transport facilities helps rural residents. An unusual result is the positive and significant effects of telephone coverage on rural Gini coefficient and the urban–rural income gap, although this is not the case for the urban Gini. This may imply that telephone usage is basically limited to urban residents and middle and high income groups in the rural regions, where in 2003 only 45 per cent of households had fixed telephones.

Finally, with respect to institutional factors, the marketization index is found to be negatively correlated with both urban and rural Gini coefficients though the estimates are not significant. The non-tax burden and the grey income index have positive impacts on urban inequality. The former is significant at the 5 per cent level, and the latter close to the 10 per cent level. It seems that inadequate government levies and corruption can change income distribution, leading to greater inequity.

The fitted curves of loglinear models and their extended counterparts are illustrated in Figures 2.2(a), 2.2(b), and 2.2(c), respectively. In each of the figures, the dotted and solid curves represent the non-extended model and extended models, respectively. Figure 2.2(a) shows a large difference between the two curves for urban China. Clearly, a large portion of urban inequality, formerly explained by GDP per capita and its quadratic term, is now explained by other variables. This, however, is not true for Figure 2.2(b). Interestingly, the two curves in Figure 2.2(c) diverge at the higher income level. This indicates that the urban–rural inequality is heavily influenced by explanatory variables for the more developed regions.

To estimate the contribution of various influential factors to income inequality, the 2002 average values of these variables are substituted into the empirical models of (1d), (2d), and (3d). The results, tabulated in Table 2.2, present some noteworthy findings. First, rural income inequality, and urban–rural inequality to some extent, is mainly due to the low levels of economic development, but this is not the case for urban inequality. As shown in Table 2.2, GDP per capita explains a major part of rural inequalities and the urban–rural gap, but only explains a minor part of urban inequality. Three-quarters of the urban Gini coefficient is explained by other factors.

Second, the direction of the effect of short run economic growth is uncertain. Some of these factors (i.e. the investment ratio, foreign investment ratio, and trade dependence), cause urban inequality to expand, but these effects are partially offset by the employment effect of growth. The trade dependence also lifts up urban–rural inequality, whereas high economic growth rate reduces rural and urban–rural inequalities. Broadly speaking, these effects led to rises in both the urban Gini and urban–rural gap by almost 10 per cent, but reduced the rural Gini by more than 10 per cent.

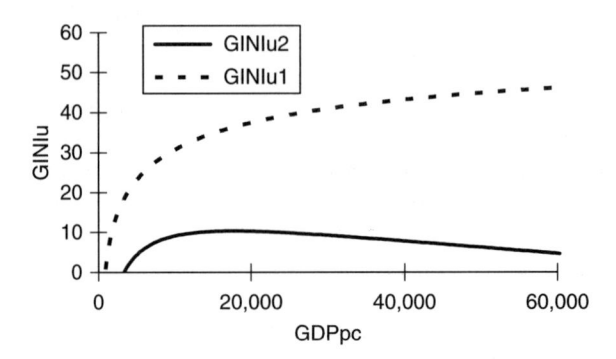

Figure 2.2a: The two urban inequality curves

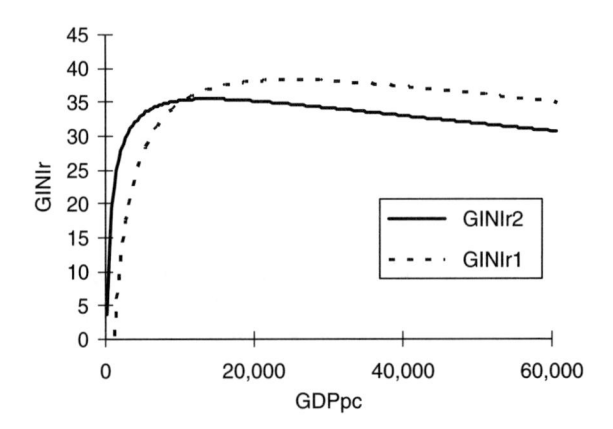

Figure 2.2b: The two rural inequality curves

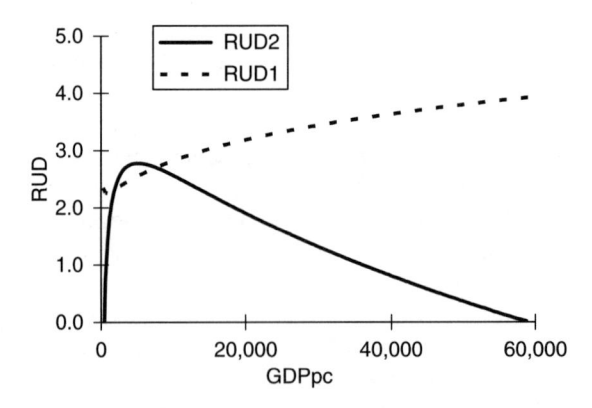

Figure 2.2c: The two rural–urban inequality curves

Note: The horizontal axis is GDP per capita (RMB), the vertical axis in Figures 2.1 and 2.2 indicates Gini coefficient (%), and that in Figure 2.3 indicates the ratio of urban per capita income to rural per capita income. GINIu1, GINIr1, and RUD1 are fitted curves based on the non-extended models; GINIu2, GINIr2, and RUD2 are that based on the extented models.

Source: Based on the modelling results.

Inequality Determinants

Third, after cancelling out the positive and negative effects of the fiscal transfer and social security systems, these factors explain roughly 5 per cent of the urban Gini and almost 10 per cent of the urban–rural gap. These positive results are due to both the low coverage of social security systems for the poor, and the inefficient use of transfer payments.

Forth, education and public infrastructure (railway and highway) are found to help reduce urban–rural gap by a quarter. But education is also the most important factor responsible for urban inequality, with a positive contribution of nearly 50 per cent. This is due to unequal opportunities, especially in higher education, and therefore unequal distribution of human resources among different social groups.

Finally, institutional environment is important for income distribution. Both enterprises' non-tax burden and the grey income index are positively related to urban inequality and responsible for 18 per cent of the Gini coefficient. To the

Table 2.2: Contribution of Variables Influencing Inequality, 2002

Influencing factors	Variable	Average value	Urban	Rural	Urban–rural
GDP per capita (RMB, 1996 prices)	Y	10,087			
Log GDP per capita	$\ln Y$	9.22	6.724	3.806	72.27
Square log GDP per capita	$(\ln Y)^2$	84.99	−3.171	−1.841	−39.07
GDP growth rate (%)	GDPR	11.70		−0.027	−0.06
Investment ratio (investment/GDP, %)	RI	39.70	0.020	0.000	
FDI ratio (FDI/fixed investment, %)	RFI	6.48	0.004	−0.009	
Trade dependence (import&export value to GDP, %)	OPEN	29.02	0.010		0.27
Urban unemployment rate (%)	UEM	3.86	0.013		
Net transfer payment (RMB, 1996 prices)	TRP	106.94	−0.004	0.008	0.03
Coverage of the pension system (%)	RPE	20.75	0.026		
Coverage of the unemployment benefit (%)	RUE	64.06	−0.020		
Coverage of the medicare system (%)	RME	60.32	0.012		0.21
Railway density (km/100 km^2)	RWD	24.87		−0.011	−0.09
Highway density (km/100 km^2)	HWD	17.74			−0.15
Telephone coverage (sets/100 people)	TEL	18.02		0.046	0.73
Years of schooling above 6 yrs old (person/year)	ED	7.82	0.141		−0.51
Marketization index	MKT	5.98	−0.039	−0.031	
Non-tax burden to enterprises' sales (%)	EB	2.42	0.049		
Grey income index (%)	GY	6.56	0.003		
Constant	C	1.00	−3.462	−1.612	−30.64
Contribution of GDP p.c.+unidentified+error			0.072	0.345	2.55
Sum contribution of other factors			0.214	−0.024	0.42
Aver. urban/rural Gini and rural-urban ratio			0.286	0.321	2.97

Notes: The railroad and highway densities are calculated as the length of network lines (km) per 100 km^2 of provincial territory, both converted into standard length of grade II highway. The conversion factor between railway and standard grade II highway is 14.7. Urban–rural income ratio is the urban per capita disposable income to rural per capita net income.

Source: Calculated from the estimation results and NBS (2003, 2004).

contrary, the marketization index is negatively related to both the urban and rural Gini coefficients, reducing them by more than 10 per cent.

2.5 Conclusion and Policy Implications

In this chapter, we examine the trend and causes of income inequality in China using a panel data modelling method. The result does not support an unconditional inverted-U curve, indicating that economic growth alone will lead a continued trend of rising inequality in the foreseeable future in China. Further analysis shows that four groups of factors are either responsible for the rising inequality, or useful measures to reduce inequality. They are related to short run growth, fiscal transfer and social security systems, education and public infrastructure, and institutional factors.

Most growth factors are disequalizing but they can help reduce inequality via their effects on employment. Unfortunately, the fiscal transfer and social security systems are found to contribute to higher inequality due to inefficient use of the transfer payment and low coverage of the social security systems for the poor. Thus, possibilities exist for enhancing these systems to lower inequality and increase economic efficiency. Education opportunities are unequally distributed in China thus supporting the disadvantaged in education can certainly help improve income distribution, although this effect is only effective in narrowing down the urban–rural gap. Finally, marketization is negatively related to urban and rural inequality. However, other institutional factors such as enterprises' non-tax burden and grey income index are positively related to inequality. Therefore, institutional reforms aiming at better governance will not only help contribute to China's sustainable development in the long run, but also help reduce inequality.

Inequality Determinants

Appendix

Table 2.A1: Estimation results

Dependent variable	Model 1c (fe) $Gini_u$	Model 1d (fe) $Gini_u$	Model 2c (fe) $GINI_r$	Model 2d (re) $GINI_r$	Model 3c (fe) RUD	Model 3d (fe) RUD
lnY		72.937 (3.092**)		41.28 (1.878′)		7.839 (4.242**)
lnY²		−3.731 (−2.795**)		−2.166 (−1.699′)		−0.4597 (−4.212**)
Y	0.000389 (0.986)		0.00163 (1.935*)		−9.11E-05 (−2.639**)	
Y²	−9.62E-09 (−1.247)		−3.22E-08 (−2.203*)		1.04E-09 (1.570)	
YR			−0.2280 (−2.319*)	−0.2327 (−2.419*)	−0.00681 (−1.751′)	−0.00532 (−1.396)
RI	0.1296 (2.925**)	0.0514 (1.116)				
RFI	0.0390 (0.697)	0.0602 (1.118)	−0.1758 (−1.543)	−0.1360 (−1.714′)		
OPEN	0.0130 (0.409)	0.0343 (1.124)			0.00716 (2.675**)	0.00930 (3.599**)
UEM	0.1782 (1.059)	0.3354 (2.060*)				
TRP	−0.00371 (−2.618**)	−0.0041 (−3.085**)	0.00760 (3.626**)	0.00738 (4.113**)	0.000384 (4.159**)	0.000238 (2.297*)
RPE	0.0889 (1.662′)	0.1249 (2.407*)				
RUE	−0.00796 (−0.517)	−0.0311 (−1.948*)				
RME	0.0360 (3.133**)	0.0192 (1.631′)			0.00367 (4.159**)	0.00352 (4.071**)
RWD			0.1012 (0.982)	−0.0450 (−1.620′)	−0.00209 (−0.485)	−0.00354 (−0.873)
HWD					−0.0112 (−1.809′)	−0.00854 (−1.681′)
TEL			−0.0614 (−0.315)	0.2544 (2.427*)	0.0421 (5.468**)	0.0403 (5.487**)
ED	2.498 (3.516**)	1.802 (2.556*)			0.0173 (0.316)	−0.0658 (−1.198)
MKT	−0.7309 (−1.378)	−0.6531 (−1.302)	0.8918 (0.812)	−0.5118 (−1.047)		
EB	1.844 (2.112*)	2.003 (2.389*)				
GY	0.0827 (2.582*)	0.0509 (1.600)				
C	−3.675 (−0.712)	−346.17 (−3.294**)	16.552 (2.523*)	−161.21 (−1.698′)	2.653 (6.728**)	−30.643 (−3.924**)
R^2 (within)	0.5914	0.6245	0.2773	0.2495	0.6790	0.6973
(between)	0.0011	0.0003	0.0051	0.6541	0.1903	0.0008
(overall)	0.0231	0.0222	0.0165	0.4312	0.2436	0.0399
Hausman test	$X^2(14) = 72.9$ $p = 0.0000$	$X^2(14) = 74.1$ $p = 0.0000$	$X^2(8) = 16.6$ $p = 0.0340$	$X^2(8) = 10.0$ $p = 0.2615$	$X^2(10) = 15.0$ $p = 0.1310$	$X^2(10) = 42.5$ $p = 0.0000$

Note: Numbers in parentheses are *t*-ratios. Those with ′ are significant at the 10% level, with * are significant at the 5% level, and with ** are at the 1% level.

Source: Author's calculations.

References

Acemoglu, D., and J. Robinson (2002). 'The Political Economy of the Kuznets Curve', *Review of Development Economics* 6(2): 183–203.

Ahluwalia, M. (1976). 'Inequality, Poverty and Development', *Journal of Development Economics* 6: 307–42.

—— N. G. Carter, and H. Chenery (1976). 'Growth and Poverty in Developing Countries', *Journal of Development Economics* 6: 299–341.

Alesina, A., and R. Perotti (1996). 'Income Distribution, Political Instability, and Investment', *European Economic Review* 40(6): 1203–28.

Bourguignon, F. (2003). 'The Poverty–Growth–Inequality Triangle', paper presented at the Agence Française de Développement/EU Development Network conference on Poverty, Inequality and Growth, Paris, 13 November.

Deininger, K., and L. Squire (1996). 'A New Dataset Measuring Income Inequality', *World Bank Economic Review* 10(3): 565–91.

Fan, G., X. Wang, and L. Zhang (2001). *NERI Index of Marketization of China's Provinces*, Economic Sciences Press: Beijing.

—— —— H. Zhu (2003, 2004). *NERI Index of Marketization of China's Provinces*, Economic Sciences Press: Beijing.

Galor, O., and J. Zeira (1993). 'Income Distribution and Macroeconomics', *Review of Economic Studies* 60: 35–52.

Kuznets, S. (1955). 'Economic Growth and Income Inequality', *The American Economic Review* 45(1): 1–28.

NBS (National Bureau of Statistics) (various years). *China Statistical Yearbook*, China Statistics Press: Beijing.

Paukert, F. (1973). 'Income Distribution at Different Levels of Development: a Survey of the Evidence', *International Labour Review* 108(2): 97–125.

Rodrik, D. (1997). *Has Globalization Gone Too Far?* Institute of International Economics: Washington, DC.

Wan, G. (2002). 'Income Inequality and Growth in Transition Economies: Are Nonlinear Models Needed?' *WIDER Research Paper* 2002/104, UNU-WIDER: Helsinki.

Wang, X., and G. Fan (2003). *Regional Disparity in China: Tendency and the Influential Factors*, Konrad-Adenauer-Stiftung Publication: Beijing.

—— —— (2004). 'Regional Disparity in China: An General Analysis on the Tendency and the Influential Factors', in X. Wang and G. Fan (eds), *Regional Disparity in China: Tendency and the Influential Factors* (in Chinese), Economic Science Press: Beijing.

WIID (UNU-WIDER World Income Inequality Database) (2000). http://www.wider.unu.edu, accessed December 2004.

Wong, C. (2005). 'Can China Change Development Paradigm for the 21st Century?' (in Chinese), *Comparison* 18.

World Bank (2001). *World Development Report 2000/2001: Attack Poverty*, World Bank: Washington, DC.

—— (2003). 'China Country Economic Memorandum: Promoting Growth with Equity', *World Bank Report* 24169-CHA, World Bank: Washington, DC.

—— (2004). *A Better Investment Climate for Everyone: World Development Report 2004*, Oxford University Press for the World Bank: New York.

3
Poverty Reduction in China: Trends and Causes

Yin Zhang and Guanghua Wan

3.1 Introduction

Poverty dynamics in China commands worldwide attention not merely because of the sheer size of its population but also because its low starting point means that China still has the second largest share of the poor in the world.[1] China's fight against poverty will continue to significantly affect global poverty trends. More intriguing, and also puzzling, is the fact that poverty reduction slowed down and at times was even reversed in the past decade or so (Ravallion and Chen 2004) while per capita real GDP frequently posted growth rates of well over 8 per cent per annum. This development contrasts with China's experience in the 1980s when growth in the same range successfully lifted hundreds of millions out of poverty. What could the weakening of the responsiveness of poverty to aggregate output growth be attributed to? Was it caused by a reduction in the household share of national income, in which case even the income of an average person would have increased more slowly than suggested by GDP growth rates? Or, was it down to an increase in inequality such that the gains from aggregate growth have failed to trickle down to those on the bottom rung of the income ladder? A theoretically less interesting yet empirically important third possibility is that the reported poverty trend is a statistical artefact arising from the inappropriate measurement of poverty.

In this study, we explore poverty changes in China in the 1990s and attempt to attribute these changes to income growth and redistribution, respectively. To address the issue of robustness, we use unit record household survey data from two separate sources rather than the grouped data published by the NBS.

---

[1] According to the World Bank's Global Poverty Monitoring database, more than 210 million people in China live with less than US$1.08 per day (in 1993 PPP) as of 2001, 99 per cent of whom are in the rural areas.

Further, we compare results from using different poverty measures, poverty lines and equivalence scales and adjust poverty lines over time and space. Urban poverty, as well as rural poverty, is considered. Our results help assess the relative importance of growth and inequality in affecting poverty, and thus shed light on the proximate causes of the lack of progress in poverty reduction in the 1990s.

The plan of this chapter is as follows. In section 3.2, we describe the decomposition methodology and discuss various uncertainties involved in assessing poverty trends and decomposition. Section 3.3 presents the time profile of poverty measures and the decomposition results. Particular attention is given to results that are consistent across alternative poverty measures, poverty lines and equivalence scales. Concluding remarks are given in the last section.

3.2 Decomposition Procedure and the Robustness of Decomposition Results

The most popular growth redistribution decomposition of poverty trends is that proposed by Datt and Ravallion (1992). Kakwani and Subbarao (1990) and Jain and Tendulkar (1990) each use a variant of the Datt-Ravallion method. All three methods are path dependent. In addition, the first two are either inexact or come with a non-vanishing residual component unless distribution remains the same or growth is absent over time. As shown below, these nuisances can be removed by a simple averaging procedure.

Let ΔP denote a change in poverty index P and assume both income Y and poverty line z are measured in real terms (changes in the poverty line can also be accommodated). A change in poverty between period 0 and period T can be written as:

$$\Delta P = P(Y_T; z) - P(Y_0; z) \tag{1}$$

By definition, the growth component is the change in poverty due to a change in the mean of Y while holding its distribution (characterized by the Lorenz curve) constant. The inequality or redistribution component is the change in poverty due to a change in the distribution of Y while holding its mean constant. Let $Y(L_i, \mu_j)$ be a hypothetical income distribution with Lorenz curve L_i and mean μ_j taken from different distributions, i.e., $i = 0$ or T, $j = 0$ or T and $i \neq j$. Let $P(L_i, \mu_j)$ represent the corresponding poverty index of $Y(L_i, \mu_j)$. The growth component of ΔP can be defined as:

$$\text{growth component} = P(L_0, \mu_T) - P(Y_0; z) \tag{2}$$

or, alternatively as:

$$\text{growth component} = P(Y_T; z) - P(L_T, \mu_0) \tag{2a}$$

Similarly, the redistribution component can either be defined as:

$$\text{redistribution component} = P(L_T; \mu_0) - P(Y_0; z) \tag{3}$$

or:

$$\text{redistribution component} = P(Y_T; z) - P(L_0, \mu_T) \tag{3a}$$

It is easy to see that different combinations of the alternative growth and redistribution components produce four distinct decompositions of ΔP. If equations (2) and (3) are used, period 0 is considered as the reference period. By contrast, choosing equations (2a) and (3a) implies that the reference period is period T. The results from the two decompositions need not agree, and both are inexact in the sense that the growth and redistribution components do add up to ΔP. If the combination (2a)–(3) or (2)–(3a) is used, the decomposition will be exact since:

$$P(Y_T; z) - P(Y_0; z) = [\text{redistribution component}] + [\text{growth component}]$$

$$= [P(Y_T; z) - P(L_0, \mu_T)] + [P(L_0, \mu_T) - P(Y_0; z)] \tag{4}$$

$$= [P(L_T; \mu_0) - P(Y_0; z)] + [P(Y_T; z) - P(L_T; \mu_0)] \tag{5}$$

However, the redistribution and growth components are measured against different reference periods in equations (4) and (5). Again, the two decompositions will produce different results in general and are thus equally arbitrary or equally justified.

A solution to the reference point problem is to take the average of equations (4) and (5) to arrive at:

$$\begin{aligned}\Delta P = &\ 0.5\{[P(Y_T; z) - P(L_0, \mu_T)] + [P(L_T; \mu_0) - P(Y_0; z)]\} \\ &+ 0.5\{[P(L_0; \mu_T) - P(Y_0; z)] + [P(Y_T; z) - P(L_T; \mu_0)]\}\end{aligned} \tag{6}$$

As it turns out, the decomposition in equation (6) is not an arithmetic gimmick; theoretical justifications can be found in the cooperative game theory (Shorrocks 1999; Kolenikov and Shorrocks 2005). Apart from notational difference, equation (6) is identical to what Shorrocks (1999) derived using Shapley value. Thus, we can decompose poverty differences into a growth component G and an inequality component I as:

$$G = 0.5\{[P(L_0, \mu_T) - P(Y_0; z)] + [P(Y_T; z) - P(L_T, \mu_0)]\} \quad (7)$$

$$I = 0.5\{[P(Y_T; z) - P(L_0, \mu_T)] + [P(L_T, \mu_0) - P(Y_0; z)]\} \quad (8)$$

The decomposition is symmetric as well as exact.

How can the poverty indices $P(L_0, \mu_T)$ and $P(L_T, \mu_0)$ of the hypothetical distributions be obtained? The method used in previous studies is to derive the functional form of the poverty index as a function of the mean and parameters governing the shape of the Lorenz curve of the distribution. The parameters are then estimated econometrically for both periods 0 and T. Plugging into the derived formula the parameter estimates for period 0 and mean income of period T gives $P(L_0, \mu_T)$. $P(L_T, \mu_0)$ can be obtained similarly. Implementing this method requires a priori specification of the parametric form of either the Lorenz curve or the probability density function of relative income. Both the specification and the estimation of parametric models can give rise to errors biasing the results, a price one is forced to pay when faced with grouped data. If unit record micro data are available, which is the case of this study, a simpler solution exists. To leave the Lorenz curve of an income distribution intact but give it a new mean, one can simply scale every observation, that is, $Y(L_T, \mu_0) = Y_T \times (\mu_0/\mu_T)$ and $Y(L_0; \mu_T) = Y_0 \times (\mu_T/\mu_0)$.

Even with unit record data, however, making poverty comparison is still subject to a host of uncertainties, many of which carry over to the decomposition of poverty changes. We consider three such uncertainties here: poverty measures, poverty lines, and equivalence scales. The three most widely used poverty measures are the head count ratio $P0$, the poverty gap index $P1$ and the squared poverty gap index $P2$, all of which belong to the Foster–Greer–Thorbecke (FGT) (Foster et al. 1984) family of poverty measures:

$$P_\alpha = \frac{1}{N} \sum_{Y_i \leq z} \left(\frac{z - Y_i}{z}\right)^\alpha \quad (9)$$

The head-count ratio ($\alpha = 0$) gives the proportion of the population whose incomes fall below the poverty line z. The poverty gap index ($\alpha = 1$) measures the average income shortfall in meeting the living standards implied by the poverty line. The average shortfall is expressed as a percentage of the poverty line, and the income shortfall of the non-poor is deemed to be zero. The squared poverty gap index ($\alpha = 2$) is the sum of the proportional poverty gaps weighted by themselves. It is well known that, depending on how inequalities among the poor have changed, the three measures may give out conflicting signals regarding changes in poverty. This in turn will lead to

Poverty Reduction

different assessment of the relative role played by income growth and redistribution in affecting poverty.[2]

The evaluation of changes in poverty may also be very sensitive to where the poverty line is drawn. For example, a poverty line set near a local mode of the income distribution might unduly exaggerate the growth component of poverty decomposition, thereby obscuring changes occurring further down the distribution. In this chapter, we consider four sets of national and international poverty lines. These include the US$1.08 and US$2.15 per capita per day poverty lines in 1993 PPP, the US$1 and US$2 per capita per day poverty lines in 1985 PPP, the urban and rural poverty lines proposed in Ravallion and Chen (2004) (1,200 yuan for urban areas, and 850 yuan for rural areas in 2002 prices), the official rural poverty line of 530 yuan in 1995 prices, and a 1995 urban poverty line obtained by adjusting the official rural line by the 2002 urban to rural poverty line ratio in Ravallion and Chen (2004). Another concern about the poverty line is whether a uniform nominal value of the poverty line is applicable to all regions under examination. The costs of living vary, sometimes widely, across Chinese provinces. Official CPIs published by the NBS, available at the provincial level, allow one to trace the changes in the costs of living within a province over time, but not the differences across provinces. Using official CPIs and price data for 1990, Brandt and Holz (2004) constructed several panels of provincial price levels for the latter purpose. One of these price deflators is adopted in this chapter to convert poverty lines at the national level to provincial poverty lines or, equivalently, to convert nominal income figures to real incomes measured in national prices of the base year.[3]

Most existing studies about China's income poverty use per capita income as the indicator of individual welfare.[4] As is known, some important household consumption items like housing, utilities, transportation, etc., are fairly non-rival.

---

[2] To take a simple example, suppose that an income distribution has changed from (1, 2, 3, 4) to (2, 2, 2, 4) and the poverty line is set at 2.5. The head count ratio would indicate an increase in poverty (from 0.5 to 0.75) whereas the poverty gap index would show a decrease (from 0.2 to 0.15). Decomposing the change in head count ratio according to equations (7) and (8) would put the contribution of growth at zero and the contribution of redistribution as poverty worsening ($I > 0$). The same decomposition applied to the change in the poverty gap index would give a negative redistribution component.

[3] For rural areas, we use the deflator obtained by applying to a rural consumption basket rural CPIs adjusted for consumption of self-produced products. For urban areas, the deflator is obtained by applying official urban CPIs to an urban consumption basket. It is necessary to note that although Brandt and Holz (2004) used separate rural and urban baskets, they applied the same compositions to all provinces throughout 1984–2000. As a result, regional differences in and changes over time of consumption patterns are ignored. In addition, consumption baskets used for deriving CPIs are meant to be representative of the consumption pattern of the entire population, and hence may well differ from the consumption pattern of the poor.

[4] In a study of urban residents in 12 cities, Gustafsson et al. (2004) found that the size and age composition of households have a modest impact on households' perception of minimum living expenditure.

The existence of scale economies due to such semi-public goods, along with the varying needs of households of different demographic compositions, means that the same amount of per capita income does not always denote the command of the same amount of real resources for individuals from different households. To account for such idiosyncrasies, we employ the constant elasticity equivalence scale to normalize household sizes. More specifically, if n_i represents the number of people in household i, the normalized household size is given by $k_i = n_i^\theta$, where θ is alternatively set to 0, 0.8, and 0.5.[5] Given a poverty line defined in per capita income, it is clear that the larger the value of θ, the lower the level of poverty. Whether and how applying a different equivalence scale will impact on the change in poverty and its decomposition is not immediately clear.

3.3 Poverty Dynamics in the 1990s

The rural and urban household surveys administered by the NBS have long been the most important data source for studying income distribution in China. Compared with other available household income data, the NBS data have two major strengths. The NBS surveys cover all mainland provinces and are thus nationally representative. Going back to 1980, the NBS data also have the longest time span. However, the NBS data have also come under criticism for excluding from houshold income many non-monetary items such as housing subsidies, various incomes in kind received by urban residents from their work units, the imputed value of owner occupied housing, and so on. The importance of these items as household income sources has varied over time. Therefore, poverty trends based on the NBS data are biased to the extent that they reflect the changing severity of the measurement error (Khan 1999). The published NBS data are invariably grouped,[6] and the format of grouping has evolved and is different across provinces and different levels of reporting.[7] As discussed earlier, obtaining poverty measures from grouped data requires estimating the Lorenz curve or probability density function. This constitutes another source for potential bias in estimated poverty trends, and the incosistnency in reporting format compounds the problem.

---

[5] $\theta = 1$ corresponds to the assumption that there exist no scale economies. Although the one parameter equivalence scale does not explicitly account for differences in household characteristics other than household size, Figini (1998) found that, for OECD countries, many two parameter equivalence scales in common use are empirically similar (when measuring inequality) to the one parameter equivalence scale with $\theta = 0.5$.

[6] Some researchers have been given access to the unit record data of the NBS surveys for selected provinces and years (e.g. Ravallion and Chen 1999; Tsui 1998).

[7] Data at the provincial level are usually reported in the form of consecutive income brackets. So are data for the 1980s at the national level. National data for later years and some province level data are reported in population percentiles. The number and division of income classes have not remained constant, either.

Poverty Reduction

Another dataset, which is closely related to the NBS data and for which household-level information is available, comprises data collected through the China Household Income Project (CHIP), a collaborative effort between an international group of economists and the Chinese Academy of Social Sciences. The CHIP has sparate rural and urban surveys, each sampling a fraction of the households covered in the corresponding NBS survey. Three rounds of CHIP surveys have been carried out, providing information about income and other household characteristics for 1988, 1995, and 2002. The number of provinces samples in each round is, respectively, 28, 19, and 21 for the rural survey and 10, 11, and 11 for the urban survey. The income definitions adopted in the CHIP surveys correct for the defects in the NBS surveys, making the CHIP data a good candidate for poverty and inequality analysis.[8] When it comes to trends in income poverty, however, the CHIP data are not particularly suitable at least as far as the 1980s and 1990s are concerned. For these two decades, only three years of CHIP data are available. Income typically fluctuates over the business cycle. For economies like China's with only rudimentary unemployment insurance and other income stabilization systems, cyclical movements of income can be quite prominent. It is therefore a stretch to infer anything about poverty trends from the income data of three sparsely spaced years. Further, the fact that the geographical coverage of the CHIP rural survey dropped sharply between 1988 and 1995 from 28 to 19 provinces calls into question whether rural data from the first two rounds are comparable.

The analysis in this chapter is based on two alternative datasets with household level income date. Our first dataset comes from the rural household survey conducted by the Research Centre for Rural Economy (RCRE) at the Ministry of Agriculture of China. The full RCRE sample covers all 31 mainland provinces and mega-cities, and dates back to 1988. We were able to obtain the 1995–2002 data for three provinces, Guangdong, Hubei, and Yunnan. These are essentially the same data used in Wan and Zhou (2005), and a brief description of the history of the RCRE survey can be found thereof. The RCRE data have been deemed as of reasonable quality and sampling approach, and have been satisfactorily used in such studies as Benjamin et al. (2005) and Giles and Yoo (2006). In addition, a long and continuous time series is a desirable property for studying trends in poverty and inequality.

Our second data source is the China Health and Nutrition Survey (CHNS), a joint project run by the Carolina Population Center at the University of North Carolina, the National Institute of Nutrition and Food Safety, and the Chinese Center for Disease Control and Prevention. Five rounds of CHNS, which distinguishs between urban and rural neighbourhoods, were conducted in

---

[8] Examples of such studies include, among others, Khan (1999), Khan and Riskin (2001), and Khan and Riskin (2005).

1989, 1991, 1993, 1997, and 2000. Each round covers around 15,000 individuals from about 4,000 households spread over nine provinces. Unlike the NBS, CHIP, and RCRE surveys where the participating households are required to keep daily records of income and expenditure items, the CHNS collects income information by soliciting answers to a pre-set questionnaire. It is debatable whether this non-diary-based approach undermines or enhances the accuracy of income data for poverty research. One one hand, the CHNS method seems rather crude in that it asks the interviewee to recollect information over the past year; on the other hand, some studies have shown (e.g., Benjamin et al. 2005) that the diary-based approach tends to underrepresent both extremes of the income distribution.[9] Since one of our concerns in this chapter is whether the slowdown in poverty reduction reported in some recent studies is sensitive to the choice of data source, the methodological feature of the CHNS is rather fit for purpose. Though not primarily an income survey, the income related part of the CHNS questionnaire is designed to enable imputing the values of incomes and subsidies received in kind, both of which are excluded in NBS surveys.[10]

The foregoing discussion shows that each of the four major household surveys has its own strengths and weaknesses. A definitive account of poverty developments in China during the 1980s and 1990s is unlikely to emerge from any of them alone. It looks, therefore, a more productive approach is to collate and compare information from different data sources, and to identify trends that are robust across different surveys. Before proceeding to the substative results, it is necessary to point out that the RCRE and CHNS surveys both have limited geographical coverage. The results below need to be qualified as such. In addition, the CHNS time series is not continuous. Poverty trends based on the CHNS are subject to contamination by cyclical movements in income.

3.3.1 *A Decade of Progress and Reverse in the Fight Against Poverty*

Against different poverty lines and equivalence scales, the three FGT poverty indices and their annual percentage changes have been calculated for our RCRE rural data and separately for the CHNS rural and urban data. These results are tabulated in Tables 3.1a, 3.1b, and 3.1c in the Appendix.

Table 3.1a traces out the as exhibited by the RCRE data. It can be seen that when per capita income is used as the indicator of living standards ($\theta = 1$), the directions of year to year changes in poverty indices are quite consistent across the six poverty lines. More specifically, over a rather wide income range (the

---

[9] Presumably, this is because poor householders do not posses the levels of literacy and numeracy requisite for diary keeping, while rich householders find it too time consuming to be worth their opportunity costs.

[10] Detailed information about the survey is available at the CHNS website http://www.cpc.unc.edu/projects/china

value of the highest poverty line is nearly four times that of the lowest poverty line), first and second order stochastic dominance can be found for most pairs of years while third order dominance always obtains.[11] The percentage changes tend to be greater in absolute value, the lower the poverty line is, suggesting concentration of per capita income at the lower end of the income spectrum. Changes in higher order poverty measures tend to be greater than those in lower order measures.[12] This indicates that the per capita income growth of households well below the poverty lines (i.e. the ultra poor) is usually positively correlated with the income growth of those around the poverty lines. As expected, allowing economies of scale within households ($\theta = 0.8, 0.5$) reduces not only the values of poverty measures, but also the magnitudes of their changes. It does not, however, alter the picture qualitatively. In particular, over the entire period between 1995 and 2002 poverty is shown to have increased.

Turning now to Table 3.1b where rural poverty indices estimated from the CHNS data are presented, the first thing that strikes one is the fluctuations of poverty levels between 1988 and 1992. There does not seem to be any historical events during this period to justify such large swings within so short a period. Upon checking the household size series in the dataset, we found that the average size of rural households was 4.31 in 1988 and 4.18 in 1992, but drops to 2.94 in 1990. Similarly, the average size of urban households was 3.92 in 1988 and 3.68 in 1992, but 2.96 in 1990. This raises serious doubts about the reliability of the 1990 data, given the high retention rates between the three rounds. We have excluded the 1990 data from subsequent analysis, but decided to retain the calculated poverty indices in Tables 3.1b and 3.1c for reference purposes. Comparing Table 3.1b with Table 3.1a, it is easily seen that not only are the estimated poverty indices for the two overlapping years of the two datasets—1996 and 1999—at comparable levels, but most of the characteristics observed above of Table 3.1a also show up in Table 3.1b, including the consistency of the directions of poverty change across poverty lines, poverty measures and equivalence scales, and the tendency for the magnitude of poverty change to be negatively related to the value of the poverty line but positively related to the order of the poverty measure. Most importantly, poverty increased between 1996 and 1999, confirming the poverty trend identified in the RCRE dataset. Thanks to the success in bringing down poverty in the late 1980s and early half of the 1990s, however, the period of 1988–99 as a whole saw a reduction in poverty.

---

[11] For the definitions of first, second, and third order stochastic dominance, see Ravallion (1992).

[12] For instance, if the official poverty line is adopted, the head count ratio declined by 10.3 per cent during 1996–97, the poverty gap index by 16.4 per cent, and the squared poverty gap index by 24.6 per cent.

Table 3.1c shows the poverty levels and changes in the urban areas covered by the CHNS. The overall level of urban poverty is still way below that found in rural areas. However, all poverty indices exhibit a worrying trend of rapid increase, especially in the second half of the 1990s. This trend seems to have broken off temporarily between 1992 and 1996. Yet the evidence is inconclusive.

Putting the results from the three tables together, the message, not incompatible with findings in studies using NBS data, emerges: while much progress was made in the first half of the 1990s in the battle against poverty in rural areas, grounds were lost in the second half of the decade. In urban areas, poverty had been creeping up throughout the 1990s and possibly at an accelerated rate in the later years.

3.3.2 Impacts of Growth and Inequality

The fact that the lack of progress in poverty reduction occurred alongside rapid output growth suggests that the nature of output growth is such that either the labour share of total output has been shrinking, and/or the part of the income distribution below the poverty line has become longer and fatter. For the first part of this proposition, we do not possess sufficient data to compute the exact metric of labour income share for testing. Nonetheless, the growth rates of rural and urban per capita income and real GDP per capita plotted in Figure 3.1 are telling. Except for one or two years, urban income growth was on average three–four percentage points lower than per capita GDP growth in the 1990s, rural

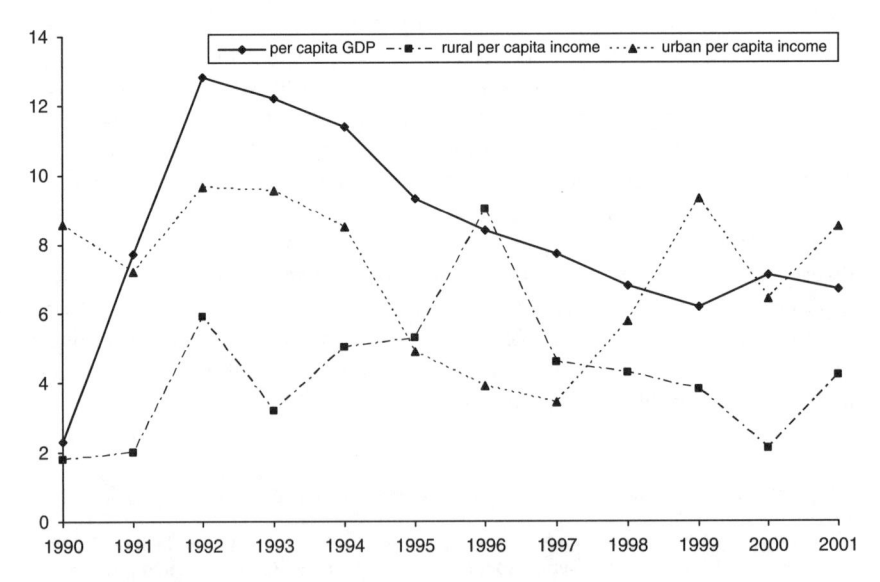

Figure 3.1: Growth rates of real GDP per capita, rural and urban per capita income

Poverty Reduction

income growth was even lower. The validity of the second part of the proposition turns partly on the assumptions about the poverty line and equivalence scale. Since we are not only interested in whether income distribution has become adverse for the poor but also the relative impact of changes in distribution vis-à-vis income growth, we now turn to decomposing poverty changes following the method described in equations (7) and (8) in section 3.2. The results of applying this procedure are in Tables 3.2a, 3.2b, and 3.2c in the Appendix.

In Table 3.2a, the welfare indicator is per capita income. The first panel presents results using the RCRE data. The signs and relative magnitudes of the growth and redistribution components are highly consistent across the three poverty indices. In most cases, the results also do not appear to be very sensitive to the choice of the poverty line. The exceptions are the 1998/99 and 2000/01 years where at higher poverty lines the redistribution component switches from poverty increasing to poverty decreasing. The growth component is mostly poverty decreasing, but is usually outweighed by the effects of adverse changes in distribution. However negative income growth occurred in 1998 and 2001, while 1997 and 1998 saw ameliorative distributional changes. Pinning down the causes for these deviations from the general pattern is beyond the scope of this chapter. But in view of the finding in Ravallion and Chen (2004) that lower inflation helps reduce poverty, our conjecture would be that rapid disinflation, or deflation in the case of 1998, in these years might have played a role.

The results in the second panel concerning the CHNS rural data also demonstrates sign consistency across poverty measures. In the two periods before 1996, poverty reduction was driven by income growth, but was also aided by distributional changes favouring the poor. During 1996–9, zero or negative income growth, compounded by adverse distributional changes reversed some of the progress made earlier. The distributional changes in this period were so large that the improvement achieved in the nine years before 1996 was completely undone. In 1999, the relative position of the poor on the income spectrum is already less favourable than that in 1988. The slow growth of rural income after 1996 was in part cyclical, as the growth of real GDP per capita declined from just under 13 per cent in 1992 to a little over 6 per cent in 1999. However, it might also be directly linked to the worsening of the income distribution in the same period as both seemed to have stemmed from the stagnation of real incomes from agricultural production. The relative price of agricultural products resumed its falling trend in 1997 when, after the hiatus of 1993–96, the liberalization of agricultural markets was restarted. With the relative decline of agricultural incomes, rural income growth had to come increasingly from non-farm activities. While the growth of agricultural incomes might be equalizing thanks to the equal distribution of land, one would expect the growth of non-farm incomes to be more disequalizing. The households most likely to be marginalized in the process are those already in a disadvantageous position: poor households without the capacity to diversify into non-farm activities or migrate to cities in poor regions lacking the infrastructure and market access to develop local rural industry.

In the third panel of Table 3.2a, where the results are for the CHNS urban data, the urban poor are found to have suffered similar misfortunes as their rural counterparts in 1996–9. In the other years covered by the sample, overall income growth seems to have left the urban poor behind. Again, the concurrence after 1996 of slow income growth and adverse distributional changes appears to be partly cyclical and partly structural. Here the structural factor was the reform of the state-owned enterprises (SOEs), which gained momentum in 1997 as the government announced an ambitious plan to turn the loss making SOE sector into profit making by the end of 2000. In the ensuing years, the state severed links with most small and medium sized SOEs. Many more SOEs shed redundant labour. A large number of laid off workers were not easily and immediately re-employable. Adding to their predicament was a social safety net that was only taking shape and hence could only provide very limited help. The income gap between the unemployed and the rest of the urban population widened quickly.

Table 3.2b and Table 3.2c in the Appendix present the results of applying the same decomposition procedure to income data adjusted by the two equivalence scales with $\theta = 0.8$ and $\theta = 0.5$ respectively. These two tables reveal qualitatively similar information to that in Table 3.2a. It appears, therefore, that the choice between these equivalence scales does not matter much to the decomposition results.

3.4 Summary

Correct assessment of poverty trend and understanding the relative roles of income growth and redistribution in affecting poverty trends often matter more to the formulation of poverty reduction policy than does the estimation of cardinal poverty measures. In addition to being vulnerable to measurement errors, the latter also hinges crucially on the choice of poverty lines, poverty measures, and equivalence scales. In principle, all these factors can also affect the evaluation of poverty trend and the results of poverty decomposition. How robust they are to these factors are not well studied empirically. Meanwhile, the most important data source for studying poverty in China—the NBS household survey—has been criticized for its exclusion of many non-monetary incomes and subsidies, the importance of which varied during the reform years. The sharp contrast between the rapid GDP growth in the 1990s and the slow progress in poverty reduction in the same period once again raised concern about the quality of the NBS data.

This chapter examines poverty trends in China in the 1990s, employing two unit record household survey datasets. One of the datasets, the CHNS data, has taken particular care to cover various incomes in kind received by households. The derived poverty changes are then decomposed into contributions due to income growth and to shifts in relative income distribution. Different poverty measures, poverty lines, and equivalence scales are considered. The following results appear to be empirically robust: poverty reduction in both rural and urban China was hampered by rising inequality in the second half of the 1990s. In urban China, worsening income distribution had been ongoing throughout the decade, while in rural China it seems to be a 'late 1990s' phenomenon. In the second half of the decade, rural and urban households also experienced slow income growth, pointing to an enlarged gap between the growth of household income and the growth of aggregate output.

Admittedly, the datasets used in this study have limited coverage. This would diminish to a certain extent the comparability of our results with those obtained from using more comprehensive surveys such as those conducted by the NBS. However, the NBS data are mostly available only in grouped format. Access to its unit record data is strictly limited. It is our view that, in the absence of nation wide observations, useful results can still be obtained from relatively selective surveys. Moreover, the possible sampling biases are less of a concern when changes in the levels of poverty rather than the levels of poverty themselves are the main subject of research. The biases will become even smaller if changes in poverty are broken down, as they have been in this chapter.

Appendix

Table 3.1a: Rural poverty levels and changes using RCRE data

<table>
<tr><th rowspan="2"></th><th rowspan="2"></th><th colspan="8">Levels of poverty measures</th><th colspan="8">Percentage changes of poverty measures</th></tr>
<tr><th>1995</th><th>1996</th><th>1997</th><th>1998</th><th>1999</th><th>2000</th><th>2001</th><th>2002</th><th>95–96</th><th>96–97</th><th>97–98</th><th>98–99</th><th>99–00</th><th>00–01</th><th>01–02</th><th>95–02</th></tr>
<tr><td colspan="18">$\theta = 1$</td></tr>
<tr><td rowspan="6">P0</td><td>(1)</td><td>9.61</td><td>10.47</td><td>9.39</td><td>8.61</td><td>12.69</td><td>10.63</td><td>12.06</td><td>10.40</td><td>8.98</td><td>-10.30</td><td>-8.33</td><td>47.34</td><td>-16.22</td><td>13.48</td><td>-13.79</td><td>8.22</td></tr>
<tr><td>(2)</td><td>16.11</td><td>17.88</td><td>17.58</td><td>16.66</td><td>19.08</td><td>16.55</td><td>17.93</td><td>19.71</td><td>10.99</td><td>-1.63</td><td>-5.27</td><td>14.55</td><td>-13.29</td><td>8.40</td><td>9.92</td><td>22.40</td></tr>
<tr><td>(3)</td><td>18.21</td><td>20.22</td><td>19.33</td><td>18.27</td><td>20.75</td><td>17.38</td><td>19.11</td><td>20.47</td><td>11.01</td><td>-4.39</td><td>-5.50</td><td>13.60</td><td>-16.24</td><td>9.96</td><td>7.10</td><td>12.39</td></tr>
<tr><td>(4)</td><td>19.49</td><td>23.14</td><td>21.42</td><td>20.26</td><td>23.52</td><td>20.11</td><td>21.05</td><td>22.94</td><td>18.69</td><td>-7.42</td><td>-5.41</td><td>16.08</td><td>-14.52</td><td>4.72</td><td>8.93</td><td>17.66</td></tr>
<tr><td>(5)</td><td>48.85</td><td>50.46</td><td>50.20</td><td>50.77</td><td>50.93</td><td>50.86</td><td>47.27</td><td>46.01</td><td>3.31</td><td>-0.53</td><td>1.14</td><td>0.32</td><td>-0.12</td><td>-7.06</td><td>-2.68</td><td>-5.81</td></tr>
<tr><td>(6)</td><td>53.21</td><td>54.55</td><td>53.82</td><td>55.31</td><td>54.53</td><td>54.50</td><td>51.94</td><td>50.96</td><td>2.52</td><td>-1.33</td><td>2.77</td><td>-1.42</td><td>-0.05</td><td>-4.70</td><td>-1.88</td><td>-4.23</td></tr>
<tr><td rowspan="6">P1</td><td>(1)</td><td>2.68</td><td>3.53</td><td>2.95</td><td>2.61</td><td>5.31</td><td>4.55</td><td>4.93</td><td>4.26</td><td>31.44</td><td>-16.43</td><td>-11.32</td><td>103.08</td><td>-14.22</td><td>8.23</td><td>-13.63</td><td>58.61</td></tr>
<tr><td>(2)</td><td>6.26</td><td>7.25</td><td>6.55</td><td>6.11</td><td>9.01</td><td>7.80</td><td>8.56</td><td>8.22</td><td>15.72</td><td>-9.69</td><td>-6.70</td><td>47.52</td><td>-13.45</td><td>9.75</td><td>-3.97</td><td>31.22</td></tr>
<tr><td>(3)</td><td>6.97</td><td>8.03</td><td>7.33</td><td>6.86</td><td>9.76</td><td>8.41</td><td>9.23</td><td>9.01</td><td>15.17</td><td>-8.72</td><td>-6.40</td><td>42.15</td><td>-13.75</td><td>9.64</td><td>-2.33</td><td>29.19</td></tr>
<tr><td>(4)</td><td>7.82</td><td>9.03</td><td>8.26</td><td>7.76</td><td>10.66</td><td>9.15</td><td>10.01</td><td>9.95</td><td>15.48</td><td>-8.47</td><td>-6.07</td><td>37.39</td><td>-14.20</td><td>9.43</td><td>-0.61</td><td>27.29</td></tr>
<tr><td>(5)</td><td>20.13</td><td>21.52</td><td>20.88</td><td>21.27</td><td>23.07</td><td>21.55</td><td>21.53</td><td>21.26</td><td>6.88</td><td>-2.95</td><td>1.86</td><td>8.44</td><td>-6.57</td><td>-0.08</td><td>-1.30</td><td>5.57</td></tr>
<tr><td>(6)</td><td>22.49</td><td>23.89</td><td>23.28</td><td>23.70</td><td>25.33</td><td>23.94</td><td>23.69</td><td>23.36</td><td>6.27</td><td>-2.56</td><td>1.79</td><td>6.90</td><td>-5.51</td><td>-1.04</td><td>-1.37</td><td>3.90</td></tr>
<tr><td rowspan="6">P2</td><td>(1)</td><td>1.02</td><td>1.58</td><td>1.19</td><td>0.98</td><td>2.75</td><td>2.40</td><td>2.61</td><td>2.07</td><td>55.59</td><td>-24.59</td><td>-17.42</td><td>179.54</td><td>-12.94</td><td>8.79</td><td>-20.43</td><td>104.15</td></tr>
<tr><td>(2)</td><td>3.16</td><td>3.91</td><td>3.35</td><td>3.04</td><td>5.50</td><td>4.73</td><td>5.17</td><td>4.63</td><td>23.76</td><td>-14.33</td><td>-9.16</td><td>80.53</td><td>-13.97</td><td>9.29</td><td>-10.45</td><td>46.40</td></tr>
<tr><td>(3)</td><td>3.60</td><td>4.39</td><td>3.81</td><td>3.48</td><td>5.99</td><td>5.16</td><td>5.64</td><td>5.14</td><td>21.80</td><td>-13.18</td><td>-8.54</td><td>71.99</td><td>-13.89</td><td>9.36</td><td>-8.97</td><td>42.60</td></tr>
<tr><td>(4)</td><td>4.13</td><td>4.97</td><td>4.37</td><td>4.02</td><td>6.58</td><td>5.66</td><td>6.20</td><td>5.74</td><td>20.15</td><td>-12.07</td><td>-7.97</td><td>63.77</td><td>-13.91</td><td>9.41</td><td>-7.34</td><td>38.98</td></tr>
<tr><td>(5)</td><td>11.32</td><td>12.55</td><td>11.90</td><td>11.76</td><td>14.10</td><td>12.75</td><td>13.22</td><td>13.11</td><td>10.82</td><td>-5.19</td><td>-1.13</td><td>19.89</td><td>-9.56</td><td>3.69</td><td>-0.86</td><td>15.79</td></tr>
<tr><td>(6)</td><td>12.79</td><td>14.05</td><td>13.40</td><td>13.34</td><td>15.59</td><td>14.23</td><td>14.61</td><td>14.47</td><td>9.78</td><td>-4.60</td><td>-0.42</td><td>16.84</td><td>-8.74</td><td>2.68</td><td>-0.98</td><td>13.06</td></tr>
<tr><td colspan="18">$\theta = 0.8$</td></tr>
<tr><td rowspan="6">P0</td><td>(1)</td><td>4.42</td><td>6.36</td><td>5.50</td><td>4.29</td><td>9.37</td><td>7.96</td><td>8.78</td><td>8.23</td><td>0.44</td><td>-0.13</td><td>-0.22</td><td>1.18</td><td>-0.15</td><td>0.10</td><td>-0.06</td><td>0.86</td></tr>
<tr><td>(2)</td><td>10.26</td><td>11.34</td><td>10.49</td><td>9.89</td><td>14.36</td><td>12.12</td><td>13.29</td><td>12.94</td><td>0.11</td><td>-0.08</td><td>-0.06</td><td>0.45</td><td>-0.16</td><td>0.10</td><td>-0.03</td><td>0.26</td></tr>
<tr><td>(3)</td><td>10.91</td><td>11.79</td><td>11.53</td><td>10.65</td><td>14.96</td><td>12.62</td><td>13.71</td><td>13.62</td><td>0.08</td><td>-0.02</td><td>-0.08</td><td>0.40</td><td>-0.16</td><td>0.09</td><td>-0.01</td><td>0.25</td></tr>
<tr><td>(4)</td><td>12.17</td><td>12.74</td><td>12.58</td><td>12.37</td><td>15.84</td><td>14.01</td><td>14.89</td><td>14.62</td><td>0.05</td><td>-0.01</td><td>-0.02</td><td>0.28</td><td>-0.12</td><td>0.06</td><td>-0.02</td><td>0.20</td></tr>
<tr><td>(5)</td><td>29.45</td><td>31.66</td><td>30.97</td><td>33.44</td><td>32.66</td><td>31.20</td><td>31.67</td><td>30.98</td><td>0.08</td><td>-0.02</td><td>0.08</td><td>-0.02</td><td>-0.04</td><td>0.02</td><td>-0.02</td><td>0.05</td></tr>
<tr><td>(6)</td><td>34.52</td><td>35.93</td><td>35.38</td><td>38.22</td><td>36.54</td><td>35.18</td><td>34.64</td><td>35.23</td><td>0.04</td><td>-0.02</td><td>0.08</td><td>-0.04</td><td>-0.04</td><td>-0.02</td><td>0.02</td><td>0.02</td></tr>
<tr><td rowspan="6">P1</td><td>(1)</td><td>0.88</td><td>1.64</td><td>1.20</td><td>0.82</td><td>3.01</td><td>2.65</td><td>2.86</td><td>2.33</td><td>0.85</td><td>-0.27</td><td>-0.31</td><td>2.65</td><td>-0.12</td><td>0.08</td><td>-0.19</td><td>1.63</td></tr>
<tr><td>(2)</td><td>3.47</td><td>4.37</td><td>3.70</td><td>3.34</td><td>6.26</td><td>5.34</td><td>5.79</td><td>5.19</td><td>0.26</td><td>-0.15</td><td>-0.10</td><td>0.87</td><td>-0.15</td><td>0.08</td><td>-0.10</td><td>0.49</td></tr>
<tr><td>(3)</td><td>3.95</td><td>4.85</td><td>4.18</td><td>3.80</td><td>6.81</td><td>5.81</td><td>6.31</td><td>5.72</td><td>0.23</td><td>-0.14</td><td>-0.09</td><td>0.79</td><td>-0.15</td><td>0.09</td><td>-0.09</td><td>0.45</td></tr>
<tr><td>(4)</td><td>4.50</td><td>5.38</td><td>4.75</td><td>4.36</td><td>7.42</td><td>6.34</td><td>6.88</td><td>6.32</td><td>0.20</td><td>-0.12</td><td>-0.08</td><td>0.70</td><td>-0.15</td><td>0.09</td><td>-0.08</td><td>0.40</td></tr>
<tr><td>(5)</td><td>11.76</td><td>13.14</td><td>12.60</td><td>12.22</td><td>14.73</td><td>13.11</td><td>13.72</td><td>13.81</td><td>0.12</td><td>-0.04</td><td>-0.03</td><td>0.21</td><td>-0.11</td><td>0.05</td><td>0.01</td><td>0.17</td></tr>
<tr><td>(6)</td><td>13.27</td><td>14.78</td><td>14.19</td><td>14.02</td><td>16.22</td><td>14.64</td><td>15.21</td><td>15.32</td><td>0.11</td><td>-0.04</td><td>-0.01</td><td>0.16</td><td>-0.10</td><td>0.04</td><td>0.01</td><td>0.15</td></tr>
</table>

		(1)	(2)	(3)	(4)	(5)	(6)						
P2	(1)	0.26	0.59	0.32	0.23	1.31	1.16	1.29	0.85	1.24	−0.45	−0.29	4.73	−0.11	0.11	−0.34	2.24
	(2)	1.44	2.09	1.65	1.38	3.40	2.94	3.19	2.68	0.45	−0.21	−0.16	1.46	−0.13	0.09	−0.16	0.86
	(3)	1.73	2.41	1.94	1.66	3.80	3.28	3.56	3.03	0.39	−0.19	−0.14	1.29	−0.14	0.09	−0.15	0.75
	(4)	2.08	2.79	2.29	2.00	4.26	3.67	3.98	3.45	0.34	−0.18	−0.13	1.13	−0.14	0.09	−0.13	0.66
	(5)	6.51	7.53	6.98	6.59	9.22	8.04	8.62	8.37	0.16	−0.07	−0.06	0.40	−0.13	0.07	−0.03	0.29
	(6)	7.39	8.47	7.93	7.55	10.14	8.90	9.48	9.29	0.15	−0.06	−0.05	0.34	−0.12	0.07	−0.02	0.26

$\theta = 0.5$

		(1)	(2)	(3)	(4)	(5)	(6)										
P0	(1)	0.83	1.82	0.68	0.33	3.58	3.40	2.91	2.44	1.20	−0.63	−0.51	9.77	−0.05	−0.14	−0.16	1.94
	(2)	3.31	5.41	5.17	3.70	8.98	7.57	7.97	7.85	0.63	−0.05	−0.28	1.42	−0.16	0.05	−0.01	1.37
	(3)	4.54	6.16	5.71	4.60	9.81	8.17	9.44	8.58	0.36	−0.07	−0.20	1.13	−0.17	0.16	−0.09	0.89
	(4)	5.39	7.23	6.57	5.62	10.29	9.29	10.07	9.29	0.34	−0.09	−0.15	0.83	−0.10	0.08	−0.08	0.72
	(5)	14.43	15.73	15.34	15.84	17.36	16.00	17.28	16.65	0.09	−0.02	0.03	0.10	−0.08	0.08	−0.04	0.15
	(6)	16.16	17.93	17.85	17.12	19.08	17.64	18.41	18.79	0.11	0.00	−0.04	0.11	−0.08	0.04	0.02	0.16
P1	(1)	0.10	0.28	0.12	0.07	0.79	0.66	0.88	0.37	1.70	−0.59	−0.41	10.34	−0.16	0.32	−0.58	2.50
	(2)	0.82	1.51	0.98	0.71	2.80	2.46	2.61	2.14	0.85	−0.35	−0.27	2.94	−0.12	0.06	−0.18	1.62
	(3)	1.02	1.80	1.27	0.94	3.24	2.82	3.01	2.55	0.76	−0.29	−0.26	2.45	−0.13	0.07	−0.15	1.49
	(4)	1.31	2.15	1.62	1.24	3.74	3.24	3.50	3.02	0.64	−0.25	−0.23	2.01	−0.13	0.08	−0.14	1.30
	(5)	5.46	6.45	5.89	5.56	8.57	7.42	7.98	7.54	0.18	−0.09	−0.06	0.54	−0.13	0.08	−0.06	0.38
	(6)	6.22	7.24	6.67	6.41	9.31	8.15	8.75	8.32	0.16	−0.08	−0.04	0.45	−0.12	0.07	−0.05	0.34
P2	(1)	0.02	0.08	0.03	0.03	0.23	0.19	0.33	0.07	2.38	−0.56	−0.16	6.91	−0.18	0.75	−0.78	2.21
	(2)	0.28	0.56	0.29	0.21	1.19	1.04	1.17	0.77	1.02	−0.48	−0.27	4.63	−0.13	0.13	−0.34	1.81
	(3)	0.36	0.70	0.40	0.29	1.42	1.24	1.38	0.98	0.95	−0.43	−0.27	3.92	−0.13	0.11	−0.29	1.73
	(4)	0.47	0.88	0.54	0.40	1.71	1.49	1.64	1.23	0.86	−0.38	−0.26	3.27	−0.13	0.10	−0.25	1.61
	(5)	2.68	3.49	2.97	2.64	5.11	4.42	4.77	4.31	0.30	−0.15	−0.11	0.93	−0.13	0.08	−0.10	0.61
	(6)	3.15	3.99	3.45	3.14	5.67	4.92	5.30	4.84	0.27	−0.13	−0.09	0.81	−0.13	0.08	−0.09	0.54

Notes: (1) the official rural poverty line of 530 yuan in 1995 prices; (2) 850 yuan in 2002 prices, equivalent to 833.85 yuan in 1995 rural prices; (3) US$1.08 per day in 1993 PPP, equivalent to 892.85 yuan in 1995 rural prices; (4) US$1 per day in 1985 PPP, equivalent to 1035.50 yuan in 1995 rural prices; (5) US$2.15 per day in 1993 PPP, equivalent to 1777.40 yuan in 1995 rural prices; (6) US$2 per day in 1985 PP, equivalent to 2071.10 yuan in 1995 rural prices.

Table 3.1b: Rural poverty levels and changes using CHNS data

		\multicolumn{6}{c}{Levels of poverty measures}	\multicolumn{6}{c}{Percentage changes of poverty measures}
		1988	1990	1992	1996	1999	88-90	90-92	88-92	92-96	96-99	88-99
							$\theta = 1$					
P0	(1)	14.81	1.59	7.26	7.44	10.86	-89.26	356.71	-103.94	2.40	46.07	-26.66
	(2)	27.71	6.21	17.82	15.11	20.35	-77.60	187.08	-55.51	-15.19	34.65	-26.57
	(3)	30.21	7.15	19.80	16.97	22.22	-76.34	176.92	-52.62	-14.27	30.93	-26.45
	(4)	35.06	9.85	25.10	21.79	26.41	-71.91	154.79	-39.70	-13.19	21.19	-24.69
	(5)	59.39	29.26	49.33	43.94	45.74	-50.74	68.59	-20.41	-10.91	4.10	-22.98
	(6)	66.30	36.29	56.60	50.79	52.84	-45.26	55.94	-17.14	-10.26	4.04	-20.29
P1	(1)	5.68	0.40	2.77	2.42	4.40	-92.90	586.49	-105.20	-12.44	81.40	-22.59
	(2)	11.36	1.55	6.22	5.56	8.39	-86.37	301.80	-82.61	-10.61	50.88	-26.14
	(3)	12.52	1.88	7.04	6.25	9.25	-84.99	274.77	-77.80	-11.30	48.03	-26.15
	(4)	15.29	2.79	9.12	8.06	11.32	-81.75	226.78	-67.68	-11.60	40.49	-25.93
	(5)	28.80	9.84	20.82	18.51	21.86	-65.84	111.66	-38.32	-11.10	18.08	-24.11
	(6)	33.65	13.09	25.36	22.62	25.73	-61.10	93.73	-32.69	-10.82	13.76	-23.54
P2	(1)	3.02	0.17	1.64	1.18	2.46	-94.32	857.32	-83.97	-28.27	108.88	-18.55
	(2)	6.40	0.62	3.34	2.89	4.85	-90.34	440.30	-91.51	-13.35	67.79	-24.08
	(3)	7.10	0.76	3.76	3.28	5.36	-89.33	396.03	-88.93	-12.81	63.55	-24.53
	(4)	8.86	1.16	4.87	4.27	6.63	-86.88	319.18	-81.89	-12.27	55.16	-25.16
	(5)	18.06	4.60	11.88	10.49	13.57	-74.54	158.52	-51.94	-11.76	29.40	-24.85
	(6)	21.55	6.42	14.86	13.16	16.28	-70.23	131.56	-45.05	-11.43	23.70	-24.47
							$\theta = 0.08$					
P0	(1)	9.53	0.83	4.28	4.05	7.40	-91.28	415.04	-122.74	-5.33	82.74	-22.33
	(2)	18.21	2.80	9.64	9.49	13.44	-84.62	244.20	-88.89	-1.59	41.72	-26.17
	(3)	20.27	3.57	11.27	10.86	14.99	-82.37	215.16	-79.96	-3.64	38.06	-26.08
	(4)	24.62	6.05	14.58	13.16	18.45	-75.42	140.88	-68.93	-9.71	40.20	-25.07
	(5)	44.91	18.42	34.57	30.56	34.72	-58.99	87.64	-29.93	-11.60	13.62	-22.70
	(6)	51.00	25.73	40.25	37.79	40.39	-49.56	56.48	-26.71	-6.13	6.90	-20.81
P1	(1)	3.36	0.22	1.80	1.32	2.89	-93.47	717.14	-87.32	-26.72	119.47	-14.14
	(2)	7.05	0.75	3.62	3.26	5.59	-89.42	385.83	-94.51	-10.09	71.71	-20.63
	(3)	7.85	0.91	4.07	3.72	6.16	-88.41	348.15	-92.57	-8.79	65.79	-21.47
	(4)	9.84	1.42	5.27	4.83	7.61	-85.53	270.45	-86.54	-8.34	57.48	-22.62

	(5)	20.29	5.70	13.42	11.94	15.67	−71.93	135.62	−51.17	−10.99	31.20	−22.75
	(6)	24.23	8.05	16.79	15.08	18.76	−66.76	108.45	−44.33	−10.14	24.38	−22.57
P2	(1)	1.69	0.11	1.13	0.59	1.53	−93.52	937.99	−48.60	−47.80	157.91	−9.39
	(2)	3.84	0.33	2.07	1.60	3.19	−91.47	532.06	−85.38	−22.73	98.90	−17.10
	(3)	4.30	0.39	2.30	1.84	3.53	−90.90	487.26	−87.14	−19.87	91.56	−17.98
	(4)	5.47	0.59	2.91	2.47	4.40	−89.27	395.52	−88.04	−15.14	77.93	−19.71
	(5)	12.13	2.54	7.27	6.48	9.41	−79.04	185.96	−66.81	−10.85	45.09	−22.46
	(6)	14.82	3.68	9.35	8.34	11.47	−75.14	153.86	−58.46	−10.78	37.54	−22.57

$\theta = 0.5$

P0	(1)	4.38	0.41	2.16	1.69	3.94	−90.68	430.13	−102.38	−21.69	132.71	−9.95
	(2)	9.22	1.29	4.59	3.94	7.93	−85.96	254.61	−100.81	−14.18	101.27	−13.98
	(3)	10.27	1.60	5.18	4.65	8.44	−84.37	222.90	−98.17	−10.25	81.63	−17.74
	(4)	12.65	1.90	6.48	6.28	10.38	−84.99	241.11	−95.27	−3.02	65.09	−18.01
	(5)	26.63	8.88	17.35	15.57	21.72	−66.66	95.38	−53.50	−10.24	39.45	−18.46
	(6)	31.88	12.48	21.63	19.84	25.66	−60.85	73.25	−47.42	−8.26	29.34	−19.51
P1	(1)	1.37	0.14	1.08	0.40	1.39	−89.95	684.57	−26.76	−62.55	243.41	1.46
	(2)	3.32	0.35	1.88	1.34	3.08	−89.40	434.85	−76.36	−28.93	130.41	−7.15
	(3)	3.75	0.42	2.08	1.54	3.42	−88.72	392.96	−79.86	−26.33	122.68	−8.78
	(4)	4.83	0.60	2.59	2.07	4.24	−87.58	332.19	−86.36	−20.09	104.80	−12.18
	(5)	10.96	2.44	6.24	5.83	9.07	−77.76	156.04	−75.64	−6.56	55.58	−17.23
	(6)	13.58	3.59	8.13	7.51	11.15	−73.59	126.53	−67.18	−7.53	48.35	−17.94
P2	(1)	0.62	0.08	0.73	0.16	0.69	−87.46	844.33	15.52	−77.53	320.42	11.81
	(2)	1.67	0.17	1.18	0.60	1.63	−89.67	580.60	−42.22	−49.41	172.83	−2.94
	(3)	1.91	0.20	1.28	0.70	1.83	−89.53	539.37	−49.37	−45.09	160.78	−4.14
	(4)	2.53	0.28	1.55	0.99	2.35	−88.88	453.24	−62.59	−36.55	138.22	−7.04
	(5)	6.19	1.07	3.45	3.00	5.28	−82.80	224.29	−79.27	−13.08	75.98	−14.68
	(6)	7.80	1.58	4.44	3.97	6.56	−79.79	181.71	−75.67	−10.60	65.29	−15.89

Notes: (1) the official rural poverty line of 530 yuan in 1995 prices; (2) 850 yuan in 2002 prices, equivalent to 833.85 yuan in 1995 rural prices; (3) US$1.08 per day in 1993 PPP, equivalent to 892.85 yuan in 1995 rural prices; (4) US$1 per day in 1985 PPP, equivalent to 1035.50 yuan in 1995 rural prices; (5) US$2.15 per day in 1993 PPP, equivalent to 1777.40 yuan in 1995 rural prices; (6) US$2 per day in 1985 PP, equivalent to 2071.10 yuan in 1995 rural prices.

Table 3.1c: Urban poverty levels and changes using CHNS data

		Levels of poverty measures					Percentage changes of poverty measures				
		1988	1990	1992	1996	1999	88–90	90–92	88–92	92–96	96–99	88–99

$\theta = 1$

P0	(1)	1.64	1.56	3.83	4.01	5.61	−4.73	144.55	57.08	4.71	40.02	241.61
	(2)	3.02	1.85	4.82	4.48	7.22	−38.79	160.73	37.34	−7.12	61.22	138.97
	(3)	5.39	3.19	9.06	6.10	10.55	−40.92	184.22	40.45	−32.60	72.83	95.61
	(4)	5.64	3.30	9.57	6.17	10.95	−41.45	189.88	41.08	−35.45	77.36	94.30
	(5)	16.10	9.08	18.09	12.89	18.22	−43.63	99.30	10.99	−28.72	41.30	13.15
	(6)	30.80	15.96	28.70	19.92	26.96	−48.18	79.82	−7.32	−30.61	35.36	−12.48
P1	(1)	0.46	0.67	1.05	1.17	2.45	46.15	55.18	55.91	11.39	109.89	430.24
	(2)	0.74	0.83	1.56	1.62	3.07	12.58	87.23	52.56	3.65	89.55	314.15
	(3)	1.52	1.23	2.73	2.45	4.45	−19.09	122.92	44.56	−10.42	81.88	193.84
	(4)	1.61	1.27	2.89	2.53	4.60	−20.89	126.66	44.23	−12.24	81.47	185.58
	(5)	4.51	2.87	6.42	4.76	7.94	−36.48	123.69	29.63	−25.83	66.86	75.86
	(6)	8.94	5.00	10.42	7.47	11.24	−44.11	108.44	14.16	−28.26	50.38	25.68
P2	(1)	0.18	0.38	0.46	0.47	1.48	116.31	22.08	62.13	1.04	217.20	746.32
	(2)	0.29	0.49	0.71	0.74	1.85	65.62	44.88	58.32	4.36	151.03	528.64
	(3)	0.63	0.71	1.28	1.27	2.63	12.32	81.39	50.92	−1.00	107.18	317.84
	(4)	0.67	0.73	1.35	1.33	2.72	8.83	84.83	50.29	−2.00	104.95	304.01
	(5)	1.97	1.46	3.21	2.59	4.73	−25.91	120.31	38.74	−19.27	82.38	140.35
	(6)	3.92	2.47	5.36	4.05	6.74	−37.05	117.48	26.96	−24.50	66.51	72.11

$\theta = 0.8$

P0	(1)	1.01	1.25	2.12	2.33	4.22	23.48	69.14	52.12	10.20	81.05	316.69
	(2)	1.38	1.59	2.35	3.25	4.78	15.55	47.31	41.25	38.58	47.07	246.91
	(3)	2.37	2.28	4.67	4.36	6.71	−4.06	105.11	49.18	−6.60	53.79	182.65
	(4)	2.84	2.28	4.85	4.57	7.17	−19.82	112.96	41.43	−5.67	56.92	152.76
	(5)	7.44	5.06	11.33	7.66	13.17	−31.95	123.68	34.31	−32.38	71.87	76.92
	(6)	14.70	8.88	16.96	12.92	18.44	−39.62	91.12	13.35	−23.87	42.78	25.44
P1	(1)	0.19	0.50	0.56	0.51	1.77	160.56	10.26	65.19	−7.67	243.46	811.07
	(2)	0.35	0.64	0.82	0.89	2.18	86.85	27.93	58.17	7.50	145.49	530.85
	(3)	0.69	0.93	1.47	1.61	3.01	35.42	57.37	53.08	9.51	87.57	337.75
	(4)	0.73	0.96	1.55	1.67	3.10	31.60	60.43	52.64	8.23	85.41	323.69
	(5)	2.11	1.77	3.68	3.10	5.51	−16.20	107.76	42.56	−15.91	78.02	160.63
	(6)	4.16	3.03	6.04	4.70	7.93	−27.27	99.76	31.17	−22.16	68.50	90.56
P2	(1)	0.07	0.28	0.26	0.19	1.07	329.76	−9.59	74.26	−27.45	473.85	1517.63
	(2)	0.12	0.37	0.38	0.33	1.33	195.78	4.27	67.58	−12.75	297.45	969.52
	(3)	0.28	0.54	0.69	0.72	1.85	89.55	27.62	58.66	3.97	157.91	548.70
	(4)	0.30	0.56	0.73	0.76	1.90	83.49	30.09	58.11	4.44	150.74	525.11
	(5)	0.92	1.00	1.75	1.68	3.26	9.49	74.58	47.68	−4.13	94.36	256.17
	(6)	1.83	1.58	3.04	2.59	4.71	−13.67	92.89	39.95	−15.04	81.89	157.34

$\theta = 0.5$

P0	(1)	0.22	0.71	0.74	0.47	2.70	218.90	4.02	69.85	−36.29	473.77	1112.62
	(2)	0.41	0.94	1.10	1.11	2.82	131.51	16.84	63.03	0.98	154.25	594.49
	(3)	1.01	1.42	2.14	2.64	4.07	40.31	50.64	52.69	23.18	54.11	301.25
	(4)	1.03	1.56	2.14	2.78	4.18	51.31	36.95	51.74	29.78	50.29	304.19
	(5)	2.43	2.82	4.85	4.64	7.33	15.76	72.09	49.80	−4.21	57.90	201.31
	(6)	5.11	4.24	8.16	6.79	11.02	−17.04	92.58	37.41	−16.85	62.34	115.66
P1	(1)	0.05	0.36	0.29	0.14	1.17	560.04	−17.61	81.61	−51.46	725.16	2077.83
	(2)	0.10	0.44	0.40	0.22	1.42	339.70	−9.14	74.97	−43.38	534.19	1334.49
	(3)	0.24	0.62	0.64	0.58	1.87	152.89	4.29	62.08	−9.96	223.28	667.65
	(4)	0.26	0.64	0.68	0.63	1.92	143.04	6.47	61.35	−7.36	206.08	633.71
	(5)	0.73	1.16	1.49	1.69	3.15	59.14	28.31	51.02	13.63	85.80	331.08
	(6)	1.44	1.71	2.64	2.62	4.56	18.73	53.97	45.30	−0.63	74.29	216.62
P2	(1)	0.02	0.20	0.15	0.06	0.67	875.49	−27.52	85.86	−62.13	1109.42	3138.30
	(2)	0.04	0.26	0.20	0.09	0.85	606.02	−21.43	81.97	−55.33	842.65	2235.94
	(3)	0.09	0.37	0.33	0.21	1.17	304.56	−10.63	72.34	−35.27	451.82	1191.39
	(4)	0.10	0.38	0.34	0.23	1.21	285.82	−9.39	71.39	−32.90	422.96	1126.68
	(5)	0.32	0.67	0.75	0.77	1.96	109.74	11.30	57.16	3.24	153.41	510.73
	(6)	0.63	0.99	1.29	1.35	2.74	57.20	30.64	51.31	4.18	103.82	336.07

Notes: (1) 689.69 yuan in 1995 urban prices; (2) US$1.08 per day in 1993 PPP, equivalent to 816.39 yuan in 1995 urban prices; (3) US$1 per day in 1985 PPP, equivalent to 1059.6 yuan in 1995 urban prices; (4) 1200 yuan in 2002 prices, equivalent to 1085.1 yuan in 1995 urban prices; (5) US$2.15 per day in 1993 PPP, equivalent to 1625.2 yuan in 1995 urban prices; (6) US$2 per day in 1985 PPP, equivalent to 2119.2 yuan in 1995 urban prices.

Table 3.2a: Decomposition and growth elasticity of poverty measures ($\theta = 1$)

		P0						P1						P2					
		(1)	(2)	(3)	(4)	(5)	(6)	(1)	(2)	(3)	(4)	(5)	(6)	(1)	(2)	(3)	(4)	(5)	(6)
RCRE rural data
95–96	G	−0.60	−1.31	−2.10	−1.06	−3.05	−2.94	−0.41	−0.64	−0.71	−0.76	−1.75	−1.82	−0.22	−0.39	−0.42	−0.47	−1.07	−1.17
	I	1.46	3.08	4.11	4.71	4.67	4.28	1.25	1.62	1.77	1.97	3.13	3.23	0.78	1.14	1.21	1.30	2.29	2.42
96–97	G	−0.29	−0.49	−0.51	−0.57	−1.28	−1.37	−0.16	−0.26	−0.29	−0.32	−0.70	−0.73	−0.09	−0.16	−0.17	−0.19	−0.43	−0.47
	I	−0.79	0.20	−0.38	−1.15	1.01	0.65	−0.42	−0.44	−0.41	−0.44	0.06	0.12	−0.30	−0.41	−0.41	−0.41	−0.22	−0.18
97–98	G	0.25	0.97	0.53	0.72	1.64	1.88	0.21	0.36	0.39	0.43	0.99	1.03	0.11	0.21	0.23	0.26	0.62	0.68
	I	−1.03	−1.90	−1.59	−1.88	−1.07	−0.39	−0.54	−0.80	−0.86	−0.93	−0.60	−0.61	−0.32	−0.52	−0.56	−0.60	−0.75	−0.73
98–99	G	−0.10	−0.54	−0.60	−0.35	−0.46	−0.66	−0.10	−0.15	−0.16	−0.18	−0.41	−0.43	−0.06	−0.09	−0.10	−0.11	−0.26	−0.29
	I	4.18	2.97	3.08	3.60	0.62	−0.13	2.79	3.05	3.06	3.08	2.21	2.07	1.83	2.55	2.61	2.67	2.60	2.53
99–00	G	−1.06	−2.85	−4.12	−4.77	−5.46	−5.63	−0.86	−1.21	−1.36	−1.61	−3.75	−3.89	−0.61	−0.86	−0.92	−1.00	−2.33	−2.55
	I	−1.00	0.31	0.75	1.36	5.40	5.61	0.11	0.00	0.02	0.10	2.23	2.50	0.26	0.10	0.08	0.08	0.99	1.19
00–01	G	0.39	0.45	0.76	0.85	1.65	1.22	0.20	0.28	0.30	0.34	0.85	0.90	0.14	0.20	0.21	0.23	0.53	0.58
	I	1.04	0.94	0.97	0.10	−5.24	−3.78	0.17	0.48	0.51	0.52	−0.86	−1.15	0.07	0.24	0.27	0.31	−0.06	−0.20
01–02	G	−4.60	−6.31	−8.12	−8.44	−14.48	−14.54	−2.18	−3.32	−3.56	−3.88	−7.91	−8.41	−1.41	−2.24	−2.39	−2.58	−5.09	−5.54
	I	2.94	8.09	9.47	10.32	13.22	13.56	1.51	2.98	3.35	3.82	7.63	8.08	0.88	1.70	1.89	2.12	4.97	5.40
95–02	G	−8.36	−11.03	−12.13	−12.65	−22.98	−22.82	−3.19	−5.34	−5.75	−6.20	−12.26	−13.07	−1.79	−3.33	−3.61	−3.94	−7.93	−8.63
	I	9.15	14.64	14.39	16.09	20.14	20.57	4.76	7.29	7.78	8.33	13.38	13.95	2.85	4.80	5.15	5.55	9.71	10.30
CHNS rural data
88–92	G	−5.21	−9.24	−10.05	−10.30	−13.34	−13.18	−1.96	−3.96	−4.34	−5.17	−8.25	−9.00	−1.05	−2.24	−2.48	−3.07	−5.63	−6.43
	I	−2.34	−0.65	−0.36	0.33	3.28	3.48	−0.96	−1.18	−1.14	−1.00	0.27	0.71	−0.33	−0.82	−0.86	−0.92	−0.54	−0.26
92–96	G	−0.86	−2.22	−2.14	−2.88	−3.66	−4.07	−0.34	−0.75	−0.84	−1.05	−1.93	−2.15	−0.17	−0.39	−0.45	−0.57	−1.21	−1.43
	I	1.04	−0.49	−0.69	−0.43	−1.73	−1.74	−0.01	0.09	0.04	−0.01	−0.38	−0.60	−0.29	−0.05	−0.04	−0.02	−0.19	−0.27
96–99	G	0.58	1.09	1.02	1.09	1.64	2.27	0.23	0.43	0.48	0.58	0.99	1.11	0.13	0.25	0.27	0.34	0.65	0.76
	I	2.85	4.15	4.23	3.53	0.16	−0.22	1.74	2.40	2.52	2.69	2.36	2.01	1.16	1.71	1.81	2.02	2.43	2.36
88–99	G	−5.77	−9.30	−9.88	−10.63	−15.19	−15.40	−2.41	−4.38	−4.72	−5.48	−8.54	−9.51	−1.42	−2.65	−2.90	−3.47	−5.95	−6.77
	I	1.82	1.93	1.88	1.97	1.54	1.95	1.12	1.42	1.45	1.52	1.60	1.59	0.86	1.11	1.15	1.24	1.46	1.50
CHNS urban data
88–92	G	−1.44	−2.89	−3.14	−3.33	−9.08	−13.77	−0.54	−0.76	−1.34	−1.38	−3.00	−5.01	−0.26	−0.36	−0.66	−0.69	−1.51	−2.55
	I	3.63	4.69	6.80	7.26	11.07	11.67	1.13	1.58	2.56	2.66	4.90	6.49	0.54	0.78	1.31	1.37	2.76	4.00
92–96	G	−0.71	−0.72	−1.96	−2.28	−3.96	−5.80	−0.34	−0.43	−0.64	−0.67	−1.40	−2.20	−0.18	−0.24	−0.36	−0.37	−0.75	−1.18
	I	0.89	0.38	−0.99	−1.11	−1.24	−2.99	0.46	0.49	0.35	0.32	−0.25	−0.75	0.19	0.27	0.34	0.34	0.13	−0.13
96–99	G	0.26	0.54	0.53	0.67	1.16	2.74	0.19	0.23	0.32	0.33	0.62	0.93	0.11	0.14	0.20	0.20	0.36	0.53
	I	1.35	2.20	3.92	4.11	4.17	4.30	1.09	1.22	1.68	1.73	2.56	2.83	0.90	0.97	1.16	1.19	1.78	2.16
88–99	G	−2.36	−3.20	−4.36	−4.77	−10.22	−15.57	−0.86	−1.15	−1.72	−1.78	−3.48	−5.73	−0.47	−0.62	−0.95	−0.99	−1.89	−3.02
	I	6.33	7.40	9.52	10.09	12.33	11.73	2.85	3.48	4.65	4.77	6.90	8.03	1.78	2.18	2.96	3.04	4.65	5.85

Table 3.2b: Decomposition and growth elasticity of poverty measures ($\theta = 0.8$)

		P0						P1						P2					
		(1)	(2)	(3)	(4)	(5)	(6)	(1)	(2)	(3)	(4)	(5)	(6)	(1)	(2)	(3)	(4)	(5)	(6)

RCRE rural data

95-96	G	-0.61	-0.29	-0.60	-1.14	-2.97	-3.73	-0.23	-0.41	-0.42	-0.46	-1.11	-1.22	-0.10	-0.25	-0.27	-0.30	-0.65	-0.72
	I	2.56	1.37	1.48	1.71	5.18	5.13	0.99	1.31	1.31	1.34	2.49	2.73	0.42	0.90	0.96	1.01	1.67	1.81
96-97	G	-0.23	-0.30	-0.18	-0.41	-1.13	-0.61	-0.09	-0.14	-0.14	-0.15	-0.37	-0.42	-0.04	-0.09	-0.09	-0.10	-0.22	-0.25
	I	-0.62	-0.55	-0.08	0.24	0.43	0.06	-0.35	-0.53	-0.52	-0.48	-0.17	-0.17	-0.23	-0.35	-0.38	-0.39	-0.32	-0.30
97-98	G	0.28	0.37	0.38	0.65	2.36	1.91	0.13	0.22	0.24	0.26	0.65	0.74	0.05	0.13	0.14	0.16	0.37	0.42
	I	-1.50	-0.97	-1.25	-0.85	0.12	0.94	-0.50	-0.59	-0.62	-0.65	-1.03	-0.90	-0.14	-0.40	-0.42	-0.45	-0.76	-0.79
98-99	G	-0.08	-0.12	0.00	-0.15	-0.40	-0.19	-0.04	-0.05	-0.06	-0.06	-0.15	-0.17	-0.02	-0.04	-0.04	-0.04	-0.08	-0.09
	I	5.16	4.58	4.30	3.63	-0.39	-1.49	2.22	2.97	3.07	3.12	2.66	2.36	1.10	2.05	2.18	2.31	2.71	2.68
99-00	G	-1.82	-1.69	-1.67	-1.71	-5.97	-6.81	-0.74	-0.96	-1.00	-1.06	-2.40	-2.71	-0.41	-0.69	-0.72	-0.77	-1.41	-1.58
	I	0.40	-0.55	-0.67	-0.13	4.52	5.45	0.38	0.04	0.00	-0.02	0.78	1.13	0.27	0.23	0.20	0.17	0.23	0.34
00-01	G	0.42	0.39	0.35	0.48	1.69	1.60	0.19	0.25	0.25	0.27	0.63	0.70	0.11	0.17	0.18	0.20	0.36	0.40
	I	0.41	0.78	0.74	0.40	-1.22	-2.15	0.02	0.20	0.25	0.27	-0.01	-0.13	0.02	0.08	0.10	0.12	0.23	0.18
01-02	G	-3.17	-4.07	-4.70	-5.19	-12.36	-12.80	-1.62	-2.28	-2.42	-2.61	-5.10	-5.65	-0.91	-1.55	-1.65	-1.77	-3.24	-3.56
	I	2.62	3.72	4.61	4.91	11.67	13.40	1.08	1.67	1.83	2.05	5.18	5.76	0.47	1.03	1.12	1.24	3.00	3.36
95-02	G	-4.22	-7.22	-7.67	-8.08	-17.61	-18.95	-1.81	-3.41	-3.69	-4.00	-8.00	-8.75	-1.02	-1.99	-2.19	-2.42	-5.00	-5.50
	I	8.04	9.90	10.37	10.54	19.14	19.66	3.25	5.12	5.46	5.83	10.05	10.80	1.61	3.24	3.50	3.80	6.87	7.40

CHNS rural data

88-92	G	-3.20	-6.37	-7.23	-8.51	-12.63	-13.43	-1.15	-2.37	-2.65	-3.37	-6.27	-7.27	-0.61	-1.31	-1.46	-1.86	-3.99	-4.73
	I	-2.05	-2.20	-1.78	-1.53	2.29	2.68	-0.42	-1.06	-1.12	-1.19	-0.59	-0.17	0.06	-0.46	-0.54	-0.70	-0.86	-0.73
92-96	G	-0.39	-0.92	-0.99	-1.52	-2.25	-2.74	-0.15	-0.36	-0.40	-0.50	-1.15	-1.33	-0.08	-0.19	-0.21	-0.27	-0.67	-0.82
	I	0.16	0.76	0.58	0.10	-1.76	0.27	-0.33	-0.01	0.04	0.06	-0.32	-0.37	-0.46	-0.29	-0.25	-0.17	-0.12	-0.19
96-99	G	0.28	0.82	0.76	1.24	1.71	2.33	0.17	0.34	0.37	0.46	0.91	1.07	0.10	0.20	0.22	0.27	0.56	0.68
	I	3.07	3.13	3.37	4.05	2.45	0.28	1.40	1.99	2.07	2.32	2.81	2.61	0.84	1.39	1.47	1.66	2.36	2.46
88-99	G	-3.66	-6.62	-7.06	-8.27	-11.34	-12.39	-1.47	-2.69	-2.97	-3.61	-6.16	-7.00	-0.85	-1.60	-1.76	-2.15	-4.09	-4.75
	I	1.53	1.86	1.77	2.10	1.15	1.78	0.99	1.24	1.28	1.38	1.55	1.53	0.69	0.94	0.99	1.07	1.37	1.41

CHNS urban data

88-92	G	-0.80	-1.49	-2.04	-2.39	-3.93	-8.33	-0.26	-0.39	-0.63	-0.67	-1.54	-2.67	-0.12	-0.18	-0.32	-0.33	-0.80	-1.33
	I	1.90	2.45	4.34	4.40	7.81	10.60	0.62	0.87	1.41	1.48	3.11	4.55	0.31	0.43	0.72	0.75	1.63	2.55
92-96	G	-0.86	-0.50	-0.86	-0.83	-1.93	-3.27	-0.20	-0.26	-0.36	-0.37	-0.75	-1.15	-0.08	-0.13	-0.20	-0.21	-0.39	-0.62
	I	1.08	1.40	0.55	0.55	-1.73	-0.78	0.16	0.32	0.49	0.49	0.17	-0.19	0.01	0.08	0.23	0.24	0.32	0.16
96-99	G	0.58	0.59	0.38	0.45	1.05	1.71	0.17	0.20	0.26	0.26	0.47	0.72	0.08	0.11	0.16	0.16	0.28	0.42
	I	1.31	0.94	1.97	2.15	4.45	3.81	1.08	1.09	1.15	1.17	1.94	2.50	0.80	0.88	0.97	0.98	1.30	1.70
88-99	G	-0.98	-1.59	-2.52	-2.67	-4.83	-8.37	-0.43	-0.58	-0.94	-0.98	-1.87	-2.93	-0.26	-0.33	-0.51	-0.53	-1.04	-1.60
	I	4.19	4.99	6.85	7.01	10.56	12.11	2.00	2.41	3.26	3.35	5.27	6.69	1.26	1.53	2.07	2.12	3.38	4.47

Table 3.2c: Decomposition and growth elasticity of poverty measures ($\theta = 0.5$)

		P0						P1						P2					
		(1)	(2)	(3)	(4)	(5)	(6)	(1)	(2)	(3)	(4)	(5)	(6)	(1)	(2)	(3)	(4)	(5)	(6)
RCRE rural data																			
95–96	G	−0.25	−0.46	−0.99	−0.56	−1.21	−1.33	−0.06	−0.19	−0.23	−0.27	−0.54	−0.61	−0.02	−0.09	−0.10	−0.12	−0.34	−0.37
	I	1.24	2.56	2.61	2.40	2.52	3.09	0.24	0.89	1.00	1.11	1.53	1.63	0.07	0.37	0.44	0.53	1.15	1.21
96–97	G	−0.16	0.00	−0.09	−0.24	−0.49	−0.42	−0.01	−0.05	−0.06	−0.07	−0.12	−0.15	0.00	−0.02	−0.03	−0.03	−0.08	−0.09
	I	−0.98	−0.24	−0.36	−0.41	0.10	0.34	−0.15	−0.48	−0.47	−0.47	−0.43	−0.42	−0.04	−0.25	−0.27	−0.30	−0.45	−0.45
97–98	G	0.12	0.38	0.27	0.48	0.56	0.56	0.01	0.11	0.12	0.14	0.30	0.34	0.00	0.04	0.05	0.06	0.18	0.20
	I	−0.46	−1.85	−1.38	−1.43	−0.06	−1.28	−0.06	−0.38	−0.46	−0.52	−0.63	−0.60	−0.01	−0.12	−0.16	−0.20	−0.50	−0.52
98–99	G	0.00	0.00	0.05	0.00	0.00	0.00	0.00	0.01	0.01	0.01	0.02	0.02	0.00	0.00	0.01	0.01	0.01	0.01
	I	3.24	5.27	5.16	4.66	1.52	1.96	0.72	2.08	2.29	2.48	2.99	2.88	0.20	0.97	1.13	1.30	2.45	2.52
99–00	G	−1.10	−1.88	−1.63	−1.08	−1.77	−2.20	−0.38	−0.72	−0.79	−0.84	−1.20	−1.25	−0.14	−0.40	−0.44	−0.50	−0.86	−0.91
	I	0.93	0.47	−0.01	0.09	0.40	0.76	0.25	0.38	0.37	0.35	0.05	0.09	0.10	0.24	0.26	0.28	0.17	0.16
00–01	G	0.21	0.24	0.79	0.24	1.00	0.48	0.10	0.23	0.24	0.27	0.38	0.41	0.04	0.12	0.14	0.15	0.26	0.28
	I	−0.70	0.17	0.49	0.54	0.29	0.28	0.11	−0.08	−0.05	−0.01	0.18	0.19	0.10	0.01	0.00	0.00	0.08	0.10
01–02	G	−2.28	−3.02	−3.26	−3.26	−5.56	−5.16	−0.72	−1.52	−1.63	−1.75	−2.67	−2.88	−0.27	−0.81	−0.91	−1.02	−1.87	−2.00
	I	1.81	2.90	2.41	2.48	4.93	5.55	0.22	1.06	1.17	1.26	2.22	2.45	0.01	0.42	0.51	0.60	1.41	1.55
95–02	G	−2.85	−3.33	−3.62	−3.93	−7.73	−8.88	−0.82	−1.67	−1.78	−1.92	−3.94	−4.27	−0.31	−0.92	−1.02	−1.14	−2.51	−2.74
	I	4.46	7.87	7.67	7.83	9.95	11.52	1.09	2.99	3.31	3.63	6.02	6.37	0.36	1.42	1.64	1.90	4.13	4.44
CHNS rural data																			
88–92	G	−1.62	−2.87	−3.20	−4.08	−8.53	−10.04	−0.53	−1.10	−1.23	−1.58	−3.60	−4.41	−0.26	−0.60	−0.68	−0.86	−2.04	−2.56
	I	−0.60	−1.76	−1.88	−2.10	−0.75	−0.21	0.24	−0.33	−0.43	−0.66	−1.12	−1.05	0.38	0.11	0.04	−0.11	−0.70	−0.80
92–96	G	−0.06	−0.32	−0.34	−0.43	−1.07	−1.17	−0.04	−0.10	−0.12	−0.15	−0.39	−0.49	−0.02	−0.06	−0.06	−0.08	−0.21	−0.27
	I	−0.41	−0.33	−0.19	0.24	−0.71	−0.62	−0.63	−0.44	−0.43	−0.37	−0.02	−0.12	−0.54	−0.53	−0.52	−0.49	−0.24	−0.20
96–99	G	0.31	0.42	0.51	0.77	1.76	1.94	0.11	0.23	0.25	0.31	0.67	0.81	0.06	0.13	0.14	0.18	0.39	0.49
	I	1.94	3.57	3.28	3.32	4.39	3.88	0.87	1.51	1.64	1.86	2.57	2.82	0.47	0.90	0.99	1.18	1.89	2.11
88–99	G	−1.93	−3.02	−3.38	−3.94	−7.20	−8.07	−0.69	−1.27	−1.40	−1.72	−3.42	−4.03	−0.35	−0.75	−0.83	−1.02	−2.09	−2.53
	I	1.49	1.73	1.55	1.66	2.28	1.85	0.71	1.03	1.07	1.14	1.54	1.59	0.42	0.71	0.75	0.84	1.18	1.29
CHNS urban data																			
88–92	G	−0.27	−0.47	−0.54	−0.63	−1.63	−2.93	−0.08	−0.12	−0.23	−0.24	−0.60	−1.06	−0.04	−0.06	−0.11	−0.12	−0.29	−0.51
	I	0.79	1.16	1.67	1.74	4.05	5.98	0.32	0.42	0.63	0.66	1.37	2.26	0.17	0.23	0.35	0.36	0.72	1.17
92–96	G	−0.06	−0.21	−0.21	−0.53	−0.90	−1.13	−0.04	−0.08	−0.16	−0.17	−0.28	−0.43	−0.02	−0.03	−0.07	−0.07	−0.15	−0.24
	I	−0.21	0.22	1.07	1.16	0.70	−0.25	−0.12	−0.09	0.10	0.12	0.48	0.41	−0.07	−0.08	−0.05	−0.04	0.17	0.29
96–99	G	0.18	0.20	0.56	0.54	0.79	1.14	0.09	0.11	0.20	0.21	0.32	0.49	0.05	0.07	0.10	0.11	0.20	0.28
	I	2.05	1.51	0.86	0.86	1.90	3.09	0.94	1.08	1.09	1.08	1.13	1.45	0.56	0.69	0.86	0.87	0.99	1.11
88–99	G	−0.13	−0.61	−0.75	−0.76	−1.91	−3.55	−0.17	−0.20	−0.35	−0.36	−0.71	−1.17	−0.13	−0.14	−0.20	−0.21	−0.39	−0.61
	I	2.61	3.02	3.80	3.90	6.81	9.46	1.29	1.53	1.97	2.02	3.13	4.29	0.77	0.96	1.28	1.32	2.02	2.72

References

Benjamin, D., L. Brandt, and J. Giles (2005). 'The Evolution of Income Inequality in Rural China', *Economic Development and Cultural Change* 53: 769–824.

Brandt, L., and C. A. Holz (2004). 'Spatial Price Differences n China: Estimates and Implications', mimeo, Social Science Division, Hong Kong University of Science and Technology: Hong Kong.

Datt, G., and M. Ravallion (1992). 'Growth and Redistribution Components of Changes in Poverty Measures: A Decomposition with Applications to Brazil and India in the 1980s', *Journal of Development Economics* 38: 275–95.

Figini, P. (1998). 'Inequality Measures, Equivalent Scales and Adjustment for Household Size and Composition', paper presented at the 50th General Conference of the International Association for Research in Income and Wealth, Cambridge, 23–9 August.

Foster, J., J. Greer, and E. Thorbecke (1984). 'A Class of Decomposable Poverty Measures', *Econometrica* 52: 761–5.

Giles, J., and K. Yoo (2006). 'Precautionary Behaviour, Migrant Networks and Household Consumption Decisions: An Empirical Analysis Using Household Panel Data from Rural China', *The Review of Economics and Statistics* 89: 534–51.

Gustafsson, B., S. Li, and H. Sato (2004). 'Can a Subjective Poverty Line Be Applied to China? Assessing Poverty among Urban Residents in 1999', *Journal of International Development* 16: 1089–107.

Jain, L. R., and S. D. Tendulkar (1990). 'Role of Growth and Distribution in the Observed Change in Headcount Ratio Measure of Poverty: A Decomposition Exercise for India', *Indian Economic Review* 25: 165–205.

Kakwani N., and K. Subbarao (1990). 'Rural Poverty and its Alleviation in India', *Economic and Political Weekly* 15: A2–16.

Khan, A. R. (1999). 'Poverty in China in the Period of Globalization: New Evidence on Trend and Pattern', Issues in Development Discussion Paper 22, ILO: Geneva.

—— C. Riskin (2001). *Inequality and Poverty in China in the Age of Globalization*, Oxford University Press: New York.

—— —— (2005). 'China's Household Income and Its Distribution, 1995 and 2002', *The China Quarterly*: 356–84.

Kolenikov, S., and A. Shorrocks (2005). 'A Decomposition Analysis of Regional Poverty in Russia', *Review of Development Economics* 9: 25–46.

Osberg, L., and K. Xu (2000). 'International Comparisons of Poverty Intensity: Index Decomposition and Bootstrap Inference', *Journal of Human Resources* 35: 51–81.

Ravallion, M. (1992). 'Poverty Comparisons: A Guide to Concepts and Methods', Living Standards Measurement Study Working Paper 88, World Bank: Washington, DC.

—— S. Chen (1999). 'When Economic Reform is Faster than Statistical Reform: Measuring and Explaining Income Inequality in Rural China', *Oxford Bulletin of Economics and Statistics* 61: 33–56.

—— —— (2004). 'China's (Uneven) Progress against Poverty', Policy Research Working Paper 3408, World Bank: Washington, DC.

Shorrocks, A. (1999). 'Decomposition Procedures for Distributional Analysis: A Unified Framework Based on the Shapley Value', mimeo, University of Essex.

Tsui, K. Y. (1998). 'Trends and Inequalities of Rural Welfare in China: Evidence from Rural Households in Guangdong and Sichuan,' *Journal of Comparative Economics* 26: 783–804.

Wan, G., and Z. Y. Zhou (2005). 'Income Inequality in Rural China: Regression-Based Decomposition Using Household Data', *Review of Development Economics* 9: 107–20.

4
Development Strategies and Regional Income Disparities in China*

Justin Yifu Lin and Peilin Liu

4.1 Introduction

Since the economic reforms began in 1978, China has achieved remarkable economic results. Real GDP per capita grew at an average annual rate of 8.1 per cent in the period of 1978–2001.[1] Maintaining such a high growth rate over such a long period of time with a population of more than one billion is truly a miracle in world economic history (Lin et al. 1994, 1998). However, as shown in Figure 4.1a—the coefficients of variation of GDP per capita and per worker—and in Figure 4.1b—the Gini coefficients of GDP per capita and per worker—the disparities among different regions within China have increased since 1990. In 2001, of the 30 provinces in China, the three metropolitan cities (Shanghai, Beijing, and Tianjin), had the highest per capita GDP in current prices: 37,382 yuan, 25,300 yuan, and 19,986 yuan, respectively; and the four coastal provinces, Zhejiang, Guangdong, Jiangsu, and Fujian, had per capita GDP of 14,550 yuan, 13,612 yuan, 12,925 yuan, and 12,375 yuan, respectively. In stark contrast, the four western provinces, Guizhou, Gansu, Guangxi, and Yunnan, had per capita GDP of 2,865 yuan, 4,173 yuan, 4,679 yuan, and 4,872 yuan, respectively. That is, the per capita GDP in Shanghai and Zhejiang were, respectively, 13 times and five times that of Guizhou.

The widening regional disparities have attracted much attention both within and beyond China. Several hypotheses have been proposed to explain the widening disparities. In their empirical study of province level growth in 1978–89, Chen and Feng (2000) stress the importance of private enterprises to

---

* The authors are grateful for the helpful comments by Guanghua Wan and two referees. Peilin Liu would like to thank the support from National Planning Office of Philosophy and Social Science of China (Grant No.: 06BJL041).

[1] The data are from NBS (2002: 14–18).

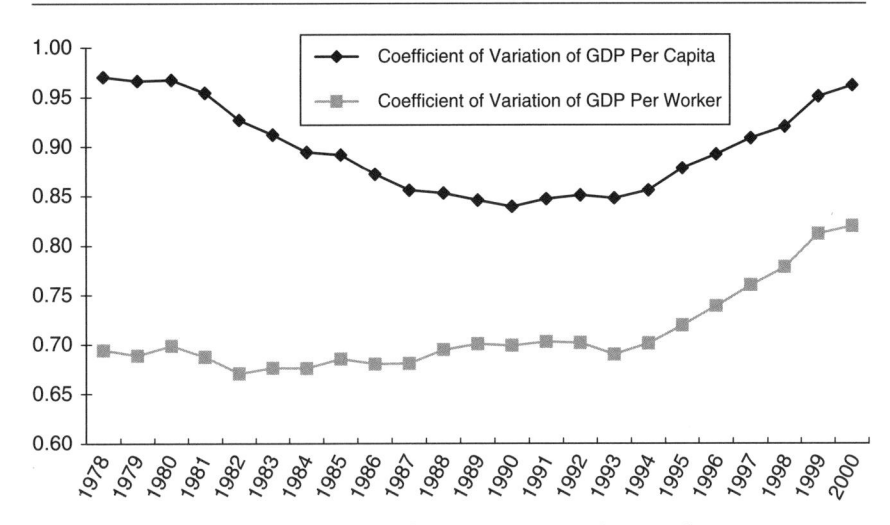

Figure 4.1a: Coefficients of variation of GDP per capita and per worker

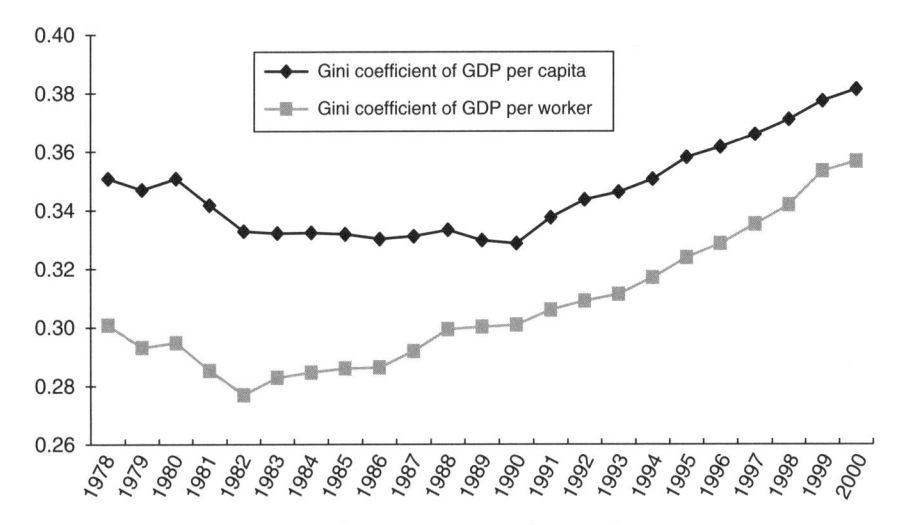

Figure 4.1b: Gini coefficients of GDP per capita and per worker

Note: The GDP in Figures 4.1(a) and 4.1(b) are measured in 1978 prices.
Sources: NBS (1999a) and NBS (*Provincial Statistics Yearbooks*, various issues).

economic growth. The differences in the extent of the development of the private economy may contribute to regional disparities. However, the experience of shock therapy in eastern Europe and the countries formerly in the Soviet Union show that privatization itself might not promote economic growth. The vitality of private enterprises in China has been due to their entry/ adoption of labour intensive industries/technologies, which are consistent with China's comparative advantages.

Lee (1994) and Dayal-Gulati and Husain (2000) emphasize the effects of foreign direct investment (FDI) on regional disparities. However, they do not analyse factors determining the location and industrial distribution of FDI. Young (2000) argues that regional protectionism was a key factor in the widening of regional disparities because the protection of local markets led to deviations in resource allocation away from regional comparative advantages. However, regional protectionism and market segmentation were endogenous to the regional development strategy.

Other studies (Fleisher and Chen 1997; Démurger et al. 2001) attribute the widening of regional disparities to the biased regional policy of the central government or to location factors. These studies argue that the central government's investment priority favouring the eastern region was the root cause for the lagging behind of the central and western regions and, at the same time, the unfavourable geographic conditions limited the development of the central and western regions. Tsui (Chapter 5, this volume) also found that physical capital is the dominant factor that affected the interprovincal differences. However, as we will point out in the following analyses, the level of central government investments in the central and western regions is no less than that in the eastern region, especially in the period just prior to the reforms. If the policy bias of central government investments is the main cause for the regional disparities, it is difficult to reconcile the fact that central and western regions received large amounts of investments in the period before the reforms, but they failed to narrow the gap with the eastern region.

In this chapter, we propose that a flawed development strategy is responsible for the increasing disparities in economic development among provinces in China. Since the founding of the People's Republic of China (PRC), the government has pushed a 'leap forward' strategy emphasizing the development of capital intensive heavy industries. In most provinces, however, the priority industries under this strategy were inconsistent with the comparative advantage determined by the factor endowments in those provinces. Many enterprises in the priority industries were not viable in competitive markets and required interventions in the markets by the government to support and protect them.[2] Consequently, this leap forward strategy retarded the functions of market, impeded capital accumulation, and hindered technology and productivity progress in the provinces. The provinces in the central and western regions continue to follow the leap forward strategy and have poor growth performance. Therefore, it is imperative to replace the comparative advantage defying leap forward strategy with a comparative advantage following strategy

[2] The concept of viability will be discussed in greater detail later in this chapter.

and restructure the existing industries in each province according to the principle of comparative advantage. This latter strategy would enhance coordinated development among regions and provinces and, in effect, work more effectively to create sustainable national economic development. The regional effects of economic strategies in China are the subject of this study.

The rest of this chapter is organized as follows. Section 4.2 reviews regional economic development policies since the founding of the PRC in 1949, especially in the period after the reforms and liberalization. In section 4.3 we discuss how the leap forward strategy has influenced regional economic development in China. Section 4.4 is an econometric analysis of the theories presented in this chapter. Some concluding remarks are provided in the last section.

4.2 An Overview of the Evolution of China's Regional Development Policies[3]

When the PRC was founded in 1949, the military chaos of the Japanese occupation and during World War II had ended and China as a nation was again ruled by a single central government. There were substantial gaps in development levels among the provinces and regions at that time.[4] Data from 28 provinces[5] in 1952 show that the average per capita GDP was 134.89 yuan with a coefficient of variance[6] of 0.59 (see Figure 4.2). Shanghai had the highest per capita GDP of 436 yuan, while Guizhou had the lowest of 58 yuan; the former is 7.5 times the latter.

---

[3] The data in this subsection are from the NBS (1999a).

[4] China has a long history of regional disparities in economic development. The Chinese civilization originated in the Yellow River area, so since early in China's history, a high concentration of economic centres emerged along the Yellow River. During the Song Dynasty, these economic centres began to move south, and major agricultural crops changed. Manufacturing in the modern sense started with the 'importing foreign industry initiative' in the 1850s, but rather than real comprehensive industrialization, this initiative was rather selective and aimed simply to build factories in riverbank and coastal areas with good transportation conditions. At the end of the nineteenth century, most of China's industry was located in the southeast, coastal regions, with 64 per cent of all factories in China being in Shanghai, Guangzhou, and Wuhan. During the ten-year period after World War I (1928–37), China's national industries experienced rapid development and quickly boosted the growth of the national economy. In this period, the economy pursued a new trend, and heavy industries in the northeast developed quickly, giving rise to industrial centres appearing in cities like Tianjin and Qingdao. When the second Sino-Japanese war broke out in 1937, some important industrial facilities were relocated to the southwestern regions, and this movement actually helped economic development in these regions. However, generally, the southeastern areas continued to lead the other areas in economic development. From World War II until the founding of the PRC, regional disparities in economic development existed.

[5] Data for Hainan and Xizang (Tibet) are not available; and statistics for Chongqing included in the data for Sichuan.

[6] The coefficient of variance is calculated by dividing the standard variance by the mean value.

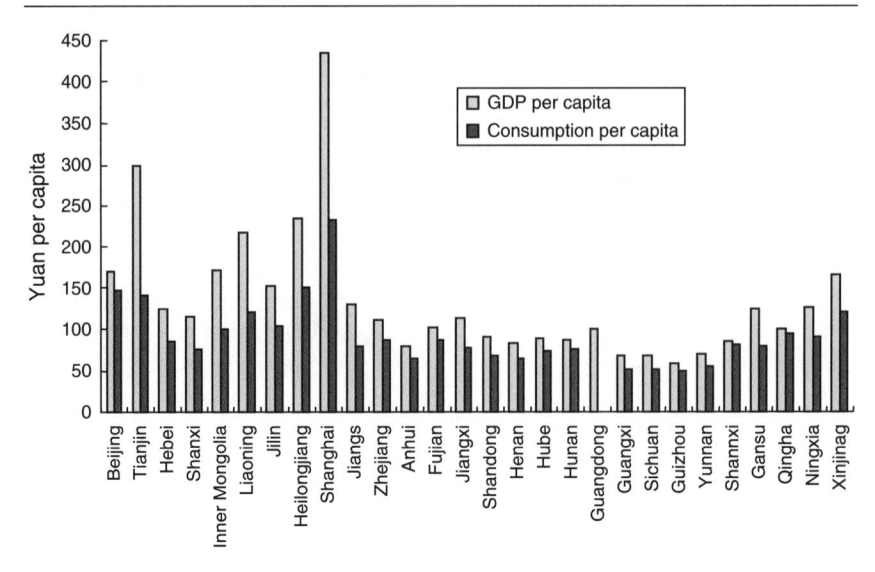

Figure 4.2: Per capita GDP and consumption expenditure in China's provinces in 1952
Source: Computed by the authors, based on data from NBS (1999b).

For the purpose of nation building, the Chinese government adopted a heavy industry oriented development strategy in its first five-year plan in 1953, focusing on the construction of 156 major projects with the assistance of the Soviet Union. Notably, due to security considerations, many of these projects were located in the northwest and southwest regions. In fact, among the 156 key projects, only one-fifth were in coastal areas.

In the second five-year plan (1958–62), the government increased its investment in the coastal areas to explore more fully the development potential of the Yangtze River delta region—with Shanghai at the helm—and of the coastal areas of northern China. The period of the third five-year plan (1966–70) included yet another strategic reallocation of China's industrial investments. As part of increased military preparedness, the central government adopted the strategy of 'third line development' and concentrated major construction projects in Sichuan, Guizhou, Shaanxi, Gansu, Shanxi, Yunnan, Hubei, and Hunan. During the fourth five-year plan, the government slowed its investment in these areas and required each province to improve industrial self-sufficiency. This change, combined with the discovery of oil in the east, prompted a resurgence of investments in the coastal provinces. This increased coastal investment continued into the early 1970s, especially after the improvement of USA–China relations.

According to standard neoclassical economic theories, intensive investment in the central and western areas, especially in the third-line regions, should have brought about economic development in those areas. The actual outcome, however, was very different. Before the reforms in 1978, economic

Development Strategy and Disparity

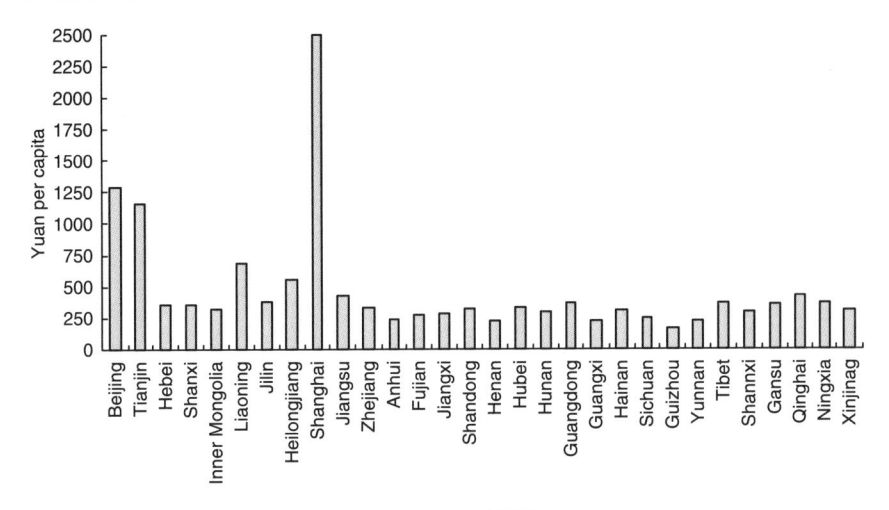

Figure 4.3: Per capita GDP in each province in 1978
Source: Computed by the authors, based on data from NBS (1999b).

development levels in the central and western areas remained behind those in the eastern areas. In 1978, Shanghai had the highest per capita GDP at 2,498 yuan, a figure 14.28 times higher than per capita GDP in Guizhou (see Figure 4.3). Besides the three municipalities directly under the central government (Beijing, Tianjin, and Shanghai), Liaoning had the highest per capita GDP of 680 yuan, a figure 3.89 times that of Guizhou. In 1978, the average overall provincial per capita GDP was 467.57 yuan with a variance of 0.96, much higher than the variance of 0.59 in 1952.

In the autumn of 1978, the Chinese government initiated the reform and liberalization policies. Under the leadership of Deng Xiaoping, the new policy allowed some people and some regions to get rich first.[7] The sixth and seventh five-year plans (1981–5, 1986–90) strategically declared that more concentrated development efforts would be allotted to the most promising growth regions. Thus, many areas along China's eastern coast enjoyed significant increases in investments. An important change in fiscal policy also occurred at this time. Starting in 1980, the government began to replace the old fiscal system of 'unified revenue and expenditure' with a decentralized fiscal responsibility system, giving partial autonomy to each province for the purpose of enhancing each province's incentives to increase revenues and reduce expenditures.

By the late 1980s, the increased development investments in the coastal regions had yielded significant gains, but relative backwardness in the central

---

[7] In a conference held in March 1980 to discuss long-term plans, Deng Xiaoping pointed out that China should 'use our comparative advantages, avoid using our disadvantages and accepting the fact of economic disparities... some people and some regions should be allowed to get rich first and in the end everyone will get rich' (Wang and Li 2000: 266).

and western areas became a challenge. To address this problem, the government entered the next decade emphasizing 'balanced regional economic development' in its long term development strategies. The ninth five-year plan and long term prospects for 2010, adopted in 1996, suggested several measures to narrow regional disparities, giving more infrastructure investments and international development agencies' loans to the central and western regions. At the end of the 1990s, the government adopted the western development strategy to promote the development of hinterland provinces. Accompanying changes in regional development policies was a reform of fiscal relations between the central and local governments in 1994, including the implementation of a tax sharing system and the establishment of a uniform income tax for all domestic enterprises.

4.3 Viability and the Effects of the Leap Forward Strategy on Regional Disparities

The priority given to the development of heavy industries before the reform resulted in intensive investments in the central and western regions. However, those investments profoundly failed to bring about a corresponding increase in per capita GDP and per worker GDP in these regions. In fact, the widening of regional income disparities after the reforms also related to the above pattern of investments in the central and western regions. In analysing the impact of development strategies on economic performance, Lin (2003: 280) formally defines the term 'viability' as follows: 'If, without any external subsidies or protections, a normally managed enterprise is expected to earn a socially acceptable profit in a free, open, and competitive market, the enterprise is viable. Otherwise, the enterprise is nonviable'. In the same paper Lin also categorizes development strategies in developing countries into two mutually exclusive groups: (1) the comparative advantage defying (CAD) strategy, which attempts to encourage firms that ignore the existing comparative advantages of the economy in their entry/choice of industry/technology; and (2) the comparative advantage following (CAF) strategy, which attempts to facilitate firms' entry/choice of industry/technology according to the economy's existing comparative advantages.

The concept of viability seems to be trivial in the context of neoclassical economics because there is a belief that, if an enterprise in the long term does not expect to earn a socially acceptable profit, the enterprise will not be set up or will be driven out of the competitive market.[8] However, if a government adopts a CAD strategy, encouraging enterprises in the economy to ignore the existing comparative advantages of the economy in their entry/choice of

---

[8] Of course, it is not unusual that during the early period of an investment, net cash flow is negative, but the sum of discounted expected net profit over the whole investment period must be non-negative. In fact, the neoclassical economic theories presume the viability of firms.

industry/technology, these enterprises will not be viable in an open, free, competitive market (Lin 2003). To establish and ensure survival of these enterprises, the Chinese government established a trinity system, including a macro environment with distorted factor and product prices, a planned and administrative resource allocation mechanism, and a micro management institution characterized by the nationalization of enterprises (Lin et al. 1994).

The viability problem endogenous to the leap forward strategy and the corresponding trinity economic system had direct impacts on increasing regional disparities in economic development before the reforms. There are several reasons for this. First, launching many highly capital intensive projects in the central and western areas required large initial investments. From the statistical data alone, one may infer such an investment pattern as attempting to narrow the gap of regional development between the developed coastal region and backward hinterland region (Yang 1990). However, only a limited portion of these investments became productive capital. And even these capital investments were quite specialized for certain production purposes and had no externality on the local economies.[9]

Second, many of China's leap forward projects required huge inputs of natural resources, raw minerals, and raw products, which were produced mostly in the central and western regions. For the purpose of subsidizing those projects, the government arbitrarily depressed prices of these goods. The central and western regions were in effect subsidizing the leap forward projects. Therefore, many construction projects in the central and western areas not only did not help economic development in these areas, but actually hampered it.

Third, although the government injected a lot of capital into the priority projects, these projects could create only limited employment opportunities for the highly educated labour force coming mainly from the developed coastal region. The local labour force was restricted to low productivity agriculture. Consequently, the indigenous local people's incomes remained low.

Because of the traditional system's low efficiency, China started a piecemeal gradual approach to reforming the economy at the end of 1978. The reforms first increased the autonomy of micro agents, farmers, and managers of state owned enterprises, and then gradually the reforms extended to the resource allocation system and to the macro policy environment (Lin et al. 1994). The gradual approach to reform enabled China to start the reforms smoothly and to have steady progress while avoiding the high costs of tumultuous social change in the reform process. But a gradual approach in reform also meant that different regions were not equal in grasping opportunities for regional development. Areas that were impacted the most by the leap forward strategies

---

[9] This is because the industry and technology of those priority projects were too intensive in capital, and local economies were too scarce in capital. Therefore, it would be difficult to transfer the technology in the priority projects to the local enterprises.

faced very challenging and more numerous difficulties and required longer periods of time to accomplish the transition because the implicit viability problems of most of their state owned enterprises (SOEs) became explicit. On the other hand, those areas that were left relatively untouched by the leap forward strategies enjoyed a much faster transition because fewer of their enterprises were burdened by viability problems.

For the purpose of subsidizing non-viable SOEs, the government continues to suppress the prices of raw materials and resource products. Suppliers of raw materials and resource products are mainly in the central and western areas. As the coastal provinces grow with the reforms, they import more of these resources from the central and western provinces. Therefore, the relatively backward central and western regions are subsidizing the growth of the relatively wealthy eastern region, causing the regional disparities to widen. Moreover, the required subsidies to the non-viable SOEs in the central and western areas have caused many problems of soft budget constraints (Lin and Tan 1999), further depressing the economic efficiency in the central and western regions.

The non-viability of many SOEs is the key issue in China's reforms (Lin et al. 1998; Lin and Tan 1999). However, the government, both at central and local levels, continues to pay insufficient attention to this problem. In assessing the performances of local leaders, the central government emphasizes technological advancement and gross and net production increases. Therefore, local leaders often make decisions that disregard market signals and continue to pursue the leap forward strategy. Fortunately, China's recent ascension to the WTO has limited the government's ability to protect/subsidize non-viable enterprises and has made all levels of government aware of the importance of following the principle of comparative advantages in developing the economy.

4.4 Regional Disparities: An Empirical Analysis

4.4.1 *A Framework for Empirical Analysis*

In order to offer deeper insights about the influence of development strategies on a region's economic development, we now present a rigorous econometric analysis. According to neoclassical growth theories (Solow 1956; Barro 1991), an economy that has lower initial per capita income will have a higher potential growth rate due to diminishing returns in capital, leading to economic convergence. However, neoclassical growth theories ignore the influence of economic structure, which is determined by the characteristics of development strategies, on growth. As discussed earlier, if a less developed economy adopts a CAD, leap forward strategy, its pace of economic growth will be hampered and its real growth rate prevented from reaching its full potential.

Development Strategy and Disparity

Lin (2003) constructs a technology choice index (TCI) to measure the characteristics of the development strategy in an economy. The idea behind the variable is as follows. If an economy adopts a CAF strategy, that is, all enterprises follow the economy's comparative advantage to choose their industries, products and technologies, the actual capital/labour ratio of the economy's manufacturing industry is endogenously determined by the capital/labour ratio of the whole economy. That is, the optimal capital intensity of the economy's manufacturing sector, K_i/L_i, can be described as a function of the economy's capital endowment, K, and labour endowment, L.

$$\left(\frac{K_i}{L_i}\right)^* = F\left(\frac{K}{L}\right) \tag{1}$$

To measure an economy's deviation from the CAF strategy, we construct the statistical indicator, TCI, the actual technology choice index of the manufacturing sector, which is defined as the actual capital/labour ratio of an economy's manufacturing industry divided by the capital/labour ratio of the whole economy. That is:

$$TCI = \frac{(K_i/L_i)}{(K/L)} \tag{2}$$

A government's choice of a development strategy will influence the economy's TCI value. We then define the optimal technology choice index of the manufacturing sector, TCI^*. Conducting the first order Taylor expansion of equation (1) at $K/L=0$ and ignoring the higher order terms, we obtain equation (3), where ω is a constant, denoting the derivative value of equation (1) at point $K/L=0$,[10]

$$\left(\frac{K_i}{L_i}\right)^* = \omega\left(\frac{K}{L}\right) \tag{3}$$

Obviously, the higher the capital/labour ratio an economy has, the higher the optimal capital/labour ratio of its manufacturing sector. That is, $\omega > 0$. Until now, we have defined the optimal technology choice index TCI^* as:

$$TCI^* = \frac{(K_i/L_i)^*}{(K/L)} = \omega \tag{4}$$

---

[10] $K/L=0$ means that the economy has no capital stock. Obviously, the optimal capital labour ratio in the manufacturing industry is zero. Equation (1) is a curve starting from the original point. ω is the tangent slope of this curve at the original point.

Given the endowment structure of an economy, TCI^* is the optimal TCI.[11] We can measure the government's deviation from the CAF strategy indirectly as follows:

$$DS = TCI - TCI^* = TCI - \omega \qquad (5)$$

If a country or area follows the CAF strategy, then $DS=0$. If the government adopts a CAD strategy to promote its capital intensive industries, we expect $DS>0$. The larger the value of DS, the stronger the CAD strategy. Furthermore, given ω, the larger the value of TCI, the stronger the CAD strategy.

From the above discussion, we construct the following econometric equation:

$$G_i = \alpha_0 + \alpha_1 \cdot \text{Ln}(GDPPL_{0,i}) + \alpha_2 \cdot DS_i + \psi X + u_i \qquad (6)$$

In equation (6), G_i, the dependent variable, is the average annual growth rate of per worker GDP of each province from 1978 to 2000. $\text{Ln}(GDPPL_{0,i})$ is the initial per worker GDP of each province in 1978, representing the initial level of development. According to the analysis we conducted before, if the convergence exists, α_1 is expect to be negative, and α_2, the coefficient of DS, is expected to be negative, too.

Because the optimal $TCI^* = \omega$ is not observable, we cannot calculate the value of DS_i directly. However, ω is a constant. We can therefore rearrange equation (6) into equation (6'), which will be used in the regression:

$$G_i = C'_k + \alpha_1 \cdot \text{Ln}(GDPPL_{0,i}) + \alpha_2 \cdot TCI_i + \psi X + u_i \qquad (6')$$

In equation (6'), $C'_k = \alpha_0 - \alpha_2\omega$, we expect the coefficient of TCI_i, α_2, to be negative.

In equations (6) and (6'), X denotes other explanatory variables, which we will describe in detail later.

4.4.2 Variables and the Data Resources

For the measurement of TCI_i, please refer to the work of the Development Strategy Research Group of the China Center for Economic Research (2002).[12] In fact, TCI_i reflects the characteristics of industries, products and the technology structure of each province. We have annual observations of TCI_i for each year in the period 1978–99 for each province. In order to describe the

---

[11] In addition to factor endowments, TCI^* is expected to be affected by the stage of development of an economy and the relative abundance of natural resource in an economy. We do not consider these factors here.

[12] The government's heavy industry oriented strategy can only absorb limited amounts of labour. Out of a concern for social stability, social policies always impose on firms the burden of absorbing excess labour. Therefore, firms hire more employees than are needed, and one person's work has to be assigned to three persons. This practice is not in accordance to the

characteristics of the development strategies for the whole period, we use the arithmetical average of TCI_i for 1978–99 and denote it $TCI7899$. In addition, we also define another indicator of development strategies, $TCI7885$, which is the arithmetical average value of TCI_i from 1978–85, in order to capture the characteristics of development strategies of each province in the initial stage of the reform.[13]

In equation (6'), the explanatory variable X differs under different situations. According to neoclassical growth theory, the stronger the propensity to save in an economy, the higher the per worker output in the steady state. Therefore, the differences in saving propensities between economies lead to different rates of convergence. To be specific, a higher savings propensity leads to a higher income level in the steady state. Therefore, the higher the saving rate, the larger the income gap between the initial income level and the steady state income level and the faster the growth rate. Savings propensity is expressed as (SAV_i) and is expected to have a positive sign. We use Mankiw's approach (Mankiw et al. 1992) and define the propensity to save in each province as follows:

$$SAV_i = \left(\sum_{t=1978}^{2000} \frac{I_i}{GDP_i} \right)$$

where the numerator denotes fixed capital and inventory investment,[14–15] while the denominator denotes current GDP. Both are measured in current prices.

In addition, in the neoclassical growth theory model, the greater the increases in the rates of labour, the lower the per worker income in the steady state tends to be. According to a principle similar to that of the propensity to save, we introduce the rate of labour increases in each province as an explanatory variable (denoted as $LABG_i$). This variable is expected to have a negative sign. Human capital is included as an explanatory variable in most studies of economic convergence. However, each researcher has a different definition of human capital. In this chapter, we take the initial level of each province's human capital as an independent variable (denoted by $HUMK82_i$), which is defined as the proportion of individuals who had completed primary school by 1982.

---

concept of a technology driven leap forward strategy that pursues priority development in capital intensive industries. Behind the appearance of high employment is a reality of large numbers of hidden, unemployed workers.

[13] The amount of labour that we use here to calculate the TCI index is larger than the real (or efficient) labour amount employed. Thus, per worker capital possession is underestimated. That is, the TCI index we get is overestimated. Nevertheless, this fact only strengthens our conclusion.

[14] Here we neglect the influences of government surplus and net export on savings. The relationship between these factors and productive capital is, after all, relatively weak.

[15] In fact, the definition of 'savings index' here is not very satisfying. In a neoclassical framework, the savings propensity refers to voluntarily savings, and all savings become investments. The savings index in the study can also be used to represent the rate of investment. And once we take this index as the rate of investment, the policy implication from the

Capital inflow, especially FDI, often brings with it new technology and management (Lee 1994; Dayal-Gulati and Husain 2000). Therefore, the greater the FDI inflow (denoted by FDI_i) into a province, the more advantages it has in technology progress. The measurement of FDI we use in our econometric analysis is the natural logarithm of total FDI from 1978–2000.[16] We expect the coefficient of FDI to be positive. Additionally, plenty of empirical research supports the point that China has experienced economic convergence since the reforms (Tsui 1991, 1993; World Bank 1995, 1997; Jian et al. 1996; Cai and Du 2000; Aziz and Christoph 2001; Zhang et al. 2001). Stretching across a vast territory, China displays great disparities between regions in natural conditions and market capacities. In order to control these factors, we introduce two dummy variables denoting the central and western areas of China.[17]

Neoclassical growth theory ignores the structure of the economy. Realizing the disadvantageous consequences of this omission, Barro attempts to remedy this deficiency in his empirical testing of neoclassical growth theory. A variable denoting the impact on structure was introduced into the regression analysis of economic convergence in US regions. The impact variable is the sum of industrial growth rates on the national level weighted by the share of each industry in each state (Barro and Sala-i-Martin 1991, 1992). The variable reflects the neoclassical growth theory's present view on economic structure. Theoretically, Barro's understanding of the impact of structure focuses on the demand side. Although it is understandable to consider the impact of demand on economic growth, Barro's understanding of the impact of economic structure on growth violates a basic principle of economics. For instance, suppose industries grow quickly on the national level, but some provinces have comparative advantages in agriculture. Then the smaller share of industry in the agricultural provinces is not necessarily negative and unfavourable to growth. In other words, that different regions have different output structures is the result of differences in regional comparative advantages and the free movement of products and

---

study should be treated carefully. After all, the mechanism of voluntary savings and automatic transforming from savings to investments is totally different from the mechanism that a government uses to create a deficit budget to expand investments.

[16] Strictly speaking, foreign direct investment can take various forms, including cash, technology, physical capital, etc. The definition of gross investment in national accounts is not exactly identical to the meaning of foreign direct investment. Therefore, the method in most research that uses the ratio of FDI over gross investment value to describe the impact of foreign investment upon economic growth is not very proper. In our opinion, from the perspective of technological progress, to use the absolute volume of foreign investment is a better choice than is the ratio mentioned above. Of course, in using this definition, we implicitly assume that all technological progress advantages from FDI occur at the initial stage of the investment. In fact, foreign invested enterprises might share further information about the parent company's R&D in the future. That is to say, one time FDI brings about continued technological progress advantages that may not initially be fully quantifiable.

[17] Here, data for Sichuan includes that for Chongqing, as systematic data for Chongqing as an independent entity could not be obtained. Systematic data for Tibet and Hainan are also not available, so these two are not included.

factors. Following the CAF strategy does not require each industry's growth rate in each region to be equal to the national growth rate, because the comparative advantages in each area are different and change constantly.

Certainly, in a mature market economy such as exists in the USA, the patterns of industry specialization between states have conformed to the regional comparative advantages over a relatively long period of time. Therefore, Barro's understanding of the impact of structure can be regarded as the impact of demand in the short run. In other words, in the USA, this variable is appropriate for describing the short run demand impact. However, in the case of China, because of the poor match between the economic structure and the comparative advantages in each region, this variable is inappropriate. Industry has undoubtedly increased most rapidly on the national level in China since 1978. But some provinces, especially those in central or western areas, do not always have comparative advantages in industry. Therefore, specializing in the development of such comparative advantage defying heavy industry will not accelerate growth but will hinder it.

Wei (1997) adopts the impact on structure variable defined by Barro in his empirical research.[18] We use data from 1978–2000 from 29 provinces in China to calculate the impact of structure variable as defined by Barro and include it in the regression.[19] Table 4.1 summarizes the data set that we used in our econometric analysis.

Cheng (2002) points out that the regression results of regional convergence in China are highly sensitive to the choice of samples. To be specific, whether to regard Beijing, Tianjin, and Shanghai as independent economies or integrate them into their respective surrounding provinces will lead to different conclusions. For example, Tsui (1996) includes Beijing, Tianjin, and Shanghai data in provincial data, and his conclusion supports the argument for regional income divergence in China since the reforms. Other studies that support the regional convergence position are all based on methods that treat these three cities as independent economies. In this chapter, we present both cases in our analysis.

---

[18] In many other studies on regional economic development in China, various kinds of structure variables are included. Cheng (2002) includes an explanatory variable, the ratio of non-agricultural GDP to total GDP, to describe the influence of economic structure in the normal Barro regression. Similarly, Jian and others (Jian et al. 1996) use initial agricultural shares. Actually, Barro and Sala-i-Martin (1991) use the structural variable of agricultural production over total state GDP in their analysis of regional convergence of states in the USA before 1929. Shen and others (Shen and Ma 2002) use a so-called industrialization index, the ratio of provincial industrial production over national total industrial production. Cai and others (Cai et al. 2001) also introduce a structural variable to describe the influence of the degree of maturity they market: the comparative productivity of agricultural labour. The definition of this index is the proportion of agricultural production over the proportions of agricultural labour. However, they do not say whether the proportions used there were set against the national total or the provincial total.

[19] Based on available data, when calculating structural variables, we divide the national economy into the primary industry, manufacturing, construction and building, trade and retailing, transportation, and other tertiary industries. There are six sectors altogether.

Table 4.1: Dataset for empirical analysis

Province (city, section)	G_i, the average annual growth rate of per worker GDP	Ln($GDPPL_0$), initial per worker GDP	TCI7899	TCI7885	SAV, the average savings rate	LABG, the average growth rate of labour	HUMK82, the rate of primary school completion, 1982	FDI	Central areas	Western areas	Structure variable defined by Barro
Anhui	0.0730	6.4107	6.1704	10.5070	0.3815	0.0294	0.4834	12.627	1	0	0.0628
Beijing	0.0789	7.8043	2.5433	3.8859	0.4032	0.0148	0.7780	14.164	0	0	0.0886
Fujian	0.0981	6.5764	3.8099	6.4157	0.3957	0.0297	0.5525	15.024	0	0	0.0698
Gansu	0.0492	6.8381	8.8154	8.6895	0.3587	0.0366	0.4674	10.794	0	1	0.0790
Guangdong	0.1017	6.7051	3.2347	4.0162	0.2610	0.0262	0.6592	16.091	0	0	0.0736
Guangxi	0.0615	6.2556	6.2663	6.9535	0.3203	0.0267	0.6147	13.366	0	1	0.0677
Guizhou	0.0599	6.0923	7.7422	11.8262	0.1714	0.0290	0.4358	10.604	0	1	0.0658
Hebei	0.0781	6.7660	3.8184	5.2152	0.2948	0.0232	0.6365	13.606	0	0	0.0598
Henan	0.0704	6.3619	5.3099	7.7140	0.3600	0.0298	0.5702	12.996	1	0	0.0745
Heilongjiang	0.0515	7.4594	3.4011	5.1687	0.3383	0.0229	0.6781	12.818	0	0	0.0672
Hubei	0.0742	6.6726	5.0769	6.9841	0.4250	0.0205	0.6251	13.364	1	0	0.0773
Hunan	0.0655	6.4688	5.9411	8.9617	0.4197	0.0227	0.6733	13.167	1	0	0.0666
Jilin	0.0647	7.1470	4.0611	4.7230	0.4366	0.0298	0.6851	12.602	0	0	0.0667
Jiangsu	0.1062	6.7994	2.9713	4.6113	0.4708	0.0131	0.6028	15.298	0	0	0.0741
Jiangxi	0.0748	6.5419	4.6175	5.7546	0.3665	0.0248	0.5784	12.505	1	0	0.0750
Liaoning	0.0611	7.5108	3.3617	4.3924	0.3084	0.0192	0.7364	14.192	0	0	0.0659
Neimeng	0.0714	6.7902	5.1472	7.0115	0.3575	0.0223	0.6009	10.506	0	0	0.0827
Ningxia	0.0533	6.8653	3.3853	3.6154	0.1916	0.0330	0.4718	9.975	0	1	0.0719
Qinghai	0.0439	6.9790	5.2507	4.8027	0.2259	0.0272	0.4558	8.645	0	1	0.0776
Shandong	0.0836	6.6321	4.2107	6.1633	0.3703	0.0278	0.5767	14.560	0	0	0.0771
Shanxi	0.0672	6.8153	3.9497	4.9722	0.3097	0.0195	0.6874	11.924	1	0	0.0712
Shaanxi	0.0657	6.6228	4.5893	6.4586	0.2764	0.0250	0.6076	12.630	0	1	0.0794
Shanghai	0.0836	8.2704	1.7581	2.4050	0.2754	0.0077	0.7706	14.940	0	0	0.0728
Tianjin	0.0771	7.7204	1.9893	2.2888	0.2379	0.0136	0.7491	14.132	0	0	0.0893
Xinjiang	0.0827	6.6787	4.6238	6.3387	0.2755	0.0172	0.5839	10.562	0	0	0.0884
Yunnan	0.0663	6.2648	6.4853	7.4401	0.2122	0.0258	0.4269	11.808	0	1	0.0693
Zhejiang	0.1048	6.5356	2.1395	2.6067	0.4214	0.0183	0.6284	13.929	0	0	0.0650
Sichuan	0.0586	6.3922	4.3966	6.1308	0.3366	0.0194	0.6133	13.051	0	0	0.0684

Notes: (1) Hainan not included because its data for TCI are not available. In the regressions, Hainan is not included; (2) TCI7899 is the average of annual TCI for the period in 1978–99; TCI7885 is the average for the period 1978–85.

Source: Nominal and real GDP index from 1978 to 1998 are available in the NBS (1999b). Nominal and real GDP indices from 1999 to 2001 are available in annual books of provincial statistics. From these statistics, timeseries data for real GDP in 1978 prices can be derived. Data for employment use in G_i and Ln($GDPPL_0$) are also taken from the above-mentioned sources. Data for FDI are from China's annual statistics books. Data for the proportion of population possessing higher than rudimentary education over the total population in 1982 (which represents human capital) are available in the CASS (1985). Savings rate data for provinces are derived from the above data by dividing nominal capital formation data by nominal GDP data.

Development Strategy and Disparity

The residual in equation (6′) is assumed to be heteroscedastic, that is, $E(u) = 0$, $Var(u) = \sigma^2 s_i$. Under this assumption, the regressions are carried out by White's method of robustness variance-covariance matrix.

4.4.3 Results of the Econometric Analysis

We report the regression results in Tables 4.2 to 4.4. Table 4.2 includes estimated results of the eight models. Model I uses the framework of neoclassical unconditional convergence. The result from this model does not support the unconditional convergence hypothesis. Moreover, the adjusted R^2 shows that the goodness of fit is not good. In model II and model III, we include the development strategies of each province in the initial stage of reform, *TCI7885*, and during the whole period of the reform, *TCI7899*. From the estimated results of these two models, we see that the stronger the leap forward characteristics in the development strategies, the slower the increase in the per worker GDP. In addition, the sign of the coefficient of the initial per worker GDP has the expected negative sign.

Model IV to model VIII are based on a framework of conditional convergence. The coefficients of the development strategy variables in these models are all significantly negative. However, the initial per worker GDP has the expected negative sign but is not significant in some cases. The signs of other explanatory variables' coefficients, such as savings rates, rates of labour increases, and FDI, are all as expected, however the significance of the variables is unstable. The coefficient of the human capital variable has an unexpected negative sign, and, in some cases, is highly significant. Of course, we cannot draw the general conclusion that human capital and per worker GDP are negatively related.

The eight models used to derive the results in Table 4.3 are the same models used in Table 4.2 except that we add another two dummy variables denoting central and western areas in Table 4.3. The inclusion of these two dummies clearly enhances the goodness of fit of all models, and the estimates for the initial per worker GDP are negative and highly significant in all models. This result indicates the existence of neoclassical convergence in China. From the regional dummies in Table 4.3, we can see that the growth rate of per worker GDP for provinces in the central region is significantly lower than in the provinces in the eastern region and higher than the provinces in the western regions, which reflects the influence of natural conditions and other unobservable regional characteristics on economic growth. The influence of development strategies has the expected negative sign and is statistically significant in all cases. These results indicate that the leap forward development strategy is detrimental to an increase of per worker GDP.

Table 4.4 shows the results of nine models, in which the structure impact variables defined by Barro are introduced. As shown, none of the estimates for

Table 4.2: Regression results

	Model I	Model II	Model III	Model IV	Model V	Model VI	Model VII	Model VIII
Constant	0.0703	0.1807	0.2267	0.0746	0.1281	0.2123	0.1413	0.2258
	(0.0290)	(0.0587)	(0.0502)	(0.0478)	(0.0503)	(0.0474)	(0.0497)	(0.0477)
	[0.0224]**	[0.0050]***	[0.0001]***	[0.1330]	[0.0188]**	[0.0002]***	[0.0098]***	[0.0001]***
Ln($GDPPI_0$)	0.0003	−0.0123	−0.0171	−0.0039	−0.0089	−0.0161	−0.0087	−0.0152
	(0.0042)	(0.0073)	(0.0063)	(0.0053)	(0.0055)	(0.0082)	(0.0052)	(0.0076)
	[0.9436]	[0.1038]	[0.0113]**	[0.4712]	[0.1223]	[0.0626]*	[0.1098]	[0.0573]*
TCI7885		−0.0042			−0.0024	−0.0033		
		(0.0017)			(0.0008)	(0.0014)		
		[0.0200]**			[0.0049]***	[0.0252]**		
TCI7899			−0.0084				−0.0047	−0.0071
			(0.0020)				(0.0012)	(0.0021)
			[0.0003]***				[0.0006]***	[0.0026]***
SAVE				0.0313	0.0395	0.0714	0.0394	0.0660
				(0.0244)	(0.0209)	(0.0330)	(0.0203)	(0.0293)
				[0.2124]	[0.0732]*	[0.0415]**	[0.0656]*	[0.0348]**
LABG				−1.2078	−1.0894	−1.1571	−0.8746	−0.7890
				(0.4221)	(0.3777)	(0.4901)	(0.3689)	(0.5323)
				[0.0078]***	[0.0089]***	[0.0275]**	[0.0274]**	[0.1525]
HUMK82				−0.0786	−0.0855	−0.0119	−0.0887	−0.0349
				(0.0269)	(0.0249)	(0.0506)	(0.0196)	(0.0424)
				[0.0078]***	[0.0025]***	[0.8157]	[0.0002]***	[0.4181]
FDI				0.0070	0.0065		0.0056	
				(0.0016)	(0.0015)		(0.0015)	
				[0.0003]***	[0.0004]***		[0.0012]***	
Adjusted R^2	−0.0384	0.1214	0.4022	0.5836	0.6330	0.3271	0.6717	0.4715

Notes: (1) The figure in the parentheses under each estimate parameter is the standard deviation of the estimation, the square brackets below shows the *p*-value of the *t*-test against the null hypotheses that 'the parameter is significantly not zero. This is the same for all other OLS estimation below. (2) As we assume that the random disturbance has heteroscedasticity, we made certain adjustments in OLS estimation. The standard deviation of the estimation reported in the table is from White's robust variance and covariance matrix. All following OLS estimations are adjusted similarly. (3) For ease of interpretation, we denote the case where the *p*-value of the two-tailed *t*-test is less than 1% with ***; cases where the *p*-values are between 1% and 5% with **; and where the *p*-value is between 5% and 10% with *.

Table 4.3: Regression results (including regional dummies)

	Model I	Model II	Model III	Model IV	Model V	Model VI	Model VII	Model VIII
Constant	0.1976	0.2354	0.2389	0.2100	0.2333	0.2723	0.2244	0.2609
	(0.0268)	(0.0316)	(0.0304)	(0.0414)	(0.0385)	(0.0285)	(0.0421)	(0.0307)
	[0.0000]***	[0.0002]***	[0.0000]***	[0.0001]***	[0.0000]***	[0.0000]***	[0.0000]***	[0.0000]***
Ln($GDPPL_0$)	−0.0152	−0.0195	−0.0196	−0.0146	−0.0166	−0.0200	−0.0155	−0.0186
	(0.0038)	(0.0044)	(0.0041)	(0.0042)	(0.0039)	(0.0043)	(0.0045)	(0.0046)
	[0.0005]***	[0.0002]***	[0.0001]***	[0.0026]***	[0.0005]***	[0.0001]***	[0.0026]***	[0.0006]***
TCI7885		−0.0018			−0.0017			
		(0.0006)			(0.0006)			
		[0.0103]**			[0.0105]**			
TCI7899			−0.0035			−0.0039	−0.0029	−0.0028
			(0.0014)			(0.0013)	(0.0012)	(0.0013)
			[0.0179]**			[0.0074]***	[0.0263]**	[0.0350]**
SAVE				0.0104	0.0142	0.0161	0.0199	0.0218
				(0.0212)	(0.0178)	(0.0196)	(0.0209)	(0.0224)
				[0.6292]	[0.4361]	[0.4212]	[0.3504]	[0.3428]
LABG				−1.0148	−0.9867	−0.9342	−0.8428	−0.7981
				(0.3483)	(0.3316)	(0.3415)	(0.3112)	(0.3266)
				[0.0086]***	[0.0078]***	[0.0128]**	[0.0140]**	[0.0239]**
HUMK82				−0.0427	−0.0577	−0.0328	−0.0557	−0.0343
				(0.0281)	(0.0286)	(0.0285)	(0.0259)	(0.0268)
				[0.1445]	[0.0581]*	[0.2643]	[0.0442]**	[0.2143]
FDI				0.0019	0.0023		0.0020	
				(0.0017)	(0.0018)		(0.0017)	
				[0.2819]	[0.2115]		[0.2459]	
Dummy for central areas	−0.0258	−0.0230	−0.0211	−0.0184	−0.0148	−0.0206	−0.0148	−0.0198
	(0.0040)	(0.0040)	(0.0043)	(0.0055)	(0.0056)	(0.0041)	(0.0058)	(0.0045)
	[0.0000]***	[0.0000]***	[0.0002]***	[0.0034]***	[0.0158]**	[0.0001]***	[0.0202]**	[0.0003]***
Dummy for western areas	−0.0377	−0.0352	−0.0303	−0.0287	−0.0257	−0.0326	−0.0229	−0.0289
	(0.0053)	(0.0055)	(0.0067)	(0.0069)	(0.0072)	(0.0062)	(0.0085)	(0.0073)
	[0.0000]***	[0.0000]***	[0.0002]***	[0.0005]***	[0.0020]***	[0.0000]***	[0.0142]**	[0.0007]***
Adjusted R^2	0.6596	0.6794	0.7070	0.7080	0.7279	0.7239	0.7320	0.7315

Table 4.4: Regression results (including Barro's structure impact variable and regional dummies)

	Model I	Model II	Model III	Model IV	Model V	Model VI	Model VII	Model VIII	Model IX
Constant	0.0608	0.1874	0.2262	0.2294	0.0841	0.2100	0.2413	0.2333	0.2251
	(0.0354)	(0.0301)	(0.0328)	(0.0336)	(0.0464)	(0.0409)	(0.0299)	(0.0382)	(0.0413)
	[0.0985]*	[0.0000]***	[0.0000]***	[0.0000]***	[0.0845]*	[0.0001]***	[0.0000]***	[0.0000]***	[0.0000]***
Ln($GDPPL_0$)	0.0077	−0.0071	−0.0099	−0.0129	−0.0108	−0.0149	−0.0157	−0.0160	−0.0173
	(0.0130)	(0.0095)	(0.0093)	(0.0089)	(0.0070)	(0.0059)	(0.0066)	(0.0058)	(0.0061)
	[0.5575]	[0.4634]	[0.2971]	[0.1618]	[0.1369]	[0.0201]**	[0.0286]**	[0.0125]**	[0.0105]**
Barro's structure variable	−0.5622	−0.6152	−0.7485	−0.4932	0.5233	0.0294	−0.1507	−0.0574	0.1628
	(0.8591)	(0.5657)	(0.5319)	(0.5177)	(0.4546)	(0.5537)	(0.4420)	(0.5322)	(0.5468)
	[0.5188]	[0.2881]	[0.1733]	[0.3511]	[0.2627]	[0.9583]	[0.7367]	[0.9153]	[0.7694]
TCI7885			−0.0019						
			(0.0006)						
			[0.0040]***						
TCI				−0.0034					−0.0030
				(0.0014)					(0.0012)
				[0.0249]**					[0.0203]**
SAVE					0.0395	0.0107	0.0106	0.0136	0.0218
					(0.0260)	(0.0206)	(0.0228)	(0.0179)	(0.0212)
					[0.1440]	[0.6111]	[0.6470]	[0.4561]	[0.3190]
LABG					−1.2643	−1.0205	−0.9430	−0.9755	−0.8715
					(0.4260)	(0.3467)	(0.3583)	(0.3054)	(0.2983)
					[0.0073]***	[0.0083]***	[0.0160]**	[0.0050]***	[0.0091]***
HUMK82					−0.0815	−0.0433	−0.0216	−0.0566	−0.0592
					(0.0279)	(0.0361)	(0.0292)	(0.0349)	(0.0335)
					[0.0081]***	[0.2450]	[0.4687]	[0.1216]	[0.0936]*
FDI					0.0070	0.0019		0.0022	0.0022
					(0.0017)	(0.0020)		(0.0020)	(0.0020)
					[0.0004]***	[0.3595]		[0.2819]	[0.2840]
Dummy for central areas		−0.0272	−0.0244	−0.0223		−0.0182	−0.0233	−0.0151	−0.0140
		(0.0044)	(0.0042)	(0.0045)		(0.0072)	(0.0045)	(0.0069)	(0.0069)
		[0.0000]***	[0.0000]***	[0.0001]***		[0.0196]**	[0.0000]***	[0.0414]**	[0.0595]*
Dummy for western areas		−0.0372	−0.0344	−0.0301		−0.0286	−0.0341	−0.0259	−0.0223
		(0.0054)	(0.0057)	(0.0067)		(0.0072)	(0.0062)	(0.0073)	(0.0084)
		[0.0000]***	[0.0000]***	[0.0002]***		[0.0008]***	[0.0000]***	[0.0023]***	[0.0163]**
Adjusted R^2	−0.0684	0.6569	0.6833	0.7017	0.5737	0.6927	0.6968	0.7129	0.7180

the structural impact variables are statistically significant. In sharp contrast to Barro's structure impact variables, the estimates for the development strategy variables are, as expected, negative and statistically significant in all models.

The regression results for the data set excluding the three municipalities are similar to those including the three municipalities. The results are not reported here but can be obtained by contacting the authors directly. The regression results strongly support our hypothesis that if a province follows a CAD strategy, causing its TCI to deviate from ω, i.e. the optimal TCI^*, the per worker GDP growth rate in the province will be reduced significantly. Table 4.4 shows that the estimates for $TCI7899$ ranged between -0.0028 and -0.0084 and most estimates are about -0.003. If we take -0.003 as the appropriate estimate for $TCI7899$, this means that with a unit deviation from ω, the per worker GDP growth rate will be reduced by 0.3 per cent per year over the 1978–99 period. The fourth column in Table 4.1 reports the $TCI7899$ for each province. The exact value of ω is unknown. The second column in Table 4.1 shows that Jiangsu province has the highest per worker GDP growth rates among all provinces in China. If we take Jiangsu's $TCI7899$, which is 2.9713, as ω, we can infer the impact of the development strategy on each province's growth. For example, Guizhou's $TCI7899$ is 7.7422, so its DS (DS is defined in equation (5)) is 4.7709. Therefore, Guizhou's per worker GDP growth rate was reduced 1.43 per cent per year over the period in 1978–99.

4.5 Concluding Remarks

In this chapter, we study regional disparities in China's economy. It is found that a province's attempt to adopt a CAD strategy in industrial development has a significantly negative effect on the province's GDP growth. Judging from the TCI in each province, shown in Table 4.3, the central and western provinces tend to follow the CAD strategy more closely than do the eastern provinces. Pursuit of the wrong industrial development strategy in the central and western regions contributed to the observed widening of regional disparities after the 1978 reforms. It is imperative for each province, especially those provinces in the central and western regions, to allocate its new additional investments and restructure its existing industries according to its regional comparative advantages so that the regional disparities can be narrowed along with the dynamic growth. As the central and western regions are endowed with less capital and more labour/resources than those of eastern provinces, the central and western provinces should pursue more labour intensive or resources intensive industries/products than those of eastern ones. Under this strategy, the enterprises are viable and central and western provinces need not to distort prices to subsidize the firms. The improved allocation efficiency would contribute to the convergence of per capita income of central and western regions to those of eastern provinces. At same time, the accession to WTO is greatly reducing the possibility for the Chinese government to protect/subsidize any enterprises. In the fact, after the WTO accession, the Chinese government has formally adopted the principle of comparative advantage as a guideline for the future development of the agriculture, manufacturing, and service industries. Regional disparities may not be eliminated totally due to the differences in natural conditions. However, in the new era after the WTO accession, the trend toward the widening of regional disparities may be mitigated.

References

Aziz, J., and D. Christoph (2001). 'China's Provincial Dynamics', IMF Working Paper WP/01/3, International Monetary Fund: Washington, DC.
Barro, R. J. (1991). 'Economic Growth in a Cross Section of Countries', *Quarterly Journal of Economics* 106(5): 407–43.
—— X. Sala-i-Martin (1991). 'Convergence Across States and Regions', *Brookings Papers on Economics Activity* 1: 107–82.
—— —— (1992). 'Convergence', *Journal of Political Economy* 100(4): 223–51.
Cai, F., and Y. Du (2000). 'The Convergence and Disparities of Regional Economic Growth in China: Implications for Western Development Strategy', *Economic Research* 10 (Jingji Yanjiu).
—— D. Wang, and Y. Du (2001). 'Impact of Labour Market Distortion on Regional Disparities', *Social Sciences in China* 2: 4–14.
CASS (Chinese Academy of Social Science) (1985). *Annual Book of Chinese Demography*, Demography Research Center of the Chinese Academy of Social Science: Beijing.
Chen, B., and Y. Feng (2000). 'Determinants of Economic Growth in China: Private Enterprise, Education and Openness', *China Economic Review* 11(1): 1–15.
Cheng, Y. (2002). 'Regional Growth Dynamics in China: A Re-examination of σ-convergence and β-convergence', paper presented at the International Workshop on the Chinese Economy, Shanghai, 7–8 August.
Dayal-Gulati, A., and A. M. Husain (2000). 'Centripetal Forces in China's Economic Take-off', IMF Working Paper WP/00/86, International Monetary Fund: Washington, DC.
Démurger, S., J. D. Sachs, W. T. Woo et al. (2001). 'Geography, Economic Policy and Regional Development in China', CID Working Paper 77, Center for International Development, University of Harvard: Cambridge, MA.
Development Strategy Research Group of the China Center for Economic Research (2002). 'The Defination and the Calculation of Technology Choice Index (TCI)', Working Paper of the China Center for Economic Research Working Paper C2002003, CCER: Beijing.
Fleisher, B. M., and J. Chen (1997). 'The Coast-Noncoast Income Gap, Productivity, and Regional Economic Policy in China', *Journal of Comparative Economics* 25(2): 220–36.

Jian, T., J. D. Sacks, and A. M. Warner (1996). 'Trends in Regional Inequality in China', NBER Working Paper 5412, National Bureau of Economic Research: Cambridge, MA.

Lee, J. (1994). 'Regional Differences in the Impact of the Open Door Policy on Income Growth in China', *Journal of Economic Development* 19(1): 215–34.

Lin, J. Y. (2003). 'Development Strategy, Viability, and Economic Convergence', *Economic Development and Cultural Change* 51(2): 277–308.

—— G. Tan (1999). 'Policy Burden, Accountability, and the Soft Budget Constraint', *American Economic Review: Papers and Proceedings* 89(2): 426–31.

—— F. Cai, and Z. Li (1994). *China Miracle: Development Strategy and Economic Reform*, Shanghai People's Press and Shanghai Sanlian Press (Chinese edition): Shanghai; Chinese University Press (English edition, 1996): Hong Kong.

—— —— —— (1998). 'Competition, Policy Burdens, and State-Owned Enterprise Reform', *American Economic Review: Papers and Proceedings* 88(2): 422–7.

Mankiw, N. G., D. Romer, and D. N. Weil (1992). 'A Contribution to the Empirics of Economic Growth', *Quarterly Journal of Economics* 107(2): 407–37.

NBS (National Bureau of Statistics) (1999a). *Comprehensive Statistical Data and Materials on 50 Years of New China*, China Statistics Press for the Department of Comprehensive Statistics of the National Bureau of Statistics: Beijing.

NBS (National Bureau of Statistics) (1999b). 'Collection of Statistical Data for 50 Years since 1949', Department of National Economic Statistics of the National Bureau of Statistics: Beijing.

NBS (National Bureau of Statistics) (various years). *Provincial Statistics Yearbooks*, China Statistics Press: Beijing.

NBS (National Bureau of Statistics) (2002). *China Statistical Abstract, 2002*, China Statistics Press: Beijing.

Shen, K., and J. Ma (2002). 'Club Convergence in China's Economic Growth: Characteristics and Causes', *Economic Research* 1: 33–9 (*Jingji Yanjiu*).

Solow, R. M. (1956). 'A Contribution to the Theory of Economic Growth', *Quarterly Journal of Economics* 70(1): 65–94.

Tsui, K. Y. (1991). 'China's Regional Inequality: 1952–1985', *Journal of Comparative Economics* 15(1): 1–21.

—— (1993). 'Decomposition of China's Regional Inequalities', *Journal of Comparative Economics* 17(3): 600–27.

—— (1996). 'Economic Reform and Interprovincial Inequalities', *Journal of Development Economics* 50(2): 353–68.

Wang, M., and S. Li (eds) (2000). *Studies on the Regional Social and Economic Disparities in China*, Shangwu Press: Beijing.

Wei, H. (1997). 'China's Regional Economic Growth and Convergence', *China Industrial Economics* 3: 31–7 (*Zhongguo Gongye Jingji*).

World Bank (1995). 'China's Regional Disparities', *WB Report* 14496-CH, Country Operations Division, East Asia and Pacific Regional Office, World Bank: Washington, DC.

—— (1997). *Sharing Rising Incomes: Disparities in China*, China 2020 Series, World Bank: Washington, DC.

Yang, D. L. (1990). 'Patterns of China's Regional Development Strategy', *The China Quarterly* 122: 230–57.

Young, A. (2000). 'The Razor's Edge: Distortions and Incremental Reform in the People's Republic of China', *Quarterly Journal of Economics* 115(4): 1091–135.

Zhang, Z., A. Liu, and S. Yao (2001). 'Convergence of China's Regional Incomes, 1952–1997', *China Economic Review* 12(2/3): 243–58.

5
Forces Shaping China's Interprovincial Inequality

Kai-yuen Tsui

5.1 Introduction

The unveiling of the western development programme[1] in 1999 by China's former Party Secretary, Jiang Zemin, is a reminder that notwithstanding China's spectacular economic success, the middle kingdom is still a country full of stark contrasts, conjuring up an image of the western periphery lagging far behind the eastern core. Uneven regional development remains a hotly debated issue half a century after Chairman Mao declared the contradictions between the coastal and inland provinces as one of the so-called ten cardinal relations (*shida guanxi*) to be addressed. There is by now a large literature on China's interprovincial inequality (Lyons 1991; Tsui 1991, 1996; Jian et al. 1996; Lin et al. 1998; Raiser 1998; Wang and Hu 1999; Fujita and Hu 2001; Naughton 2002: 57–86; Lin and Cai 2003; Aroca et al., Chapter 7, this volume—the list is by no means exhaustive). This study extends previous works along two fronts. First, in view of the problems plaguing Chinese official data, this chapter tries seriously to address the problems with Chinese statistics and comes up with adjusted data for the analysis of the trend in interprovincial inequality since the 1950s. Second, and more importantly, we introduce a framework for quantitatively identifying the contributions of different forces behind the oscillation of interprovincial inequality.

With regard to the first issue, previous studies rarely treat the problem of China's data seriously, though the quality of the data has recently been the subject of much scrutiny (e.g. Young 2000; Rawski 2001; Holz 2004). Recent scepticism about Chinese official data coupled with the anomalies we have discovered in provincial statistics has prompted us to experiment with different

---

[1] For background information see, e.g., Naughton (2004) and Goodman (2004).

ways of adjusting the official figures to identify a trend in interprovincial inequality. The results turn out to be somewhat different from those in previous studies.

The present study also fills the lacuna in existing literature by proposing a coherent framework not only to identify the forces shaping interprovincial inequality, but also to assess their relative importance by quantitatively decomposing China's interprovincial inequality. In this connection, a novel method building a bridge between growth accounting, often invoked to study the sources of growth, and the dynamics of regional inequality is introduced. To be more precise, let $I(\mathbf{y})$ be some measure of interprovincial inequality, where $\mathbf{y}$ is a vector of provincial GDP per capita. In so far as provincial output and factor inputs may be summarized by provincial production functions (see equation (1)), the change in interprovincial inequality, $dI(\mathbf{y})/dt$, may be expressed as a function of provincial growth rates. Employing the growth accounting technique, the latter in turn may be decomposed into contributions by the growth of total factor productivity (TFP) and such factor inputs as physical and human capital. $dI(\mathbf{y})/dt$ may thus be attributable to the changing pattern of interprovincial allocation in investment captured by the interprovincial differential growth in physical and human capital as well as the impact of institutional innovations encapsulated in the growth of TFP.

To motivate the subsequent empirical exercise, a historical sketch of the forces shaping interprovincial inequality is the subject of section 5.2. Experimenting with different ways of adjusting the official data, section 5.3 arrives at trajectories of interprovincial inequality that may be compared with the one based on official data. Section 5.3 introduces the conceptual framework that is employed to explain the evolution of regional disparities. The empirical results based on the conceptual framework and adjusted data are summarized in section 5.4. The concluding section highlights and interprets our salient findings and proposes possible extensions of the chapter.

5.2 Background

There is a common perception that regional development strategy in the last four decades went through a number of phases, inducing different forces that impinged ultimately on interprovincial inequalities. This section is a historical synopsis of these forces that might have exerted effect on the dynamics of interprovincial inequalities. These forces are incorporated in the decomposition exercise in the next section. In the pre-reform era, the Chinese government saw it as one of their goals to reduce the gap between the coastal and inland provinces, a goal reinforced by defence considerations. Lardy (1978) and later Naughton (2002) have pointed out that the apparatus of central planning gave the Chinese government a handle to mobilize resources for achieving that goal, as witnessed by state appropriations as the dominant source of investment funds

Interprovincial Inequality

(see Table 5.1). However, the spatial allocation of investment funds often was not concerned with such efficiency considerations as comparative advantages and economies of scale. A case in point is the 'third front campaign', which was a defence related programme to relocate industries to inland provinces in the mid-1960s and the early 1970s (Naughton 1988). With state investments pouring into some inland provinces, the campaign is often perceived as an extreme manifestation of such an apparently egalitarian development strategy. Such a massive plan to transfer industrial capacities to less developed regions in complete disregard of their comparative advantages and their poor infrastructure turned out to be a recipe for economic waste.[2] Inefficient regional development policies were reinforced by the need for self-reliance and the formation of a cellular economy (Donnithorne 1972) that militated against specialization and the emergence of efficient economic structures. The effect of increases in investment favouring some inland provinces was thus offset by all the other forces that undercut efficiency and productivity.

Notwithstanding the political turmoil and radical economic experiments with disastrous consequences at times, the spread of basic education to less developed provinces was a legacy of the Maoist period that has prompted some scholars, among them Bramall (2000), to argue that the investment in education in the Maoist era undergirds the rapid economic growth in the reform era. At the beginning of the reform era, China had a population that was more educated than those in countries with comparable levels of development. In so far as education boosts productivity, the spread of education may increase the productivity of labour forces in poor provinces and may help reduce gaps between rich and poor provinces.[3]

Table 5.1: Proportion of investment in fixed assets of state owned units by sources of funds (10,000 yuan)

	State appropriation	Domestic loans	Foreign funds	Self-raised funds and other sources
1953–57	543.48			68.10
1958–62	956.91			350.09
1963–65	424.80	3.30		71.35
1966–70	923.86	13.40		271.83
1971–75	1,519.28	21.86		735.23
1976–80	1,831.85	142.40	111.27	1,100.68
1981–85	1,680.68	932.86	320.43	2,396.50
1986–90	2,171.19	3,095.28	1,143.29	6,932.95
1991–95	2,238.46	9,880.60	2,804.89	23,290.60
1996–2000	5,525.28	17,335.27	3,151	45,892.56

Source: NSB (2002).

[2] Lin and Liu, Chapter 4 in this volume, also point out that the central and western provinces pursued comparative defying development strategy.
[3] However, the rapid expansion of basic education raises questions about the quality of pre-reform education.

The reform era has witnessed a policy break with the past. New forces unleashed by the economic reform have fundamentally changed the spatial distribution of investment funds and induced a spatial restructuring of industries. With the retreat of central planning, the state's role in the allocation of investment has been diminishing in importance, as shown in Table 5.1. Fiscal decentralization has allowed local governments, administrative agencies and state owned enterprises to retain more of the revenue generated within their jurisdictions and has opened up more opportunities to boost their fiscal intake (e.g., through township and village enterprises). In the case of Guangdong and Fujian, their high powered fiscal contracting system (*dabaogan*) was the envy of other provinces (Wong et al. 1995). The result was an explosion of self-raised funds, the distribution of which is highly skewed in favour of the richer coastal provinces.

Other than inducing a change in the spatial allocation of investment, productivity boosting institutional innovations set off by reforms were often localized with spatially differentiated effects. For example, the household responsibility system had its origin in Anhui and initially spread faster in the poor provinces. Greater reliance on market forces channels industries to regions with comparative advantage and economies of scale, in contrast to politically motivated strategies such as the 'third front' campaign that could be detrimental to economic efficiency. Richer provinces have also benefited from a faster pace of market reforms and opening up to the outside world. Guangdong and Fujian have been one step ahead of other provinces, attracting preponderant shares of foreign direct investment. The 'special economic zones' have helped some coastal provinces to attract foreign investments that not only increased physical capital for production but also introduced technology and management knowhow, boosting productivity. Some of the institutional innovations benefited the poor provinces, others boosted productivity of the richer provinces, reinforcing the effect of the new spatial pattern of investment distribution.

What emerges from the discussion is that different policy regimes emerging in the last four decades unleashed different forces with differential and, at times, opposing impacts on interprovincial inequality. Different policy regimes brought about different spatial distribution of such factors of production as human and physical capital. This translated into different rates of provincial economic growth. Furthermore, development strategies and institutional environment have also exerted spatially differential impacts on aggregate productivities of the provincial economies. The complex dynamics of interprovincial inequality by the different forces do not indicate a pattern of a monotonic change in interprovincial inequality over the last four decades. This is indeed the case, as is shown in the next section when we look into the trend of interprovincial inequality.

5.3 Interprovincial Inequality: The Trend

With the above background in mind and as a prelude to the subsequent decomposition analysis, this section turns to the historical trend in China's interprovincial inequality for the period 1952–99.[4] But first, an introduction of our notation is in order. The basic unit of our analysis is a province.[5] Following the Chinese convention, the provinces may be partitioned further into three regions: east, central, and west.[6] The nominal provincial GDP of the mth province in the gth region is Y_{gm}. Let the real provincial GDP per capita, y_{gm}, be defined as $Y_{gm}/(\Pi_{gm} P_{gm})$, where P_{gm} is the total population and Π_{gm} is the GDP deflator of the mth province in the gth region.

Notwithstanding the many studies that have derived the trend in interprovincial inequality, there remains a number of nagging problems with respect to official data. It is customary to measure interprovincial inequality in terms of real provincial GDP per capita, y_{gm}.[7] There are at least two potential problems with using such a measure. With the release of provincial real growth rates (e.g., see NBS 1997), most studies have used the official growth rates for deriving provincial real GDP. However, much has been written on the defects of these growth rates (e.g. Xu 1999, 2000; Young 2000; Keidel 2001; Rawski 2001; Wu 2001). Though much less is known about the accuracy of the growth rates for the Maoist period, there is a common perception that official real growth rates for the reform era are overestimated.[8] It is also to be noted that the provincial implicit deflators derived from the growth rates seem to indicate price variability to be larger than one would expect for the Maoist period, known to be largely an era of price stability except for a period in the early 1960s after the 'great leap forward'.

The second data problem is that official population figures used to estimate the per capita GDP have become less accurate in the reform era. Post-reform figures based on household registration fail to keep track of inward or outward migration. In this chapter, official population data are used for the pre-reform

---

[4] The period under study stops at 1999. While it is possible in theory to extend the study using more recent data, there are problems with changing definitions, especially for provincial populations after 2000, which render some data inter-temporally incomparable.

[5] The directly administered municipalities are incorporated into their neighbouring provinces. Hainan and Xizang are excluded. Directly administered municipalities (i.e. Shanghai, Tianjin, Beijing, and Chongqing) are merged with their neighbouring provinces.

[6] The former practice was to include Guangxi in the eastern region. We follow the recent practice of assigning it to the western region. Formerly classified as a province in the central region, Neimenggu has officially been included in the west region after the introduction of the western development programme.

[7] Earlier studies such as Lyons (1991) and Tsui (1991) use national income (*guomin shouru*) figures drawn from the socialist national income accounting framework that excludes the service sector.

[8] In the pre-reform era, inflation was low except for the years surrounding the 'great leap forward' in the early 1960s.

era, inter-census population figures are derived based on the three censuses after 1982 (see Appendix 5.A).

To estimate the trend in interprovincial inequality, this chapter departs from previous studies by experimenting with different GDP deflators and estimates of provincial population figures. An alternative to using the official real growth rates is to deflate expenditure components by their respective price indices collected from other sources, an approach suggested by Keidel (2001). Next is a brief summary of how the data are adjusted; a detailed explanation is given in Appendix 5.A.[9] The different expenditure categories to be individually deflated are rural consumption, urban consumption, government consumption, capital formation, and net exports. For the period since the mid-1980s, provincial CPIs, together with their rural and urban counterparts, are available for all provinces and are used to deflate the various categories of consumption. For the pre-1985 period, we use provincial retail price indices (RPIs) as deflators whenever provincial consumer price indices (CPIs) are not available. The next component is gross capital formation (*ziben xingcheng zhonge*). Provincial price indices for fixed asset investment are available only for the period 1992–9. The official implicit deflators for gross capital formation are used until 1984. Between 1985 and 1991, deflators based on prices of capital goods released by the National Bureau of Statistics (NBS) are constructed. Details on deriving the provincial price indices for capital formation are given in Appendix 5.A.

The adjusted data are used to examine how interprovincial inequality changes over time. The results are then compared with those based on official data. For this purpose, we resort to a population-weighted version of Theil's entropy measure:

$$I(\mathbf{y}) = \sum_{g=1}^{G} \sum_{m=1}^{M_g} f_{gm} \ln\left(\frac{\bar{y}}{y_{gm}}\right), \quad \bar{y} = \sum_{g=1}^{G} \sum_{m=1}^{M_g} f_{gm} y_{gm} \tag{1}$$

where G is the number of regions, M_g is the number of provinces in the gth region, $\mathbf{y} = (\mathbf{y}_1, \ldots, \mathbf{y}_G)$ where $\mathbf{y}_g = (y_{g1}, \ldots, y_{gM_g})$, $f_{gm} = P_{gm} / \sum_{g=1}^{G} \sum_{k=1}^{M_g} P_{gk}$. In the present context, the provinces are categorized into the eastern, central and western regions so that G is equal to 3. Figure 5.1 reports three set of results. *EN1* is based on unadjusted official data. *EN2* and *EN3* are derived using our estimates of provincial GDP deflators and population figures as detailed in Appendix 5.A. *EN3* is different from *EN2* in the deflation of capital formation so as to come up with the provincial GDP deflators. While *EN3* adopts the official implicit deflators for capital formation, we adjust some anomalous figures of the official deflators in arriving at *EN2*. This does not appear to make too great a difference.

---

[9] For another approach, see Young (2000).

Interprovincial Inequality

Next, we focus only on *EN1* and *EN2*. A striking feature is that the magnitude of *EN1* is distinctly higher than those of the other trend. What is even more interesting is that the two trajectories diverge in certain subperiods even though their overall oscillation patterns share certain salient features. Until 1967 and with the exception of the anomalous years of the 'great leap forward', *EN1* based on official data ratchets upwards while *EN2* etches downwards. Inequality shoots up in 1968, which may be due to production disruptions caused by the chaos of the Cultural Revolution. During the period between 1968 and the early 1970s, *EN2* moves downwards while *EN1* is almost stationary. This period coincides with the 'third front' campaign when investment funds were poured into inland provinces. But by 1973, all the trajectories move upward, reaching a peak in 1976. The start of the reform era sets off a conspicuous decline in interprovincial inequalities until the mid-1980s for both *EN1* and *EN2*. Thereafter, the two trends initially crawl upwards, followed by sharp increases in the first half of the 1990s. Unlike the trend for *EN2*, which remains by and large stable from 1995, the trend using official data continues to climb upwards. This finding seems to suggest that the richer provinces underestimate their rates of inflation, thereby exaggerating the increase in inequality.

Is the trend robust with respect to the inequality indices used? The parameter dependent class of generalized entropy (GE) measures reduces to the Theil entropy measure above when the parameter a equals zero.[10] We repeat the above exercise using the GE measures when $a = 1$ and 2 for the case that corresponds to *EN2*. The case when a is equal to 2 is the square of the coefficient of variation. The smaller a, the more sensitive the measure is to transfers at the

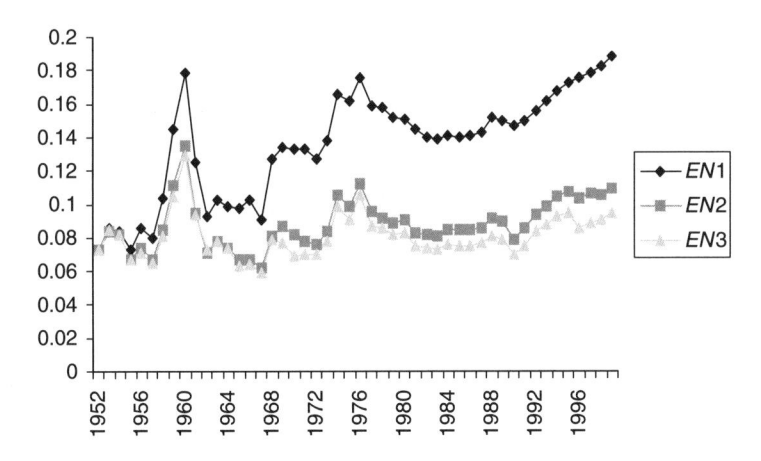

Figure 5.1: Overall inter-provincial inequality

Source: Computed by author from data sources cited in Appendix 5.A.

[10] See, for example, Shorrocks (1984).

bottom of the income distribution (Shorrocks and Foster 1987). The three cases are reported in Figure 5.2. They are normalized to 100 in 1952. The trend of interprovincial inequality is, by and large, robust to the inequality indices used.

Since much attention has been focused on the income gap between the coastal and inland provinces, it is informative to isolate such a gap from overall inequality. The class of entropy measures is susceptible to decomposition into within region and between region inequality, i.e.:[11]

$$I(y) = WG(y) + BG(y) \qquad (2)$$

where the within region inequality is defined as:

$$WG(y) = \sum_{g=1}^{G} f_g I(y_g), \quad f_g = \sum_{m=1}^{M_g} P_{gm} / \sum_{g=1}^{G} \sum_{m=1}^{M_g} P_{gm}$$

while the between region inequality assumes the following form:

$$BG(y) = \sum_{g=1}^{G} f_g \ln\left(\frac{\bar{y}}{\bar{y}_g}\right), \quad \bar{y}_g = \sum_{m=1}^{M_g} Y_{gm} / \sum_{m=1}^{M_g} P_{gm}$$

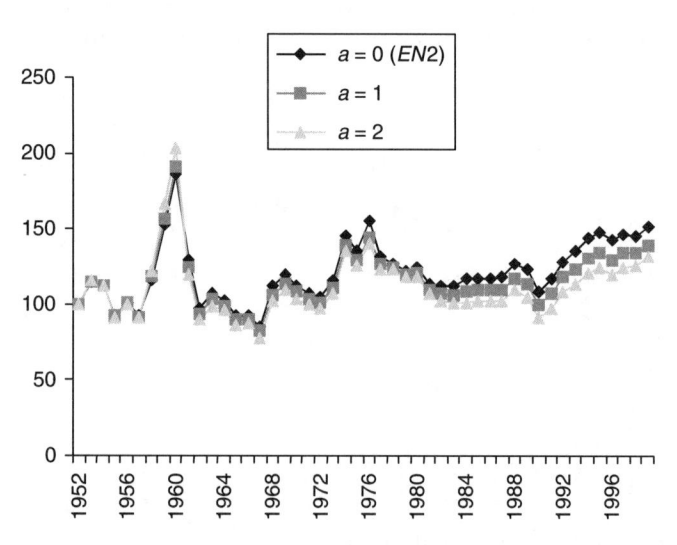

Figure 5.2: Trends in overall inter-provincial inequality based on official and adjusted data
Source: Computed by author from data sources cited in Appendix 5.A.

[11] See Shorrocks (1984).

Interprovincial Inequality

Figures 5.3 and 5.4 report the trends in the within region inequality and between region inequality, respectively, using different deflators, where *WGi* and *BGi* correspond to *ENi*, $i = 1, 2, 3$. Careful scrutiny suggests that the trajectories based on adjusted data differ from the one based on official data. Pre-reform within region inequality, inequality based on adjusted data (i.e., *WG2* and *WG3*) moves downward with spikes in the second half of the 1970s. This is to be contrasted with *WG1* that seems, despite oscillations, to be on an upward trend. For all three cases, *WGi*, $i = 1, 2, 3$, decrease and then taper off in the reform era.

With regard to *BGi*, $i = 1, 2, 3$, the trends based on the adjusted data fluctuate, as opposed to an increasing trend based on official data. The jumps around the early 1950s and in 1968 capture the policy shocks of those chaotic years. Then the short interlude when downward trends are discernible coincides with the 'third front campaign'. Inequality increases thereafter for all three cases, reaching a peak in 1976. The reform era introduces a period of mildly declining or almost stationary between region inequality. From the mid-1980s, the between region inequality for the three trends increases slowly at first and then accelerates. The three trajectories, however, diverge in the second half of the 1990s, with the trend based on official data still exhibiting a distinctly increasing trend while the other two series are much less pronounced.

What are the forces driving the aggregate trend in interprovincial inequality? The last section reviews the different forces which were created by policy regime switching and which have shaped spatial inequalities over the last four

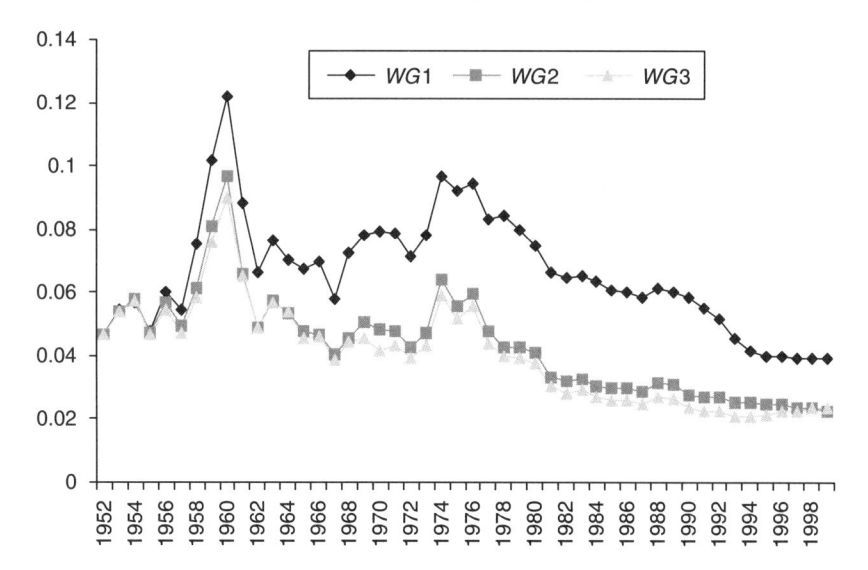

Figure 5.3: Within region inequality

Source: Computed by author from data sources cited in Appendix 5.A.

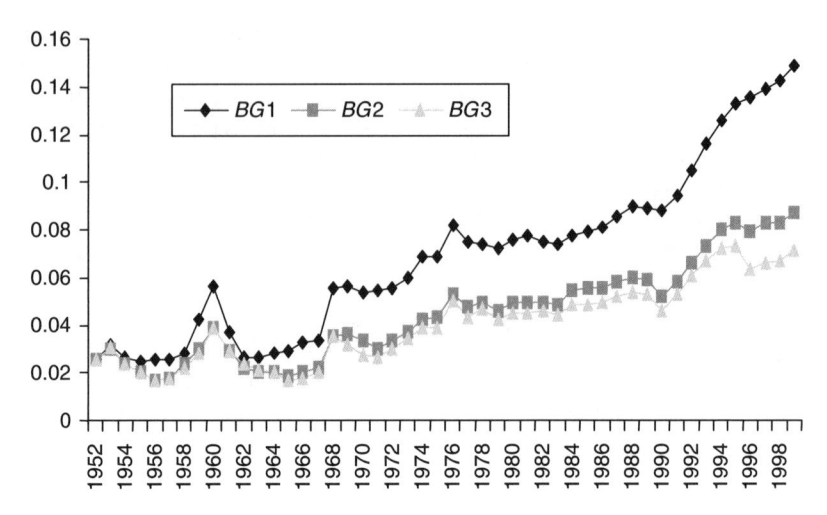

Figure 5.4: Between region inequality
Source: Computed by author from data sources cited in Appendix 5.A.

decades. The aggregate trend in interprovincial inequality is the convergence of all these forces, some having a reinforcing effect, others having a counteracting effect. However, simply observing the aggregate trend in interprovincial inequality is not enough to understand the underlying dynamics when a confluence of factors are at work. What seems missing in previous studies (e.g. Donnithorne 1972; Lardy 1978; Tsui 1991, 1996; Naughton 2002; Aroca et al., Chapter 7, this volume) is a better tool for isolating the effects of these forces on interprovincial inequality. These factors include, for example, the changing spatial distribution of physical investment and the spread of basic education. But physical and human capital do not exhaust the list of factors that affect interprovincial inequality. As mentioned earlier, spatial distribution of resources induced by different institutional arrangements may have implications for comparative advantages and economies of agglomeration inducing higher or lower productivity at the aggregate level. Institutional changes were pertinent to interprovincial inequality not least because many of these changes were region specific. Next, we introduce a framework to examine more precisely the different forces driving interprovincial inequality.

5.4 The Conceptual Framework: Growth Accounting and Interprovincial Inequality

This section introduces a framework for the decomposition of changes in interprovincial inequality. The discussion in section 5.2 highlights the links between the spatial distribution of factors of production, e.g. physical and human capital, under different policy regimes and regional inequality. No less important is the effect of policy shifts on productivity. It is convenient to think in terms of provincial production functions:

$$Y_{gm} = A_{gm}F_{gm}(K_{gm}, H_{gm}), \quad H_{gm} = S_{gm}L_{gm} \tag{3}$$

where K_{gm} is the capital stock, H_{gm} is quality adjusted labour force being a product of an index of schooling, S_{gm} and the labour force, L_{gm}. F_{gm} is an increasing function of K_{gm} and H_{gm}, and A_{gm} is the term capturing the total factor productivity (TFP) of the mth province in the gth region. To make our notation less cumbersome, we omit the time subscript. For each province, provincial economic growth may then be decomposed into the contribution of the growth of TFP and factor inputs:[12]

$$\frac{\dot{Y}_{gm}}{Y_{gm}} = \frac{\dot{A}_{gm}}{A_{gm}} + \left(\frac{\partial F_{gm}/\partial K_{gm}}{Y_{gm}}\right)\frac{\dot{K}_{gm}}{K_{gm}} + \left(\frac{\partial F_{gm}/\partial H_{gm}}{Y_{gm}}\right)\frac{\dot{H}_{gm}}{H_{gm}} \tag{4}$$

Interprovincial differences in the growth of A_{gm}, K_{gm}, and H_{gm} result in provincial outputs expanding at different pace, contributing ultimately to the change in interprovincial inequality. In this connection, it is to be noted that:

$$\dot{y}_{gm}/y_{gm} = (\dot{Y}_{gm}/Y_{gm}) - (\dot{P}_{gm}/P_{gm}) \tag{5}$$

Substituting (5) into (4) results in:

$$\frac{\dot{y}_{gm}}{y_{gm}} = \frac{\dot{A}_{gm}}{A_{gm}} + \alpha_{gm}^K \frac{\dot{K}_{gm}}{K_{gm}} + \alpha_{gm}^H \frac{\dot{H}_{gm}}{H_{gm}} - \frac{\dot{P}_{gm}}{P_{gm}} \tag{6}$$

where $\alpha_{gm}^K = (\partial F_{gm}/\partial K_{gm})/Y_{gm}$ and $\alpha_{gm}^H = (\partial F_{gm}/\partial H_{gm})/Y_{gm}$. Differential growth rates in TFP, physical capital, human capital, and population result in different growth rates in provincial GDP per capita. The change in inequality index $I(\mathbf{y})$ may ultimately be decomposed into contributions of A_{gm}, K_{gm}, H_{gm}, and P_{gm}.

To operationalize the above intuition, the first step is to differentiate equation (1) with respect to time:

$$\frac{dI(\mathbf{y})}{dt} = \sum_{g=1}^{G}\sum_{m=1}^{M_g}(s_{gm} - f_{gm})\frac{\dot{y}_{gm}}{y_{gm}} + \sum_{g=1}^{G}\sum_{m=1}^{M_g}(s_{gm} - f_{gm}\ln(y_{gm}))\frac{\dot{f}_{gm}}{f_{gm}} \tag{7}$$

where t is time and $s_{gm} = Y_{gm}/\sum_{g=1}^{G}\sum_{k=1}^{M_g}Y_{gk}$.[13] The first term on the right-hand side of equation (7) captures the impact on interprovincial inequality of

---

[12] Throughout this chapter, $\dot{X}/X$ refers to the growth rate of the variable X.
[13] Details for deriving equation (7), see Appendix 5.B.

differential growth rates across provinces, while the second term summarizes the impact of changing population shares. It is interesting to note that the impact of $\dot{y}_{gm}/y_{gm}$ on inequality hinges on the sign of the term $(s_{gm} - f_{gm})$. Behind this term is the implicit ethical judgement that, with income share of a province, s_{gm}, falling below its population share, f_{gm}, transferring more income to that province reduces inequality. The ethical judgement is thus analogous to the Pigou–Dalton transfer principle well known in the literature on inequality measurement.[14]

Substituting equation (6) into equation (7), the change in inequality then depends on the growth of TFP and factor inputs, i.e.:

$$\frac{dI(\mathbf{y})}{dt} = CA + CK + CH + CP + CF \qquad (8)$$

where:

$$CA = \sum_{g=1}^{G} \sum_{m=1}^{M_g} (s_{gm} - f_{gm}) \frac{\dot{A}_{gm}}{A_{gm}}, \quad CK = \sum_{g=1}^{G} \sum_{m=1}^{M_g} (s_{gm} - f_{gm}) \alpha_{gm}^K \frac{\dot{K}_{gm}}{K_{gm}}$$

$$CH = \sum_{g=1}^{G} \sum_{m=1}^{M_g} (s_{gm} - f_{gm}) \alpha_{gm}^H \frac{\dot{H}_{gm}}{H_{gm}}, \quad CP = -\sum_{g=1}^{G} \sum_{m=1}^{M_g} (s_{gm} - f_{gm}) \frac{\dot{P}_{gm}}{P_{gm}}$$

$$CF = \sum_{g=1}^{G} \sum_{m=1}^{M_g} (s_{gm} - f_{gm} \ln(y_{gm})) \frac{\dot{f}_{gm}}{f_{gm}}$$

Whenever any of the above components are positive, they contribute to an increase in interprovincial inequality. It is natural to interpret CA, CK, CH as the contributions of growth in TFP, physical capital, and human capital to the *change* in interprovincial inequality. Capturing the effect of population growth on inequality is the term CP. Faster population growth in a poor region, *ceteris paribus*, results in an increase in interprovincial inequality. Finally, CF summarizes the effect of changing population shares on inequality.

An important dimension of interprovincial inequality that has generated a lot of debate is the gap between the coastal provinces as opposed to the central and western provinces. Indeed, as shown above, hidden behind *overall* interprovincial inequality may be divergent changes in between region and within region inequalities. To gain a richer picture of interprovincial inequality, the terms in equation (8) may be further decomposed into between and within region contributions. Recalling equation (2), the term $dWG(\mathbf{y})/dt$ may in turn be decomposed as in equation (8):

---

[14] An inequality measure satisfies the Pigou-Dalton principle if a transfer of US$1 from a richer to a poorer person leads, without changing their total income, to a fall in inequality (see, e.g., Sen 1997).

Interprovincial Inequality

$$\frac{dWG(\mathbf{y})}{dt} = WCA + WCK + WCH + WCP + WCF \qquad (9)$$

where:

$$WCA = \sum_{g=1}^{G} f_g \left[\sum_{m=1}^{M_g} (\hat{s}_{gm} - \hat{f}_{gm}) \frac{\dot{A}_{gm}}{A_{gm}} \right], \quad WCK = \sum_{g=1}^{G} f_g \left[\sum_{m=1}^{M_g} (\hat{s}_{gm} - \hat{f}_{gm}) \alpha_{gm}^K \frac{\dot{K}_{gm}}{K_{gm}} \right]$$

$$WCH = \sum_{g=1}^{G} f_g \left[\sum_{m=1}^{M_g} (\hat{s}_{gm} - \hat{f}_{gm}) \alpha_{gm}^H \frac{\dot{H}_{gm}}{H_{gm}} \right], \quad WCP = -\sum_{g=1}^{G} f_g \left[\sum_{m=1}^{M_g} (\hat{s}_{gm} - \hat{f}_{gm}) \frac{\dot{P}_{gm}}{P_{gm}} \right]$$

$$WCF = \sum_{g=1}^{G} f_g \left[\sum_{m=1}^{M_g} (\hat{s}_{gm} - \hat{f}_{gm} \ln(y_{gm})) \frac{\dot{\hat{f}}_{gm}}{\hat{f}_{gm}} + I(\mathbf{y}_g) \frac{\dot{f}_g}{f_g} \right]$$

where $\hat{s}_{gm} = Y_{gm} / \sum_{k=1}^{M_j} Y_{gk}$, $\hat{f}_{gm} = P_{gm} / \sum_{k=1}^{M_g} P_{gk}$. Similarly, in the case of between region inequality:

$$\frac{dBG(\mathbf{y})}{dt} = BCA + BCK + BCH + BCP + BCF \qquad (10)$$

where:

$$BCA = \sum_{g=1}^{G} \sum_{m=1}^{M_g} (s_{gm} - f_g \hat{s}_{gm}) \frac{\dot{A}_{gm}}{A_{gm}}, \quad BCK = \sum_{g=1}^{G} \sum_{m=1}^{M_g} (s_{gm} - f_g \hat{s}_{gm}) \frac{\dot{K}_{gm}}{K_{gm}}$$

$$BCH = \sum_{g=1}^{G} \sum_{m=1}^{M_g} (s_{gm} - f_g \hat{s}_{gm}) \frac{\dot{H}_{gm}}{H_{gm}}, \quad BCP = -\sum_{g=1}^{G} \sum_{m=1}^{M_g} (s_{gm} - f_g \hat{s}_{gm}) \frac{\dot{P}_{gm}}{P_{gm}}$$

$$BCF = \sum_{g=1}^{G} \left[\sum_{m=1}^{M_g} \left(s_{gm} \frac{\dot{\hat{f}}_{gm}}{\hat{f}_{gm}} - f_g \hat{s}_{gm} \frac{\dot{\hat{f}}_{gm}}{\hat{f}_{gm}} \right) - f_g \ln(\bar{y}_g) \frac{\dot{f}_g}{f_g} \right], \quad \bar{y}_g = \sum_{m=1}^{M_g} \hat{f}_{gm} y_{gm}$$

Variables with '^' denote shares or averages with respect to a region. The term $(\hat{s}_{gm} - \hat{f}_{gm})$ is the difference between the income share and population share of the *m*th province *within the g*th region and its interpretation is similar to $(s_{gm} - f_{gm})$ discussed above. In the case of the between region contribution, since $(s_{gm} - f_g \hat{s}_{gm}) = \hat{s}_{gm}(s_{gm}/\hat{s}_{gm} - f_g)$ and $s_{gm}/\hat{s}_{gm}$ is in fact the share of income accruing to region *g*, so that $(s_{gm}/\hat{s}_{gm} - f_g)$ turns out to be the difference between the income share and the population share of the *g*th region.

Finally, to facilitate our discussion in subsequent sections, it is helpful to derive *cumulative* changes in inequality induced by the different components above. For example, in the case of TFP, its cumulative contribution is defined as follows:

$$CCA_T = \sum_{s=T_0}^{T} CA_s, \quad WCCA_T = \sum_{s=T_0}^{T} WCA_s, \quad BCCA_T = \sum_{s=T_0}^{T} BCA_s \qquad (11)$$

where CCA_T, $WCCA_T$, and $BCCA_T$ are the *cumulative* contribution by TFP to the *change* in overall, within region, and between region inequality from T_0 up to the period T. Cumulative changes with respect to components other than TFP in equations (8), (9), and (10) may be defined accordingly.

5.5 Estimation of Provincial Production Functions

As a prelude to the derivation of those components in equation (8) to equation (10), the provincial production functions have to be estimated. To render the estimation manageable, the provincial production functions are assumed to be loglinear. Furthermore, to explore the black box of TFP, we assume that A depends on a R-vector $z_{gm} = (z_{gm1}, \ldots, z_{gmk})$.

$$Y_{gm} = \left(e^{\lambda_{gm} + \sum_{r=1}^{R} \lambda_r z_{gmr}} \right) K_{gm}^{\alpha_K} H_{gm}^{\alpha_H} \qquad (12)$$

It follows that the contribution of TFP may further be decomposed:

$$CA = \Sigma_r \, Cz_r, \quad Cz_r = \sum_{r=1}^{R} (s_{gm} - f_{gm}) \lambda_r \frac{dz_{gmr}}{dt} \qquad (13)$$

WCA and *BCA* may be decomposed analogously.

With regard to z_{gm}, data availability has limited the factors we can include in z_{gm}. An important dimension of China's reform is the open door policy as manifested in the huge influx of foreign direct investments (FDI). The spatial distribution of FDI is skewed towards the coastal provinces not only because of spatially differential policies (e.g. all the special economic zones are in the coastal region only), but possibly because coastal provinces are farther advanced with regard to reform. Therefore as a proxy for openness, we incorporate FDI as a share of GDP into z_{gm}. In recent years, many studies have tried to establish the nexus between openness and growth. In the present context, we try to determine how differential degrees of openness impact on interprovincial inequality via their effect on provincial economic growth.

Another factor that possibly affects TFP is the spatial reshuffling of industries mentioned in section 5.2. With the retreat of central planning, the spatial flows of investments have conformed with comparative advantages and economies of scale. Fujita and Hu (2001) argue that industrial agglomeration in the coastal region has become stronger in the reform era and may even be a direct source of regional inequality. On the other hand, by blocking the free flow of resources between jurisdictions, local protectionism may have weakened the effect of agglomeration and comparative advantage on regional inequality. How serious market fragmentation is in the reform era is still an unsettled issue (see, e.g., Naughton 2002 and Young 2000). Empirical evidence seems to suggest that China has yet to fully exploit the effect of agglomeration on productivity (Au and Henderson 2004). It is also useful to note that the re-orientation of industrial strategy from an excessive focus on heavy industries to the judicious exploitation of China's comparative advantage in labour intensive industries has boosted some provinces, such as Guangdong and Fujian, that were lagging behind in the pre-reform era. This has triggered a decline in such industrial powerhouses as Liaoning. In view of these complicated dynamics, without an empirical analysis it is a priori difficult to ascertain how industrial restructuring affects regional inequality. In the present context, we treat the effect induced by the industrial reshuffling as among z_{gm} that may affect productivity. The effect is measured by the share of that province's secondary sector output to the national total, i.e., $Y_{2k}/\Sigma_m Y_{2m}$, where Y_{2k} is the kth province's output of the secondary sector and the denominator is the national total.[15] As an illustration, Figure 5.10 summarizes the shares for Guangdong and Liaoning for the period under study. The underlying increase in the share of Guangdong since 1978 may expand the productivity of the province due to the exploitation of comparative advantage and economies of scale producing for the world market.

In addition to these two key variables, a dummy variable for the initial years of the Cultural Revolution and a time trend for the reform era are also included in z_{gm}.[16] The included variables do not exhaust all the factors driving TFP growth. However, data limitations prevent us from embarking on a more comprehensive investigation. Much remains to be done in future work to explore the forces driving TFP.

5.6 Empirical Findings

Before implementing the decomposition exercise, we first estimate equation (12). We briefly summarize how a number of econometric issues are dealt with. Covering the period from 1964 to 1999, the provincial data are pooled to increase the degree of freedom. First, the panel unit root test proposed by Im et al. (2003) suggests that the timeseries for the regression is not stationary.[17]

---

[15] In the literature on agglomeration, the regional share of industry is often used as a measure for agglomeration (see, e.g., Brakman et al. 2001).

[16] We have also experimented with the share of primary output. The rationale is that TFP growth in many developing countries is due to structural transformation. However, in the present context, this variable does not seem to be significant.

[17] Results are available on request.

Table 5.2: Regression results from production function estimation

	Log-linear		Constant returns	
Ln(K)	0.5243 (5.8585)	0.4765 (5.1743)		
Ln(H)	0.5846 (2.4991)	0.5989 (2.5311)		
Ln(K/H)			0.4884 (4.0531)	0.4513 (3.6700)
FDI	0.7087 (2.7690)	0.4525 (0.2457)	0.7236 (2.7610)	0.4606 (1.8581)
IND		7.1664 (12.2763)		7.2270 (12.8106)
CRV	−0.1017 (−6.1104)	−0.1030 (−6.8251)	−0.1032 (−9.4339)	−0.1041 (−9.5102)
TD	0.0076 (0.6008)	0.0117 (0.9156)	0.0144 (1.4702)	0.0164 (1.6503)

Notes: K = capital stock; H = quality-adjusted labourforce; FDI = share of foreign direct investment to GDP; IND = share of the secondary sector; CRV = dummy for the Cultural Revolution; TD = time trend for the reform era. The estimates are based by pooling the provincial data and estimating the first-difference form of the log-linear production, i.e. equation (12). The variance–covariance matrix is robust to autocorrelation and heteroscedasticity following Arellano (2003). Figures in parentheses are t-statistics.

To avoid the potential problem of spurious correlation based on level data, we estimate the first difference form of equation (12). To test whether the right-hand side (RHS) variables are exogenous, we apply the Wooldridge (2002) test for strict exogeneity. The test suggests that the bias induced by endogeneity of RHS variables is not serious. The above tests and procedures result in the two sets of estimates given in Table 5.2, one for the loglinear case and the other for the case of constant returns to scale, i.e., $\alpha_K + \alpha_H = 1$. Robust t statistics are based on variance–covariance matrices taking into account autocorrelation and heteroscedasticity proposed by Arellano (2003). Finally, using the Wald test for linear restrictions, the hypothesis of constant returns to scale is accepted.[18]

The results of the above regressions are summarized in Table 5.2. Two sets of estimates are presented, one for the panel regression without and the other with the constant returns to scale restriction. As suggested above, the Wald test for linear restrictions accepts the hypothesis of constant returns to scale. Estimates for λ_r, α_K, and α_H are plugged into the equations for the various contributions to inequality. The contributions by the different factors are summarized in Figure 5.5: *CCK* and *CCH* are the contributions of the growth in physical capital and quality adjusted labour. Decomposing the contribution of TFP growth, *CCFDI* pertains to the contribution of openness and *CCIND* to that of spatial industrial restructuring. What remains after deducting *CCFDI* and *CCIND* is *CCOTH*.

Being a dominating factor and the focus of many previous studies (e.g., Naughton 2002), the cumulative contribution of physical capital (*CCK*) unambiguously declines until 1972 and then starts to climb until the end of period under review. As shown in Figure 5.6, the initial decline is attributable to the fall in both within-region contribution of capital (*WCCK*) and between region contribution of capital (*BCCK*), though the magnitude of the latter is

---

[18] In any case, the magnitudes of the estimates are quite similar. The Wald test is used because of the robust variance–covariance matrix.

Interprovincial Inequality

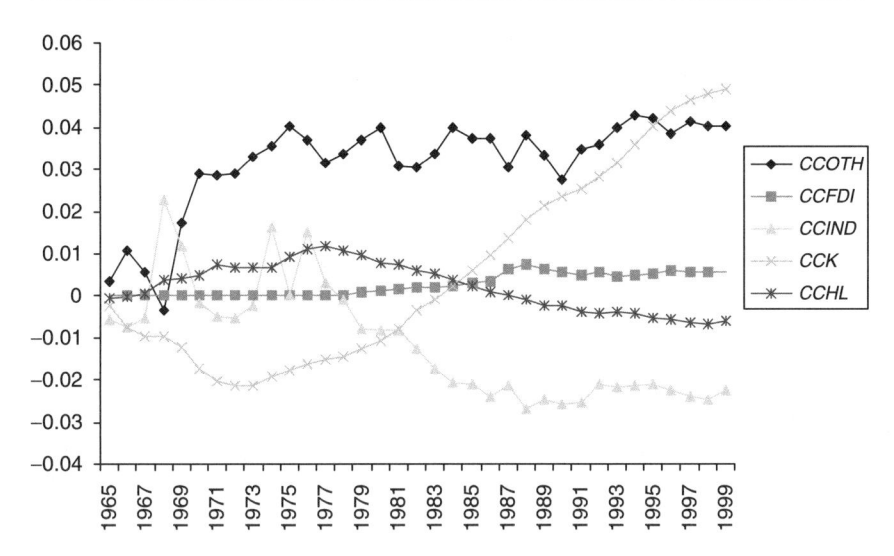

Figure 5.5: Contributions to inter-provincial inequality
Source: Computed by author from data sources cited in Appendix 5.A.

much larger. The decline in *BCCK* coincides with the 'third front' campaign, a period when massive state investments were directed to the inland provinces.

The increasing trajectory of *CCK* after 1973 is largely explained by the widening gap among the coastal, central, and western regions, so much so that by the 1990s, the upward trend in *CCK* is entirely propelled by *BCCK*. The peak of the 'third front' campaign was over in the 1970s (Naughton 1988,

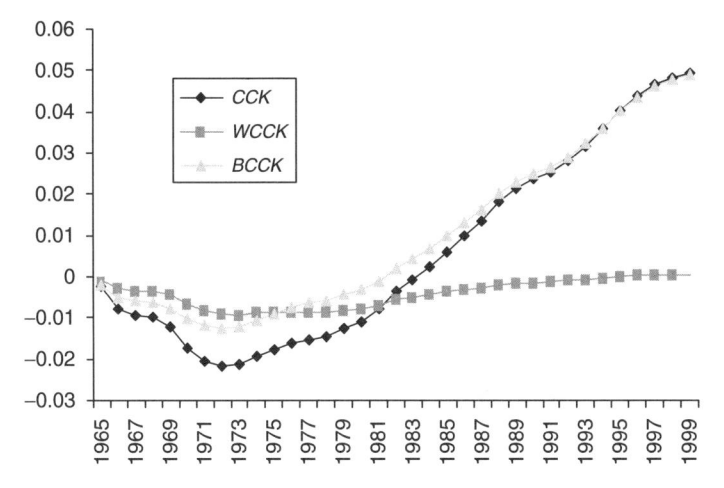

Figure 5.6: Overall between regional and within region contributions of capital
Source: Computed by author from data sources cited in Appendix 5.A.

2002) and the result is captured by *CCK* moving upward again. As shown in Figure 5.6, the sharp increase in *CCK* progressively driven by the between region contribution of capital (*BCCK*) is the major force in the reform era pushing interprovincial inequality upwards. This is consistent with the interspatial reshuffling of investment funds outlined in section 5.2 above.

Even though the above discussion has confirmed that contribution of physical capital is, *ceter paribus*, important in explaining interprovincial inequality, it is interesting to note that changes in *CCK* do not always track the trend in overall interprovincial inequality. Our results suggest that the cumulative contribution to inequality of TFP growth before deducting the impact of FDI and industrial restructuring, i.e. *CCA*, is equally if not more important in certain subperiods and has a trajectory that is divergent from that of *CCK*. Figure 5.7 summarizes the contribution of TFP (*CCA*) based on equation (13). During the Cultural Revolution (1967–77), the magnitude of the upward trend in *CCA* is so large that it surpasses *CCK* so that overall inequality increases. Decomposing *CCA* using equation (13), and the proxy for the distribution of industries exhibits some spikes but no discernible trajectory. *CCOTH* (equal to *CCA-CCFDI-CCIND*) in Figure 5.5 is the remainder after the contributions of FDI and *IND* are deduced and exhibits, by and large, an increasing trend up to the mid-1970s.

Using equation (13), the effects of FDI and industrial restructuring may be extracted from *CCA*. There was no FDI in the pre-reform era. FDI initially contributes to an increase in inequality but the effect tapers off from the mid-1980s

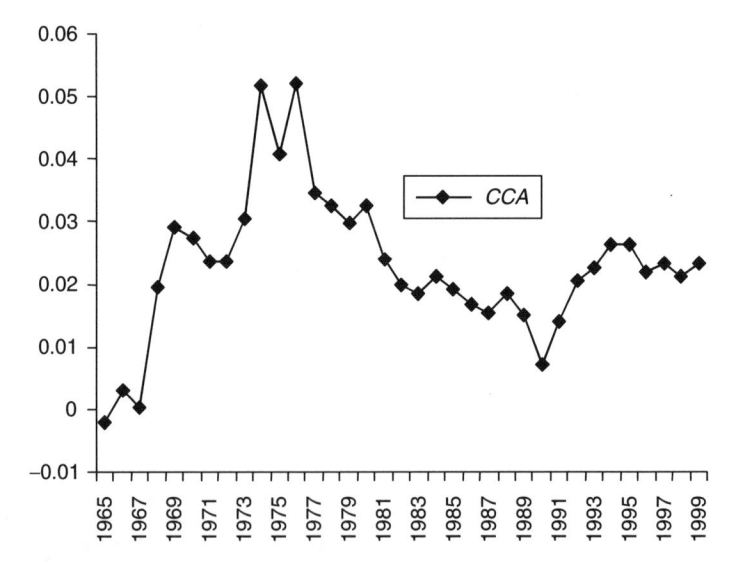

Figure 5.7: Total factor productivity (before deducting the effects of FDI and agglomerative effects)

Source: Computed by author from data sources cited in Appendix 5.A.

Interprovincial Inequality

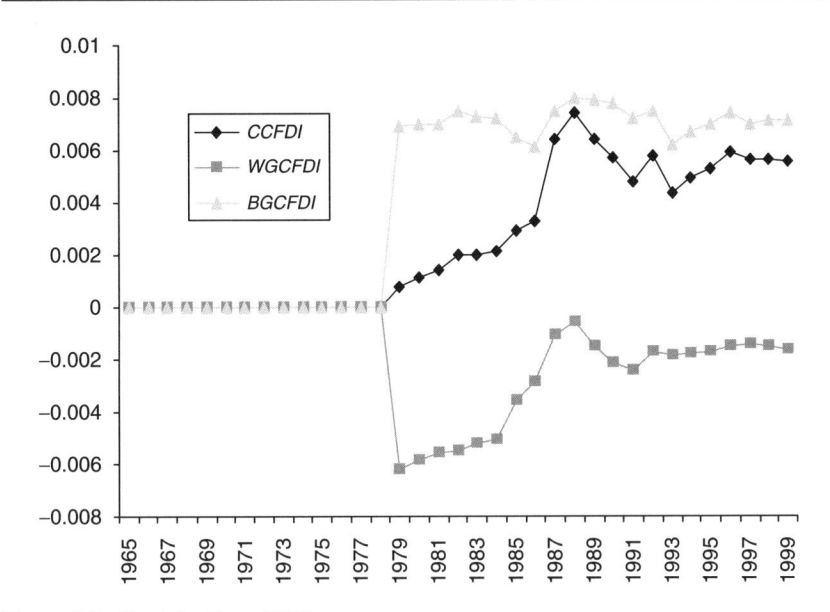

Figure 5.8: Contribution of FDI
Source: Computed by author from data sources cited in Appendix 5.A.

onwards (see Figure 5.8). After a jump induced by initial FDI flows into the coastal provinces (such as Guangdong), the between region contribution of FDI (*BCCFDI*) does not exhibit a discernible trend. The trajectory of the within region contribution (*WCCFDI*) exhibits a one off decrease, followed by an upward trend. This is consistent with the fact that the initial beneficiaries of FDI are the poorer coastal provinces, such as Guangdong and Fujian which constitute the special economic zones. Foreign capital subsequently spread to other coastal provinces. On the whole, these contributions are relatively small in magnitude.

Figure 5.9 summarizes the overall (*CCIND*), between (*BCCIND*) and within (*WCCIND*) region contributions of industrial restructuring. In the pre-reform era, there are a number of inequality increasing spikes but no discernible trends are detected. Since the late 1970s, *CCIND* contributes to a reduction in overall interprovincial inequality, though its inequality reducing effect tapers off in the 1990s. In decomposing *CCIND* further into between and within region contributions, the declining trend is largely attributable to *WCCIND* and, to a much smaller extent, to *BCCIND*. In the latter case, the trend of *BCCIND* seems to have become modest in the 1990s. In a further breakdown of *WCCIND* into contributions by the three regions, the decline is concentrated largely within the eastern region.[19] The reform period has witnessed the decline of such industrial powerhouses as Liaoning that relied on heavy industries. In their place are

---

[19] Recall (9); the figures are not reported but are available on request.

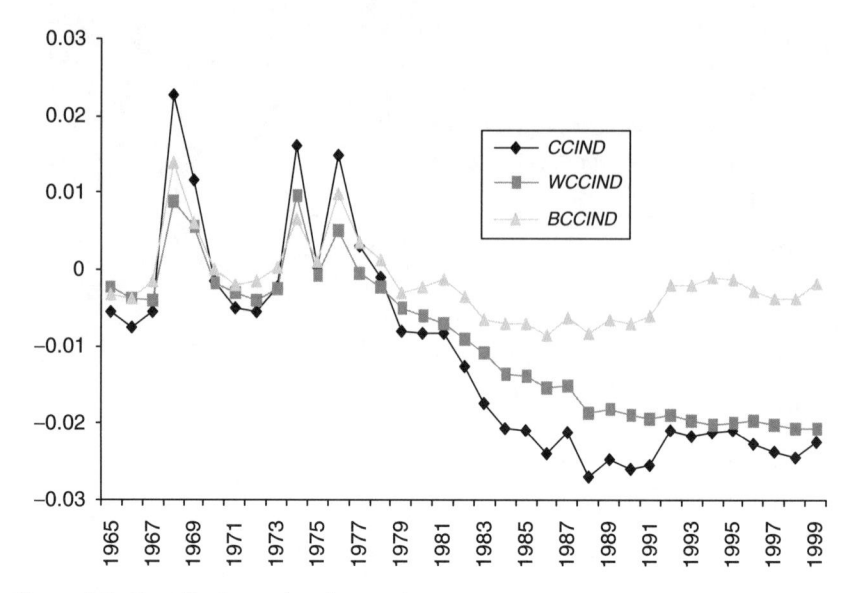

Figure 5.9: Contributions of agglomeration
Source: Computed by author from data sources cited in Appendix 5.A.

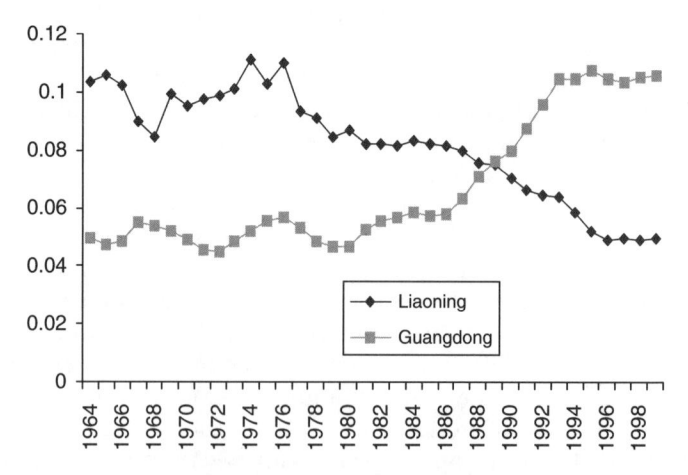

Figure 5.10: Shares of secondary sectors in Liaoning and Guangdong
Source: Computed by author from data sources cited in Appendix 5.A.

Interprovincial Inequality

new industrial growth poles such as Guangdong, translating their comparative advantage and economies of scale in labour intensive industries (see Figure 5.10) into faster TFP growth. As these newly industrializing provinces were less developed in the initial stages of the reform era, industrial restructuring has thus reduced interprovincial inequality.

Next, as depicted in Figure 5.11, quality adjusted labour (H) contributes to an increase in interprovincial inequality until the mid-1970s, after which the trend is reversed. The trajectories of between region ($BCCH$) and within region contributions ($WCCH$) are similar, with the inequality reducing effect of the between region contributions being more prominent. Two forces are at work. First, growth of the labour force is faster in poor provinces. The second factor is the spread of education. As better educated children in the poor provinces gradually entered the labour force in the 1960s and 1970s, the rapid improvement in labour quality S leads to a faster growth in H. Our empirical findings suggest that this translates into a decline in interprovincial inequality but the impact is small relative to the contributions of TFP and physical capital (see Figure 5.5).

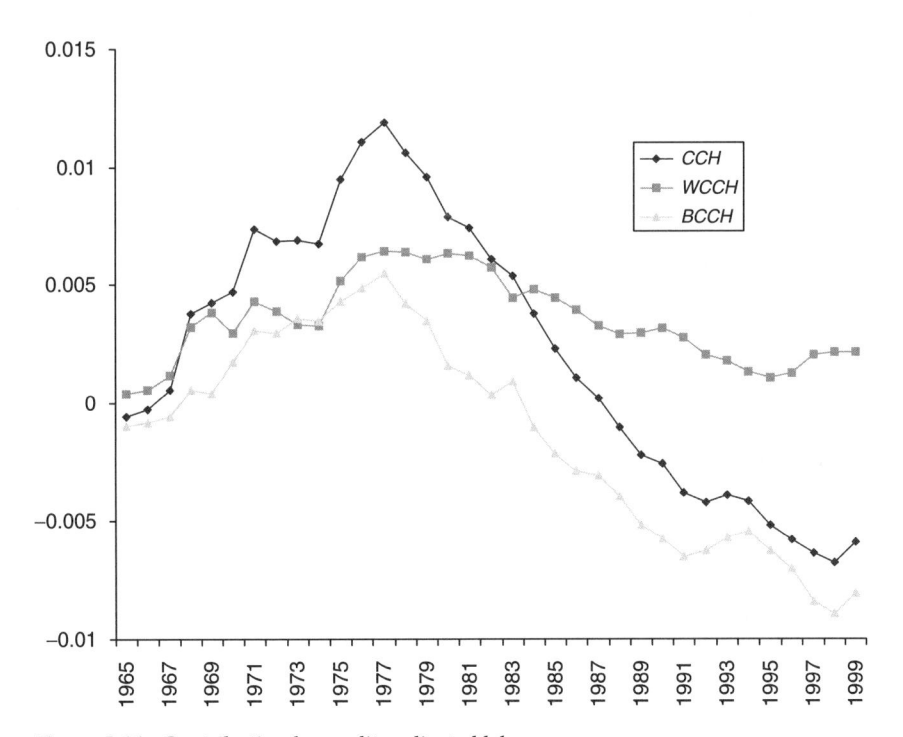

Figure 5.11: Contribution by quality adjusted labour
Source: Computed by author from data sources cited in Appendix 5.A.

5.7 Salient Findings and Concluding Remarks

The main objective of this chapter is to better link the forces induced by policy regime switching to the fluctuation in interprovincial inequality. This is done with the help of data that have been adjusted to hopefully take into account the data problems that are of concern to many experts on China. As our empirical results suggest, the vicissitude of interprovincial inequality reflects the paradigm shifts in China's development strategies over the last four decades that reshuffled resources and induced spatially differential impacts. The rest of this section highlights three major clusters of results. The first pertains to the contribution of capital vis-à-vis TFP growth. The second set of results indicates a more complex picture than can be captured by the coastal–inland divide in explaining interprovincial inequality. The final set of results sheds light on the effect of pre-reform spread of education on growth in the reform era.

First, the contribution of physical capital has a trajectory that, at times, is divergent from that of TFP. In the pre-reform era, especially during the ten-year period of the Cultural Revolution, the contribution of TFP growth surpasses that of physical investment, and seems to coincide with the shocks induced by political turmoil as well as the policy environment in the pre-reform era. As pointed out by Donnithorne (1972), the 'cellular economy' induced by a policy of self-reliance militated against the convergence of TFP, in so far as the inter-jurisdictional flow of resources, ranging from factors of production to ideas and knowledge, was discouraged. The roles of TFP growth and of investment have been reversed since the late 1970s; the decreasing contribution of TFP more than offsets the increasing contribution of capital, accounting for the decline in interprovincial inequality in the 1980s. The inequality decreasing contribution of TFP fades in the 1990s, with the trajectory of the contribution of capital becoming dominant.

Spatial industrial restructuring, with the evolution of provincial shares of secondary sector output as a proxy, turns out to be important in explaining much of the decline in the contribution of TFP in the post-Mao era. As summarized by our empirical results, industrial reshuffling in the 1980s probably had the effect of rectifying a distorted spatial industrial structure and induced a decline both in within region and between region inequality. This effect is so powerful that it overrides the other inequality increasing forces, leading to an overall decrease in interprovincial inequality. Once the spatial restructuring of industries was complete and the effect exhausted, our findings seem to suggest that the spatial distribution of TFP growth contributes to an increase in between region inequality in the 1990s. Institutional changes seem to be moving at a much faster pace in the coastal provinces, probably reinforced by agglomeration economies.

With regard to the coastal–inland disparity captured by the changes in the overall between region contribution, the inequality reducing between region contribution of capital (CCK) in the pre-reform era is more than offset by the increase in the between region contribution of TFP. Since the mid-1970s, changing spatial patterns of investment are the major factor behind the between region inequality. However, other forces at times counteract this tendency. Among these are the investments in education in the pre-reform period, the effect of which began to show up in the late 1970s, and industrial restructuring in the 1980s. Their impact, however, is modest in comparison with the contribution of capital.

There is more to interprovincial inequality than the coastal–inland dichotomy. As shown in Figure 5.3, there is a sustained decline in the within region inequality. Careful scrutiny suggests that the fluctuation of provinces within the coastal region can, at times, be the dominant force behind the trajectory of overall interprovincial inequality. Worthy of particular mention is the industrial restructuring among the coastal provinces that triggers a fall in interprovincial inequality in the 1980s. The emerging new growth poles in the eastern region have capitalized on the development of non-state industrial enterprises (e.g. township and village enterprises) and the open-door policy. In sharp contrast is the decline in the old industrial centres (especially those in the northeast) as their moribund state-owned enterprises failed to meet the competition brought about by market reform. The above transformation translates into a decline in overall interprovincial inequality in the 1980s, with the within region contribution of industrial restructuring exhibiting a downward trend.

Last but not least, the effect of schooling on China's interprovincial inequality is discussed much less, although human capital is often in the limelight in connection with economic growth. Notwithstanding the political calamities communism inflicted on the people, there is no denying that much had been done before 1978 in spreading education to the less developed provinces. Some scholars (e.g. Bramall 2000) have even gone so far as to argue that the pre-reform investment in education laid the foundation for the spectacular growth of the reform era. This chapter is a preliminary attempt to incorporate this issue into the analysis of interprovincial inequalities, though much remains to be done to improve the measure of schooling. The empirical results suggest that contribution of schooling first increases and then reduces interprovincial inequality. In so far as school-aged children in less developed provinces entered the labour force in the 1970s only gradually, our interpretation is that the inequality reducing effect of schooling is a consequence of the pre-reform expansion of basic education. The contribution of quality adjusted labour to growth is, however, small relative to capital and TFP.

This chapter attempts to extend the research on China's regional inequality first by resorting to a more careful use of China's data and then introducing a framework that enhances our understanding of the forces behind the changes in the country's interprovincial inequality. In particular, quantitative estimates of the contributions of factors affecting inequality are presented. Much, however, remains to be done. The experimentation with adjusting official data leaves room for improvement. Nor is our method of adjustment the only one conceivable.

For example, Young (2000) tackles the problem by first coming up with deflators for different sectors of the national economy, an approach that may be applied to provincial data. Another potential extension of our study is to experiment with different ways to construct provincial indices for human capital, a subject too complex to be elaborated in this chapter.[20] Finally, our study of the factors behind TFP growth is crude and tentative. There are certainly other important variables in the equation. Among them are the effects of interprovincial migration, local protectionism and improvement in transportation network, etc. All these extensions may be topics for future research.

Appendix 5.A

5.A1 *Real Provincial GDP*

The nominal GDP for the period 1952–98 are from NBS (2001a). Data for 1999 are collected from the provincial yearbooks.[21] Care has been exercised in ensuring that the 1999 data are consistent with those of previous years because provincial statistical bureaux periodically update the GDP figures. In case of a province update on its GDP series, we use the new series (this involves very few cases). Details are available on request.

To deflate the provincial GDP, we experiment with different methods (recall Figure 5.1). Official real growth rates are available in NBS (1997). Provincial yearbooks may be used to deflate nominal GDP. However, as pointed earlier, many China experts suspect that official data underestimate inflation in the reform period. This chapter follows the suggestion of Keidel (2001) by deflating the different categories of expenditure by their respective price indices. Specifically:

$$Y_{gm} = CR_{gm} + CU_{gm} + CG_{gm} + CF_{gm} + NX_{gm}$$

where the subscript *gm* refers to the *m*th province in the *g*th region, Y_{gm} = GDP, CR_{gm} = rural consumption, CU_{gm} = urban consumption, CG_{gm} = government consumption, CF_{gm} = capital formation, and NX_{gm} = net export. The data are from NBS (2001a).[22] These expenditure components can be found in NBS (2001b). For the period from the

---

[20] Appendix 5.A has a discussion on the derivation of provincial average years of schooling. In this chapter, we have mainly used age specific data from censuses to estimate the average years of schooling of the labour force for each province. Another way is to integrate census figures with the annual enrolment data.

[21] Another source of national income data is from NSB (1997). However, the data cover the period until 1995. A cross-check of our data with this source of data shows that they are approximately the same.

[22] Jiangxi and Guangdong do not have data for the pre-reform period. However, information is available for these provinces on consumption (*xiaofei*) and accumulation (*jilei*) under the socialist material product system (MPS); see NBS (1987). To derive deflators for these provinces, the best option is to deflate consumption and accumulation as defined in the MPS by their respective price indices. The national implicit deflator for capital formation is used to deflate accumulation. The implicit deflators so derived are then used to deflate the prereform GDP series for these two provinces. Details are available on request (NSB 2001a).

Interprovincial Inequality

mid-1980s onwards, provincial rural and urban CPIs are used to deflate CR_{gm} and CU_{gm}, respectively, because better alternatives are hard to come by. Provincial CPI indices are used to deflate CG_{gm}. For the preceding period, only provincial cost of living indices for staff and workers are available for deflating CU_{gm} (NBS 2001a, b). We have no choice but to resort to provincial retail price indices (RPIs). Theoretically, the biases with this expediency are twofold. First, changes in the prices of services are not taken into account. Second, RPIs reflect changes in both rural and urban prices. However, casual comparisons of RPIs and CPIs for a few provinces when both indices are available seem to suggest that their movements are very similar for the pre-reform period (with the possible exception of the years surrounding the 'great leap forward'). This, in fact, is not surprising because the shares of urban and rural expenditures on services might be relatively insignificant. In any case, prices were administratively fixed and rarely changed.

Ideally, provincial capital formation should be deflated using price indices for capital goods. This is the case when provincial price indices for fixed asset investment are available for the period from 1992 to 1999. For the period 1985–91, the price indices for capital goods recently released by NBS (2001b) are used to estimate the price indices for construction (*jianzhu anzhuang*) and equipment (*shebi*). Then, we derive an overall price index for capital investment by weighting the indices for construction and equipment (*shebi*) by their respective shares in total investment.[23] From 1964 to 1984, owing to data limitations, two sets of deflators are used for the period until the mid-1980s. One set involves using official implicit deflators for capital formation without adjustments.[24] Using the official implicit deflators for gross capital formation, we can derive provincial real GDP per capita series that are used to estimate *EN3* in Figure 5.1. Another set includes adjusted official implicit deflators for capital formation that takes into account data anomalies. Specifically, there are some years when the implicit rates of changes in the prices of capital goods are incredibly high even though the pre-reform era is known to be a period of price stability. Our rule of thumb is to replace price increase rates exceeding 20 percent with the national rates for the same year. For the years around the 'great leap forward' that were affected by high price increases, we refrain from such adjustments. The use of these adjusted deflators corresponds to *EN2* in Figure 5.1. Finally, provincial RPIs are used to deflate net exports.

5.A2 Real Capital Stock

The main difficulty with the estimation of provincial physical capital stock is to derive at the initial capital stock for each of the provinces. We follow the procedure proposed by Nehru and Dhareshwar (1993). If, as a first approximation, the capital–output ratio is constant, then it can easily be shown that $K_{gm,t-1} = FA_{gmt}/(g + \delta)$, where K is capital stock, FA_{gmt} is *real* fixed asset investment, δ is the depreciation rate, and g is the output growth rate. We assume that $\delta = 0.05$. To smooth out fluctuations, a three-year average

---

[23] The publication consists of *national* price indices for specific capital goods classified under construction and equipment. For each category, we take the average of the price increases of the specific capital goods to arrive at the price indices for construction and equipment, respectively. To arrive at the province specific indices, the two indices are weighted by the respective shares of construction and equipment in total fixed asset investment.

[24] Pre-reform provincial real growth rates are from NBS (1997).

growth rate (the three years being 1953, 1954, and 1955), and the corresponding three-year average investment level are used to estimate the 1954 capital stock. Then, the capital stock figures for 1953 and 1952 can be derived recursively. To arrive at the real provincial capital stock series, the perpetual inventory approach is used:

$$K_{gmt} = (1-\delta)K_{gm,t-1} + FA_{gmt}$$

To arrive at the real fixed asset investment, the nominal data used are those of capital formation in fixed assets (*guding zichan xingcheng zonge*) from NBS (2001a, b). The same method for the deflation of capital formation (see above) is also applied to arrive at FA_{gmt}. Since the sample period of our econometric estimation is 1964–99, whatever biases are embedded in the initial capital stocks are hopefully ameliorated after 12 years.

Pre-reform data on fixed asset capital formation are not available for Guangdong and Jiangxi. We use an admittedly crude method to estimate the pre-reform data utilizing the fixed asset accumulation figures under the socialist material product system from NBS (1987). First, ratios of fixed asset capital formation under the current national accounting system (i.e., SNA) and fixed-asset accumulation under MPS are derived for the period 1978–85. The averages of these ratios are then applied to the fixed-asset accumulation data for the pre-reform period to arrive at estimates of fixed-asset capital formation under SNA.

5.A3 *Quality Adjusted Labour Force*

Quality adjusted provincial labour force is the product of the labour force (*congye renyuan*) multiplied by the average year of schooling. Provincial labour force statistics are found in NSB (1999) and provincial yearbooks. For a few provinces where data are missing for a few years, estimates for those years are derived by using linear extrapolations. Details are available on request. One problem with the labour force statistics is that workers on leave (*xiagang*) were included before 1998. The problem of *xiagang* began in the early 1990s and reached a peak in the late 1990s. Provincial *xiagang* figures can be obtained from various issues of NBS's Department of Population, Social, and Technological Statistics. *Xiagang* workers were subtracted from total labour force for the post-1994 period based on the assumption that these figures are relatively small before 1994.

To arrive at provincial estimates of years of schooling, we utilize information from the 1982, 1990, and 2000 censuses on the working aged population with different levels of education, viz., primary (*xiaoxue*), junior high (*chuzhong*), senior high (*gaozhong*), and university (*daxue*). For any period between two censuses, age specific population for a given level of education is projected forward using the survival rate of that age group. For example, let $x(a, e, T)$ be the population at age a with the eth level of education derived from the population census in year T (e.g. 1982) for a given province (to ease exposition, subscripts for provinces are omitted). In theory, the population at age $a + 1$ in year $T + 1$ with the eth level of education is:

$$x(a+1, e, T+1) = x(a, e, T) \times s(a, T) + d(a+1, T+1)$$

where $s(a, T)$ is the rate of those surviving in $T + 1$ and $d(a + 1, T + 1)$ is the volume of net migration between T and $T + 1$. Then, the following recursive formula can be used to

Interprovincial Inequality

$$x(a+k, e, T+k) = x(a+k-1, e, T+k-1) \times s(a, T+k-1) + d(a+k, t+k) \quad \text{(A1)}$$

Survival rates from provincial life tables, $\hat{s}(a)$, can be used to approximate $s(a,t)$.[25] Annual information on age specific net migration data is, however, hard to obtain. Thus, we have made use of the figures from two consecutive censuses to arrive at the total volume of net migration for each age group for the intervening period as a whole. Then, the total volume of net migration is evenly distributed among the intervening years. To be precise, we first assume that $d(a+k, t) = d(a)$ for the period between the census in year T and the next census K year from T. Then, using the recursive formula above, the estimate of $x(a+K, e, T+K)$, denoted by $\hat{x}(a+K, e, T+K, d(a))$, is an unknown function of $d(a)$. In theory, if our assumption that $d(a+k, t)$ is equal to $d(a)$ were correct, then $x(a+K, e, t+K) = \hat{x}(a+K, e, T+K, d(a))$. Since $x(a+K, e, t+K)$ is a figure that may be derived from the census in $T+K$, we can solve the equation for some *implicit* net migration figure $\hat{d}(a)$, which can be substituted into (A1) to arrive at estimates of $x(a+k, e, t+k)$ between the two censuses:

$$\hat{x}(a+k, e, t+k) = x(a, e, t) \times \hat{s}(a) + \hat{d}(a)$$

The above method is used to arrive at the estimates for different education levels for the period after 1982 making use of data from the 1982, 1990, and 2000 censuses. The number of years of schooling for the working aged population is then equal to:

$$\hat{X}(t+k) = \sum_e \sum_{a=15}^{60} w_e \hat{x}(a+k, e, t+k), \quad k = 0, 1, \ldots, K \quad \text{(A2)}$$

where w_e is the number of years of schooling for the eth level of education. The years for primary, junior high, senior high, and university education are 6, 9, 12, and 16, respectively.

For the period before 1982, age specific data required for implementing the above method are not available.[26] To arrive at estimates before 1982, $x(a, e, t)$ may, in theory, be projected recursively backward, i.e.:

$$\hat{x}(a-k, e, 1982\text{-}k)$$
$$= [\hat{x}(a-k+1, 1982\text{-}k+1) - d(a-k+1, 1982\text{-}k+1)]/\hat{s}(a-k)$$
$$= f(a, e, k, 1982) - g(a, k)$$

where:

$$f(a, e, k, 1982) = x(a, e, 1982) / \left(\prod_{j=1}^{k} \hat{s}(a-j) \right), \quad g(a, k) = \left(\sum_{j=0}^{k-1} \frac{d(a-j)}{\prod_{i=j}^{k-1} \hat{s}(a-i)} \right)$$

---

[25] $\hat{s}(a)$ is equal to $L(a+1)/L(a)$, where $L(a)$ is the population surviving to age a in a life table.
[26] The census prior to 1982 was undertaken in 1964. However, age specific figures by education levels are not available.

$f(a, e, k, 1982)$ may be derived using the 1982 census data and survival rates from life tables. The figures for each level of education are then multiplied by their respective years of schooling, w_e, to arrive at the total years of schooling before deducting the second term, i.e. $F(k, 1982) = \sum_e \sum_{a=15}^{60} w_e f(a, e, k, 1982)$.

However, information again on $d(a)$ is not available. There are only provincial figures on the total volume of net migration, denoted by $m(t)$, each year. We apply a rule to apportion the total to different levels of education. First, we decompose net migration in year t, $m(t)$, into different education levels. We assume that the share of net migration with working ages is equal to the share of the labour force of the population of the province in question, denoted by $r(t)$. Next, we assume that the share of migrants with the eth level of education is the same as that of the share of $f(a, e, k, 1982)$ in the workforce, denoted by s_e. Then, $r(t)m(t)s_e$ is the component of $m(t)$ with the eth level of education. Finally the total number of years of schooling with respect to net migration is $\sum_e w_e r(t) m(t) s_e$. This term is then subtracted from $F(k, 1982)$ to arrive at the total number of years of schooling $\hat{X}$ (1982-k). This method is applied to recover the total number of years of schooling only up to 1964. One reason is that the 'great leap forward' had a great impact on population figures and large margins of errors may result if $\hat{X}(t)$ is projected back into the 1950s. Second, frequent changes in provincial boundaries and large scale population migration in the 1950s may further reduce the accuracy of the estimation.

There are, no doubt, weak spots in constructing $\hat{X}(t)$, $t = 1964, \ldots, 1999$, using the method delineated above. However, given the data available, this is the best we can do. There is much room for further fine tuning of the method and experimenting with other methods (e.g. using enrolment data). To arrive at the average years of schooling S, $\hat{X}(t)$ is divided by the working aged population (estimated based on census data)

5.A4 Population

Population data used to derive provincial GDP per capita, especially figures based on household registration in the reform era, are not without problems because of the failure to take proper account of inward or outward migration. In so far as the data problems created by migration are not so serious for the pre-reform period, the official population figures from NBS (1999) and from provincial yearbooks are used. From 1982 onwards, we extrapolate population figures made up of age specific data from the 1982, 1990, and 2000 population censuses. Essentially, we have age specific populations for all the provinces from the 1982, 1990, and 2000 censuses. Using the survival rates from the provincial life tables, we project the age specific population groups forward from one census to the next. The difference between the projected and actual figures of the next census is assumed to be due to net migration. Such differences are allocated evenly to the inter-census years as in the case of schooling.[27]

Appendix 5.B

This Appendix illustrates how the equations in the text are derived. The population weighted version of Theil's entropy measure is as follows:

[27] Details available on request.

Interprovincial Inequality

$$I(\mathbf{y}) = \sum_{g=1}^{G} \sum_{m=1}^{M_g} f_{gm} \ln\left(\frac{\bar{y}}{y_{gm}}\right) = \ln(\bar{y}) - \sum_{g=1}^{G} \sum_{m=1}^{M_g} f_{gm} y_{gm} \tag{B1}$$

where $\bar{y} = \sum_{g=1}^{G} \sum_{m=1}^{M_g} f_{gm} y_{gm}$.

Differentiate equation (B1):

$$\frac{dI}{dt} = \frac{\dot{\bar{y}}}{\bar{y}} - \sum_{g=1}^{G} \sum_{m=1}^{M_g} \left(f_{gm} \frac{\dot{y}_{gm}}{y_{gm}} + \dot{f}_{gm} \ln(y_{gm}) \right) \tag{B2}$$

where, for any variable x, $\dot{x} = dx/dt$. It is to be noted that:

$$\frac{\dot{\bar{y}}}{\bar{y}} = \sum_{g}^{G} \sum_{m}^{M_g} \left(\frac{\dot{f}_{gm} y_{gm} + f_{gm} \dot{y}_{gm}}{\bar{y}} \right) = \sum_{g}^{G} \sum_{m}^{M_g} \left(\frac{f_{gm} y_{gm}}{\bar{y}} \frac{\dot{f}_{gm} y_{gm} + f_{gm} \dot{y}_{gm}}{f_{gm} y_{gm}} \right) \tag{B3}$$

Since:

$$s_{gm} = \frac{f_{gm} y_{gm}}{\bar{y}} = \frac{P f_{gm} y_{gm}}{P \bar{y}}$$

P being the total population. It follows that the term is equal the share of GDP accruing to the m province in the gth region. Thus equation (B3) becomes:

$$\frac{\dot{\bar{y}}}{\bar{y}} = \sum_{g}^{G} \sum_{m}^{M_g} \left(\frac{f_{gm} y_{gm}}{\bar{y}} \frac{\dot{f}_{gm} y_{gm} + f_{gm} \dot{y}_{gm}}{f_{gm} y_{gm}} \right) = \sum_{g}^{G} \sum_{m}^{M_g} s_{gm} \left(\frac{\dot{f}_{gm}}{f_{gm}} + \frac{\dot{y}_{gm}}{y_{gm}} \right)$$

Thus, equation (B2) becomes:

$$\frac{dI}{dt} = \sum_{g}^{G} \sum_{m}^{M_g} s_{gm} \left(\frac{\dot{f}_{gm}}{f_{gm}} + \frac{\dot{y}_{gm}}{y_{gm}} \right) - \sum_{g=1}^{G} \sum_{m=1}^{M_g} \left(f_{gm} \frac{\dot{y}_{gm}}{y_{gm}} + \dot{f}_{gm} \ln(y_{gm}) \right)$$

Re-grouping the terms:

$$\frac{dI}{dt} = \sum_{g}^{G} \sum_{m}^{M_g} \left((s_{gm} - f_{gm}) \frac{\dot{y}_{gm}}{y_{gm}} \right) - \sum_{g=1}^{G} \sum_{m=1}^{M_g} \left((s_{gm} - f_{gm} \ln(y_{gm})) \frac{\dot{f}_{gm}}{f_{gm}} \right)$$

Since:

$$\dot{y}_{gm}/y_{gm} = (\dot{Y}_{gm}/Y_{gm}) - (\dot{P}_{gm}/P_{gm}) \text{ and} \tag{B4}$$

$$\frac{\dot{Y}_{gm}}{Y_{gm}} = \frac{\dot{A}_{gm}}{A_{gm}} + \left(\frac{\partial F_{gm}/\partial K_{gm}}{Y_{gm}} \right) \frac{\dot{K}_{gm}}{K_{gm}} + \left(\frac{\partial F_{gm}/\partial H_{gm}}{Y_{gm}} \right) \frac{\dot{H}_{gm}}{H_{gm}} \tag{B5}$$

dI/dt may easily be rewritten as equation (7) in the text.

Tsui

The within region component is:

$$WG(y) = \sum_g^G f_g I(y_g), \quad f_g = \sum_m^{M_g} f_{gm}$$

$$\frac{WG(y)}{dt} = \sum_g^G \left(f_g \frac{dI_g}{dt} + I_g \dot{f}_g \right), \quad I_g = I(y_g)$$

Using the results above:

$$\frac{dI_g}{dt} = \sum_m^{M_g} \left[(\hat{s}_{gm} - \hat{f}_{gm}) \frac{\dot{y}_{gm}}{y_{gm}} \right] + \sum_m^{M_g} \left[(\hat{s}_{gm} - \hat{f}_{gm}) \ln(y_{gm}) \right) \frac{\dot{\hat{f}}_{gm}}{\hat{f}_{gm}} \right]$$

where the notation is the same as in the text. Thus:

$$\frac{WG(y)}{dt} = \sum_g f_g \sum_m \left[(\hat{s}_{gm} - \hat{f}_{gm}) \frac{\dot{y}_{gm}}{y_{gm}} \right] + \sum_g \left\{ I_g \dot{f}_g + f_g \sum_m \left[(\hat{s}_{gm} - \hat{f}_{gm}) \ln(y_{gm}) \frac{\dot{\hat{f}}_{gm}}{\hat{f}_{gm}} \right] \right\}$$

$$= \sum_g f_g \sum_m \left[(\hat{s}_{gm} - \hat{f}_{gm}) \frac{\dot{y}_{gm}}{y_{gm}} \right] + \sum_g f_g \left\{ I_g \frac{\dot{f}_g}{f_g} + \sum_m \left[(\hat{s}_{gm} - \hat{f}_{gm}) \ln(y_{gm}) \frac{\dot{\hat{f}}_{gm}}{\hat{f}_{gm}} \right] \right\}$$

Again, using (B4) and (B5), the above expression is reduced to equation (9). The between region component is:

$$BG(y) = \sum_g^G f_g (\ln(\bar{y}) - \ln(\bar{y}_g))$$

Thus:

$$\frac{BG(y)}{dt} = \sum_g^G \left[f_g \left(\frac{\dot{\bar{y}}}{\bar{y}} - \frac{\dot{\bar{y}}_g}{\bar{y}_g} \right) + \dot{f}_g (\ln(\bar{y}) - \ln(\bar{y}_g)) \right]$$

$$= \frac{\dot{\bar{y}}}{\bar{y}} - \sum_g^G f_g \frac{\dot{\bar{y}}_g}{\bar{y}_g} + \left(\sum_g^G \dot{f}_g (\ln(\bar{y}) - \ln(\bar{y}_g)) \right)$$

$$= \frac{\dot{\bar{y}}}{\bar{y}} - \sum_g^G f_g \frac{\dot{\bar{y}}_g}{\bar{y}_g} + \left(\sum_g^G \dot{f}_g \ln(\bar{y}_g) \right)$$

where $\sum_g^G \dot{f}_g = 0$.

Since:

$$\frac{\dot{\bar{y}}_g}{\bar{y}_g} = \sum_m^{M_g} \hat{s}_{gm} \left(\frac{\dot{\bar{f}}_{gm}}{\hat{f}_{gm}} + \frac{\dot{y}_{gm}}{y_{gm}} \right)$$

$$\frac{BG(\mathbf{y})}{dt} = \sum_g^G \sum_m^{M_g} s_{gm} \left(\frac{\dot{f}_{gm}}{f_{gm}} + \frac{\dot{y}_{gm}}{y_{gm}} \right) - \sum_g^G f_g \sum_m^{M_g} \hat{s}_{gm} \left(\frac{\dot{\hat{f}}_{gm}}{\hat{f}_{gm}} + \frac{\dot{y}_{gm}}{y_{gm}} \right) - \left(\sum_g^G \dot{f}_g \ln(\bar{y}_g) \right)$$

$$= \sum_g^G \sum_m^{M_g} \left[(s_{gm} - f_g \hat{s}_{gm}) \frac{\dot{y}_{gm}}{y_{gm}} \right] + \sum_g^G \left\{ \sum_m^{M_g} \left[s_{gm} \frac{\dot{f}_{gm}}{f_{gm}} - f_g \hat{s}_{gm} \frac{\dot{\hat{f}}_{gm}}{\hat{f}_{gm}} \right] - \dot{f}_g \ln(\bar{y}_g) \right\}$$

where the notation as the same as in the text. Using (B4) and (B5), the above expression is reduced to equation (10).

References

Arellano, M. (2003). *Panel Data Econometrics*, Oxford University Press: Oxford.
Au, C. C., and V. Henderson (2004). 'Estimating Net Urban Agglomeration Economies with an Application to China', mimeo, Brown University: Providence, RI.
Brakman, S., H. Garretsen, and C. van Marrewijk (2001). *An Introduction to Geographical Economics*, Cambridge University Press: Cambridge.
Bramall, C. (2000). *Sources of Chinese Economic Growth, 1978–1996*. Oxford University Press.
Donnithorne, A. (1972). 'China's Cellular Economy: Some Economic Trends since the Cultural Revolution', *The China Quarterly* 52: 605–19.
Fujita, M., and D. Hu (2001). 'Regional Disparity in China, 1985–1994: The Effects of Globalization and Economic Liberalization', *The Annals of Regional Science* 35(1): 3–37.
Goodman, D. S. G. (2004). 'The Campaign to "Open Up the West": National, Provincial-level and Local Perspectives', *The China Quarterly* 178: 317–34.
Holz, C. A. (2004). 'Deconstructing China's GDP Statistics', *China Economic Review* 15(2): 164–202.
Im, K. S., M. H. Pesaran, and Y. Shin (2003). 'Testing for Unit Roots in Heterogeneous Panels', *Journal of Econometrics* 115(1): 53–74.
Jian, T., J. D. Sachs, and A. M. Warner (1996). 'Trends in Regional Inequality in China', *China Economic Review* 7(1): 1–21.
Keidel, A. (2001). 'China's GDP Expenditure Accounts', *China Economic Review* 12(4): 355–67.
Lardy, N. (1978). *Economic Growth and Distribution in China*, Cambridge University Press.
Lin, Y., and F. Cai (2003). *Zhongguo jingji: gaige yu fazhan* (Chinese Economy: Reform and Development), Zhongguo caizheng jingji chubanshe: Beijing.
—— —— Z. Li (1998). 'Zhongguo jingji zhuanxingqi de diqu chayi fenxi' (Analysis of China's Regional Inequality in the Period of Transition). *Jingji Yanjiu* (*Economic Research*) 6: 3–10.

Lyons, T. P. (1991). 'Interprovincial Disparities in China: Output and Consumption', *Economic Development and Cultural Change* 39(3): 471–506.

NBS (National Bureau of Statistics) (1987). *Guomin shouru tongji ziliao huibian, 1949–1985* (Collection of National Income Statistics), Zhonggou tongji chubanshe: Beijing.

—— (1997). *Zhonggou guonei shangchan zongzhi hesuan lishi ziliu* 1952–1995 (Gross National Product of China), Zhonggou tongji chubanshe: Beijing.

—— (1999). *Xin zhongguo wushinian tongji ziliao huibian* (Comprehensive Statistical Data and Materials on 50 Years of New China), Zhongguo tongji chubanshe: Beijing.

—— (2001a). *Zhongguo guding zichan touzi shudian* 2000 (A Statistical Compendium of Chinese Fixed Asset Investment), Tongji chubanshe: Beijing.

—— (2001b). *Quanguo guding zichan jiazhi chonggu xishu biaozhun mulu, 1984–2000* (A Catalogue of Parameters for the National Revaluation of Fixed Asset Investments 1984–2000), Zhongguo tongji chubanshe: Beijing.

—— (various issues). *Zhonggou laodong tongji nianjian* (Chinese Labour Statistical Yearbook), Zhongguo tongji nianjian: Beijing:

Naughton, B. (1988). 'The Third Front: Defence Industrialization in the Chinese Interior'. *The China Quarterly* (115): 351–86.

—— (2002). 'Provincial Economic Growth in China: Causes and Consequences of Regional Differentiation', in M-F. Renard (ed.), *China and Its Regions: Economic Growth and Reform in Chinese Provinces*, Edward Elgar: Cheltenham.

—— (2004). 'The Western Development Programme', in B. Naughton and D. Yang (eds) *Holding China Together: Diversity and National Integration in the Post-Deng Era*, Cambridge University Press.

Nehru, V., and A. Dhareshwar (1993). 'A New Database on Physical Capital Stock: Sources, Methodology and Results', *Revista de Analisis Economico* 8: 37–59.

Raiser, M. (1998). 'Subsidising Inequality: Economic Reforms, Fiscal Transfers and Convergence Across Chinese Provinces', *Journal of Development Studies* 34(3): 1–26.

Rawski, T. G. (2001). 'What is Happening to China's GDP Statistics', *China Economic Review* 12: 347–54.

Sen, A. (1997). *On Economic Inequality*, Clarendon Press: Oxford.

Shorrocks, A. (1984). 'Inequality Decomposition by Population Subgroups', *Econometrica* 52(6): 1369–85.

—— J. E. Foster (1987). 'Transfer Sensitive Inequality Measures', *Review of Economic Studies* 54(3): 485–97.

Tsui, K. Y. (1991). 'China's Regional Inequality, 1952–85', *Journal of Comparative Economics* 15: 1–21.

—— (1996). 'Economic Reform and Interprovincal Inequalities in China', *Journal of Development Economics* 50(2): 353–68.

Wang, S., and A. Hu (1999). *The Political Economy of Uneven Development. The Case of China*, M. E. Sharpe: Armonk.

Wong, C., C. Heady, and W. T. Woo (1995). *Fiscal Management and Economic Reform in the People's Republic of China*, Oxford University Press for ADB: Oxford.

Wooldridge, J. M. (2002). *Econometric Analysis of Cross Section and Panel Data*, MIT Press: Cambridge, MA.

Wu, H. X. (2001). 'China's GDP Level and Growth Performance: Alternative Estimates and the Implications', *Review of Income and Wealth* 46(4): 475–99.

Xu, X. (1999). *Zhongguo guomin jingji hesuan lilun fangfa yu shijian* (Theory and Practice of China's National Income Accounting), Zhongguo tongji chubanshe: Beijing.

—— (2000). 'Zhongwei jingji xuejia dui zhongguo jingji zengzhan de pinglun' (Reviews by Chinese and Foreign Economists on China's Economic Growth), *Caimao Jingji (Journal of Finance and Trade)* 2.

Young, A. (2000). 'Gold into Base Metals: Productivity Growth in the People's Republic of China during the Reform Period', NBER Working Paper 7856, National Bureau of Economic Research: Cambridge, MA.

6
Financial Development, Growth, and Regional Disparity in Post-Reform China

Zhicheng Liang

6.1 Introduction

Since economic reforms initiated in 1978, coastal China has witnessed rapid economic growth while the poor inland regions have been largely left behind, resulting in widening coastal–inland income disparity. The coast–interior dichotomy and the rising regional disparity have posed serious challenges to China's future development and attracted considerable attention (Wan et al. 2007). Various factors have been identified to be contributors to the rising disparity, such as fiscal decentralization (Tsui 1991); foreign direct investment (Lee 1994); geography reinforced by biased policies (Fleisher and Chen 1997; Démurger et al. 2001); and local protectionism (Young 2000). Zhang and Fan (2004) conclude that public investments in the less developed western regions help reduce regional inequality, whereas additional investments in the coastal and central regions tend to widen regional inequality. More recently, Wan et al. (2007) apply the newly developed regression-based decomposition technique to quantify contributions of various variables to regional inequality. They find that uneven distribution of domestic capital stock is the largest contributor to regional inequality and its relative contribution increases over time.

The finding of Wan et al. (2007) naturally leads to the policy recommendation of increasing capital formation in less developed areas. This, in turn, implies that unevenness in financial development may be a root cause of the rising regional inequality as financial development is a necessary condition for capital formation. The relationship between inequality and financial development, however, has been largely neglected in the literature despite recognition of the importance of financial deepening in promoting growth and productivity (see Hasan and Zhou 2006; Zhang et al. 2007).

This chapter intends to fill this gap in the literature by focusing on the role of financial development in affecting regional disparity in China. Towards this objective, we model the finance–growth relationship separately for coastal and inland China in order to guage any spatial differences in the impact of financial development on growth. As concluded later, financial development is found to significantly promote economic growth in coastal regions, but not the inland regions. Thus, uneven development in the financial sector of China (see section 6.3 below) has exacerbated China's regional disparity.

The rest of this chapter is organized as follows. The next section provides a brief literature review on the finance–growth relationship. Section 6.3 outlines recent trends of financial reforms and regional disparity in China. Econometric model and method of estimation are discussed in section 6.4. Empirical results are presented in section 6.5. Finally, this chapter concludes with section 6.6.

6.2 Financial Development and Economic Growth: A Brief Literature Review

The importance of financial development in determining economic growth has long been recognized (e.g. McKinnon 1973; Shaw 1973; King and Levine 1993a, b; Arestis and Demetriades 1997; Levine 1997; World Bank 2001; Green et al. 2005). A well functioning financial system is crucial for clearing and settling payments, pooling savings, facilitating resource allocation across space and time, pooling risk, and reducing information costs (Merton and Bodie 1995: 12–16). In addition, portfolio diversification and risking sharing via stock markets help accelerate economic growth (Levine 1991; Saint-Paul 1992).

Specifically, Greenwood and Jovanovic (1990) highlight two essential functions of financial intermediaries in promoting growth, in other words, collecting and analysing information of alternative investment projects, and increasing investment efficiency by allocating funds to projects with higher expected returns. According to Bencivenga and Smith (1991), the development of financial intermediaries can help enhance liquidity and mitigate idiosyncratic risk through risk diversification and pooling. These would help reduce households' unproductive reserve of liquid assets and facilitate the allocation of such reserve toward illiquid but more productive activities. Roubini and Sala-i-Martin (1992, 1995) argue that the financial sector is an 'easy' source for financing government's public budget. In order to increase revenue from money creation, governments subject to large income tax evasion may choose to increase seigniorage by repressing the financial sector and increasing inflation rates. Financial repression will therefore be associated with high tax evasion, low growth, and high inflation.

Empirical evidences on the relationship between finance and growth are mixed. Using 1960–89 data from 80 countries, King and Levine (1993a) find that financial development is positively associated with faster current and future rates of economic growth, physical capital accumulation, and economic efficiency improvement. Based on 1960–95 data of 63 countries, Beck et al. (2000) conclude that development of financial intermediary leads to faster economic growth and improved total factor productivity. Similar results can also be found in Levine et al. (2000). However, Demetriades and Hussein (1996) criticize the practice of heavily relying on cross-country regressions, where countries with very different experiences in economic growth and financial development are implicitly treated as homogeneous entities despite the fact that they have very different institutional characteristics and take on different development strategies and policies. This criticism is supported by Ram (1999), who compiled a large dataset covering 95 countries and found a negligible or weakly negative covariation between financial development and economic growth. When the sample of Ram is split into three subgroups (i.e. low, medium, and high growth countries), substantial parametric heterogeneity is observed for the finance–growth relationship. Andersen and Tarp (2003) use the data from Levine et al. (2000), but estimate the finance–growth model with both the full sample and regional subsamples. While a positive and significant relationship is confirmed with the full sample, the correlation is negative in the poorest countries. Within individual countries, different causal patterns exist. Further, estimation results are sensitive to the type of estimator used.

6.3 Financial Reforms and Regional Disparity in China

During the transition from a centrally planned economy to a market oriented economy, China's financial sector has experienced successive structural reforms and institutional changes. However, the development levels of financial sector are rather uneven across Chinese regions, which may have contributed to the increases in the income gap between the coastal and inland regions. To better understand the relationship between financial development and regional inequality, in this section we first present the evolution of China's financial reforms and regional disparity over the last two decades, and then investigate how uneven financial development may affect regional income inequality in post-reform China.

6.3.1 *Financial Reforms in China*

During the pre-reform period, a mono banking system prevailed in China, where the People's Bank of China (PBC) acted as an all inclusive financial institution. Since the late 1970s, when financial reforms began, substantial changes have occurred, notably including institutional reforms in the banking system and intensive development in the capital markets. In particular, four state owned specialized banks, serving different economic activities, were separated from the PBC, and the PBC was re-organized as the central bank of

China in the mid-1980s. These four state owned banks are: the Agricultural Bank of China (ABC), the China Construction Bank (CCB), the Bank of China (BOC), and the Industrial and Commercial Bank of China (ICBC). Meanwhile, two other institutions, the People's Insurance Corporation of China (CPIC) and the China International Trust and Investment Corporation (CITIC) were established. In addition, China's stock markets were set up and have experienced fast growth in the last decade although they remain relatively small in size and scale relative to the entire financial sector.

In 1995, the promulgation of the central bank law and the commercial bank law laid the basis for building a modern banking system in China. The central bank law legally confirms the independent status of the PBC. Similarly, the commercial bank law ensures and protects independent operations of commercial banks. Nevertheless, China's banking sector has been dominated by the state owned banks, resulting in a highly state monopolized and bank-based financial structure. Consequently, the banking system has become an important instrument for the government to finance its policy lending targets. This is largely responsible for a huge number of non-performing loans, which is also attributable to poor banking operation and management, soft budget constraints, and lack of efficient regulation and surveillance system. To solve the problem of non-performing loans, the central government injected a total of 270 billion yuan (US$32.6 billion) into the four state owned banks in 1998. In addition, four asset management corporations were established in 1999 to take over the 1.4 trillion yuan (US$169 billion) of non-performing loans and bad debts from the four banks.

Under China's commitment to the WTO, China's banking sector was opened up for foreign competition in 2006. Meanwhile, a series of new policy measures have been implemented to strengthen banks' corporate governance, to reduce non-performing loans, to improve banking efficiency, and to enhance their competitiveness. For example, in December 2003, the Chinese government injected US$45 billion of its foreign reserve into the Bank of China (BOC) and the China Construction Bank (CCB), to increase the adequacy of bank reserves and to strengthen the banks' capital base in preparation for their restructuring into joint stock commercial banks and stock market public listing. In an attempt to turn China's state owned banks into competitive and modern commercial banks, the joint stock system reforms of these state owned banks have been put on the agenda.

6.3.2 Regional Disparity in China

Since the implementation of economic reforms and the Open Door policies in 1978, China began its market oriented transformation. This was first experimented in Guangdong and Fujian provinces in the late 1970s with the establishment of four special economic zones (i.e. Shenzhen, Zhuhai, and Shantou in Guangdong province, and Xiameng in Fujian province). This was followed by the opening up of the coastal areas (i.e. the successive establishment of 14 coastal open cities, a number of coastal open development zone and open belt, and Hainan special economic zones) and then of the inland regions. Prioritizing coastal development was clearly stipulated in the government's sixth (1981–5) and seventh (1986–90) five-year plan. This is partly because the coastal regions are closer to international market and more advanced in terms of human capital and social development. As such they were expected to better take advantage of favourable policies to exploit comparative advantages and improve economic efficiency. These policies were formulated to promote international trade, attract foreign direct investment, and accelerate economic development. Preferential policies provided to the coastal regions and their inherent geographical advantages have promoted coastal growth, but largely left the inland region behind.[1] Figure 6.1 presents the coast–inland income ratio, which demonstrates widening regional disparity over the last two decades. Such a growing inequality has significantly contributed to the increases in aggregate inequality in post-reform China. A World Bank study (1997)

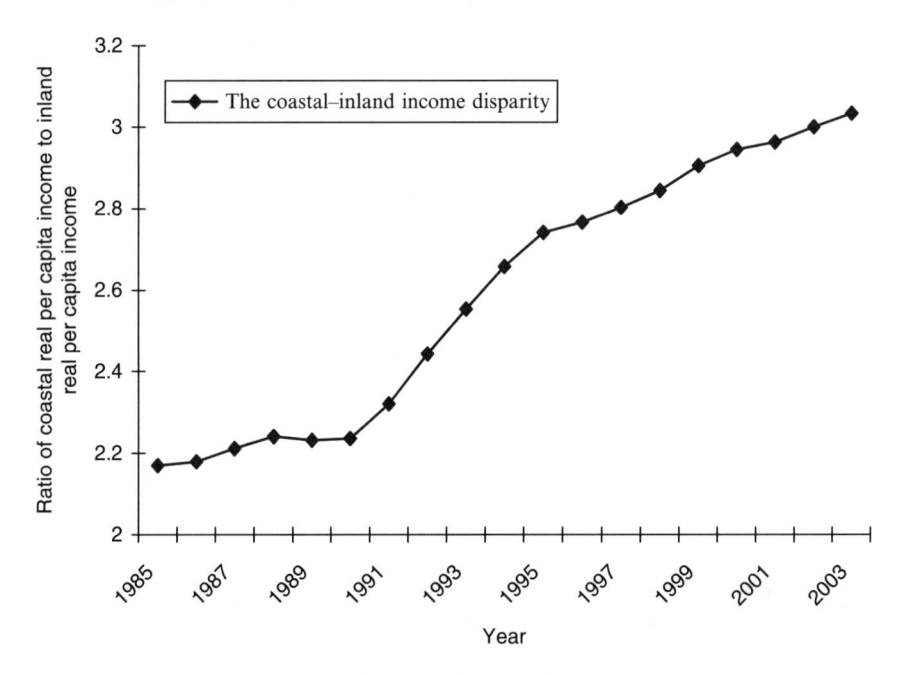

Figure 6.1: China's coastal–inland income disparity, 1985–2003

Source: China Statistical Yearbook (NBS various years), and author's calculations.

[1] Following the conventional classification, the Chinese provinces are divided into two groups, namely the coastal regions and the inland regions. The coastal region is composed of eleven provinces that are situated along the coast of China, including Beijing, Tianjin, Hebei, Liaoning, Shanghai, Jiangsu, Zhejiang, Fujian, Shandong, Guangdong, and Hainan. The remaining provinces are grouped as inland regions.

Financial Deepening and Inequality

shows that inter-provincial inequality accounted for almost one-quarter of total inequality in 1995 and one-third of the increase in inequality since 1985.

In order to lower regional disparity, the Chinese government has implemented various policies to develop the inland regions. In its ninth five-year plan, narrowing down regional income gaps was formally placed on the government agenda. By the end of the 1990s, the central government began to implement the strategy for the development of the western regions. The strategy consisted of accelerating infrastructure construction, especially in water conservancy; communications and transportation; tourism and broadcasting; ecological construction and environmental protection; adjusting industrial structure, giving priority to the industries that are consistent with comparative advantages of inland regions; stimulating technology innovation and enhancing education; and creating better environment to attract domestic and foreign investments. It is imperative to note, however, that without well-functioning financial systems, capital resources cannot be efficiently mobilized and intermediated to generate productive investments required to meet the need of economic growth. This is likely to be particularly severe for inland regions. As a result, efforts in reducing regional inequality may have been compromised due to possible capital misallocation in inland regions that were resulted from their poor financial systems.

6.3.3 Linking Financial Reforms and Regional Disparity in China

A number of recent studies have highlighted the important role of capital input variation in determining income inequality (Zhang and Zhang 2003; Wan 2004; Wan and Zhou, 2005). Variation in capital input has emerged as the most significant and increasingly important contributor to China's regional inequality, which constitutes almost 20 per cent of total inequality, making it the largest contributor since 1995 (Wan et al. 2007). It is known that the less developed areas suffer from capital scarcity, resulting in serious development bottleneck in both investment and production. It is in this context that financial markets are expected to play a pivotal role in narrowing down gaps in capital possession across regions by breaking the vicious circle existing in capital formation and accumulation in the less developed regions.

Meanwhile, despite more than two decades of economic reforms, the level of China's domestic financial integration is still quite low, and China's capital markets remain seriously fragmented. There is evidence that profit rates and returns to capital differ widely across Chinese localities and sectors (Boyreau-Debray 2003; World Bank 2003; Boyreau-Debray and Wei 2004). Moreover, real interest rates significantly differ from one province to another (Guillaumont Jeanneney and Hua 2002; Zhang and Wan 2002). Worse still, financial integration is found to have decreased in the 1990s, resulting in greater fragmentation of capital markets in China (Boyreau-Debray and Wei 2004; Zhang and Tan 2004).

Given the fragmentation of China's capital market, the development level of local financial intermediaries may play an important role in determining local economic performance (Boyreau-Debray 2003). This requires and justifies our separate modelling of the finance–growth relationship in coastal and inland China.[2]

6.4 Model, Estimation Technique, and Data Sources

In this section, we attempt to assess the extent to which financial development may affect regional disparity in China using 1991–2003 provincial data. Towards this end, we will specify and estimate growth models for coastal and inland China, with the growth rate of real per capita income ($GD\dot{P}PC$) as the dependent variable. The explanatory variables include: (1) development level of financial sector to be denoted by *FDEV*, defined as the natural logarithm of real per worker output in financial sector;[3] (2) the growth rate of real per capita fixed asset investment (*INV*); (3) openness (*OPEN*), defined as the ratio of total exports to GDP; (4) education (*EDU*), measured by the proportion of population with junior secondary school and higher level of schooling; (5) non-state sector development (*NSOE*), measured by the ratio of fixed investment in non-state sector to total fixed investment. Panel A of Table 6.1 presents descriptive statistics for these variables and panel B reports correlations between the variables. We find that financial development (*FDEV*) is significantly correlated with GDP per capita growth. Meanwhile, the correlation between openness (*OPEN*) and growth is also significant. In addition, investment growth (*INV*) and non-state sector development (*NSOE*) are found to be positively and significantly correlated with economic growth.

Our empirical model can be written as follows:

$$GD\dot{P}PC_{i,t} = \alpha + \beta_1 INITGDPPC_{i,t-1} + \beta_2 FDEV_{i,t} + \beta_3 INV_{i,t} \\ + \beta_4 OPEN_{i,t} + \beta_5 EDU_{i,t} + \beta_6 NSOE_{i,t} + \mu_i + \varepsilon_{i,t} \quad (1)$$

where subscripts i and t index provinces and time respectively; *INITGDPPC* denotes the natural logarithm of initial value of real per capita income.

Model (1) may suffer from endogeneity problem as bi-directional causality between finance and growth has been suggested in recent empirical works. Thus, instrumental variable or generalized method of moment (GMM) is the appropriate estimation technique. In the present study, we use the GMM

---

[2] Regional variations in informal finance may also have important effects on regional disparity in China. Unfortunately, data on informal finance are not available at the provincial level.
[3] More specifically, we have: $FDEV = \ln(FGDP/FEMP)$, where *FGDP* is the gross domestic product of the financial sector, and *FEMP* is the total number of staff and workers employed in the financial sector.

Financial Deepening and Inequality

Table 6.1: Descriptive statistics and correlation

	Mean	Std Dev.	Minimum	Maximum	Observation	
Panel A: Descriptive statistics						
GDṖPC	0.0988	0.0373	−0.033	0.381	377	
FDEV	10.4517	0.6041	8.6900	12.3819	377	
INV	0.1404	0.1465	−0.2201	0.7647	377	
OPEN	0.1407	0.1629	0.0224	1.0165	377	
EDU	0.4638	0.1250	0.1914	0.8091	377	
NSOE	0.4150	0.1465	0.0877	0.7086	377	
Panel B: Correlation						
	GDṖPC	FDEV	INV	OPEN	EDU	NSOE
GDṖPC	1					
FDEV	0.2262***	1				
INV	0.5039***	−0.0412	1			
OPEN	0.2293***	0.4656***	−0.0164	1		
EDU	0.0152	0.3481***	−0.1252**	0.3313***	1	
NSOE	0.2092***	0.2887***	−0.0213	0.3086***	0.3331***	1

Notes: (1) GDṖPC: Growth rate of real per capita income; FDEV, the indicator of financial development; INV: growth rate of real per capita fixed asset investment; OPEN: trade openness; EDU: the level of education development; NSOE: the level of non-state sector development. (2) *** significant at the 1% level; ** significant at the 5% level; * significant at the 10% level.
Source: Author's calculations.

system estimators for panel data, which was proposed by Arellano and Bond (1991) and further developed by Blundell and Bond (1998). To illustrate this technique, assume the following simple model:

$$y_{i,t} = \gamma_1 EX_{i,t} + \gamma_2 EW_{i,t} + \mu_i + \varepsilon_{i,t}, \quad i=1,\ldots,N;\ t=1,\ldots,T \quad (2)$$

where EX is a vector of strictly exogenous covariates; EW denotes a vector of predetermined covariates and endogenous covariates (predetermined variables are assumed to be correlated with past errors, while endogenous ones are assumed to be correlated with past and present errors); μ_i is the unobserved group level effect, and ε_{it} is the error term with the assumption that μ_i and ε_{it} are independent for each i over all t, and that there is no autocorrelation in the ε_{it}.

In order to eliminate the unobservable group-specific effects, equation (2) can be differenced:

$$y_{i,t} - y_{i,t-1} = \gamma_1(EX_{i,t} - EX_{i,t-1}) + \gamma_2(EW_{i,t} - EW_{i,t-1}) + (\varepsilon_{i,t} - \varepsilon_{i,t-1}) \quad (3)$$

It is possible to estimate (3) with the instrumental–variable approach, where the predetermined and endogenous variables in first differences are instrumented with appropriate lags of the specified variables in levels, while strictly exogenous regressors are first differenced for use as instruments in (3). However, the efficiency of this instrumental approach can be weak since lagged levels are often poor instruments for first differences. Therefore, Blundell and Bond (1998) propose the System-GMM approach, in which the first differenced equation

(3) is combined with the levels equation (2) so that a more efficient 'system estimator' can be obtained. For the first differenced equation, the instruments are the same as that discussed above. For the levels equation, predetermined and endogenous variables in levels are instrumented with appropriate lags of their own first differences while the strictly exogenous regressors can directly enter the instrument matrix for use in the levels equation. The GMM method has a number of advantages. It exploits the time series variation in the data, accounts for unobserved individual specific effects, and provides better control for potential endogeneity of all explanatory variables (Beck et al. 2000).

The data to be used cover 29 Chinese provinces over the period of 1991–2003.[4] The primary sources of our data are from *China Statistical Yearbook* (NBS various years), *China Population Statistics Yearbook* (NBS various years), and *Comprehensive Statistical Data and Materials on 50 Years of China* (NBS 1999), *Accounting Data and Materials on Gross Domestic Product in China: 1952–1995*, plus individual provincial statistical yearbooks.

6.5 Empirical Results

We first estimate our regression model using data from all provinces, and then re-examine the model using data from the coastal regions and inland regions separately. Empirical results are presented in Table 6.2. For each regression, we test model specification with the Hansen test for overidentifying restrictions, and with the Arellano-Bond test for second order serial correlation. The test results show that none of the estimated models suffers second order serial correlation or is misspecified, implying validity of our instruments.

Focusing on column 1 of Table 6.2 that shows results for all Chinese provinces, financial development is found to be significantly and positively associated with economic growth. In other words, regions with higher level of financial development tend to enjoy faster economic growth. Consistent with a priori expectations, highly significant and positive coefficient estimates are obtained for fixed asset investment (*INV*) and trade openness (*OPEN*). In addition, both the development of non-state sector (*NSOE*) and education enhancement (*EDU*) help accelerate economic growth in China.

Turning to the finance–growth nexus for coastal and inland regions, we find that financial development (*FDEV*) enters positively and significantly into the growth model (see column 2 of Table 6.2) for coastal provinces. However, for inland regions, we find a rather weak correlation between finance and growth (see column 3 of Table 6.2). More importantly, the weak relationship is statistically insignificant. Therefore, our empirical results suggest that financial

---

[4] Tibet has been excluded from our sample due to data incompleteness; Chongqing is merged with Sichuan province.

Financial Deepening and Inequality

Table 6.2: Financial development and economic growth in China

	All Chinese provinces	Coastal provinces	Inland provinces
$INITGDPPC_{i,t-1}$	−0.0376***	−0.0605***	−0.0396
	(0.001)	(0.006)	(0.001)
$FDEV_i$	0.0131**	0.0304***	−0.0001
	(0.017)	(0.006)	(0.985)
$INV_{i,t}$	0.1445***	0.1638***	0.0695***
	(0.000)	(0.000)	(0.000)
$OPEN_{i,t}$	0.0791***	0.0739***	−0.0585
	(0.003)	(0.006)	(0.278)
$EDU_{i,t}$	0.1022***	0.0976	0.1340***
	(0.003)	(0.117)	(0.001)
$NSOE_{i,t}$	0.0686**	0.0444	0.0550***
	(0.024)	(0.321)	(0.008)
Constant	0.1412**	0.1609	0.2936***
	(0.042)	(0.308)	(0.000)
Hansen Test of over identifying restrictions	Chi2=27.45 Prob.>Chi2=0.195	Chi2=9.98 Prob.>Chi2=0.987	Chi2=14.88 Prob.>Chi2=0.629
Arellano-Bond test for the second order serial correlation	Z=1.09 Prob.>Z=0.274	Z=0.64 Prob.>Z=0.522	Z=−0.48 Prob.>Z=0.629
Observations	377	143	234
Provinces	29	11	18

Notes: (1) $GD\dot{P}PC$: Growth rate of real per capita income; $INITGDPPC$: the natural logarithm of initial value of real per capita income; $FDEV$: the indicator of financial development; INV: growth rate of real per capita fixed asset investment; $OPEN$: trade openness; EDU: the level of education development; $NSOE$: the level of non-state sector development. (2) ***: significant at the 1% level; **: significant at the 5% level; *: significant at the 10% level. (3) For all regressions, p-values are presented in parentheses. Dependent variable = $GD\dot{P}PC_{i,t}$: the growth rate of real per capita income.
Source: Author's calculations.

development significantly promotes economic growth in coastal regions but not in inland regions. This absence of finance–growth nexus in the less developed regions has helped widen the coastal–inland income gap in China.

Similar patterns of coast–interior differences are found for the relationship between trade openness and economic growth. The coefficient of *OPEN* is positive and statistically significant in the growth regression for the coastal regions. However, for the inland regions, it is insignificant. Thus, trade has been a driving force for economic growth for the coastal regions, but not for the inland regions. These results are consistent with Fu (2004).

6.6 Conclusion

A number of recent studies show that regional variations in capital inputs have become the largest contributor to China's regional inequality, and the contribution of the capital inputs to regional inequality is likely to continue to increase unless governments establish effective financial markets to assist poor regions to obtain capital (Wan 2004; Wan and Zhou 2005; Wan et al. 2007). Thus, the development of financial markets in China, especially in less-developed regions and poor areas, is expected to help curb the rising regional disparity.

In this chapter, we investigate the relationship between financial sector development and regional economic growth in China. Our empirical results show that financial development significantly promotes economic growth in coastal regions but not in inland regions. The absence of finance–growth linkage in inland provinces must have contributed to China's regional disparities. These results have important implications for China's future development. First, effective policy measures have to be made to strengthen the financial sector in inland regions, so as to reduce income disparity among regions. Second, more efforts are required to improve the efficiency of capital allocation by creating more flexible financial systems and promoting domestic financial integration. Finally, to accelerate banking commercialization in China, there is an urgent need to improve banking regulatory and supervisory systems and to strengthen governance infrastructure through institutional reforms in accounting, auditing, and information disclosure system. These reforms can help reduce financial sector vulnerability, facilitate economic restructuring, and promote inclusive growth.

Reference

Andersen T. B., and F. Tarp (2003). 'Financial Liberalization, Financial Development and Economic growth in LDCs', *Journal of International Development* 15(2): 189–209.

Arellano, M., and S. Bond (1991). 'Some Tests of Specification for Panel Data: Monte Carlo Evidence and an Application to Employment Equations', *Review of Economic Studies* 58: 277–97.

Arestis, P., and P. Demetriades (1997). 'Financial Development and Economic Growth: Assessing the Evidence', *Economic Journal* 107: 783–99.

Beck, T., R. Levine, and N. Loayza (2000). 'Finance and The Sources of Growth', *Journal of Financial Economics* 58: 261–310.

Bencivenga, V. R., and B. D. Smith (1991). 'Financial Intermediation and Endogenous Growth', *Review of Economic Studies* 58(2): 195–209.

Blundell, R., and S. Bond (1998). 'Initial Conditions and Moment Restrictions in Dynamic Panel Data Models', *Journal of Econometrics* 87(1): 115–43.

Boyreau-Debray, G. (2003). 'Financial Intermediation and Growth: Chinese Style', World Bank Policy Research Working Paper 3027, World Bank: Washington, DC.

—— S. Wei (2004). 'Can China Grow Faster? A Diagnosis of the Fragmentation of Its Domestic Capital Market', IMF Working Paper 04/76, International Monetary Fund: Washington, DC.

Demetriades, P. O., and K. A. Hussein (1996). 'Does Financial Development Cause Economic Growth? Time-series Evidence from 16 Countries', *Journal of Development Economics* 51: 387–411.

Démurger, S., J. D. Sachs, W. T. Woo et al. (2001). 'Geography, Economic Policy and Regional Development in China', CID Working Paper 77, Center for International Development at Harvard University: Cambridge, MA.

Fleisher, B. M., and J. Chen (1997). 'The Coast–Noncoast Income Gap, Productivity, and Regional Economic Policy in China', *Journal of Comparative Economics* 25(2): 220–36.

Fu, X. (2004). 'Limited Linkages from Growth Engines and Regional Disparities in China', *Journal of Comparative Economics* 32: 148–64.

Green, C. J., C. Kirkpatrick, and V. Murinde (2005). *Finance and Development: Surveys of Theory, Evidence and Policy*, Edward Elgar: Cheltenham.

Greenwood, J., and B. Jovanovic, (1990). 'Financial Development, Growth, and the Distribution of Income', *Journal of Political Economy* 98(5): 1076–107.

Guillaumont Jeanneney, S., and P. Hua (2002). 'The Balassa–Samuelson Effect and Inflation in the Chinese Provinces', *China Economic Review* 13: 134–60.

Hasan, I., and M. Zhou (2006). 'Financial Sector Development and Growth: The Chinese Experience', WIDER Research Paper 2006/85, UNU-WIDER: Helsinki.

King, R. G., and R. Levine (1993a). 'Finance and Growth: Schumpeter Might Be Right', *Quarterly Journal of Econmics* 108: 717–37

—— —— (1993b). 'Finance, Entrepreneurship, and Growth: Theory and Evidence', *Journal of Monetary Economics* 32: 513–42.

Lee, J. (1994). 'Regional Differences in the Impact of the Open Door Policy on Income Growth in China', *Journal of Economic Development* 19(1): 215–34.

Levine, R. (1991). 'Stock Markets, Growth, and Tax Policy', *Journal of Finance* 46: 1445–65.

—— (1997). 'Financial Development and Economic Growth: View and Agenda', *Journal of Economic Literature* 35: 688–726.

—— N. Loayza, and T. Beck (2000). 'Financial Intermediation and Growth: Causality and Causes', *Journal of Monetary Economics* 46(1): 31–77.

McKinnon, R. L. (1973). *Money and Capital in Economic Development*, Brookings Institution: Washington, DC.

Merton, R. C., and Z. Bodie (1995). 'A Conceptual Framework for Analysing the Financial Environment', in D. B. Crane et al. (eds), *The Global Financial System, a Functional Perspective*, Harvard Business School Press: Cambridge, MA.

Ram, R. (1999). 'Financial Development and Economic Growth: Additional Evidence', *Journal of Development Studies* 35(4): 164–74.

Roubini, N., and X. Sala-i-Martin (1992). 'Financial Repression and Economic Growth', *Journal of Development Economics* 39(1): 5–30.

—— —— (1995). 'A Growth Model of Inflation, Tax Evasion, and Financial Repression', *Journal of Monetary Economics* 35: 275–301.

Saint-Paul, G. (1992). 'Technological Choice, Financial Markets and Economic Development', *European Economic Review* 36(4): 763–81.

Shaw E. S. (1973). *Financial Deepening in Economic Development*, Oxford University Press: New York.

Tsui, K. (1991). 'China's Regional Inequality, 1952–1985', *Journal of Comparative Economics* 15(1): 1–21.

Wan, G. H. (2004). 'Accounting for Income Inequality in Rural China', *Journal of Comparative Economics* 32(2): 348–63.

Wan, G. H., and Z. Y. Zhou (2005). 'Income Inequality in Rural China: Regression-based Decomposition Using Household Data', *Review of Development Economics* 9(1): 107–20.

—— M. Lu, and Z. Chen (2007). 'Globalization and Regional Inequality in China: Empirical Evidence from within China', *Review of Income and Wealth* 53(1): 35–59.

World Bank (1997). *Sharing Rising Incomes: Disparities in China*, World Bank: Washington, DC.

—— (2001). *Finance for Growth: Policy Choices in a Volatile World*, Oxford University Press: New York.

—— (2003). *China: Promoting Growth with Equity*, World Bank: Washington, DC.

Young, A. (2000). 'The Razor's Edge: Distortions and Incremental Reform in the People Republic of China', *Quarterly Journal of Economics* CXV: 1091–135.

Zhang, J., G. H. Wan, and Y. Jin (2007). 'The Financial Deepening–Productivity Nexus in China: 1987–2001', WIDER Research Paper 2007/08, UNU-WIDER: Helsinki.

Zhang, X., and S. Fan (2004). 'Public Investment and Regional Inequality in Rural China', *Agricultural Economics* 30: 89–100.

—— K. Tan (2004). 'Blunt to Sharpened Razor: Incremental Reform and Distortions in the Product and Capital Markets in China', Development Strategy and Governance Division Discussion Paper 13, International Food Policy Research Institute: Washington, DC.

—— K. Zhang (2003). 'How does Globalization Affect Regional Inequality within a Developing Country? Evidence from China', *Journal of Development Studies* 39: 47–67.

Zhang, Y., and G. H. Wan (2002). 'Household Consumption and Monetary Policy in China', *China Economic Review* 13: 27–52.

7
Spatial Convergence in China: 1952–99

Patricio A. Aroca, Dong Guo, and Geoffrey J. D. Hewings

7.1 Introduction

The study of regional income convergence is gaining more attention as scholars explore the impacts of globalization on income disparity among countries. The issue is stressed within countries because of the accumulating evidence which suggests that increased economic growth has generated increasing regional income inequalities, especially in many developing economies, see Mossi et al. (2003) and Aroca et al. (2006). In the case of China, regional income convergence has generated a great deal of attention because it would appear that regional income disparities have increased at the same time as the country has been growing rapidly after the economic reform. For example, in 1980 the per capita GDP of Shanghai, the richest region in China, was 11.6 times that of Guizhou, one of the poorest regions in the western part of the country, while in 1952 the difference was 7.5 times. However, by 1999, the difference had increased to 12.5 times.

If one considers that the country is at an early state of development, the situation in China confirms the inverted-U shape relationship between regional development and regional income disparity described by Kuznets (1955) for different countries and Williamson (1965) when he investigated the same issue in the USA. In other words, when regions grow, income inequality first increases, and then they decrease over time. Hence, it would appear that increased regional income disparities may be an unavoidable characteristic at the earlier stage of regional development. Since initial concentrations of income in certain geographic regions were attributed to unequal natural resource endowments, Williamson (1965) argues that these concentrations attracted selective skilled labour migration from the peripheral regions and generated rapid income growth in the core regions. This led to the widening differentials in per capita income between the core and the peripheral regions. Over time, however, a diffusion of income generating factors leads to the subsequent slowing down and eventual decline in regional income inequality. This is reflected in the convergence prediction of growth and income from the perspective of neoclassical economics in the sense that poor regions will grow faster and catch up with the richer regions. Therefore, neoclassical economic theory predicts the converging of regional income if all regions share similar steady states.

The new economic geography represented by Krugman (1991) and Fujita et al. (1999) stress the importance of geography by proposing a regional scheme of development pattern similar to Williamson (1965), in terms of a core–periphery regional dichotomy but with an explanatory emphasis on increasing returns to scale and the resulting agglomeration of economic activity. In contrast to the convergence perspective, they argue that regions with natural advantage tend to grow faster than other regions over a relatively long period because of the effect of increasing returns to scale and resulting agglomeration effects. Under such circumstances, a long lasting regional income disparity will be the expected result (Rey 2001).

China, as a geographically diverse country, exhibits vast differences among regions in terms of natural endowments. Undisputedly, the coastal area (the eastern part of the country) enjoys the advantage of climate and geographical accessibility compared to inland regions. What is more, the coastal area was able to capture significant advantages when the country started to implement a more liberal trade policy. In this case, the coastal region can be regarded as the core area while the inland area can be considered as the periphery area. In fact, within the framework of neoclassical economic theory, there has been some research on regional income convergence in China. Whether or not a trend of regional income convergence exists is still disputed, but most analyses acknowledge the importance of the divergence between the coastal and non-coastal area (i.e. the core region and the periphery region), especially in the current period of reform.

For example, based on the Solow growth model, Weeks and Yao (2003) find conditional convergence in both the pre-reform (1953–78) and reform (1978–97) period with the convergence speed in the reform era being much faster than during the pre-reform time. Applying two methods for detecting convergence (σ-convergence and β-convergence), Jian et al. (1996), on the other hand, find that China's real income convergence has emerged strongly since the 1978 reform, a period strongly associated with the adoption of market economy and openness to external trade. However, they note a divergence in regional income between the coastal and non-coastal regions since 1990. Using an augmented Solow growth model, Chen and Fleisher (1996) measure regional inequality and project that overall regional inequality in the near term is likely to decline modestly but the coast/non-coast income difference is likely to increase somewhat. Fujita and Hu (2001) analyse the problem by relating it to the process of globalization and economic agglomerations in China. They argue that

Spatial Convergence

income disparity between the coastal area and the interior is increasing, while there was a trend towards convergence within the coastal area. Zhang et al. (2001) and Wang and Ge (2004) suggest that China's regions, especially the eastern and the western regions, have converged to their own specific steady states over the past 40 years, while the differences between the east and the west regions have widened. Yao and Zhang (2001) propose a production model to explain regional divergence based on the hypothesis that in developing countries where technology and capital are scarce, initial economic growth depends on the economic spillover from growth centres. Furthermore, they provide alternative tests to demonstrate that regional divergence can be associated with different geo-economic clubs. In contrast to some previous studies, they find that regions in China did not converge in the reform period.

However, one element missing from the analysis of regional income convergence in China is that researchers have not considered the influence of spatial effects even though issues of different spatial scales have been considered (Ying 1999; Yao and Zhang 2001; Zhang et al. 2001; Lu and Wang 2002; Bhalla et al. 2003; among others). In fact, it has been widely acknowledged that the role of spatial effects has been ignored in regional income convergence analyses. So far, only Bao et al. (2002) and Ying (2003) integrate spatial effects in their analyses of regional growth in China. Rey and Montouri (1999) point out those spatial effects have been largely ignored in regional analyses dealing with a cross-section or panel data of regional or national data. Sachs (1997) stresses the importance of spatial effects in the sense that physical geography itself is a factor in terms of the distance to markets, variations in topography, climate, and other geographical variables that may determine factor productivity. Krugman (1991) and Puga (1999) emphasize the importance of spatial effects within the frame of the 'new economic geography' by illuminating that two regions with similar economic characteristics in different locations may end up with different economic structures and performance profiles. Benabou (1993) and Durlauf (1996) highlight the importance of space by taking into account neighbouring spillover effects in which space is understood as a relative term.

The importance of spatial effects in economic analysis has recently captured attention with regard to regional income convergence (for example, Armstrong 1995; Fingleton 1999; López-Bazo et al. 1999; Rey and Montouri 1999; Rey 2001, 2004; Bickenbach and Bode 2003; Le Gallo and Ertur 2003; Le Gallo et al. 2003; Mossi et al. 2003; Le Gallo 2004; among others). Parametric estimation for β- and σ-convergence (Barro and Sala-i-Martin 1995) incorporating spatial effects has been widely used. Note that empirically β-convergence is usually investigated by regressing the growth rate of per capita GDP on initial levels after the addition of other variables while maintaining the steady-state of each region as constant. A negative regression coefficient is interpreted as an indication of conditional β-convergence, implying that each region converges to its own steady state. The concept of σ-convergence refers to a reduction of dispersion within the GDP per capita cross-sectional distribution over time. It is usually measured as the standard deviation of log GDP per capita of the sample regions (Le Gallo 2004). As Quah (1993) points out, both β- and σ-convergence cannot provide insights into the behaviour of the entire regional income distribution over time, since the two convergence measures could not provide reliable inference on the dynamics of convergence (Rey 2004). Rey (2001), Aroca et al. (2006), and Baumont et al. (2006) show the impact on the parametric approach results of taking the spatial interaction or spatial heterogeneity into account. On the other hand, Quah (1993, 1997, 2000) and Rey (2000, 2004) suggest that the complete distribution of the growth rate should be studied, instead of the mean and variance that are featured in the usual approaches.

At least three topics are relevant in our application of a non-parametric approach. The first is the *persistence* of the process (Durlauf 1996), referring to the measurement of stability of a region's position in the regional income distribution across the country. *Mobility* is also considered in this study and is the complement of persistence, and is taken to represent the change of a region's position in the income distribution. It is also expected that the shape of the regional income distribution will be influenced by economic policy over time. In particular, two hypotheses on the regional growth process will be explored: one is *polarization* (Esteban and Ray 1994; Quah 1997), and the other one is *stratification* or *club convergence* (Chatterji and Dewhurst 1996; Quah 1997). According to Quah (1997: 2), it is important to show how the shape of the distribution has changed over time

> What also matters is that these features have a natural interpretation in terms of polarization: those portions of the underlying population of economies collecting in the different peaks may be said to be polarized, one group versus another. More generally, if more than two peaks emerged, it might be natural to call the situation stratification.

Two non-parametric tools commonly used to study the distribution of a random variable and its mobility across time are the Markov transition matrix approach and stochastic densities (Silverman 1986). The former measures persistence or mobility among a discrete number of states, while the later estimates the probability density function in a continuous framework. Based on Quah, non-parametric estimation is recognized (Quah 1996; Fingleton 1999; Bickenbach and Bode 2003; Mossi et al. 2003; Le Gallo 2004; Rey 2004). Concerned about the reliability of the estimated transition probabilities that may influence the income distribution, Bickenbach and Bode (2003) propose a series of reliability tests, which includes tests of time homogeneity, time independence, spatial homogeneity, and spatial independence in order to evaluate the estimated transition probabilities.

While previous literature recognizes the importance of space and geography in China's growth process, none has used techniques which had been tailored specifically to take spatial effects into account. In this chapter, we expect to fill that gap and to report new information derived from the application of spatial techniques in the analysis of income convergence in China. The chapter is structured as follows: the next section introduces the data sources used, followed by a description of the methodology applied. The applications to China are reported in the subsequent section. Discussion on the results is given next and the last section concludes.

7.2 Data

The source data for the regional GDP and population figures used in this chapter are derived from the National Bureau of Statistics (NBS 1999), which provides the data series from 1952 to 1999. It is possible to calculate the GDP per capita at 1999 prices in Renminbi (RMB) yuan, and then convert these to 1999 US dollar value according to the official exchange rate given in the *China Statistical Yearbook 2000*. Some administrative changes have taken place in China. For example, the current Hainan province was separated from Guangdong province in 1985 while Chongqing was annexed from Sichuan province in 1996. Therefore, in order for the data to be comparable, the figure for Guangdong after 1985 includes the nominal GDP of both Guangdong and Hainan; similarly, Sichuan and Chongqing were combined after 1996 to obtain the figure for Sichuan. Data for some provinces and auto-administrative districts such as Tibet, Taiwan, and Hong Kong were not available for the entire period considered. Therefore, these are excluded from the study.

7.3 Results

7.3.1 *Changes in GDP Inequalities*

Earlier studies recognize the importance of the space and geography in China's growth process. However, none has used techniques that have been specifically tailored to take spatial effects into account. In this chapter we hope to fill that gap and report the additional information derived from the application of the spatial techniques to the analysis of growth in China.

7.3.2 Spatial Univariate Measure

The spatial dependence measure for each period t is provided by a global statistic such as Moran's I, which can be represented by equation (1).

$$I_t = \frac{n}{S} \frac{\sum_{i=1}^{n}\sum_{j=1}^{n} w_{ij} z_i z_j}{\sum_{i=1}^{n} z_i^2}, \forall \text{ all } t = 1, 2, \ldots, T \qquad (1)$$

where n is the number of regions; w_{ij} are the elements of a binary contiguity matrix $W(n \times n)$, taking the value 1 if regions i and j share a common border and 0 if they do not; and z_i and z_j are normalized[1] vectors of the log of per capita GDP of regions i and j, respectively. Values around 1 represent strong and positive (clustering of similar values) spatial dependence, whereas values around -1 show negative spatial correlation (clustering of different values).

In Figure 7.1, the Moran's I shows that there is an increasing spatial interaction among the Chinese regions. This pattern become stronger in the 1990s; it is statistically significant[2] and has been rapidly growing since 1978, the year coinciding with the start of market reforms in China (Jian et al. 1996). It is also clear from Figure 7.1 that during 1952–78 there is no evidence of spatial clustering in the growth process of the regions. On the other hand, there is a high standard deviation, particularly in 1960 and the mid-1970s. One can note that the standard deviation, which is currently used to measure sigma convergence in the literature based on the Solow-Swan model (Barro and Sala-i-Martin 1995), has a different behaviour pattern to Moran's I statistics, implying that they measure different concepts. During the period 1965–78, termed as the cultural revolution by Jian et al. (1996), there is an important increment in the standard deviation of the regional GDP per capita that again can be interpreted as evidence of the sigma convergence. This is said by Jian et al. (1996: 9–10) to be the 'anti-agricultural bias of the cultural revolution' which in the next decade tends to decrease the standard deviation. However, there is again a large increment in the 1990s that follows the Moran's I pattern very closely. On the other hand, in this period the Moran's I statistic is stable. This indicates that there was a low level of spatial interaction among the regions, a fact that can be associated with one of the five crucial economic components of the Cultural Revolution mentioned by Jian et al. (1996), i.e. the regions were forced into near autarky.

---

[1] The $z_i = \ln(GDP_{it}/GDP_t)$ denotes the logarithm of the GDP per capita of region i in period t, (GDP_{it}), normalized by the country sample mean of the same variable, GDP_t (de la Fuentes 1997).
[2] The statistical significance was calculated according to Anselin and Bera (1998).

Spatial Convergence

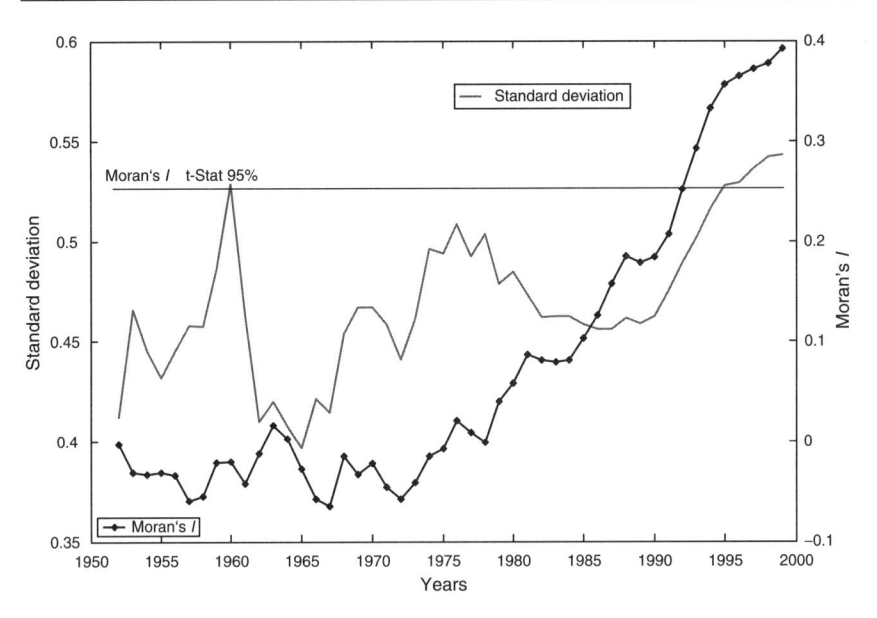

Figure 7.1: Moran's *I* for regional GDP per capita, China 1952–99
Source: Compiled by the authors based on data from NBS (various years).

Though Moran's *I* provides important information about the aggregate spatial growth process taking place in China, it does not help to pinpoint where spatial linkages were strong. Moran scatterplots and local Moran index (Anselin 1995) are two techniques that can be used for this purpose. The Moran scatterplot is used to provide a graphical presentation of the spatial distribution of regional GDP per capita for three periods: 1957, 1978, and 1999.

Figures 7.2, 7.3, and 7.4, having the same axes, show the three time points associated with the evolution of the spatial pattern of the relative GDP per capita in China. Figure 7.2 shows that in 1957 there was no relation between the regional GDP per capita and its spatial lag, which is calculated as the average of its neighbours' GDP per capita. Figure 7.3 shows that in 1978 there is more dispersion compared to 1957, but still no spatial pattern can be deducted. However, in both graphs, certain regions—Shanghai, Beijing, Sichuan, Heilongjiang—have an above average GDP per capita in both periods. In addition, these regions in 1978 are bordering on areas with below national average GDP, implying rich regions with poor neighbours. Figure 7.4 shows the 1999 situation, in which the emerging positive relation between regional GDP per capita and its spatial lag can be noted.

One interesting point here is the situation of Shanghai and Beijing. In 1978 these cities are in the IV quadrant, indicating that their neighbours, on average, have a GDP per capita lower than the national average, but in 1999 they

Aroca, Guo, and Hewings

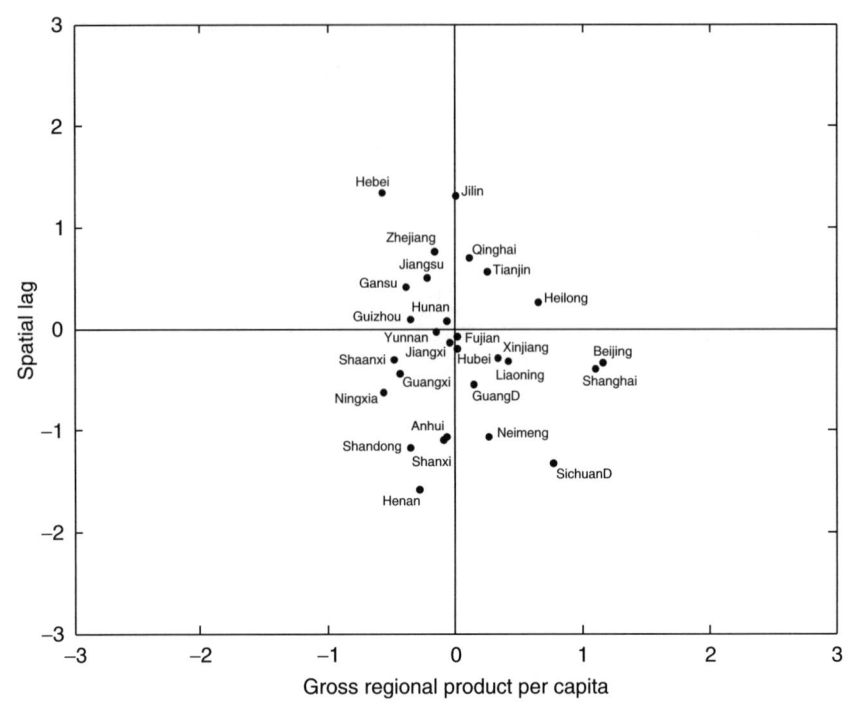

Figure 7.2: Moran scatterplot for regional GDP per capita, China 1957
Source: Compiled by the authors based on data from NBS (various years).

are in the I quadrant, implying that their neighbours, on average, have increased their GDP per capita above the national average. It is a clear indication that these regions are a part of the explanation for the high growth of the Moran's *I* in the last decade and the creation of the so-called 'hot spots' (i.e. economic zones growing faster than the rest of the country).

On the other hand, 14 provinces are located in the III quadrant, indicating regions having a GDP per capita below the national average and bordered with neighbouring regions with similar characteristic, i.e. depressed zones. For more precise results, we calculate the local Moran:

$$I_i = \frac{z_i \sum_j w_{ij} z_j}{\sum z_i^2 / n} \qquad (2)$$

Local indicators of spatial association (*LISA*) can be interpreted as an indicator of spatial cluster, using the indicator itself as the basis of a test where

Spatial Convergence

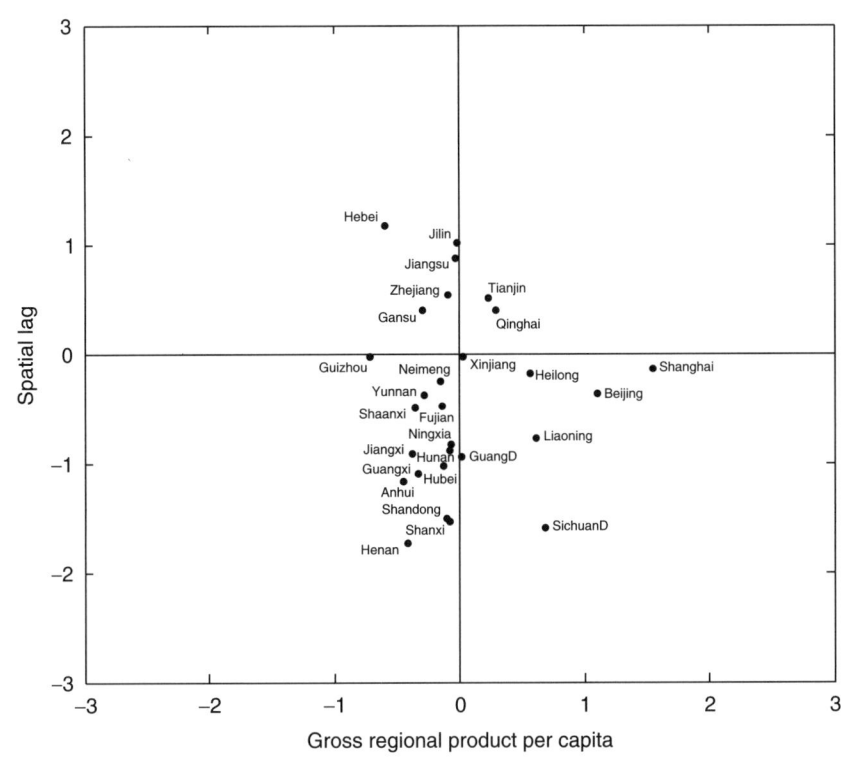

Figure 7.3: Moran scatterplot for regional GDP per capita, China 1978
Source: Compiled by the authors based on data from NBS (various years).

the null hypothesis is the lack of spatial dependence. These local clusters can be identified for those observations in which the *LISA* is significantly different from zero. However, *LISA* distributions are usually unknown. Anselin (1995) suggests a method to generate an empirical distribution for *LISA* consisting of the conditional randomization of the vector z_j. It is conditional in the sense that z_i remains fixed. The reasoning behind the randomization procedure lies in the need to assess the statistical significance of the linkage of one region to its neighbours. Generation of a region's *LISA* distribution is inferred by the permutation of the neighbours that surround region *i* (obviously, region *i* is not used in the permutation). This empirical distribution provides the basis for a statement on the extremeness of the observed *LISA* (Aroca et al. 2006). When we put these results on the map a clear spatial pattern emerges indicating that the coast regions are conforming to 'hot spots' in China (see Figure 7.5).

133

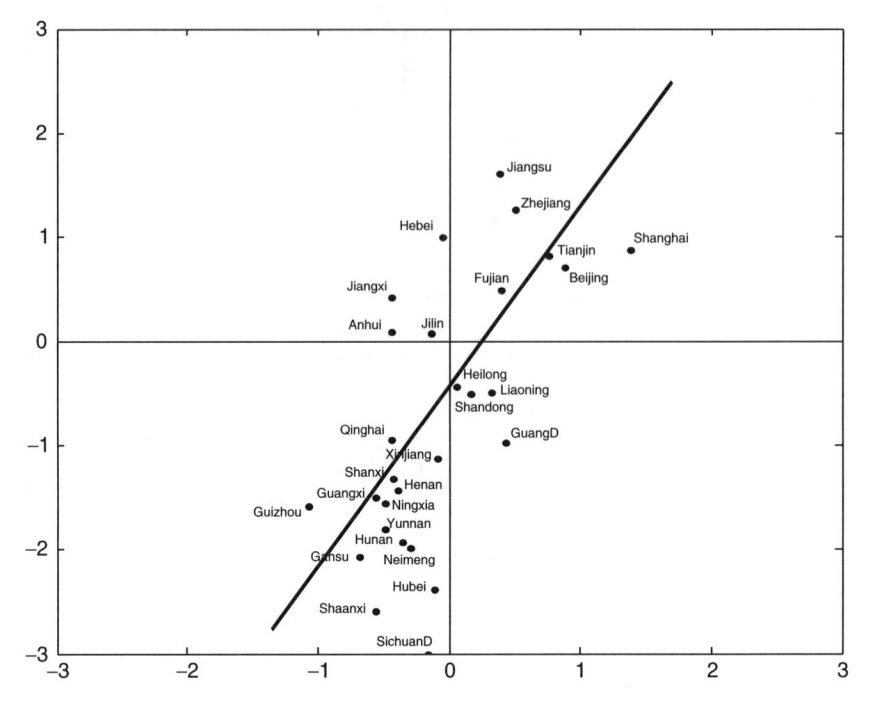

Figure 7.4: Moran scatterplot for regional GDP per capita, China 1999
Source: Compiled by the authors based on data from NBS (various years).

7.3.3 Distributional Description of GDP Inequalities

In the previous section we have shown that the interaction of space was important in China's growth process in the last decade, therefore all the parametric approaches that were mentioned in the section on literature should take this fact into account in the last period of analysis, because we could say that the results are at least inefficient and they may even be biased. In addition, Jian et al. (1996), Zhang et al. (2001), and Fujita and Hu (2001) obtain their results according to the traditional parametric approach of convergence based on the mean (conditional and unconditional) and the variance of growth, which assumes that this will be a good representation if each observation of the growth rate is identical, independently distributed and follows a normal distribution. However, if the assumption of independency or normality does not hold, then this instrument could lead to erroneous conclusions.

Rey and Montouri (1999), Aroca et al. (2006), and Baumont et al. (2006) show the impact on the parametric approach results of taking account the

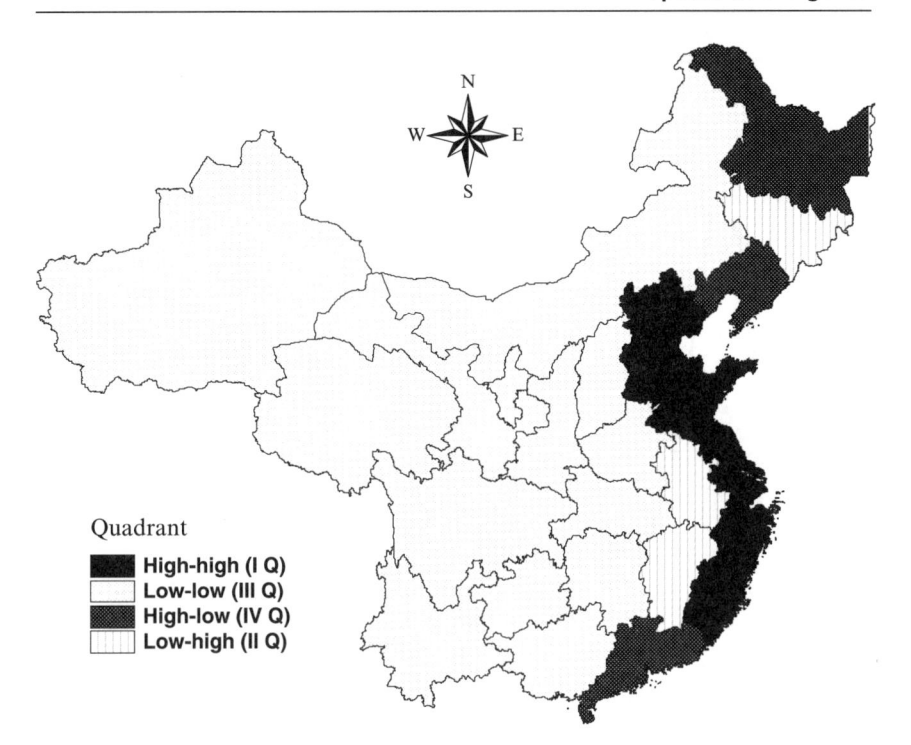

Figure 7.5: Moran scatterplot map for regional GDP per capita, China 1999

Note: This is a partial map of China including only the regions for which data were available.
Source: Compiled by the authors.

spatial interaction or spatial heterogeneity. On the other hand, Quah (1993, 1997, and 2000), López-Bazo et al. (1999) and Rey (2000, 2001) suggest studying the complete distribution of the growth rate instead of the mean and variance, as is done in the non-parametric approach.

To study the Chinese growth process with special focus on the concepts described above, we examine the behaviour pattern of the distribution of income per capita across the provinces of the country. According to Quah (1997: 2), it is important to show how the shape of the distribution has changed over time

> What also matters is that these features have a natural interpretation in terms of polarization: those portions of the underlying population of economies collecting in the different peaks may be said to be polarized, one group versus another. More generally, if more than two peaks emerged, it might be natural to call the situation stratification.

Two tools are commonly used to study the distribution of a random variable and their mobility across time: Markov transition matrix and stochastic

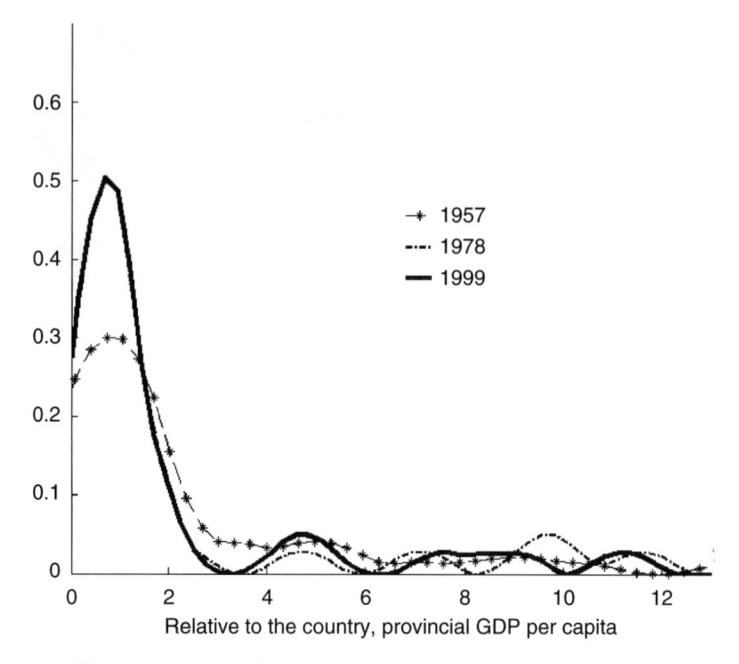

Figure 7.6: Chinese empirical density, 1957, 1978, and 1999

Source: Compiled by the authors based on data from NBS (various years).

densities (see Silverman 1986). The former is believed to measure persistence or mobility among a discrete number of states, while the latter was built to estimate the probability density function in a continuous framework.

First, we estimate the densities function for different years in order to determine how this function has changed over time. Figure 7.6 shows the empirical densities functions for 1957, 1978, and 1999. Quah (1997) uses the term 'emerging twin peaks' to describe a situation where there is a clustering of the very rich, a clustering of the very poor, and a disappearance of the middle income class. In Figure 7.6, the year 1957 clearly showed a one peak distribution with a long flat right tail. However, for the year 1978, there were several peaks emerging in the tail of the empirical density distribution for China. According to the previous definition, this could be called *stratification*. It means that a group of Chinese province are converging to different levels relative to the country's GDP per capita.

The second peak for the year 1999 emerged stronger than in 1978, while the other peaks in the distribution tail were fewer and smaller in 1999 than in 1978. If this trend continues into the future, we can predict that Quah's hypothesis of two emerging peaks to hold. In contrast, Rey (2000) finds for the USA that the change in the distribution over the years was dramatic, 'going from the twin peaks distribution of 1929 to a more unimodal distribution' in 1994. In addition, the direction of this distribution change was favourable, and increased the income of the poorer states and relatively decreased the income of the richer. On the other hand, China exhibits the opposite: it is moving from a unimodal distribution to a multimodal distribution, and possibly to a bi-modal in the future.

Another interesting point is that in 1957 the unimodal distribution peaked around 1, with a high concentration ranging from 0 to 3. However in 1978 and 1999, this first peak was less than 1 and the first range went from 0 to around 2. On the other side, maximum significant values of the distribution were around 6, while in 1978 and 1999 these values were almost around 12, showing an increase in variance and a difference between the poor and the rich.

7.3.4 Conditioning by Space

In the previous section we standardized the provincial GDP with the national average. Quah (1993) proposes alternative conditions that could help to better understand the GDP evolution. In this section we condition the income per capita distribution with space, which means that we standardize the GDP per capita of each province by the average per capita GDP of its neighbours. If there is no spatial effect on the distribution of GDP per capita, then we should find a situation similar to the one described in the previous section. In contrast, if spatial effects exist and differences in income are smoothly distributed across space, then we should find a one peak distribution.

Figure 7.7 shows changes over time. In 1957 there was just a small rise in the distribution indicating the existence of a zone where the difference between the GDP per capita of those provinces and their neighbours was five times larger. However, the main peak was centred on one. In 1978, even though the distributional characteristics remained unchanged, the difference was seven times larger than before. In 1999, the distribution had a stratification shape, indicating three different zones; zones in which the difference of the per capita GDP between the provinces and its neighbours is about seven times greater, zones with differences of about five times greater, and finally zones where there is no significant difference. Lin and Liu (2005) state that a global strategy for the whole country could have significant heterogeneity in pushing growth across provinces due to large differences in their endowments.

7.3.5 Transitions in the Distribution

Once we have established that there have been changes in the distribution of provincial GDP per capita, we would like to find the specific provinces that have

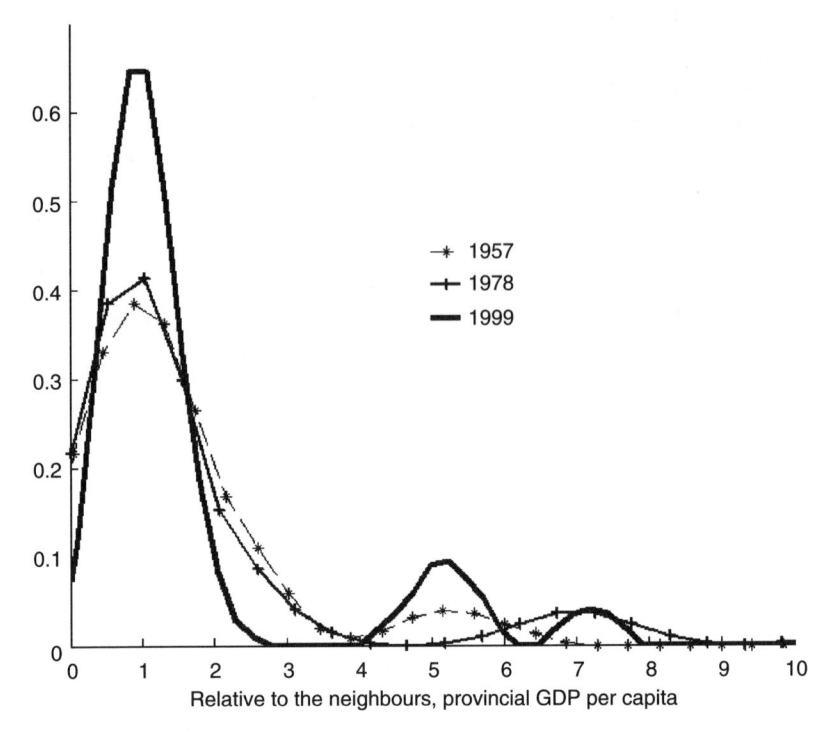

Figure 7.7: Chinese empirical density conditioned by space, 1957, 1978, and 1999

Source: Compiled by the authors based on data from NBS (various years).

been affected and the direction of change. We have two tools for studying transition in distribution: the Markov transition matrix and the stochastic kernel. First, we estimate the Markov transition matrix (*MTM*) conditioned by space as in Rey (2000). We define five feasible income levels for each province: poor (*P*), low income (*L*), medium income (*M*), upper income (*U*), and rich (*R*).

The matrix is calculated based on changes over intervals of four years. Table 7.1 shows that there is much more mobility among the lower income provinces than the high income ones. For example, if a province was rich in the initial stage, the probability of being rich at the end of the period is almost 1, regardless of the economic standing of its neighbours. However, if a province's origin state is poor, then there is more than 40 per cent chance of it achieving the lower income level if its neighbouring provinces are at the upper income level. But if the neighbouring regions are poor, the province has only about 10 per cent chance of reaching the lower income level. In general, the Markov transition matrix shows that there is some transition especially in the low end of the distribution, however the possibility is

Spatial Convergence

Table 7.1: Conditioned by space

t0	Lag	Obs.	P	L	M	U	R
	P	74	89.2%	10.8%	0.0%	0.0%	0.0%
	L	78	75.6%	24.4%	0.0%	0.0%	0.0%
P	M	79	87.3%	12.7%	0.0%	0.0%	0.0%
	U	15	60.0%	40.0%	0.0%	0.0%	0.0%
	R	0	0.0%	0.0%	0.0%	0.0%	0.0%
	P	32	18.8%	78.1%	3.1%	0.0%	0.0%
	L	101	13.9%	73.3%	12.9%	0.0%	0.0%
L	M	89	10.1%	70.8%	19.1%	0.0%	0.0%
	U	25	0.0%	68.0%	32.0%	0.0%	0.0%
	R	0	0.0%	0.0%	0.0%	0.0%	0.0%
	P	26	0.0%	15.4%	65.4%	19.2%	0.0%
	L	68	0.0%	13.2%	73.5%	13.2%	0.0%
M	M	92	2.2%	20.7%	69.6%	7.6%	0.0%
	U	60	0.0%	0.0%	91.7%	8.3%	0.0%
	R	0	0.0%	0.0%	0.0%	0.0%	0.0%
	P	0	0.0%	0.0%	0.0%	0.0%	0.0%
	L	15	0.0%	0.0%	40.0%	60.0%	0.0%
U	M	113	1.8%	0.0%	8.0%	90.3%	0.0%
	U	119	0.0%	0.0%	0.8%	95.8%	3.4%
	R	0	0.0%	0.0%	0.0%	0.0%	0.0%
	P	15	0.0%	0.0%	0.0%	0.0%	100.0%
	L	18	0.0%	0.0%	5.6%	0.0%	94.4%
R	M	109	0.0%	0.0%	0.0%	0.0%	100.0%
	U	101	0.0%	0.0%	0.0%	8.9%	91.1%
	R	3	0.0%	0.0%	0.0%	0.0%	100.0%

Source: Authors' calculation.

higher at the larger income level of distribution. Nevertheless, these results could be the outcome of the limited definition for income levels, because there is no further category beyond rich or lower category after poor. This fact could, thus, account for the larger mobility among the middle income levels and lower mobility in the extreme levels.

An alternative way to deal with this problem is the stochastic kernel. Figures 7.8 and 7.9 show the results for China's GDP per capita conditioned by space. The stochastic kernel shows a high persistence with some small variability at high levels of relative income, which confirms the results from the Markov transition matrix with respect to the persistence. On the other hand, the contour shows that the neighbouring effect is strong, given that the shape of the contour is biased to the lower part of the main diagonal. This implies that the provinces in comparison to the national level are in a worse position than in comparison to neighbours.

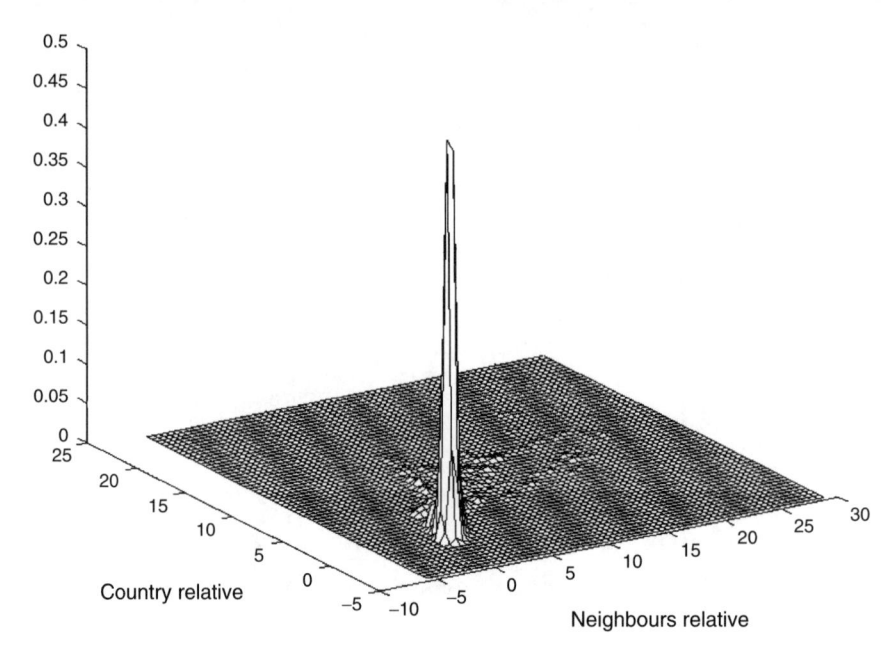

Figure 7.8: Stochastic kernel for Chinese regions relative to the per capita GDP of the neighbouring provinces

Source: Compiled by the authors based on data from NBS (various years).

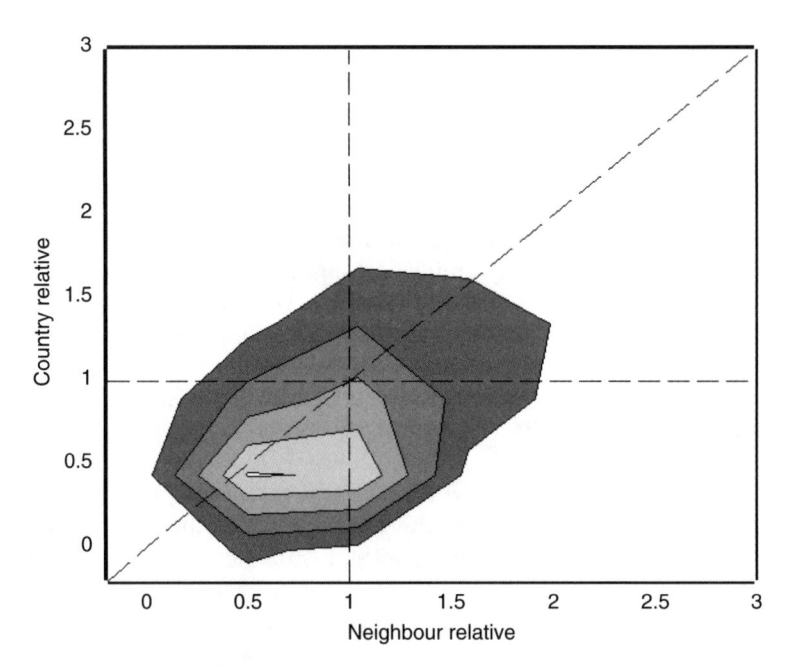

Figure 7.9: Contour for Chinese regions relative to the neighbours' per capita GDP

Source: Compiled by the authors based on data from NBS (various years).

7.4 Conclusions

The purpose of this chapter has been to examine the regional income convergence process in China by using non-parametric methods that take into account the influence of spatial interaction. The methods include density function and Markov chain analysis integrated with spatial analysis. The chapter shows that in China there has been an increase over the last 20 years in the spatial dependence of the per capita GDP. Consequences of the spatial effect play an important role, as is shown by the positive impact that neighbouring effect has on regional income distribution. The dynamics of the process provide evidence that China's regional income distribution has moved from convergence to stratification and from stratification to polarization. This is revealed in the widening income difference between the coastal (core) and the inner land (periphery) regions. Especially the strong probability of the rich staying rich and the poor staying poor may sustain this trend, resulting in long-lasting regional income disparities between the core and the periphery regions. China's regional income distribution may prove to be a confirmation of the new economic geography's prediction, namely a sharp polarization in the presence of high interregional transportation costs.

References

Anselin, L. (1995). 'Local Indicators of Spatial Association—LISA', *Geographical Analysis* 27: 93–116.

—— A. K. Bera (1998). 'Spatial Dependence in Linear Regression Models with and Introduction to Spatial Econometrics', in A. Ullah and D. Giles (eds.), *Handbook of Applied Economic Statistics*, Marcel Ockker: New York.

Armstrong, H. W. (1995). 'Convergence among the Regions of the European Union', *Papers in Regional Science* 74: 143–52.

Aroca, P., M. Bosch, and G. J. D. Hewings (2006). 'Regional Growth and Convergence in Chile 1960–1998: The Role of Public and Foreign Direct Investment', in P. Aroca and G. J. D. Hewings (eds), *Structure and Structural Change in the Chilean Economy*, Palgrave Macmillan: Basingstoke.

Bao, S., G. H. Chang, J. D. Sachs, and W. T. Wood (2002). 'Geographic Factors and China's Regional Development under Market Reforms, 1978–1998', *China Economic Review* 13: 89–111.

Barro, R., and X. Sala-i-Martin (1995). *Economic Growth*, MIT Press: Cambridge, MA.

Baumont, C., C. Ertur, and J. Le Gallo (2006). 'The European Regional Convergence Process, 1980–1995: Do Spatial Regimes and Spatial Dependence Matter?' *International Regional Science Review* 29(1): 3–34.

Benabou, R. (1993). 'Workings of a City: Location, Education, and Production', *Quarterly Journal of Economics* 108(3): 619–52.

Bhalla, A., S. Yao, and Z. Zhang (2003). 'Regional Economic Performance in China', *Economics of Transition* 11(1): 25–39.

Bickenbach, F., and E. Bode (2003). 'Evaluating the Markov Property in Studies of Economic Convergence', *International Regional Science Review* 26(3): 363–92.

Chatterji, M., and J. Dewhurst (1996). 'Convergence Clubs and Relative Economic Performance in Great Britain', *Regional Studies* 30(1): 31–40.

Chen, J., and B. M. Fleisher (1996). 'Regional Income Inequality and Economic Growth in China', *Journal of Comparative Economic* 22(2): 141–64.

de la Fuentes, A. (1997). 'The Empirics of Growth and Convergence: A Selective Review', *Journal of Economic Dynamics and Control* 21(1): 23–73.

Durlauf, S. (1996). 'A Theory of Persistent Income Inequality', *Journal of Economic Growth* 1: 75–93.

Esteban, J., and D. Ray (1994). 'On the Measurement of Polarization', *Econometrica* 62(4): 819–51.

Fingleton, B. (1999). 'Estimates of Time to Economic Convergence: An Analysis of Regions of the European Union', *International Regional Science Review* 22(1): 5–34.

Fujita, M., and D. Hu (2001). 'Regional Disparity in China 1985–1994: The Effects of Globalization and Economic Liberalization', *The Annals of Regional Science* 35(1): 3–37.

—— P. Krugman, and A. J. Venables (1999). *The Spatial Economy: Cities, Regions and International Trade*, MIT Press: Cambridge, MA.

Jian, T., J. D. Sachs, and A. M. Warner (1996). 'Trends in Regional Inequality in China', *China Economic Review* 7(1): 1–21.

Krugman, P. (1991). 'Increasing Returns and Economic Geography', *Journal of Political Economy* 99(3): 483–99.

Kuznets, S. (1955). 'Economic Growth and Income Inequality', *American Economic Review* 45(1): 1–28.

Le Gallo, J. (2004). 'Space–time Analysis of GDP Disparities among European Regions: a Markov Chains Approach', *International Regional Science Review* 27(2): 138–63.

—— C. Ertur (2003). 'Exploratory Spatial Data Analysis of the Distribution of the Regional per capita GDP in Europe, 1980–1995', *Papers in Regional Science* 82: 175–202.

—— —— C. Baumont (2003). 'A Spatial Econometric Analysis of Convergence across European Regions, 1980–1995', in B. Fingleton (ed.), *European Regional Growth*, Springer Verlag: New York.

Lin, J. Y., and P. Liu (2005). 'Development Strategies and Regional Income Disparities in China', East Asian Bureau of Economic Research Development Economics Working Papers 656.

López-Bazo, E., E. Vayà, A.J. Mora, and J. Suriñach (1999). 'Regional Economic Dynamics and Convergence in the European Union', *The Annals of Regional Science* 33: 343–70.

Lu, M., and E. Wang (2002). 'Forging Ahead and Falling Behind: Changing Regional Inequalities in Post-reform China', *Growth and Change* 33(1): 42–71.

Mossi, M. B., P. Aroca, I. J. Fernandez, and C. R. Azzoni (2003). 'Growth Dynamics and Space in Brazil', *International Regional Science Review* 26: 393–418.

NBS (National Bureau of Statistics) (1999). *Comprehensive Statistical Data and Material on 50 years of New China*, China Statistics Press: Beijing.

—— (various years). *China Statistical Yearbook*, China Statistics Press: Beijing.

Puga, D. (1999). 'The Rise and Fall of Regional Inequalities', *European Economic Review* 43: 303–34.
Quah, D. (1993). 'Empirical Cross-Section Dynamics in Economic Growth', *European Economic Review* 37: 426–34.
—— (1996). 'Empirics for Economic Growth and Convergence', *European Economic Review* 40: 1353–75.
—— (1997). 'Empirics for Growth and Distribution: Stratification, Polarization and Convergence Clubs', CEP Discussion Paper 324, Centre for Economic Performance, London School of Economics and Political Science: London.
—— (2000). 'Cross-country Growth Comparison: Theory to Empirics', CEP Discussion Paper 442, Centre for Economic Performance, London School of Economics and Political Science: London.
Rey, S. (2000). 'Spatial Analysis of Regional Income Inequality', REAL Discussion Paper, University of Illinois and the Federal Reserve Bank of Chicago: Urbana and Chicago.
—— (2001). 'Spatial Empirics for Economic Growth and Convergence', *Geographical Analysis* 33: 195–214.
—— (2004). 'Spatial Dependence in the Evolution of Regional Income Distributions', in M. F. Goodchild, and D. G. Jannelle (eds), *Spatially Integrated Social Science*, Oxford University Press: Oxford.
—— B. D. Montouri (1999). 'US Regional Income Convergence: A Spatial Econometric Perspective', *Regional Studies* 33(2): 143–56.
Sachs, J. (1997). 'Geography and Economic Transition' (mimeo), CID/HIID Research on Geography and Economic Growth, Center for International Development at Harvard University: Cambridge, MA.
Silverman, B. W. (1986). *Density Estimation for Statistics and Data Analysis*, Chapman & Hall: New York.
Wang, Z., and Z. Ge (2004). 'Convergence and Transition Auspices of Chinese Regional Growth', *The Annuals of Regional Science* 38: 727–39.
Weeks, M., and J. Y. Yao (2003). 'Provincial Income Convergence in China, 1953–1997: A Panel Data Approach', *Econometrics Reviews* 22: 59–77.
Williamson, J. G. (1965). 'Regional Inequality and the Process of National Development: A Description of the Patterns', *Economic Development and Cultural Change* 13(2): 2–84.
Yao, S., and Z. Zhang (2001). 'On Regional Inequality and Diverging Clubs: A Case Study of Contemporary China', *Journal of Comparative Economics* 29(3): 446–84.
Ying, L. (1999). 'China's Changing Regional Disparities during the Reform Period', *Economic Geography* 75: 59–70.
—— (2003). 'Understanding China's Recent Growth Experience: A Spatial Econometric Perspective', *The Annals of Regional Science* 37: 613–28.
Zhang, Z., A. Liu, and S. Yao (2001). 'Convergence of China's Regional Incomes', *China Economic Review* 12(2–3): 243–58.

8
China's Regional Inequality in Innovation Capability: 1995-2004

Peilei Fan and Guanghua Wan

8.1 Introduction

It has been widely acknowledged that innovation has become an increasingly important determinant of economic growth (Schumpeter 1942; Barsberg 1987; Malecki 1987; Fargerberg 1994; Fargerberg et al. 1997; Malecki 1997). OECD (1988, 2001) documents the contributions of innovation to GDP growth for several of its member countries. For instance, Japan's miraculous development after World War II was fuelled by its technical progress. Especially in the 1960s, technological advances constituted 6.1 percent of Japan's GDP growth, with the remaining 3.5 percent attributable to labour and capital inputs. Similarly, a substantial proportion of growth in the USA can be attributed to technological progress, particularly in the late 1990s, when the USA led the world in information and communication technology (ICT).

Recognizing the importance of innovation, the Chinese government has been instrumental in directing the country towards a knowledge economy. Recent policy initiatives include the National High-tech Research and Development Plan (863 Plan), the National Basic Sciences Initiative (973 Plan), and the Torch programme that specifically aims at facilitating commercialization of scientific research outcomes. Furthermore, the government has set up 53 national high-tech parks to attract foreign high-tech firms and to encourage the development of domestic high-tech companies. These policy initiatives have undoubtedly promoted innovation activities in China. According to a recent study, technological progress contributed more than 40 percent of the remarkable economic growth rate in China during the period 1981-2000 (Fan and Watanabe 2006).

Given the predominant role of innovation in economic growth in China and the fast rising regional inequality in China (Wan et al. 2006, 2007), two issues deserve special research attention. First, it is interesting to examine innovation inequality in China. This has been undertaken in terms of patent application (Sun 2000). Second, more importantly, it is crucial to analyse sources or contributing factors of innovation inequality. Although studies exist, which focus on determinants of innovation capabilities in China and elsewhere (Guerrero and Sero 1997), no previous attempt has been made to quantify contributions of various determinants to the inequality of innovation. The typical regression model in the current literature (e.g. Sun 2000; Guerrero and Sero 1997) can only be used to gauge the impacts of independent variables on the level of innovation, not the inequality of innovation. The latter requires the regression-based inequality decomposition of Wan (2002, 2004).

This chapter represents a first attempt to measure and analyse factor contributions to China's regional inequality in innovation capability from 1995 to 2004. To be more precise, we intend to focus on the following research questions: What was the status of China's regional inequality in innovation capability and how did it change from 1995 to 2004? How much did the relevant factors contribute to the level of innovation capability and how much did they contribute to the regional inequality in innovation capability?

The plan of the chapter is as follows. In section 8.2, we will review the limited literature on innovation inequality in China and provide preliminary data analysis. This is followed by measurement of innovation inequality in China in section 8.3. Section 8.4 presents regression analysis as well as decomposition of innovation inequality. The summary and policy recommendations are provided in section 8.5.

8.2 Literature Review and Preliminary Data Analysis

Few studies explored innovation inequality in China with the exception of Sun (2000, 2003), who used a primary index, top-five index, top-ten index, and coefficient of variation to indicate spatial pattern of innovation. Sun (2000) found that patents in China were highly clustered in the east–coastal region and the inland provinces, although the degree of spatial concentration declined during 1985–95. When other indicators of innovation such as new products sales and R&D spending were used, the spatial concentration is found to be on the rise in the 1990s (Sun 2003).

Sun (2003) classifies the provinces into two groups and applies the logistic regression to model the cluster membership resulting from the classification. Provinces in cluster 1 spend more on in-house R&D, and those in cluster 2 spend more on imported technologies. The four independent variables for the logistic regression are GDP per capita, size of S&T (science and technology) staff, ratio of international trade to GDP, and a coast–inland dummy variable. However, the model did not work well as none of the independent variables were significant.

Innovation capability can be measured by different indexes such as R&D inputs, patent counts, patent citations, and new product announcement. In this chapter, we follow Audretsch and Feldman (2004: 2713–39) and use patent data as a proxy measure for innovation capability.[1] Hagedoorn and Cloodt (2003) find that statistical overlap between various innovativeness indicators is strong and any of these indicators, including patent, may be used to measure innovation capability. In fact, patent is generally accepted as one of the most appropriate measures for innovation capability (Mansfield 1986; Barsberg 1987; Griliches 1990).

In China, the State Bureau of Intellectual Properties examines and certifies different types of patents. The invention patents refer to those that show 'novelty' and have been developed to the point where they can be utilized in industry. The utility model patents are creations or improvements relating to the form, construction, or fitting of an object, with a lower technical requirement than invention patents. The design patents refer to original designs relating to the shape, pattern, colour or a combination thereof of objects.[2]

Relying on *China Statistical Yearbook on Science and Technology* (1995–2005) and *China Statistical Yearbook* (1994–2005),[3] we compiled a set of data on innovation and relevant determinants at the regional (by region, in this chapter we mean east, central, and west China) or provincial level. Table 8.1 displays numbers of granted patents in 1995 and 2004, including numbers of invention, utility model, and design. The table reveals that eastern China dominated certified patents, especially Beijing, Liaoning, Shandong, and Guangdong. In sharp contrast, central and particularly west China fell behind. To deal with bias in population distribution, we also report regional per capita patents relative to the national average, denoted by R. Thus a region with $R > 1$ performs better in creating patents than the national average, and vice versa.

Eliminating bias in population distribution, the R values for a particular year indicate innovation inequality between regions in China. Over time, eastern China increased its R value from 1.60 in 1995 to 1.82 in 2004, which means that the gap between the eastern regions and others had expanded. Looking into individual regions, some provinces/cities (e.g. Beijing, Tianjin, Heilongjiang, and Shaanxi) underwent significant drop while others (such as Shanghai, Guangdong, and Zhejiang) experienced substantial gains in R values. In 2004, all provinces in eastern China, except Hebei, Shandong, Guangxi, and Hainan, possessed R values greater than 1. On the contrary, provinces in central and western China all had R values smaller than 1.

---

[1] Patent data have some weaknesses, such as sectoral difference in patenting behaviour, difference in patenting between large and small firms. Further, not all the innovations are patented and the patent counts equalize the economic significance of different new technologies.
[2] China State Intellectual Property Office, see website at www.sipo.gov.cn
[3] NBS (1994–2005a, b).

Table 8.1: Patents in China, 1995 and 2004

	1995				2004				R	
Province	Total	Inventions	Utility models	Designs	Total	Inventions	Utility models	Designs	1995	2004
Beijing	4,025	328	3,169	528	9,005	3,216	3,956	1,833	10.40	5.72
Tianjin	1,034	63	785	186	2,578	432	1,587	559	3.55	2.36
Hebei	1,580	56	1,341	183	3,407	357	2,064	986	0.79	0.47
Liaoning	2,745	131	2,362	252	5,749	911	3,752	1,086	2.17	1.26
Shanghai	1,436	72	1,025	339	10,625	1,687	4,040	4,898	3.28	5.74
Jiangsu	2,413	72	1,884	457	11,330	1,026	5,474	4,830	1.10	1.41
Zhejiang	2,131	54	1,455	622	15,249	785	5,492	8,972	1.59	3.01
Fujian	933	17	439	477	4,758	160	1,776	2,822	0.93	1.26
Shandong	2,861	84	2,222	555	9,733	788	6,028	2,917	1.06	0.99
Guangdong	4,611	56	1,447	3,108	31,446	1,941	9,307	20,198	2.17	3.66
Guangxi	665	20	457	188	1,272	127	666	479	0.47	0.24
Hainan	108	4	44	60	278	36	93	149	0.48	0.32
Shanxi	569	47	480	42	1,189	295	636	258	0.60	0.33
Inner Mongolia	415	8	293	114	831	108	437	286	0.59	0.32
Jilin	824	38	723	63	2,145	451	1,179	515	1.03	0.73
Heilongjiang	1,403	44	1,248	111	2,809	326	1,997	486	1.23	0.68
Anhui	574	18	469	87	1,607	150	972	485	0.31	0.23
Jiangxi	509	19	402	88	1,169	105	625	439	0.40	0.25
Henan	1,145	34	1,009	102	3,318	306	2,117	895	0.41	0.32
Hubei	1,017	55	868	94	3,280	744	1,966	570	0.57	0.51
Hunan	1,515	51	1,318	146	3,281	436	1,801	1,044	0.77	0.46
Sichuan	2,019	79	1,486	454	8,031	730	3,069	4,232	0.58	0.63
Guizhou	274	12	207	55	737	179	364	194	0.25	0.18
Yunnan	569	35	346	188	1,264	235	586	443	0.46	0.27
Shaanxi	1,085	52	934	99	2,007	459	1,193	355	1.00	0.50
Gansu	257	7	215	35	514	127	322	65	0.34	0.18
Qinghai	65	2	61	2	70	21	30	19	0.44	0.12
Ningxia	111	4	98	9	293	46	119	128	0.70	0.47
Xinjiang	312	9	286	17	792	75	530	187	0.61	0.38
E. China	24,542	957	16,630	6,955	105,430	11,466	44,235	49,729	1.60	1.82
C. China	7,971	314	6,810	847	19,629	2,921	11,730	4,978	0.60	0.40
W. China	4,692	200	3,633	859	13,708	1,872	6,213	5,623	0.55	0.43
Total	37,205	1,471	27,073	8,661	138,767	16,259	62,178	60,330	1.00	1.00

Notes: (1) Because of unavailable data for Tibet for early years, we exclude Tibet from our analysis. (2) The total patents granted do not include Hong Kong, Macau, and Taiwan. The figures of Sichuan include the figures of Chongqing City. (3) n.a. = not applicable or not available. Location quotient is calculated for total patents only. (4) The total population used in our calculation does not include the military population, nor the population of Hong Kong, Macau, and Taiwan.

Source: National Bureau of Statistics (various years).

8.3 Measuring Innovation Inequality

To formally measure innovation inequality, we use the following five indices: the Atkinson index (A), the generalized entropy family $GE(0)$ and $GE(1)$, the squared coefficient of variation (CV^2), and the Gini coefficient $(Gini)$.

Let y denote the number of patents per 10,000 persons, N denote the total number of the provinces/regions, and $\bar{y}$ denote the mean of y. The Atkinson index is defined as:

$$A = 1 - \frac{1}{\bar{y}} \left(\prod_{i=1}^{N} y_i \right)^{1/N} \qquad (1)$$

$$GE(0) = \frac{1}{N} \sum_{i=1}^{N} \ln \frac{\bar{y}}{y_i} \qquad (2)$$

$$GE(1) = \frac{1}{N} \sum_{i=1}^{N} \frac{y_i}{\bar{y}} \ln \frac{\bar{y}}{y_i} \qquad (3)$$

The squared coefficient of variation (CV^2) can be expressed as:

$$CV^2 = \frac{1}{\bar{y}^2} \left[\frac{1}{N} \sum_{j=1}^{N} (y_i - \bar{y})^2 \right] \qquad (4)$$

The Gini index is defined as:

$$Gini = \frac{\sum_{i=1}^{N} \sum_{j=1}^{N} |y_i - y_j|}{2N\bar{y}^2} \qquad (5)$$

Regional inequality in innovation in terms of total patent number and its components are displayed in Figures 8.1 and 8.2. All indexes show that the inequality increased from 1995 to 2004 (Figure 8.1) with a notable drop in 2000, although the trend differs somehow for different indicators of innovation. Interestingly, design patents are found to be distributed most unequally. On the

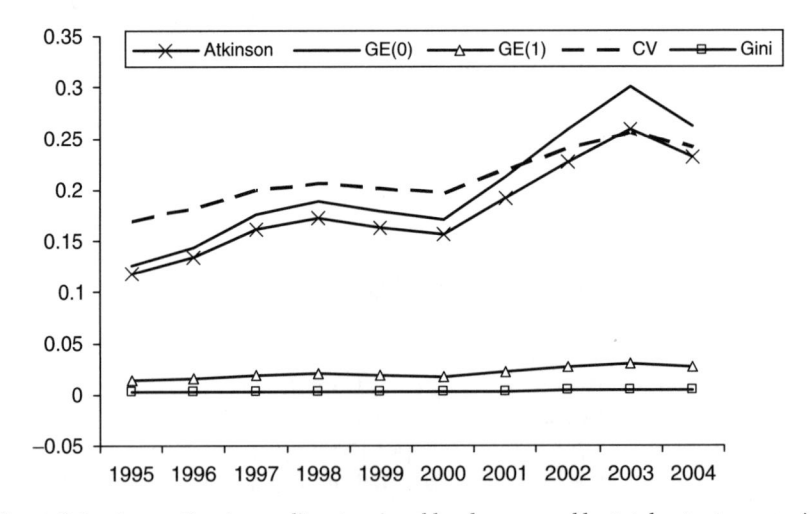

Figure 8.1a: Innovation inequality at regional level, measured by total patents per capita

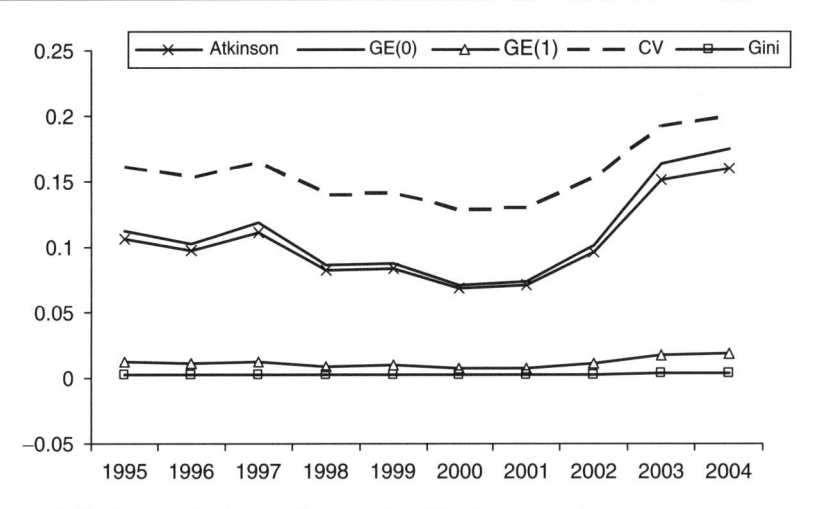

Figure 8.1b: Innovation inequality at regional level, measured by invention patents per capita

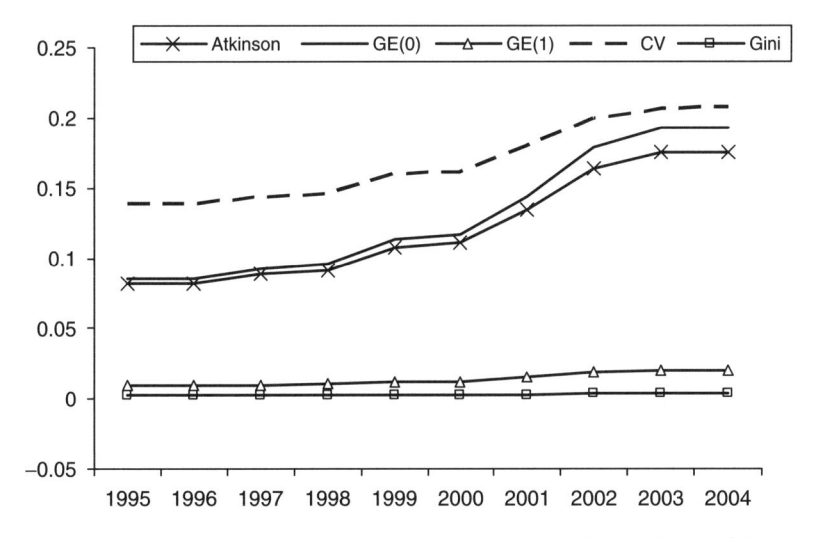

Figure 8.1c: Innovation inequality at regional level, measured by utility model patents per capita

other hand, Figure 8.2 conveys a mixed message. For invention patents, all indexes showed that inequality oscillated around the same level. For utility model and design patents, the inequality decreased from 1995 to 2000, but increased from 2000 to 2004. This pattern is shared by the total patent, which is not surprising as utility model and design patents constitute a great portion of

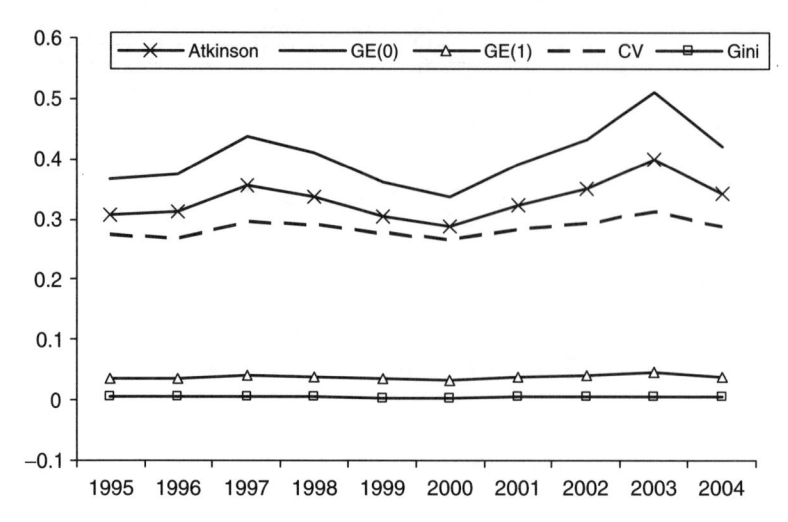

Figure 8.1d: Innovation inequality at regional level, measured by design patents per capita

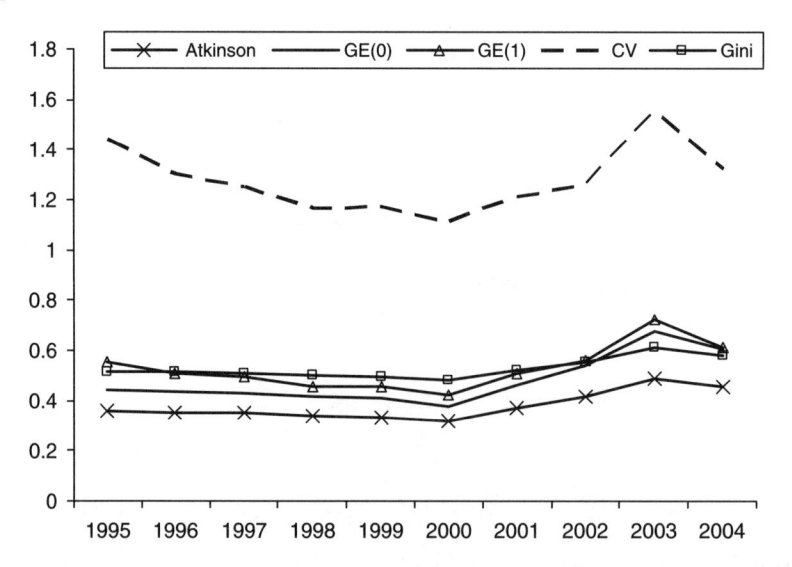

Figure 8.2a: Innovation inequality at provincial level, measured by total patents per capita

the total patent. These results seem to be in line with Sun (2000, 2003), which found a decline in patent concentration from 1985 to 1995 and an increasing concentration afterwards. It should be noted that Sun used total patent number rather than patent per capita in calculating the inequality indexes.

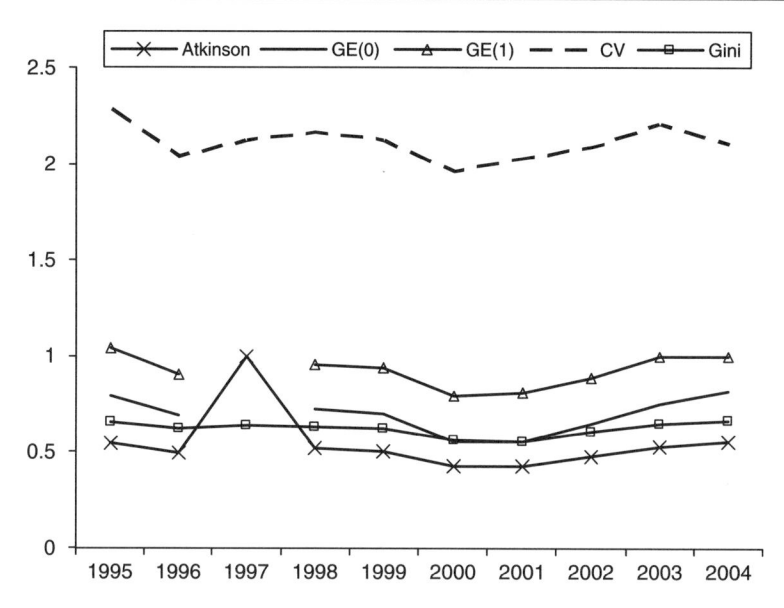

Figure 8.2b: Innovation inequality at provincial level, measured by invention patents per capita

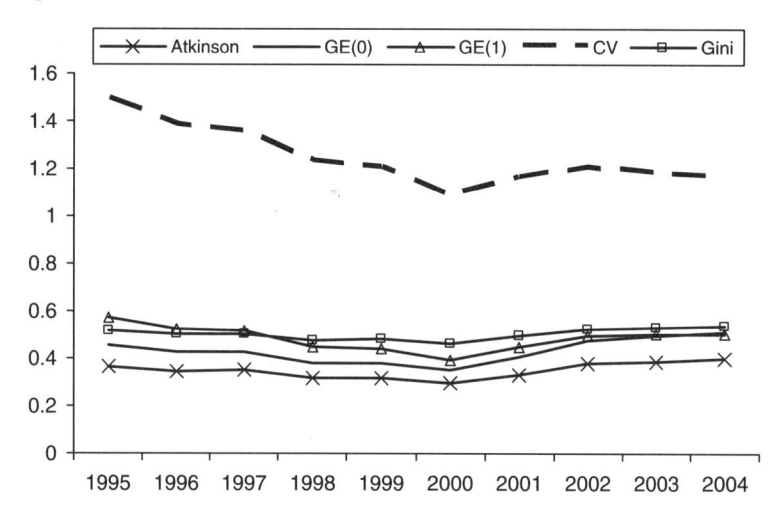

Figure 8.2c: Innovation inequality at provincial level, measured by utility model patents per capita

8.4 Decomposing Innovation Inequality

In order to implement regression-based inequality decomposition, it is necessary to model innovation as a knowledge production function. A conventional functional form is:

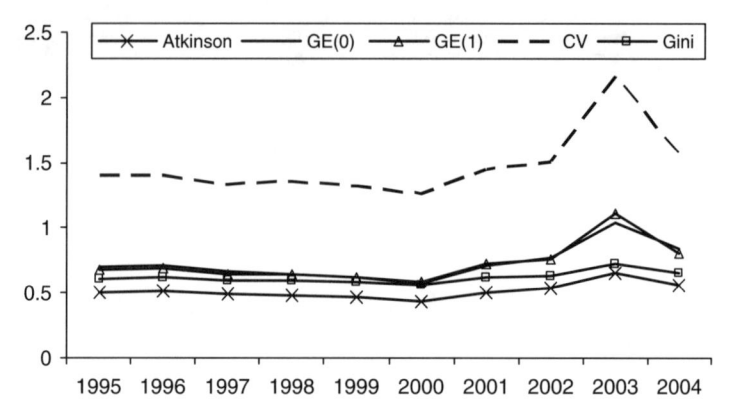

Figure 8.2d: Innovation inequality at pronvincial level, measured by design patents per capita

$$Y_i = \alpha RD_i^\beta HK_i^\gamma \varepsilon_i \tag{6}$$

where *Y* stands for the output of innovation activity, *RD* represents R&D inputs, *HK* represents human capital inputs. The subscript *i* represents the unit of observation, such as regions, industries, or enterprises (Audretsch and Feldman 2004). To incorporate the spatial dimension, Jaffe (1989) modified the above traditional model and used:

$$Y_{si} = \alpha IRD^{\beta 1} * UR_{si}^{\beta 2} * (UR_{si} * GC_{si}^{\beta 3}) * \varepsilon_{si} \tag{7}$$

where *IRD* is private corporate expenditure on R&D, *UR* is the research expenditures occurred at universities, and *GC* measures the geographic coincidence of university and corporate research. The subscripts *s* (*i*) represents a state (industry). Equation (7) was also employed by Acs et al. (1992) and Feldman (1994) in modelling innovation.

In studying China's patent distribution, Sun (2000) used the same model specification and found that the level of regional development, R&D, openness (import, export, and presence of foreign enterprises), and agglomeration (urbanization) are significant determinants of patent production. However, Sun's study and the alike do not permit quantification of the impacts of various input factors on the spatial inequality of innovations. This is because the regression model can only be used to explain the level of innovation capability, not its spatial variation. In what follows, we will first estimate a flexible regression model and then use the estimated model to conduct inequality decomposition.

8.4.1 *Regression Analysis: Innovation Capability*

Using the published consumer price indexes (CPIs) and the spatial price index of Brandt and Holz (2006) for 2004, we deflated all observations in value terms. To deal with the delay between innovation inputs and output, we follow Guerrero and Sero (1997) by lagging independent variables by one year in our empirical model. This also helps to address the possible endogeneity problem.

We follow the 'general to specific' modelling strategy in this study. In other words, we start with as many explanatory variables as possible subject to data availability. To explain the per capita number of patents (*Y*), education and R&D funding ought to be considered. Consequently, average years of schooling of labour force (*Edu*) and per capita public R&D funding (*RD*) are included as independent variables. Following Sun (2000), rate of urbanization (*Urban*) is used to capture possible agglomeration effects. Since most inventions occur in the non-farming sectors, it is necessary to control for structure of economic activities. For this purpose, share of agricultural GDP (*Stru*) is taken as an independent variable. We also included per capita GDP (*GDP*) and the trade/GDP ratio (*Opent*) and FDI/GDP ratio (*Openf*). *GDP* represents level of development and *Opent* and *Opentf* may crowd out domestic innovative capability. Needless to say, it is necessary to incorporate location dummy variables. In this study, we define *DB*, *DG*, *DS*, and *DT* for Beijing, Guangdong, Shanghai, and Tianjin, respectively. To allow for non-linearity, we also include the squares of education and R&D in the model. Difference in the impacts of education and R&D on inventions across regional belts are considered by adding *D1*Edu* and *D2*Edu*, where *D1* is the dummy for east China and *D2* for central China. Finally, time trend (*Year*) is used to denote reform and other time dependent forces underlying innovation. To facilitate robustness test, several variables are considered and they include total population (*POP*), consumer price index (*CPI*), and per capita value of high-tech product (*HT*). Population size may bring about economies of scale or economies of specialization in innovative activities. *CPI* signals macroeconomic environment and *HT* may reflect non-public R&D inputs.

Regarding functional forms, we consider four possibilities instead of, as in almost all earlier studies of innovation, sticking to a particular specification. The Lin-Lin specification involves no transformation to the dependent or independent variables. The Log-Log specification involves taking logarithms to both the dependent and independent variables, with the exception of dummy variables. As discussed earlier, this specification is commonly used in the literature. By the same token, we can have the Lin-Log and Log-Lin specifications.

Fitting the four specifications to the Chinese data produce results as tabulated in Table 8.2. Models with the same dependent variable can be easily compared by examining the log-likelihood values. In doing so, we eliminate the Lin-Log and Log-Log models. To choose between the Lin-Lin and Log-Lin models, the χ^2 test of Cox can be utilized. The test result indicates preference of the Log-Lin model. Based on the Log-Lin model, R&D is not a significant determinant of innovation in China. This is understandable for at least two reasons. First, public R&D accounts for a fairly small percentage of total R&D input. More importantly, R&D in China is not appropriately managed. Misallocation and corruption are well known. To many academics, it would be surprising to find R&D to be significant. It is useful to note that this insignificance is robust to model specification (Table 8.2). Like R&D, the variables *POP*, *CPI*, and *D2*Edu* are not significant in any of the equations.

Now, we drop the five variables which are insignificant (*RD*, *RD²*, *POP*, *CPI*, and *D2*Edu*) and estimate the four models again, with results tabulated in Table 8.3. Repeating the earlier model selection procedure, we end up with the Log-Lin functional form again. As is evident from Table 8.3, the selected model is of good quality in terms of common sense, statistical properties and innovation production theory. The only insignificant variable is the HT variable. However, HT is significant in other models and in earlier estimation (see Table 8.3). More importantly, we believe that HT is a relevant and important determinant of innovation outputs. Therefore, we decide to keep this variable in the model.

As the final step in our modelling procedure, robustness test is conducted by adding some possibly relevant variables into the selected Log-Lin model. We added both *POP* and *CPI*, and added each separately. The results are presented in Table 8.4. Clearly, our selected model is fairly robust. In passing, it is noted that the commonly used double log model is rejected here thus earlier studies adopting this functional form are likely to suffer from misspecification errors.

8.4.2 Regression-Based Inequality Decomposition

Based on the selected regression model, we now conduct the decomposition exercise to quantify contributions of relevant factors to the inequality of innovation capability in China. It is known that different measures of inequality often produce different results, which may carry over to inequality decomposition. Consequently, we consider the four of the five inequality measures defined earlier in this chapter. These include $GE(0)$, $GE(1)$, the squared coefficient of variation (CV^2), and the *Gini* coefficient.

Following Wan et al. (2007), we collect all regional dummy variables terms, and name it *Loc* to represent location, the *D1*Edu* is merged with *Edu* and *Edu2* to form *HC*, human capital. Naturally, *Opent* and *Openf* are combined to represent globalization denoted by *Open*. All other variables retain their original definitions. To measure the inequality of innovation, not inequality of its

Table 8.2: Summary of regression models, with initial 19 variables

Variable name	Log-Lin Standardized coefficient	Log-Lin t-ratio	Log-Lin p-value	Lin-Lin Standardized coefficient	Lin-Lin t-ratio	Lin-Lin p-value	Log-Log Standardized coefficient	Log-Log t-ratio	Log-Log p-value	Lin-Log Standardized coefficient	Lin-Log t-ratio	Lin-Log p-value
RD	−0.02	−0.53	0.600	0.02	0.28	0.782	0.07	0.98	0.328	0.13	1.00	0.317
RD²	0.01	0.32	0.746	0.00	−0.06	0.952	−0.07	−0.93	0.353	−0.10	−0.80	0.424
EDU	0.72	2.45	0.014	−0.51	−1.10	0.270	0.30	0.67	0.505	−2.38	−2.72	0.006
EDU²	−0.90	−2.98	0.003	0.42	0.88	0.377	−0.34	−0.73	0.468	2.27	2.55	0.011
OPENF	−0.13	−4.34	0.000	−0.06	−1.08	0.279	−0.03	−0.85	0.396	−0.01	−0.09	0.930
OPENT	−0.02	−1.42	0.156	0.01	0.41	0.685	−0.06	−2.16	0.031	−0.06	−1.38	0.168
Urban	0.15	4.01	0.000	0.05	0.60	0.547	0.15	5.01	0.000	0.05	0.56	0.578
STRU	−0.31	−9.85	0.000	0.22	1.94	0.053	−0.57	−11.73	0.000	−0.83	−5.01	0.000
GDP	0.06	2.65	0.008	−0.02	−0.44	0.657	0.05	2.17	0.030	0.00	−0.03	0.979
Year	0.24	8.31	0.000	0.22	3.49	0.000	0.09	4.19	0.000	0.10	1.97	0.049
DB	0.25	8.01	0.000	0.31	4.79	0.000	0.09	2.75	0.006	0.13	1.48	0.138
DG	0.20	6.73	0.000	0.24	2.38	0.017	0.18	3.74	0.000	0.13	1.21	0.226
DS	0.13	2.98	0.003	0.35	5.55	0.000	−0.13	−3.05	0.002	−0.17	−1.52	0.130
DT	0.07	3.26	0.001	0.10	1.63	0.102	−0.07	−3.00	0.003	−0.22	−3.07	0.002
HT	0.04	1.50	0.133	0.34	6.76	0.000	0.28	8.69	0.000	0.21	2.99	0.003
POP	−0.01	−0.53	0.594	−0.04	−1.57	0.117	−0.02	−1.03	0.304	−0.03	−1.01	0.312
CPI	0.00	0.00	0.997	−0.03	−0.61	0.540	0.02	0.67	0.503	0.03	0.57	0.570
D1*EDU	0.50	10.04	0.000	0.43	3.65	0.000	0.23	4.09	0.000	0.22	1.54	0.123
D2*EDU	0.05	1.27	0.205	0.03	0.24	0.809	0.00	−0.03	0.977	0.05	0.33	0.743
Constant	0.00	−3.15	0.002	0.00	0.80	0.421	0.00	−0.61	0.539	0.00	3.46	0.001
Same estimated ρ for all cross-sections		0.87			0.67			0.84			0.72	
BUSE [1973] R^2		0.91			0.79			0.89			0.63	
BUSE raw moment R^2		0.92			0.87			0.92			0.77	
Variance of the estimate-σ^2		0.03			0.14			0.03			0.17	
Standard error of the estimate-σ		0.18			0.37			0.19			0.41	
Sum of squared errors (SSE)		9.00			40.46			10.03			47.96	
Mean of dependant variable		−0.85			0.76			−0.85			0.76	
Log of the likelihood function		74.42			−151.97			61.74			−179.09	

Source: Authors' calculations.

Table 8.3: Summary of regression models, with 14 variables

Variable name	Log-Lin Standardized coefficient	Log-Lin t-ratio	Log-Lin p-value	Lin-Lin Standardized coefficient	Lin-Lin t-ratio	Lin-Lin p-value	Log-Log Standardized coefficient	Log-Log t-ratio	Log-Log p-value	Lin-Log Standardized coefficient	Lin-Log t-ratio	Lin-Log p-value
EDU	0.70	2.34	0.019	-0.25	-0.49	0.621	0.29	0.65	0.516	-2.43	-2.79	0.005
EDU^2	-0.87	-2.84	0.005	0.15	0.30	0.766	-0.33	-0.71	0.481	2.35	2.65	0.008
OPENF	-0.13	-4.25	0.000	-0.07	-1.25	0.211	-0.03	-0.88	0.381	-0.01	-0.10	0.922
OPENT	-0.02	-2.01	0.044	0.00	0.07	0.944	-0.03	-2.07	0.038	-0.02	-0.69	0.491
Urban	0.14	3.76	0.000	0.00	0.05	0.961	0.14	4.82	0.000	0.04	0.55	0.580
STRU	-0.31	-9.80	0.000	0.20	1.81	0.071	-0.57	-11.84	0.000	-0.80	-4.71	0.000
GDP	0.05	2.67	0.008	0.00	-0.04	0.968	0.06	2.64	0.008	0.01	0.21	0.836
Year	0.24	8.27	0.000	0.23	3.47	0.001	0.09	4.21	0.000	0.09	1.84	0.066
DB	0.25	7.87	0.000	0.35	5.17	0.000	0.08	2.65	0.008	0.20	2.98	0.003
DG	0.20	6.73	0.000	0.23	2.39	0.017	0.17	3.79	0.000	0.20	1.93	0.053
DS	0.14	3.01	0.003	0.37	5.50	0.000	-0.13	-3.02	0.003	-0.07	-0.76	0.449
DT	0.07	3.22	0.001	0.11	1.94	0.053	-0.07	-3.02	0.003	-0.13	-2.47	0.013
HT	0.04	1.48	0.139	0.34	6.61	0.000	0.28	8.83	0.000	0.20	3.03	0.002
D1*EDU	0.46	11.75	0.000	0.41	3.99	0.000	0.24	6.13	0.000	0.01	0.08	0.937
Constant	0.00	-2.96	0.003	0.00	0.21	0.837	0.00	-0.61	0.544	0.00	3.47	0.001
Same estimated ρ for all cross-sections		0.88			0.67			0.84			0.74	
BUSE [1973] R^2		0.91			0.78			0.88			0.61	
BUSE raw moment R^2		0.92			0.87			0.92			0.76	
Variance of the estimate-σ^2		0.03			0.14			0.03			0.17	
Standard error of the estimate-σ		0.18			0.37			0.19			0.41	
Sum of squared errors (SSE)		9.03			40.68			10.10			48.20	
Mean of dependant variable		-0.85			0.76			-0.85			0.76	
Log of the likelihood function		73.87			-152.13			60.78			-179.84	

Source: Authors' calculations.

Table 8.4: Robustness test

Variable name	Add POP and CPI			Add POP			Add CPI		
	Standardized coefficient	t-ratio	p-value	Standardized coefficient	t-ratio	p-value	Standardized coefficient	t-ratio	p-value
EDU	0.66	2.31	0.021	0.66	2.31	0.021	0.66	2.33	0.020
EDU^2	−0.05	−2.81	0.005	−0.05	−2.81	0.005	−0.05	−2.83	0.005
OPENF	−0.03	−4.31	0.000	−0.03	−4.27	0.000	−0.03	−4.25	0.000
OPENT	0.00	−1.36	0.173	0.00	−2.08	0.038	0.00	−1.66	0.098
Urban	0.01	3.63	0.000	0.01	3.76	0.000	0.01	3.75	0.000
STRU	−0.04	−9.75	0.000	−0.04	−9.74	0.000	−0.04	−9.80	0.000
GDP	0.12	2.59	0.010	0.11	2.57	0.010	0.11	2.50	0.013
Year	0.08	8.37	0.000	0.08	8.34	0.000	0.08	8.27	0.000
DB	1.31	7.96	0.000	1.31	7.91	0.000	1.31	7.85	0.000
DG	1.03	6.56	0.000	1.04	6.56	0.000	1.04	6.72	0.000
DS	0.73	3.14	0.002	0.71	3.09	0.002	0.71	3.00	0.003
DT	0.39	3.38	0.001	0.38	3.30	0.001	0.38	3.20	0.001
HT	0.00	1.48	0.138	0.00	1.48	0.138	0.00	1.48	0.139
D1*EDU	0.12	11.89	0.000	0.12	11.79	0.000	0.12	11.72	0.000
POP	0.00	−0.86	0.389	0.00	−0.76	0.447			
CPI	−0.05	−0.41	0.685				0.01	0.08	0.940
Constant	−3.07	−2.87	0.004	−3.12	−2.93	0.003	−3.17	−2.96	0.003
Same estimated ρ for all cross-sections		0.88			0.88			0.88	
BUSE [1973] R^2		0.91			0.91			0.91	
BUSE raw moment R^2		0.92			0.92			0.92	
Variance of the estimate-σ^2		0.03			0.03			0.03	
Standard error of the estimate-σ		0.18			0.18			0.18	
Sum of squared errors (SSE)		9.00			9.01			9.03	
Mean of dependant variable		−0.85			−0.85			−0.85	
Log of the likelihood function		74.16			74.08			73.87	

Source: Authors' calculations.

logarithm, we solve the estimated model for Y and then proceed to inequality decomposition using the technique developed by Wan (2004). To briefly explain, the contribution of the residual represents those made by variables not included in our model. All remaining inequalities are explainable by variables included in our regression. See Wan (2004), Wan and Zhou (2005), and Wan et al. (2007). The decomposition results are tabulated in Tables 8.5 a and b.

Several findings deserve particular discussion. First, location is found to contribute the most to the inequality (around 30–40 per cent). This is not surprising as location captures the effects of culture, tradition and even policy biases. For example, Beijing, Tianjin, Guangdong, and Shanghai are China's traditional and emerging innovation centres. As the national political and manufacturing centres of the Huabei Area, Beijing, and Tianjin have enjoyed more higher education institutions, national research institutes, and national industrial bases. Guangdong rose to a local power house economically due to the economic reform and open policy in the 1980s. Shanghai has gained ever more rapid development since Pudong New Area was established in the 1990s. It is worth mentioning that all these locations belong to east China. The location variable may also capture other socioeconomic or institutional factors that are critical to innovation but were not included in our model.

Second, economic structure (share of agricultural GDP) has a significant impact on inequality. This essentially reflects the impact of different pace of industrialization on innovation inequality. A positive contribution of this variable echoes well the significant contribution of the urbanization variable. Both of these findings support our earlier argument that China's certified patent are generated mainly by industrial/service sectors, which are mostly located in urban areas. Although China is advanced in agricultural research and technology, most innovations in the agricultural sector are created by public research institutes in Beijing and those provinces which do not have a high share of agricultural GDP.

Third, human capital is found to be the third most important factor in driving the inequality in China's innovation capability. This finding is consistent with a priori expectation that human resource is an important input of knowledge production (Audretsch and Feldman 2004). Silicon Valley and the Boston metropolitan area are typical examples to illustrate the crucial importance of human capital in affecting knowledge-based industries. They are clustered by computing and biomedical industries which take advantage of the rich human resources that the regions can supply through prominent universities and research institutes. Similarly, in China, high-tech firms, regardless of whether they are domestic or multinational, tend to locate in places such as Beijing, Shanghai, and coastal provinces where there exists a large skilled labour force.

Fourth, the negative contribution of openness implies that trade and foreign direct investment (FDI) can help mitigate disparity in innovation.

Inequality in Innovation

Table 8.5a: Result of decomposition, 1995–2000

1995	GE 0	GE 1	CV	Gini	1996	GE 0	GE 1	CV	Gini
Inequality contribution (%)	0.45	0.55	1.44	0.52	Inequality contribution (%)	0.44	0.51	1.31	0.51
Human capital	28	25	27	29	Human capital	28	26	28	29
Open	−9	−8	−10	−3	Open	−8	−7	−8	−2
Urban	11	12	17	11	Urban	12	14	20	11
Struc	30	28	34	30	Struc	33	33	41	31
GDP	−2	−2	−2	0	GDP	−1	−1	−2	0
Location	34	36	46	30	Location	37	42	56	31
High-tech	1	1	1	1	High-tech	1	1	2	1
Subtotal	94	91	113	97	Subtotal	102	107	139	101
Residue	6	9	−13	3	Residue	−2	−7	−39	−1
1997	GE 0	GE 1	CV	Gini	1998	GE 0	GE 1	CV	Gini
Inequality contribution (%)	0.43	0.49	1.25	0.51	Inequality contribution (%)	0.41	0.46	1.17	0.50
Human capital	27	25	25	28	Human capital	30	28	29	30
Open	−10	−9	−10	−4	Open	−10	−9	−10	−4
Urban	11	13	19	11	Urban	12	14	21	11
Struc	33	33	42	31	Struc	33	34	43	31
GDP	−1	−1	−2	0	GDP	−1	−2	−2	0
Location	36	41	56	31	Location	39	46	62	32
High-tech	1	1	2	1	High-tech	1	2	3	1
Subtotal	97	102	131	98	Subtotal	104	114	147	102
Residue	3	−2	−31	2	Residue	−4	−14	−47	−2
1999	GE 0	GE 1	CV	Gini	2000	GE 0	GE 1	CV	Gini
Inequality contribution (%)	0.41	0.46	1.17	0.50	Inequality contribution (%)	0.38	0.43	1.12	0.48
Human capital	30	28	27	30	Human capital	29	26	23	30
Open	−10	−10	−11	−4	Open	−8	−8	−10	−3
Urban	12	14	20	11	Urban	12	14	19	11
Struc	32	33	41	30	Struc	32	32	38	30
GDP	−1	−1	−2	0	GDP	−1	−2	−2	0
Location	38	44	57	32	Location	40	46	57	33
High-tech	131	138	70	97	High-tech	4	5	7	3
Subtotal	104	111	136	102	Subtotal	107	113	134	103
Residue	−4	−11	−36	−2	Residue	−7	−13	−34	−3

Source: Authors' calculations.

Our regression model indicates that both trade and FDI are negatively associated with innovation, confirming the crowding out effects frequently discussed in the literature. Finally, we observe that the contribution of high-tech development (per capita revenue from high-tech parks) to innovation disparity increased from 1 per cent in 1995 to 6–10 per cent in 2004. The increase demonstrates that high-tech parks, initiated by the national government, have successfully stimulated high-tech industrial development in the respective regions, leading to higher regional inequality in innovative capability.

It seems pertinent to placing results from the regression and decomposition analysis in the context of the changing national innovation system (NIS) in China. More engagement from the business sectors, especially large and

Table 8.5b: Result of decomposition, 2001–04

2001	GE 0	GE 1	CV	Gini	2002	GE 0	GE 1	CV	Gini
Inequality contribution (%)	0.46	0.51	1.22	0.52	Inequality contribution (%)	0.54	0.56	1.26	0.56
Human capital	26	24	24	29	Human capital	21	20	20	27
Open	−6	−5	−7	−3	Open	−5	−5	−6	−3
Urban	12	13	20	12	Urban	9	10	16	10
Struc	25	26	34	26	Struc	20	22	30	23
GDP	−1	−2	−3	0	GDP	−1	−2	−3	0
Location	34	40	55	31	Location	28	34	50	28
High-tech	4	5	8	3	High-tech	3	4	6	3
Subtotal	95	101	132	98	Subtotal	74	83	114	89
Residue	5	−1	−32	2	Residue	26	17	−14	11
2003	**GE 0**	**GE 1**	**CV**	**Gini**	**2004**	**GE 0**	**GE 1**	**CV**	**Gini**
Inequality contribution (%)	0.68	0.73	1.55	0.61	Inequality contribution (%)	0.61	0.61	1.32	0.58
Human capital	17	16	16	24	Human capital	19	18	19	26
Open	−3	−3	−3	−2	Open	−4	−4	−5	−2
Urban	7	9	15	9	Urban	8	10	16	9
Struc	16	17	25	20	Struc	17	19	28	20
GDP	−1	−1	−2	0	GDP	0	−1	−2	1
Location	24	29	45	27	Location	26	34	53	28
High-tech	4	5	10	4	High-tech	6	8	14	6
Subtotal	65	71	107	83	Subtotal	72	84	123	88
Residue	35	29	−7	17	Residue	28	16	−23	12

Source: Authors' calculations.

medium sized enterprises, represents the most prominent change of China's NIS. As a result, industrial enterprises generated most utility model and design patents. Though universities and colleges are major owners of invention patents, the role of industrial enterprises has increased significantly over time (Fan and Watanabe 2006). In fact, enterprises invested heavily in innovation activities, reflected by its share of S&T funding and R&D expenditure. While China's S&T funding increased to 258 billion yuan in 2001, more than six times of that in 1991, the contribution of enterprises grew more than ten times, reaching 56 per cent of the total in 2001. Similarly, large and medium sized enterprises increased their R&D spending from 14 billion yuan in 1995 to 42 billion yuan in 2001, contributing to 42 per cent of the national R&D expenditure (Fan and Watanabe 2006). Furthermore, building innovation capability has become the first priority of some domestic high-tech companies. A study on these firms, such as Huawei Technology Corporation, Shenzhen Zhongxin Technology Corporations, Datang Telecom, and Great Dragon Information Technology, found that innovation capability and self-developed technologies have been the key to leading domestic firms catching up with the multinational corporations (Fan 2006).

Our research findings are at odds with those of Sun (2000), who found that R&D and agglomeration are not significant factors for innovations in

China. This inconsistency can be largely attributed to the inefficiency in China's innovation system in the early period examined by Sun. Our results suggest that China has improved the effectiveness of its R&D activities in the past decade.

8.5 Summary

This study uses several indexes to measure the inequality in innovation capability in China from 1995 to 2004. It reveals that the east–central–west inequality has increased over time, whereas the inter-provincial inequality showed a V-pattern. Major factors driving these inequality trends are location, industrialization and urbanization, human capital, and openness (foreign direct investment). The location variable is found to contribute the most to the innovation inequality. The variable is a collection of regional dummies for Beijing, Guangdong, Shanghai, and Tianjin, as well as east coastal region and central region. It captures the effects of culture, tradition, and even policy biases of regions which can hardly be quantified. Unbalanced development in high-tech parks is found to play an increasing role in causing innovation disparity in China. As innovation capability plays a vital role for growth, the found increasing inequality can seriously affect lagging region's catching up in economic development. Accordingly, policymakers in China should focus on promoting enterprises' involvement in innovation and nurturing domestic high-tech companies in the inland provinces. Also, our results appeal for a more equalized approach in human capital investment.

References

Acs, Z. J., D. B. Audretsch, and M. P. Feldman (1992). 'Real Effects of Academic Research', *American Economic Review* 82: 363–7.

Audretsch, D., and M. Feldman (2004). 'Knowledge Spillovers and the Geography of Innovation', in J. V. Henderson and J. F. Thisse (eds), *Handbook of Regional and Urban Economics* Vol. 4, Elsevier: Amsterdam.

Barsberg, B. L. (1987). 'Patents and the Measurement of Technological Change: A Survey of the Literature', *Research Policy* 16: 131–41.

Brandt, L., and C. Holz (2006). 'Spatial Price Differentiation in China: Estimates and Implications', *Economic Development and Cultural Change* 55: 43–86.

Fan, P. (2006). 'Catching Up Through Developing Innovation Capability: Evidence From China's Telecom Equipment Industry', *Technovation* 26: 359–68.

—— C. Watanabe (2006). 'Promoting Industrial Development Through Technology Policy: Lessons From Japan and China', *Technology in Society* 28(3): 303–20.

Fargerberg, J. (1994). 'Technology and International Differences in Growth Rates', *Journal of Economic Literature* 31(1): 147–75.

—— B. Verspagen, and M. Caniels (1997). 'Technology, Growth and Unemployment across European Regions', *Regional Studies* 31: 457–66.
Feldman, M. (1994). *The Geography of Innovation*, Kluwer Academic: Boston, MA.
Griliches, Z. (1990). 'Patent Statistics as Economic Indicators: A Survey', *Journal of Economic Literature* 28: 1661–707.
Guerrero, D. C., and M. A. Sero (1997). 'Spatial Distribution of Patents in Spain: Determining Factors and Consequences on Regional Development', *Regional Studies* 31: 381–90.
Hagedoorn, J., and M. Cloodt (2003). 'Measuring Innovative Performance: Is There an Advantage in Using Multiple Indicators?', *Research Policy* 32: 1365–79.
Jaffe, A. B. (1989). 'Real Effects of Academic Research', *American Economic Review* 79: 967–70.
Malecki, E. J. (1987). 'Hope or Hyperbole? High Tech and Economic Development,' *Technology Review* 90: 44–51.
—— (1997). *Technology and Economic Development*, Longman: London.
Mansfield, E. (1986). 'Patents and Innovation: An Empirical Study', *Management Science* 32: 173–81.
NBS (National Bureau of Statistics) (1994–2005a). *China Statistic Year Book*, China National Bureau of Statistics: Beijing.
—— (1995–2005b). *China Statistical Yearbook on Science and Technology*, China National Bureau of Statistics: Beijing.
OECD (Organization for Economic Co-operation and Development) (1988). *OECD Economic Studies*, OECD: Paris.
—— (2001). *European Competitive Report*, OECD: Paris.
Schumpeter, J. (1942). *Capitalism, Socialism, and Democracy*, HarperCollins: London.
Sun, Y. (2000). 'Spatial Distribution of Patents in China', *Regional Studies* 34(5): 441–54.
—— (2003). 'Geographic Patterns of Industrial Innovation in China During the 1990s', *Journal of Economic and Social Geography* 94(3): 376–89.
Wan, G. H. (2002). 'Regression-based Inequality Decomposition: Pitfalls and a Solution Procedure', *Discussion Paper* 2002/101, UNU-WIDER: Helsinki.
—— (2004). 'Accounting for Income Inequality in Rural China: A Regression-based Approach', *Journal of Comparative Economics* 32: 348–63.
—— Z. Y. Zhou (2005). 'Income Inequality in Rural China: Regression-based Decomposition Using Household Data', *Review of Development Economics* 9: 107–20.
—— M. Lu, and Z. Chen (2006). 'The Inequality–Growth Nexus in the Short and Long Run: Empirical Evidence from China', *Journal of Comparative Economics* 34(4): 654–67.
—— —— —— (2007). 'Globalization and Regional Inequality: Evidence from within China', *Review of Income and Wealth* 53(1): 35–59.

9

Widening Gap of Educational Opportunity? A Study of the Changing Patterns of Educational Attainment in China

Min-Dong Paul Lee

9.1 Introduction

Recently, rapidly growing income inequality in China has generated significant interest as well as alarm among China scholars around the world (Kanbur and Zhang 1999; Yang 1999; Ravallion and Chen 2004; Meng et al. 2005). A World Bank study reports that the estimated Gini coefficient of national income inequality after cost of living adjustment grew from 25.91 in 1981 to 39.45 in 2001 (Ravallion and Chen 2004). However, the interest in income inequality has not triggered a similar surge of interest in educational inequality. This lack of interest in educational inequality is rather puzzling given that the positive relationship between education and earnings is arguably the most well documented finding in social science (Becker 1964; Blau and Duncan 1967; Sewell et al. 1969; Deng and Treiman 1997). Without understanding the state of educational inequality, it would be difficult to predict future patterns of income inequality or formulate effective policy to curb growing inequality.

Education is indeed one of the most consistent predictors of a person's future income (Mincer 1974; Ashenfelter and Rouse 1999), and China is no exception to this rule. As Nee (1989, 1996) argues, as China continues its transformation into a market economy, education, or human capital would emerge as more and more the central mechanism behind social stratification based on income. Recent empirical studies find clear evidence for the increased earnings returns to education in a reforming country such as China (Bian and Logan 1996; Zhou 2000; Wu and Xie 2003). The most recent study on the returns to education estimates that a return of an additional year of schooling of 4 per cent in 1988 has made a huge jump to 10.2 per cent in 2001. Education has clearly emerged as an important causal factor shaping income stratification in China.

Understanding educational inequality in China is important not only in terms of identifying the source of economic and social inequality, but also in terms of devising a solution to reduce overall inequality. In the tradition of Horace Mann, education is often perceived to be the 'great equalizer' in society (Cremin 1951). This belief in education as the equalizer has facilitated the rapid diffusion of public education around the world during the last century (Meyer et al. 1992). China also adopted this philosophy when the government passed legislation on compulsory education in 1986, which guaranteed all school age children the right to receive nine years of schooling. How did the law affect the distribution of educational attainment? Do Chinese students today have more or less equal opportunity to education regardless of their personal and environmental characteristics? If there is educational inequality, is it increasing or decreasing? The time is ripe for asking and answering these critical questions.

The aim of this study is twofold. First, the study examines and describes the current distribution of educational attainment in China from both static and dynamic perspectives. Second, it tests whether the urban biased policy and institution, which is purported to be the main source of economic inequality (Yang 1999), is also the source of educational inequality. It then examines whether the continuing economic growth and accompanying urban expansion will eventually reduce educational inequality without other policy interventions. The structure of chapter is as follows. The next section briefly introduces the history of education in China after the establishment of a communist government in 1949. Section 9.3 describes the data, measurement, and methods. Section 9.4 analyses the within cohort inequality (i.e. static inequality). Section 9.5 explores the between cohort inequality (i.e. dynamic inequality or changes in inequality over time). Section 9.6 tests the urban bias hypothesis by decomposing the differences in transition rates and estimating the proportion that population composition contributes to total inequality. The last section concludes with summary of results and some theoretical and policy related implications.

9.2 Historical Background

Education has been an important channel of social mobility in China for over a thousand years (Wang 1960). Since the founding of the People's Republic of China in 1949, however, education has been subject to a series of disruptions under various political manipulations and state policies (Pepper 1980; Zhou et al. 1998). First, disruption came immediately after the complete failure of the 'great leap forward' economic policy in the late 1950s. The failed economic

Educational Inequality

plan resulted in severe economic contraction which, in turn, ushered in one of the worst famines in human history. Prolonged starvation sharply raised mortality rates all over China. By the end of the famine in 1961, it had already claimed millions of lives. During this period when most rural residents did not even have enough to eat, education was a luxury they simply could not afford. The new student enrolment rate for school age children dropped 38 per cent in 1961 and another 5 per cent in 1962. Even 20 per cent of the students who had already been enrolled in school dropped out. During this period more than one-third of China's population was deprived of even basic education.

The second major disruption came during the infamous Cultural Revolution (1966–76). The main causal force that affected educational attainment during this period was political rather than economic. Soon after Mao declared the 'great proletarian cultural revolution', many secondary and post-secondary schools were forcibly closed down. Individuals with high education were often labelled as 'bourgeoisie' and became the target of political persecution. The original intention of the Cultural Revolution was to level the opportunity structure between rural peasants and workers versus urban intelligentsia and cadre families. The Revolution probably did achieve its intended effect of more egalitarian educational attainment between classes (Deng and Treiman 1997), but the unintended side effect was serious disruption of the entire education system, and national enrolment which was gradually recovering after the great famine dropped almost 60 per cent of the 1957 level. The drop in new student enrolment rate extended also to the primary school.

The effect of these two major disruptions on the educational system is clearly evident in the relatively high proportion of the population over 6 years of age who have never attended school—these are people who have had no formal schooling experience during their lifetime. About 10 per cent of the population aged over 6 years have never attended school and the figure goes as high as 46.4 per cent in Xizang (Tibet).

Figure 9.1 presents the current state of educational inequality in six large geographic regions of China.[1] The interregional variation of educational attainment is clearly visible. The percentage of the population who never attended school in the western provinces is almost four times higher than that of the northeastern provinces. In general, the coastal provinces have much smaller percentage of uneducated people than the inland provinces. The figure also indicates sharp gender inequality in educational attainment.

---

[1] The north region includes the provinces of Beijing, Tianjin, Hebei, Shanxi, and Neimenggu. The northeast region includes the provinces of Liaoning, Heilongjiang, and Jilin. The eastern region includes the provinces of Shanghai, Jiangsu, Zhejiang, Shandong, Anhui, Fujian, and Jiangxi. The southern region includes the provinces of Henan, Hubei, Hunan, Guangdong, Guangxi, and Hainan. The western region includes the provinces of Sichuan, Chongqing, Guizhou, Xizang (Tibet), and Yunnan. The northwest region includes the provinces of Shaanxi, Gansu, Ningxia, Qinghai, and Xinjiang.

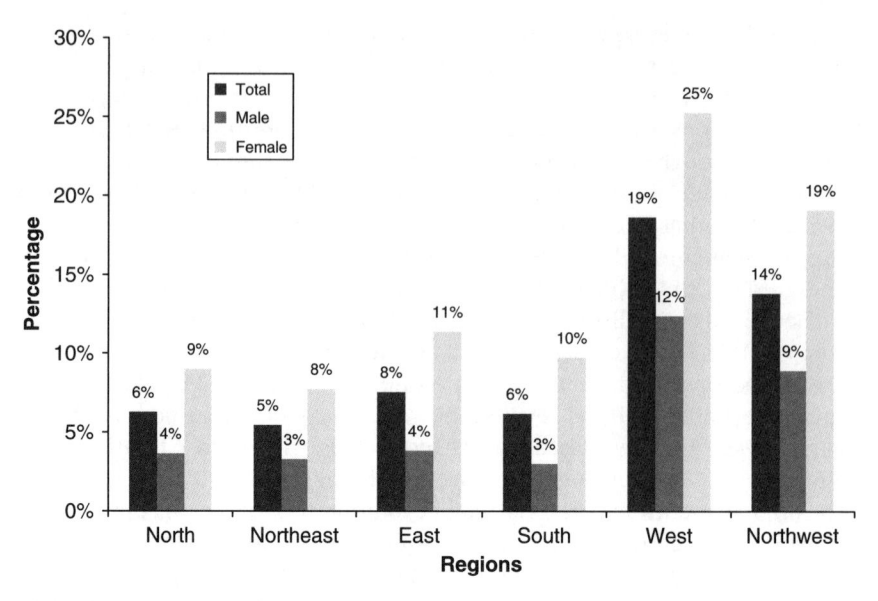

Figure 9.1: Percentage of the population aged over 6 years who never attended school

Note: Data are based on the fifth national population census in 2000.
Source: SSB (2002).

The proportion of female population who never attended school is more than twice as large as that of the males. One caveat in interpreting the observed gender inequality is that the statistics are affected by differences in male–female population composition due to the longer life expectancy of females. However, considering that significant gender differences in the population composition occur mostly after 70 years of age, which accounts for less than 3 per cent of the population, the gender gap in education after age composition standardization still remains very large.

In order to remedy the high regional disparity in educational attainment, the Chinese government passed legislation on compulsory education in 1986, which guaranteed all school age children the right to receive nine years of schooling. Although the government did not immediately offer nine years of free education for all, it significantly stepped up the effort to improve education in the semi-urban and rural areas in terms of both quantity and quality. The government's effort to expand education is clearly evident in the increased annual education budget which grew almost 26 times from 1978 to 1998 (nominal). The share of the educational budget in total government expenditure also grew from 6.8 per cent in 1978 to 18.8 per cent in 1998. The increasing willingness to invest in education among individuals and families is also evident from the fact that a sharp increase in tuition had no effect on enrolment rates between 1990 and 1998. Tuition continued to

Educational Inequality

increase much faster than income—especially at higher educational levels of schooling—but enrolment in post-secondary educational institutions continued to skyrocket, doubling in every four years (Studwell and Kroeber 2004).

The increased educational investment resulted in a rapid expansion of education over the last two decades. Elementary school enrolment rate for school age children grew from 93.9 per cent in 1980 to 98.9 per cent in 1998, and the percentage of primary school graduates entering junior high grew from 75.9 per cent in 1980 to 94.3 per cent in 1998 (Ministry of Education various). According to almost every measure, China's overall performance in improving the educational system is impressive. The question is whether the expansion of education has been consistent and distributed fairly throughout China. Interestingly, in spite of the importance of education in the study of inequality, surprisingly little attention has been paid to the trend and extent of educational inequality in China. There are a small number of studies on educational inequality that draw insightful and eclectic pictures of educational inequality in China. Yet, most of the existing studies examine educational inequality through a magnifying glass focused on subjects such as the urban area and political shift (Zhou et al. 1998), ethnicity and education (Hannum and Xie 1998; Hannum 2002), and labour market and education (Wu and Xie 2003). There has yet to be a systematic analysis on the trend and source of educational inequality at the national level.

9.3 Data and Method

The quantitative analysis is based on a nine-year longitudinal province level data, which is derived from the *Educational Statistics Yearbook of China* and the *China Statistical Yearbook* between 1994 and 2002. Ideal data for examining educational inequality would be longitudinal individual level data from a nationally representative sample. However, such data are not yet available in China. There are, however, cross-sectional household data such as the Chinese Household Income Project (Khan and Riskin 1998) data or the household survey data collected by the National Bureau of Statistics (Song et al. 2006). Because this study aims to investigate the trend of educational inequality over time, we use the aggregate province[2] level data and employ what Kanbur and Zhang call the spatial inequality approach, in other words, the examination of variations across 31 provinces (Zhang and Kanbur 2003). After the decentralization reform was initiated in 1980, each province in China took a very different development trajectory. The administration and financing of education

---

[2] The main administrative divisions in the statistical yearbooks include 22 provinces, four municipalities (province level cities), and five autonomous regions. For simplicity, we use 'province' as the generic inclusive term to cover all three types of administrative divisions.

were also effectively decentralized as of 1985. Since then, provinces have been independently making the most of the core decisions regarding educational policies and financing. Moreover, the migration of population between provinces is still quite limited due to the persistence of the household registration system (*hukou*). From this perspective, provinces can be conceived to constitute a form of restricted social system which effectively shapes the differential opportunity structure and aspirations of individuals. Therefore, provinces are an appropriate unit for examining the pattern of educational inequality in China. The *Educational Statistics Yearbook of China* reports detailed data on student enrolments in each grade at the province level, thus offering the advantage that the data are not limited to the sample data, but cover the entire population. Therefore, there are no problems concerning sampling bias. I augment the enrolment data with other economic and social characteristic data on the provinces from the *China Statistical Yearbooks*.

The standard method in investigating educational inequality is the sequential logit model of educational transition developed by Mare (1980, 1981). Mare suggests that the best method of measuring educational inequality is to observe student transition in the educational attainment process. At each level of the process, a student decides whether to continue to the next level or to drop out. Thus, educational attainment can be measured by a series of probabilities of continuation which represent the probability of a student continuing to a specific level of schooling, given that the preceding level has been completed. The obvious advantage of dividing the attainment process into separate grade transitions is that it allows us to analyse the differentials in schooling at various stages. The model enables the efficient estimation of the impact of social environment on the variation in the transition process. Although we do not fully adopt Mare's statistical model in this chapter, we apply his measurement method for educational attainment, i.e. the probability of a student making the transition to the next level, given that they have completed the previous level.

It is clear that significant variations in educational inequality exist between geographic regions and gender among the adult population of China today. The question we want to examine in detail is whether gender-based and regional-based inequality has been diminished or increased with the expansion of education since 1978. Educational inequality over time can be measured in two different ways. The first measure used is the within cohort variation over time, which primarily provides information on whether children from a particular gender group or geographical location are more likely to stay in school longer than others. From the spatial inequality perspective, the within cohort inequality measure will tell us whether growing up in a certain province will impact differently on the child's likelihood of staying in school and obtaining higher education than growing up in other provinces.

Educational Inequality

The second measure employed is the inter-cohort variation over time. By focusing on just one schooling transition point over time, we observe the variations in transition rates between cohorts. The inter-cohort inequality measure reveals whether children from successive cohorts face more inequality or less inequality over time.

9.4 Within Cohort Inequality

In spite of the nine-year compulsory education law promulgated over 15 years ago, the national average of the probability of making the transition from grade 1 to grade 9 between 1994 and 2002 was less than 75 per cent. The nine-year compulsory education programme achieved almost immediate results in some provinces, but had slow effects in others. Since 1997, the central government exerted greater pressure on local school authorities to implement the nine-year compulsory education through the so-called 'Two Basics' (*liangji*) movement. The probability of making the transition to ninth grade among the cohort who entered primary school in 1994 can be calculated using a simple conditional probability measure:

$$\Pr(T) = \Pr(N_9|N_1) = \frac{\text{Number of students among the cohort } C_{94} \text{ who remained through grade 9}}{\text{Number of students in the cohort } C_{94} \text{ entering grade 1}} \quad (1)$$

where $\Pr(T)$ is the conditional probability of graduating to grade 9 in 2002 given that the person entered grade 1 in 1994, N_9 is the number of enrolled ninth grade students in 2002, and N_1 is the number of enrolled first grade students in 1994. Table 9.1 presents the computed within cohort transition probabilities by provinces and gender. The results show that a high level of inter-provincial disparity exists in educational attainment, and the transition probabilities vary significantly, ranging from 0.93 in Zhejiang to 0.20 in Xizang (Tibet). In other words, if students entered the first grade in 1994 in Zhejiang, they are almost five times more likely to stay in school through ninth grade than students from Xizang in the same cohort.

What accounts for such low transition rates in some provinces? The difference in the number of students between grade 1 and grade 9 is not caused simply by dropouts. Several other factors, such as death rate, contribute to the difference, as the following formula shows:

$$N_9 = N_1 + \text{immigrants} - \text{emigrants} - \text{number of deaths} - \text{dropouts} \quad (2)$$

However, the mortality rate for this age group is very low, and the difference in mortality rate between provinces is almost negligible. Therefore, we can assume

Table 9.1: Transition probability from grade 1 to 9 among the cohort who entered primary school in 1994, by provinces

Provinces (i)	Total Pr(T_i)	Female Pr($T_{i,f}$)	Male Pr($T_{i,m}$)	Gender inequality index, Pr($T_{i,m}$)=1	Inter-provincial inequality index, Pr(T_{Xizang})=1
Xizang (Tibet)	0.20	0.24	0.17	1.38	1.00
Guizhou	0.46	0.44	0.47	0.94	2.29
Qinghai	0.47	0.49	0.46	1.07	2.37
Hainan	0.49	0.47	0.50	0.95	2.43
Gansu	0.52	0.52	0.53	0.97	2.60
Ningxia	0.52	0.55	0.50	1.11	2.62
Guangxi	0.56	0.57	0.56	1.02	2.82
Yunnan	0.57	0.57	0.57	1.00	2.86
Shaanxi	0.68	0.69	0.67	1.03	3.38
Hubei	0.69	0.66	0.72	0.92	3.44
Xinjiang	0.71	0.74	0.68	1.08	3.54
Neimenggu	0.73	0.75	0.71	1.06	3.63
Jiangxi	0.73	0.69	0.76	0.91	3.64
Jilin	0.75	0.76	0.74	1.03	3.73
Sichuan/Chongqing	0.75	0.76	0.75	1.01	3.76
Jiangsu	0.78	0.76	0.80	0.95	3.89
Hebei	0.79	0.83	0.76	1.08	3.94
Henan	0.79	0.80	0.78	1.01	3.97
Liaoning	0.80	0.81	0.78	1.04	3.98
Hunan	0.80	0.80	0.79	1.01	3.98
Shanxi	0.81	0.83	0.80	1.04	4.05
Guangdong	0.81	0.80	0.82	0.97	4.07
Heilongjiang	0.83	0.85	0.81	1.04	4.15
Anhui	0.83	0.81	0.85	0.95	4.15
Shandong	0.87	0.86	0.87	0.98	4.33
Tianjin	0.91	0.92	0.90	1.02	4.54
Fujian	0.92	0.90	0.93	0.97	4.59
Zhejiang	0.93	0.93	0.92	1.00	4.63
Beijing	0.96	0.98	0.95	1.04	4.81
Shanghai	0.98	0.99	0.97	1.02	4.89

Source: Ministry of Education (various years).

that proportion of students who have died before completing the transition is constant over the provinces. What is more difficult to deal with is the contribution of immigration and emigration between provinces to the inter-provincial differences in transition probabilities. Recently, there has been a huge number of migrant manual labourers moving from rural to urban areas. However, the migration trend until 2002 still lacks long term commitment, and very few of these labourers settle down for extended stays in the cities (Zhao 1999). Workers usually leave their families behind on the farms and return home during periods of unemployment. Moreover, because of the continuing existence of the *hukou* system, it was difficult for rural migrant workers to permanently settle in the urban areas and send their children to local school where they worked. Because of the high cost of uncertainty (Todaro 1969), at least until 2002, permanent inter-provincial migration of families with school aged children was not too common in China. Therefore, we argue that most of the difference in enrolment numbers between grade 1 and 9 can be mostly attributed to dropouts. If school aged children themselves migrate to find work (in the case of some of the older students), they are then counted as dropouts.

The first surprising outcome revealed by the within cohort probability of making the transition from grade 1 to 9 among those who entered primary school in 1994 is that gender inequality has been almost completely eliminated. The gender inequality index, which is calculated using the following equation, shows that female students in most provinces are even more likely to stay in school than male students:

$$\text{Gender inequality index for province } i = 1 + \frac{\Pr(T_{i,f}) - \Pr(T_{i,m})}{\Pr(T_{i,m})} \qquad (3)$$

where $\Pr(T_{i,f})$ is the probability of female students making the transition in province i, and $\Pr(T_{i,m})$ is the probability of male students making the transition in province i. The gender inequality index is simply a standardized ratio of the female probability of transition from grade 1 to 9 in province i by setting the male transition probability in the same province as 1.

In some provinces, the substantial gender inequality presently existing among the adult population is reversed among students in this particular cohort. This reversal occurs not only in rich provinces with a high proportion of well educated people, but also in poor provinces. For example, in Tibet, the probability of a female student graduating from grade 9 is 38 per cent higher than for a male student. Overall, it is clear that gender inequality has been significantly reduced. This result is a surprising reversal of the gender inequality that persisted throughout the early 1990s, as earlier research points out (Zhou et al. 1998). The expansion of education has clearly had a favourable effect on female students. The finding is also supported by a recent study that used a household survey data (Song et al. 2006).

The reversal of gender inequality may reflect the government's conscious effort to decrease educational inequality between genders. Since 1997, the Chinse government has aggressively pushed for the 'Two Basics' (*liangji*) movement targeting elimination of illiteracy and universalization of nine-year compulsory education. The elimination of gender inequality has been an important element in the movement from the beginning. In order to encourage schools to place a greater emphasis on gender equality, the education ministry has even included gender ratio as a category for evaluating school performance. I suggest that the virtual elimination of gender inequality in education reported above partly refects the effects of government initiated propaganda as well as the policy changes in favour of girls. As Song et al. (2006) reports, however, gender inequality in education begins to increase after ninth grade.

Inter-provincial educational inequality, however, still remains very high. The inter-provincial inequality index, which is calculated according to the same standardization method as the gender inequality index, shows that a student attending school in Beijing in the 1994 cohort is 4.89 times more likely to make the transition to ninth grade than a student in Xizang:

$$\text{Inter-provincial inequality index for province } i = 1 + \frac{\Pr(T_i) - \Pr(T_{Xizang})}{\Pr(T_{Xizang})} \quad (4)$$

where $\Pr(T_{i,Xizang})$ is the average transition probability in the province of Xizang (Tibet) which is used as the comparison province, and $\Pr(T_i)$ is the average transition probability in province i which is being compared with Xizang. What is clear from the figures in the index is that unlike the reduced gender bias against girls, a huge inter-provincial gap in terms of educational attainment still remains. Students in the coastal provinces have a much better probability of making the transition to grade 9 than students in the inland

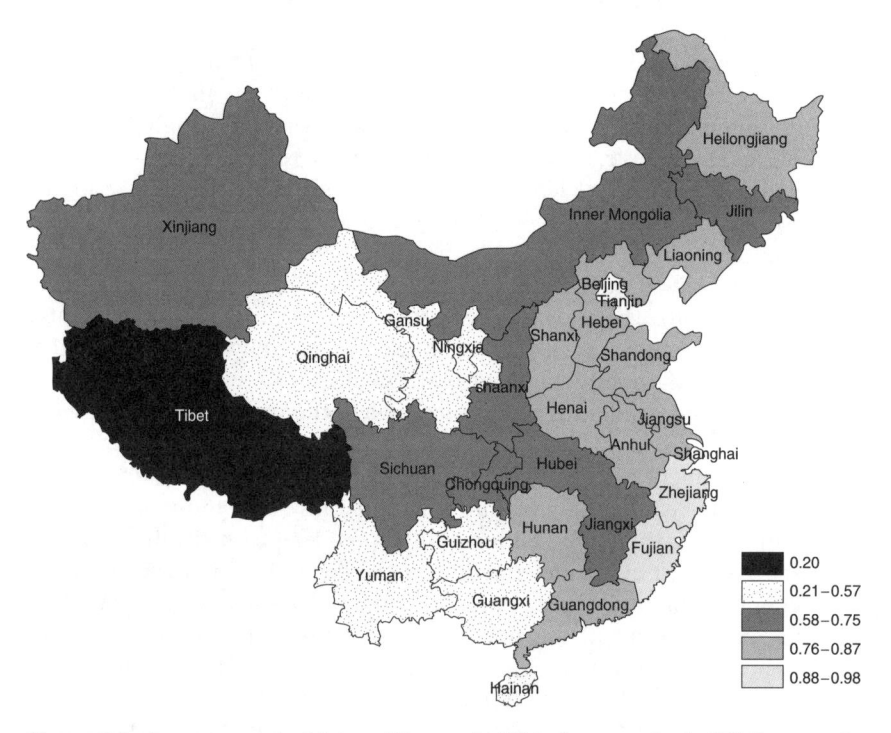

Figure 9.2: Average provincial transition probability from grade 1 (1994) to grade 9 (2002)

Source: Ministry of Education (1995–2003).

provinces. The pattern of coastal–inland inequality is clearly visible from the GIS projection where light shading indicate high transition probability and darker shading indicate lower probability (see Figure 9.2).

9.5 Inter-cohort Inequality

In most western societies, the inequality of educational opportunity, as measured by differences in educational attainment of children from advantaged and disadvantaged families has declined steadily during industrialization (Boudon 1974; Brooks-Gunn et al. 1997). In other words, with economic growth, younger generation of students face less inequality in educational opportunities regardless of their socioeconomic background. How is the educational opportunity changing for the successive generations of Chinese students? Is the existing inter-provincial inequality increasing or decreasing over time? In order to measure the inter-cohort variations over the years, we examine the variations in each cohort's first major education transition (i.e. going from elementary school to junior high). Junior highschools in China are divided into academic and vocational tracks, and the enrolment number used here for junior highschools is the total of both tracks.

The national average transition probability between grades 6 and 7 has increased steadily over successive cohorts, as the positive slope of the fitted least squares line over the mean indicates. The mean transition rate increased substantially from 89.5 per cent for the 1994–5 cohort to 95.1 per cent for the 2001–2 cohort. What this result confirms is that elementary education has indeed been expanding over the nine-year period under observation, and that with each successive generation, a greater proportion of students are graduating from elementary school to junior high: more and more students are receiving a basic education in literacy. Not only has there been a general upward trend of the mean transition probability, but the distribution gap of the transition probability between provinces has also been narrowing. As the converging pattern of scatterplot in Figure 9.3 shows, the overall differences in transition probabilities between provinces are diminishing. The decreasing divergence of provincial transition rates within each cohort is clear evidence of China's diminishing regional inequality for this particular schooling transition point. The relative ranking of provinces, however, did not change significantly. In other words, students from Xizang province are still disadvantaged compared to those from Zhejiang province, but the degree of disadvantage has been significantly reduced. Overall, evidence indicates that inequality is clearly in decline.

Judging from the inter-cohort trend at this particular transition point, China has successfully achieved the primary objective of educational expansion (i.e. greater equality in educational opportunity). The question is

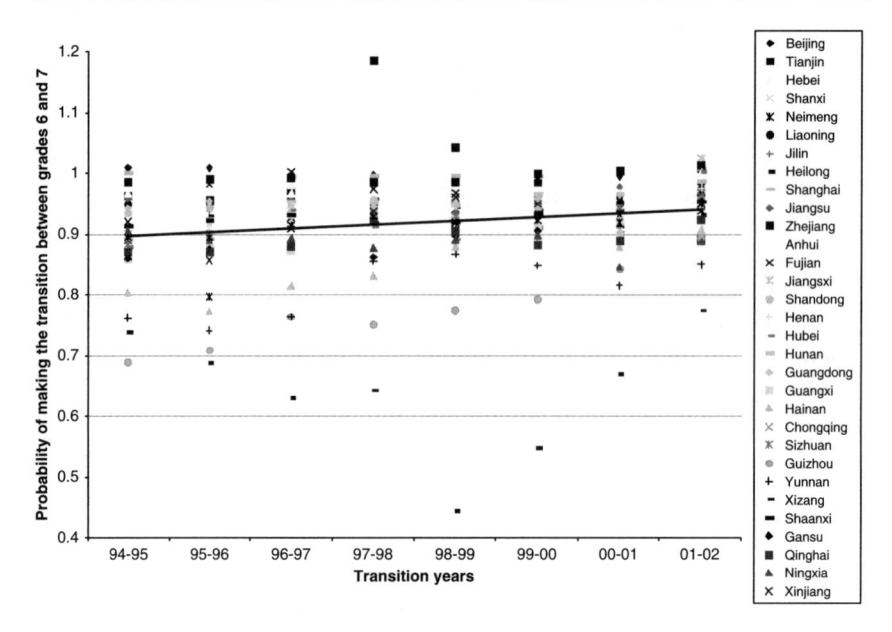

Figure 9.3: Inter-cohort comparison of transition probability from elementary to junior highschool, between provinces, 1994–2002

Source: Compiled from *Educational Yearbook of China*, 1995–2002, Ministry of Education.

whether this trend will continue into upper-year schooling. Are the students who achieved the junior highschool level equally likely to stay until grade 9 and graduate? To answer this question, we trace the trend for two more years for the same cohorts who made the transition from elementary school to junior high. The results are presented in Figure 9.4 below.

Two striking features stand out in comparison to the two sets of inter-cohort transition probabilities presented in Figures 9.3 and 9.4. Figure 9.4, which plots the inter-cohort comparison of transition probabilities in upper school years (from grade 7 to 9), shows a completely opposite pattern to that in Figure 9.3. First of all, the fitted least squares line over the mean shows a downward trend in the inter-cohort variations, indicating that the transition probability for the successive cohorts actually deteriorated slightly (from 90.2 per cent for the 1995–7 cohort to 89.4 per cent for the 2000–2 cohort). These are the same first six cohorts of students observed in the previous analysis depicted on Figure 9.3.

Whereas a greater number of younger cohort of students are gradually making the transition from elementary school to junior high, a smaller number of students from younger cohorts are staying in school until grade 9. Although the difference is not huge in percentages, in absolute numbers, among the cohort of students who entered junior high in 2000, almost

Educational Inequality

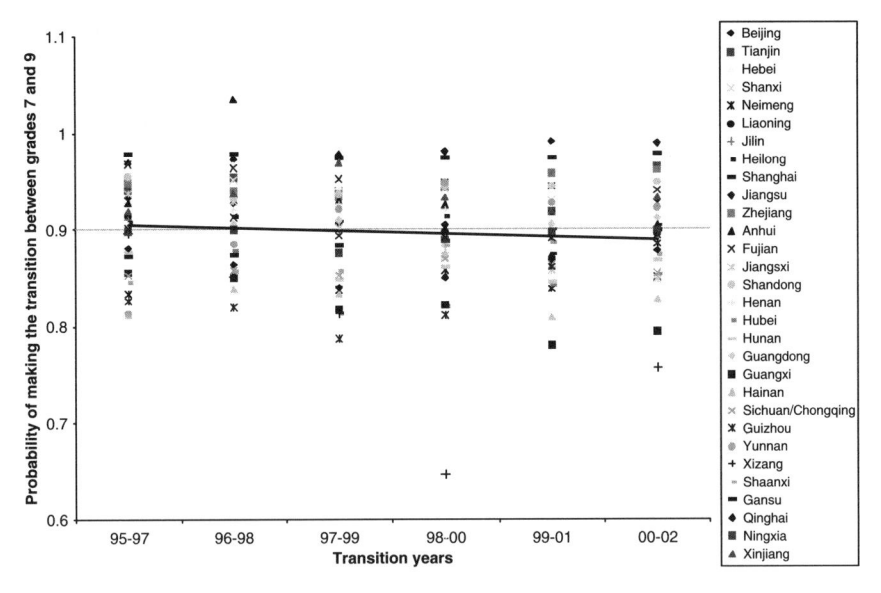

Figure 9.4: Inter-cohort comparison of transition probability from grade 7 to grade 9, between provinces, 1995–2002

Source: Compiled from *Educational Yearbook of China, 1995–2002*, Ministry of Education.

800,000 more pupils dropped out versus the 1995 cohort. What is even more surprising is that the dropout rate increased *in spite of* the sharp increase in the government's educational spending and the growing demand for more skilled and educated workers due to rapid economic expansion. The rational choice theory in the sociology of education predicts that an individual's educational decision is based on their expectation of the related costs and benefits (Breen and Goldthorpe 1997; Morgan 1998). Therefore, individuals will stay in school longer when the potential future payoff from an additional year of schooling becomes greater while the cost of education remains steady or decreases. Yet, quite interestingly, in China today, we see an opposite trend.

The second striking difference between the two transition patterns is that the dispersion of transition probability between provinces shows a gradually diverging pattern over time, indicating that the inter-provincial inequality of educational attainment at junior high-school level is being aggravated. The diverging pattern is clearly visible in the scatterplot, where the standard deviations increase from 0.47 for the 1995–7 cohorts to 0.52 for the 2000–2 cohorts (see Figure 9.4). In fact, the rise in the national dropout rate in successive cohorts is mostly due to the increasing dropout rates in provinces where the transition rate had already been comparatively low. Students in provinces with already high transition rates are continuing to stay in school,

175

while successive cohorts in the already disadvantaged provinces are dropping out in greater numbers.

The patterns presented in Figures 9.3 and 9.4 indicate that while educational inequality is decreasing during the earlier years of school, it is increasing in the later years. Evidence from the analysis indicates that the situation is becoming worse. This implies that even though China is moving towards greater equality in terms of basic literacy, inequality is increasing with regard to more advanced technical skills and knowledge. Technical skills and expertise in certain fields often necessitate longer training than nine years of schooling, and those dropping out before ninth grade will not do well in the modern labour market. If markets continue to expand and employers place greater emphasis on the skill and knowledge that require higher education, as Nee (1989) predicts, then income inequality will continue to increase in China.

9.6 Decomposition

A theoretical as well as a policy related issue that arises from this analysis is the source of the existing inequality and whether it is something that policy-makers should be concerned about. The primary candidate for the source of educational inequality is the urban bias evident in the government's policies and institutional investment. Previous studies find that students living in large cities have a significant advantage over those in small cities or rural areas with regard to the odds of obtaining higher education (Knight and Li 1996; Zhou et al. 1998; Kanbur and Zhang 1999; Zhang and Kanbur 2003). The main locus of income inequality is also argued to be between urban and rural areas (Yang 1999). Looking at the transition probability between grade 7 and 9 for the period 2000–2, there is clear urban–rural difference: the average national transition probability for urban students was 0.95, whereas it was 0.77 for rural students. Consequently, the inference that emerges from this is that the different ratio of urban and rural population composition should explain a big portion of the spatial educational differential.

A central empirical question needs to be addressed for theoretically confirming the urban bias hypothesis for spatial inequality: how much of the inter-provincial difference in transition probability among provinces is attributable to variations in their urban–rural population composition? The within province difference in enrolment rate between two points in time (ΔE_i) can be separated into three sectoral components that represent differences in urban, semi-urban (*xiang/zhen*), and rural areas:

$$\sum_i \frac{\Delta E_i}{N} = \sum_i \frac{\Delta E_{iU}}{N} + \sum_i \frac{\Delta E_{iX}}{N} + \sum_i \frac{\Delta E_{iR}}{N}, \quad (i = 1, \ldots, N) \qquad (5)$$

Educational Inequality

where N represents the number of provinces and ΔE_i denotes the difference in enrolment rate in province i during the period under observation. The sectoral subscripts U, X, and R denote urban, semi-urban (*xiang/zhen*), and rural areas, respectively. Each province has a very different population composition between urban and rural areas. For example, in Beijing which is essentially an extended city with some annexed rural counties, over 44 per cent of students live in urban areas where the educational system is usually better. On the other hand, in the neighbouring province of Hebei, only 10 per cent of the students live in urban areas. The urban–rural difference hypothesis assumes that each component contributes unequal weights to the total difference. In order to isolate the different contribution of the population composition to the inter-provincial totals in educational attainment, we use a standard demographic technique of decomposing the differences in rate (Kitagawa 1955; Kim and Strobino 1984; Preston et al. 2001). Let the original difference between two provinces be defined as Δ:

$$\Delta = T_A - T_B = \sum_i C_i^A \cdot D_i^A - \sum_i C_i^B \cdot D_i^B \qquad (6)$$

where T_A denotes the transition probability of province A and T_B the transition probability of province B. C_i^A is the proportion of population in sector i in province A, and D_i^A is the sector specific transition probability in sector i in province A, and vice versa. Using simple algebraic methods, we can recombine the terms on the right-hand side of equation (6) and produce:

$$\Delta = \sum_i (C_i^A - C_i^B) \cdot \left[\frac{D_i^A + D_i^B}{2}\right] + \sum_i (D_i^A - D_i^B) \cdot \left[\frac{C_i^A + C_i^B}{2}\right] \qquad (7)$$

The first part of equation (7) is the contribution of the sectoral population composition difference to the total Δ and the second part of the equation (7) is the contribution of the rate schedule differences to Δ. Due to space limitations, only a few sample results are presented in Table 9.2. For this decomposition analysis, we use the transition probability from grade 1 to 4 among the cohort who entered grade 1 in 1994. This particular transition period is used because this is the age when the student population is more or less stable. For older pupils (especially from grade 6 or 7), there is substantial inter-sectoral movement because many rural areas do not have schools for older students. However, most children in grade 4 or lower still attend the local school.

The first set of provinces to be compared is Xizang (Tibet) and Zhejiang. Xizang has the lowest average transition probability between grade 1 and 4 at 0.56, and Zhejiang has the highest among all the provinces at 0.99 (excluding the three province level municipalities). Is the difference in rates mainly attributed to differences in the urban–rural population composition? As the population composition data in Table 9.2 indicate, the two provinces have

Table 9.2: Decomposition results and population compositions in the sampled provinces

	Xizang	Zhejiang	Xizang	Xinjiang
Provincial transition rate	0.56	0.99	0.56	0.83
Urban population composition, %	5.2	13.4	5.2	11.6
Xiang/Zhen population composition, %	10.4	62.8	10.4	9.9
Rural population composition, %	84.4	23.8	84.4	78.5
Contribution of population composition, %	36.4		6.8	
Contribution of other inter-provincial differences, %	63.6		93.2	
	Hunan	Guizhou	Sichuan/CQ	Gansu
Provincial transition rate	0.98	0.73	0.98	0.71
Urban population composition, %	9.2	4.6	6.7	7.3
Xiang/Zhen population composition, %	13.9	7.2	26.6	7.0
Rural population composition, %	76.9	88.2	66.6	85.6
Contribution of population composition, %	28.2		1.4	
Contribution of other inter-provincial differences, %	71.8		98.6	

Source: Ministry of Education (various years).

significantly diverging urban–rural population composition: in Xizang nearly 85 per cent of the students live in rural communities whereas the corresponding figure for Zhejiang is only 24 per cent. The difference in population composition does indeed account for over 36 per cent of the variance. However, the remaining 64 per cent constitutes a difference in rates that cannot be explained by the different population composition. In other words, even if the population composition between Xizang and Zhejiang were identical, the differential in transition rate between the two would still be 0.27, implying that 27 per cent more students in Xizang will *not* make the transition from grade 1 to 4.

The population composition controlled difference in rates is much more pronounced if we compare Xizang with Xinjiang. The two are neighbouring provinces in northwestern China with similar urban–rural population structure. However, the average provincial transition probability between grade 1 and 4 shows a large gap. When the same decomposition technique is applied to these two provinces, the variance in population composition accounts for only 7 per cent of the total difference in rates; 93 per cent of the difference in rates comes from other factors. I also compare two sets of neighbouring provinces with shared borders: Hunan and Guizhou, and Sichuan (including Chongqing) and Gansu. There were, however, marked differences in their respective transition rates between grade 1 and 4. Again, population composition contributes a rather small amount to the overall inter-provincial differences in transition probabilities.

The cases above were chosen to illustrate the point that, contrary to the urban bias hypothesis, the inter-provincial difference does not primarily originate from differences in the population or geographical composition. Although the urban–rural divide indeed plays a significant role in aggravating educational inequality (Knight and Li 1996), the source of inequality is much more complex and systemic. Students in the rural areas of Zhejing or Jiangsu have a much better chance of making the transition from grade 1 to 4 than students in rural Xizang or Guizhou. Part of the reason is related to the differences in income and living standard between the rural areas in coastal and inland provinces. Even rural areas tend to be much more affluent and developed in coastal provinces than in inland provinces. The current analysis does not fully account for the heterogeneity in living standards between rural areas. Nonetheless, the result does paint a rather complex picture of educational inequality in China. There are other, yet unidentified, structural barriers that discourage students in inland provinces from staying in school, and economic expansion of inland provinces will not automatically solve the problem.

9.7 Conclusion

This study attempts to achieve two objectives: (1) to examine and present an accurate picture of the current distribution of education attainment in China from both static and dynamic perspectives; and (2) to test the urban bias hypothesis. On the one hand, there is clear evidence of the rapid expansion of education, and younger students all over China are benefiting from the expansion. One of the most notable achievements is the virtual elimination of gender bias against girls in educational attainment. On the other hand, however, inter-provincial inequality of educational attainment still remains large, and has even grown worse among upper grade students. Students from inland provinces continue to face considerable structural inequality in educational opportunity, and this becomes more pronounced in the upper grades.

The decomposition analysis shows that this inter-provincial inequality does not originate from differences in urban–rural population composition, as can be inferred from earlier research on income inequality. The source is much more complex. From a policymaker's perspective, this is a worrisome outcome. One hypothesis on the trend of educational inequality implies that it follows the famous Kuznets inverted-U-shaped curve. As the economy expands and the overall level of schooling increases, educational inequality initially increases but diminishes after a certain threshold (Ram 1990). However, the results from this study suggest that economic expansion, as represented by the size of urban population, is unlikely to automatically reduce educational inequality—a much more sophisticated and province specific measure is needed.

The natural next step in research is to identify the causal influences on differential transition probabilities among provinces using multivariate methods. Several scholars have indirectly suggested potential causal variables. Zhang and Kanbur (2003) suggest that the fiscal decentralization of educational funding resulted in unbalanced educational investments among the provinces, and aggravated inter-provincial inequality. Hannum's study (2002) suggests that the proportion of minorities in each province would affect inter-provincial differences. Nee's theory of transition economy (1989, 1996) suggests that the different level of marketization in each province will affect the importance of educational credential, which in turn produces variations in educational attainment between provinces. The existing inequality in university entrance quotas between provinces may also affect student aspirations for pursuance of further education. The current system requires students from interior provinces to obtain much higher national exam scores to enter top universities than students from large coastal cities. Moreover, the probability of entering university is much lower for students in interior provinces compared to their counterparts in large coastal cities due to structural limitations created educational policies. Therefore, the incentive to remain in school is much lower of students in inland provinces. The next research project extending on this study will involve multivariate analyses of these various causal factors that are purported to affect inter-provincial differences in educational attainment.

Another research direction highlighted by this study is the relationship between the present educational inequality and future earnings inequality. Classical economic theory postulates that the expansion of education will negatively affect inequality through the increased supply of skilled workforce which in turn reduces the educational premium (Knight and Sabot 1983; Gottschalk and Smeeding 1997). But the expansion of education in China had no impact on earnings inequality, and even in some cases aggravated inequality (Hannum and Xie 1998). This study shows that educational expansion in China did not have the well known equalizing effect because expansion was highly uneven and opportunities unequally distributed. Such an uneven educational development has strong implications for China's future socioeconomic inequality. Education has repeatedly been proven to be the most consistent and significant predictor of future earnings for individuals (Becker 1964; Blau and Duncan 1967; Sewell et al. 1969; Mincer 1974; Polacheck and Siebert 1993; Ashenfelter and Rouse 1999). Therefore, assuming that reform polices for greater marketization and privatization will continue in China, the growing inter-provincial educational inequality at the upper level of schooling will fuel greater earnings inequality between provinces (Nee 1996, 2004; Nee and Matthews 1996; Wu and Xie 2003). This hypothesis is waiting to be tested with a more adequate dataset.

There are largely two types of policy interventions to address the problem of inequality. The first approach directly targets the outcome through stratified collection and redistribution of resources by central authority (Jencks et al. 1972; Moller et al. 2003). The second approach focuses on the equalization of opportunity by removing structural barriers to social mobility. Being an important predictor of social status and economic well-being, education is often linked to the opportunity for social mobility. Equal opportunity in education will not eliminate inequality in outcome (Coleman 1990), but *unequal* opportunity in education will most likely solidify, if not increase, social and economic inequality. China has experimented with direct redistribution to an extreme degree but without success, and is now moving away from the redistribution system in favour of market economy that places greater emphasis on market mechanisms and individual freedom in the redistribution of resources. It is unlikely that the Chinese government will go back to equal outcome for all. Therefore, an important question is how to implement policy to reduce inequality without reversing the direction of reform? We hope this study is an important initial step toward finding an answer to this essential question.

References

Ashenfelter, O., and C. Rouse (1999). 'Schooling, Intelligence, and Income in America: Cracks in the Bell Curve', NBER Working Paper 6902, National Bureau of Economic Research: Cambridge, MA.

Becker, G. (1964). *Human Capital*, National Bureau of Economic Research: Cambridge, MA.

Bian, Y., and J. Logan (1996). 'Market Transition and the Persistence of Power: The Changing Stratification System in Urban China', *American Sociological Review* 61: 739–58.

Blau, P. M., and O. D. Duncan (1967). *The American Occupational Structure*, Wiley: New York.

Boudon, R. (1974). *Education, Opportunity, and Social Inequality: Changing Prospects in Western Society*, Wiley: New York.

Breen, R., and J. H. Goldthorpe (1997). 'Explaining Educational Differentials: Towards a Formal Rational Action Theory', *Rationality and Society* 9: 275–305.

Brooks-Gunn, J., G. J. Duncan, and J. L. Aber (1997). *Neighborhood Poverty*, Russell Sage Foundation: New York.

Coleman, J. S. (1990). *Equality and Achievement in Education*, Westview Press: Boulder.

Cremin, L. (1951). *The American Common School: A Historic Conception*, Teachers College Press: New York.

Deng, Z., and D. J. Treiman (1997). 'The Impact of the Cultural Revolution on Trends in Educational Attainment in the People's Republic of China', *American Journal of Sociology* 103: 391–428.

Gottschalk, P., and T. M. Smeeding (1997). 'Cross-National Comparisons of Earnings and Income Inequality', *Journal of Economic Literature* 35: 633–87.

Hannum, E. (2002). 'Educational Stratification by Ethnicity in China: Enrollment and Attainment in the Early Reform Years', *Demography* 39: 95–117.

—— Y. Xie (1998). 'Ethnic Stratification in Northwest China: Occupational Differences between Han Chinese and National Minorities in Xinjiang, 1982–1990', *Demography* 35: 323–33.

Jencks, C., M. Smith, H. Acland et al. (eds) (1972). *Inequality: A Reassessment of the Effect of Family and Schooling in America*, Basic Books: New York.

Kanbur, R., and X. Zhang (1999). 'Which Regional Inequality? The Evolution of Rural–Urban and Coast–Inland Inequality in China', *Journal of Comparative Economics* 27: 686–907.

Khan, A., and C. Riskin (1998). 'Income and Inequality in China: Composition, Distribution and Growth of Household Income, 1988 to 1995', *The China Quarterly* 154: 221–53.

Kim, Y. J., and D. M. Strobino (1984). 'Decomposition of the Difference between Two Rates with Hierarchical Factors', *Demography* 21: 361–72.

Kitagawa, E. M. (1955). 'Components of a Difference Between Two Rates', *Journal of American Statistical Association* 50: 1168–94.

Knight, J. B., and R. H. Sabot (1983). 'Educational Expansion and the Kuznets Effect', *American Economic Review* 73: 1132–6.

—— S. Li (1996). 'Educational Attainment and the Rural–Urban Divide in China', *Oxford Bulletin of Economics and Statistics* 58: 83–117.

Mare, R. D. (1980). 'Social Background and School Continuation Decisions', *Journal of the American Statistical Association* 75: 295–305.

—— (1981). 'Chanage and Stability in Eduational Stratification', *American Sociological Review* 46.

Meng, X., R. Gregory, and Y. Wang (2005). 'Poverty, Inequality, and Growth in Urban China, 1986–2000', *Journal of Comparative Economics* 33: 710–29.

Meyer, J. W., F. O. Ramirez, and Y. N. Soysal (1992). 'World Expansion of Mass Education, 1870–1980', *Sociology of Education* 65: 128–49.

Mincer, J. (1974). *Schooling, Experience, and Earnings*, Kluwer: New York.

Ministry of Education (various). *Educational Statistics Yearbook of China*, People's Education Press: Beijing.

Moller, S., D. Bradley, E. Huber, F. Nielsen, and J. D. Stephens (2003). 'Determinants of Relative Poverty in Advanced Capitalist Democracies', *American Sociological Review* 68: 22–51.

Morgan, S. L. (1998). 'Adolescent Educational Expectations', *Rationality and Society* 10: 131–62.

Nee, V. (1989). 'Theory of Market Transition: from Redistribution to Markets in State Socialism', *American Sociological Review* 54: 663–81.

—— (1996). 'The Emergence of a Market Society: Changing Mechanisms of Stratification in China', *American Journal of Sociology* 101: 908–49.

—— (2004). 'Market Transition and the Firm: Institutional Change and Income Inequality in Urban China', *Management and Organization Review* 1: 19–52.

—— R. Matthews (1996). 'Market Transition and Societal Transformation in Reforming State Socialism', *Annual Review of Sociology* 22: 401–35.

Pepper, S. (1980). 'Chinese Education after Mao: Two Steps Forward, Two Steps Back and Begin Again?', *The China Quarterly* 81: 1–65.

Polacheck, S. W., and W. S. Siebert (1993). *The Economics of Earnings*, Cambridge University Press.

Preston, S. H., P. Heuveline, and M. Guillot (2001). *Demography: Measuring and Modeling Population Processes*, Blackwell Publishers: Oxford.

Ram, R. (1990). 'Educational Expansion and Schooling Inequality: International Evidence and Some Implications', *The Review of Economics and Statistics* 72: 266–74.

Ravallion, M., and S. Chen (2004). 'China's (Uneven) Progress Against Poverty', World Bank Working Paper 3408, World Bank: Washington, DC.

Sewell, W. H., A. O. Haller, and A. Portes (1969). 'The Educational and Early Occupational Attainment Process', *American Sociological Review* 34: 82–92.

Song, L., S. Appleton, and J. Knight (2006). 'Why Do Girls in Rural China Have Lower School Enrollment?' *World Development* 34: 1639–53.

Studwell, J., and A. Kroeber (2004). 'The Economics of Education in China', *The Financial Times*: London.

Todaro, M. P. (1969). 'A Model of Labor Migration and Urban Unemployment in Less Developed Countries', *American Economic Review* 59: 138–48.

Wang, Y. C. (1960). 'Western Impact and Social Mobility in China', *American Sociological Review* 25: 843–55.

Wu, X., and Y. Xie (2003). 'Does the Market Pay Off? Earning Returns to Education in Urban China', *American Sociological Review* 68: 425–42.

Yang, D. T. (1999). 'Urban-Based Policies and Rising Income Inequality in China', *American Economic Review* 89: 306–10.

Zhang, X., and R. Kanbur (2003). 'Spatial Inequality in Education and Health Care in China', CEPR Discussion Paper 4136, Centre for Economic Policy Research: London.

Zhao, Y. (1999). 'Labor Migration and Earnings Differences: The Case of Rural China', *Economic Development and Cultural Change* 47: 767–82.

Zhou, X. (2000). 'Economic Transformation and Income Inequality in Urban China', *American Journal of Sociology* 105: 1135–74.

—— P. Moen, and N. B. Tuma (1998). 'Educational Stratification in Urban China: 1949–94', *Sociology of Education* 71: 199–222.

10

Poverty Accounting by Factor Components: With an Empirical Illustration Using Rural Chinese Data*

Guanghua Wan

10.1 Introduction

Culminating in the Millennium Declaration, poverty reduction has been the most important and overarching goal of development for a decade or so. Despite controversies over the roles of growth versus redistribution (Dollar and Kraay 2002), one cannot refute the use of redistribution[1] as a powerful weapon in the fight against poverty when the size of the economic pie is given. On the other hand, growth is bound to benefit the poor even if it does not induce more inequality. At any particular point of time, the size of the pie or resource base is pre-determined. Under this static circumstance, redistribution is the only option for reducing poverty. Over time, however, growth may occur, leading to the expansion in the size of the resource base or the pie. Under this dynamic circumstance, the nature of growth has intrinsic bearings on the poverty profile. An equitable growth process or a fair distribution of extra resources or welfares generated by growth is needed to ensure that poverty does not rise over time. To reduce poverty requires progressive redistribution of the initial and/or expanded pie or resources.

Thus, the fundamental issue is not so much about '*if* growth or redistribution helps reduce poverty', of more significance and urgency is to address '*what factor* growth and redistribution for poverty reduction?' Since economic outputs are produced by factor inputs and output distributions are essentially driven by

---

* The author acknowledges useful comments from Tony Shorrocks, Erik Thorbecke, Nanak Kakwani, James Foster, and colleagues at UNU-WIDER.

[1] In this chapter, redistribution is not only referred to transfer or reallocation of outputs from, but also re-allocation of inputs into, economic activities.

factor distributions, it would be particularly interesting and indeed important to ascertain by how much poverty would increase or decrease when these fundamental inputs or determinants of outputs are redistributed and/or their quantities alter. This can produce valuable insights regarding which factor growth and/or redistribution is more important in affecting poverty or its changes.

Clearly, what is needed is a prescriptive rather than descriptive approach to poverty decomposition. While valuable, the descriptive approach which has so far prevailed in the literature largely focuses on the symptoms of poverty such as measuring overall poverty and decomposing it by sector, location, or population subgroups. The prescriptive decomposition, as will be proposed in this chapter, directly identifies and quantifies the causes or sources of poverty. To better comprehend the prescriptive approach requires a change of perception on growth vs. redistribution effects from being output-based to being input-based. From the output-based perspective, the concepts of 'growth' and 'redistribution' are in terms of outputs of economic activities, such as GDP, income, and consumption. In contrast, from the input-based perspective, growth and redistribution are in terms of factor inputs or determinants of economic outputs. Under the conventional output-based perspective, research findings and policy recommendations are confined to either 'more output growth' or 'progressive output redistribution'. This perception seems somehow restrictive, rendering the findings too general or too broad for policymakers who, in all likelihood, would ask: what factors to 'grow' or redistribute—capital, education, infrastructure, or other factor inputs?

To answer this kind of vital and pragmatic questions appeals for poverty decomposition by factor components—attributing poverty and poverty changes to fundamental determinants of economic activities. Two such decompositions will be developed in this chapter, respectively corresponding to the static and dynamic cases discussed at the onset of this chapter. In the static case, accounting for the *level* of poverty (or simply level accounting/decomposition) can help reveal the compositions of a given poverty, which provides information on the consequences of factor redistributions on poverty. In the dynamic case, accounting for the *change* in poverty (or simply difference accounting/decomposition) can help discover sources of increased or decreased poverty, which yields information on the impacts of growths and distributions of various fundamental determinants on poverty dynamics. Both forms of accounting offer useful ingredients for the formulation and execution of development policies and strategies. In fact, they are complementary to each other given that the current level of poverty may affect subsequent growth and that policymakers are confronted with both the level of and the changes in poverty. As long as redistribution remains a policy option, the level decomposition is relevant. It is interesting to note the parallel literature on inequality accounting where attention has been mostly focused on the level decomposition.

Poverty decomposition by factor components appears to be absent in the current literature. A related contribution is that by Datt and Ravallion (1992), who popularized the growth vs. redistribution decomposition of a poverty change. This useful contribution falls within the output-based perception; the critical link of poverty with its fundamental determinants was not considered. As mentioned earlier, insofar as income or expenditure (or any other output variable of human well being)[2] is a function of more fundamental variables, it is possible and indeed important to establish such a link, which will enable identification of the growth and redistribution effects of these individual factors on poverty.

This chapter is written with two major objectives in mind. First, we develop two poverty accounting frameworks. The level decomposition is presented in section 10.2 while changes of poverty or the dynamic decomposition is considered in section 10.3. Second, we illustrate the applicability of these decomposition techniques in section 10.4, where we decompose poverty levels and a poverty change in rural China. Section 10.5 concludes the chapter.

10.2 Accounting for the Level of Poverty[3]

It has been rigorously established that for a given poverty line z, the level of poverty $P(Y; z)$, measured in terms of income or expenditure Y, is completely determined by the distribution of Y. The distribution of Y can be characterized by its mean and its Lorenz curve. Assuming, for ease of exposition, there are two or two groups of fundamental variables used for producing Y, say X_i and X_j, such that $Y = f(X_i, X_j)$, then the poverty level $P(Y; z)$ can be equivalently expressed as $P(X_i, X_j; z)$.

When all factors are distributed evenly among all N agents or recipients (i.e. $X_i = \mu_i$ and $X_j = \mu_j$), Y is identical for everyone and inequality in Y disappears. As a consequence, all recipients receive $\mu_Y = f(\mu_i, \mu_j)$ where μ denotes mean or expected values appropriately indexed. The corresponding poverty $P(\mu_Y; z)$,[4] if any remaining at all, is then entirely attributable to the shortage of resource endowments. Consequently, we can define $P_E(Y; z) \equiv P(\mu_Y; z)$ as the endowment component of poverty, any reduction of which cannot be achieved by redistribution but only by increasing resources. Since $P_E(Y; z)$ represents poverty with completely even distributions of all resources and $P(Y; z)$ represents poverty with existing (most likely uneven) distributions of the same resources,

---

[2] Income or expenditure will be used as the target variable in this chapter, but use of other measures of human well being does not change the thrust of the study.

[3] In a different context, the level of poverty can be decomposed into chronic and transitory components. See Thorbecke (2004). Poverty can also be decomposed by sectors or population subgroups. Both decompositions are essentially descriptive in nature rather than prescriptive.

[4] μ_Y is a scalar but will be treated as a vector whenever necessary and appropriate. Such an abuse of notation does not seem to cause confusion.

the difference $P(Y;z) - P_E(Y;z)$ naturally represents contributions due to resource redistributions. Therefore, we can define $P_R(Y;z) \equiv P(Y;z) - P_E(Y;z)$ as the redistribution or inequality component of poverty. Such a definition is consistent with the 'before and after' principle of Cancian and Reed (1998). It is also used by Shorrocks (1980, 1982, 1984) for developing the classic frameworks of inequality decomposition by factor components or population subgroups. $P_R(Y;z)$ measures how much poverty could be reduced if all factors were evenly distributed. In other words, it measures that part of poverty caused by unequal distribution of resources.

Following the above discussions, the observed poverty level can be expressed as:

$$P(Y;z) = P_E(Y;z) + P_R(Y;z) \qquad (1)$$

When redistributions of Xs are sufficient for eliminating poverty, $P_E(Y;z) \equiv P(\mu_Y;z) = 0$ and $P(Y;z) = P_R(Y;z)$. This corroborates the scenario that there are sufficient resources; but poverty exists merely due to unequal distribution of these resources or production factors.

Equation (1) might be useful, but it is not very interesting. In particular, when the headcount ratio is used, $P_E(Y;z) = P(\mu_Y;z)$ can only take two values: 0 per cent if $\mu_Y > z$ or 100 per cent otherwise. What is more challenging and useful is to further decompose $P_R(Y;z)$ and $P_E(Y;z)$ into finer components associated with individual determinants of Y. That is, to work out:

$$P_R(Y;z) = P_R(X_i) + P_R(X_j) \qquad (2)$$

$$P_E(Y;z) = P_E(X_i) + P_E(X_j) \qquad (3)$$

where subscript R indexes a redistribution component and E an endowment component.[5]

By definition, $P_R(X_i)$ represents poverty that is caused by unequal distribution of X_i. To obtain its value, the so-called before–after principle can be used. This principle is widely used in different contexts by others, in addition to Shorrocks (1980, 1982, 1984) and Cancian and Reed (1998). Here, it involves constructing counterfactuals with and without the equal distribution of X_i and then measuring the corresponding poverty levels. The difference between these two levels is defined as the marginal contribution of X_i to the redistribution component of poverty, denoted by $MC_R(X_i)$:

$$MC_R(X_i) = P(X_i, X_j) - P(\mu_i, X_j) \qquad (4)$$

---

[5] To simplify notations but also maintain consistency, z will be dropped hereafter from expressions where input variables rather than Y are used as arguments of a poverty measure.

Similarly:

$$MC_R(X_j) = P(X_i, X_j) - P(X_i, \mu_j) \qquad (5)$$

These marginal contributions are termed first round effects because the before–after principle can also be used to obtain:

$$MC_R(X_i) = P(X_i, \mu_j) - P(\mu_i, \mu_j) \qquad (6)$$

$$MC_R(X_j) = P(\mu_i, X_j) - P(\mu_i, \mu_j) \qquad (7)$$

Faced with multiple estimates of the same marginal contribution, an average can be obtained and defined as the contribution of factor X to the distributional component of poverty:

$$P_R(X_i) = 0.5\{[P(X_i, X_j) - P(\mu_i, X_j)] + [P(X_i, \mu_j) - P(\mu_i, \mu_j)]\} \qquad (8)$$

$$P_R(X_j) = 0.5\{[P(X_i, X_j) - P(X_i, \mu_j)] + [P(\mu_i, X_j) - P(\mu_i, \mu_j)]\} \qquad (9)$$

Is the above an arbitrary or ad hoc procedure? No, according to the Shapley value founded on the cooperative game theory (Shapley 1953; Moulin 1988; Shorrocks 1999; Sastre and Trannoy 2002). The Shapley value also ensures the validity of (2) and (3) when the poverty components are obtained according to (4)–(9).

Figure 10.1 illustrates the Shapley procedure when there are three input variables $X1$–$X3$. In the Figure, crossed Xs denote mean values of Xs, $P(Y)$ represents poverty levels for a given poverty line when Y are obtained by substituting Xs or crossed Xs into the underlying function $Y = f(X1 - X3)$. The symbols $C1$–$C3$ represent marginal contributions of Xs, calculated as the difference in poverty between the relevant two boxes. It is noted that the same procedure will be used in decomposing the overall endowment component and also for constructing the framework of poverty difference accounting in section 10.3. Readers are referred to Shorrocks (1999) for technical details, including various proofs.

The key feature of the Shapley procedure lies in the replacement of arguments in the relevant function, for example replacing Xs by their mean values. In the first round (corresponding to the first layer of Figure 10.1), one argument is replaced at a time. In the second round (second layer of Figure 10.1), two arguments are replaced at a time. This continues until the Kth round where all arguments are replaced at once. At each round, all possible combinations of replacement must be exhausted and estimates for the same marginal contribution are averaged to obtain an expected contribution. The expected contributions from different rounds are then averaged again to produce the final contribution.

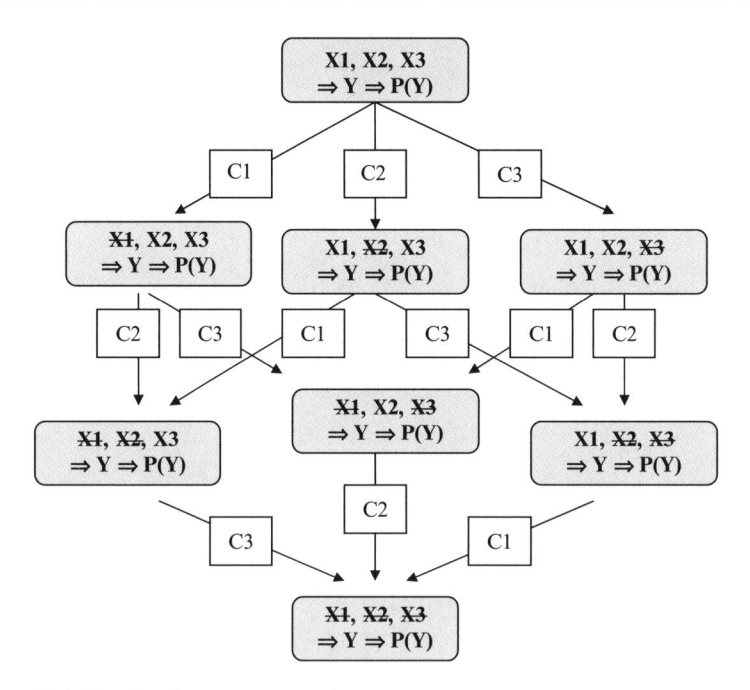

Figure 10.1: Shapley decomposition of poverty

It is possible that redistribution of one factor, say X, is sufficient to wipe out poverty. In this case, two scenarios must be considered. In the first scenario, all factor redistributions except that of X contribute nothing to poverty reduction. Consequently, the Shapley procedure assigns 100 per cent contributions to X, zero to other factors, say $\underline{X}$. In the second scenario where redistributions of $\underline{X}$ contribute q per cent to poverty reduction, it is conceivable that policymakers may choose to redistribute these factors. Consequently, the marginal contribution of factor X equals to 100 minus q. Thus, the averaged percentage contribution of factor X is $0.5(100 + 100 - q) = 100 - 0.5q$.

We now turn to the decomposition of the endowment component. Recall that when redistributions are sufficient for poverty elimination, this component is zero. In this case, its decomposition is not needed. Only when redistributions of all factors fail to completely eliminate poverty, such decompositions are useful in the sense that it will provide information on the relative importance of additional resources for poverty eradication. Referring to Figure 10.2, after accounting for the redistribution component, every agent is now operating at the same point in the production space, say C, where average Xs are used to produce μ_Y. Using Y^* to denote the indifference curve or isoquant given by $Y^* = f(X_i, X_j) = z$, the distance from C to the line Y^* indicates poverty severity after redistributing Xs. This distance signifies the shortfall of resources Xs needed for reaching the poverty line.

To eliminate poverty, point C must be moved onto or beyond Y^*. Since any point beyond Y^* is the same as those on Y^* as far as poverty elimination is concerned and the ultimate objective is poverty elimination with limited and costly resources, the optimal action is to simply move to a point on Y^*, say C^*. Consequently, the difference in poverty between points C and C^* can be defined as the endowment component of poverty. It must be kept in mind that no inequality is to be reintroduced when constructing the framework for decomposing the endowment component. That is, every agent must be assumed to possess equal amounts of resources at both C and C^*.

Once point C^* is located, decomposing the endowment component can proceed as follows. From C^* to B, no change occurs to X_i, thus the difference in poverty between C^* and B is due to shortfall in X_j. We can define this difference as the marginal contribution of X_j to the endowment component. The same marginal contribution can be obtained for the movement from B^* to C. Similarly, X_j remains unchanged from C to B, thus the difference in poverty between B and C can be defined as the marginal contribution of X_i, so is the difference in poverty between C^* and B^*. Based on the Shapley value, averages can be computed and defined as the final estimates of factor contributions to the overall endowment component. Since for any X it is always valid to write $X^* = \mu_X + \Delta X$, where X^* denote inputs at point C^*. The Shapley procedure described earlier can be applied here by replacing X^*s by the mean values of Xs or μ_X (point C in Figure 10.2).

How to identify C^* or X^* then? By theory of production, the optimal strategy is to move along the expansion paths of the function $Y = f(X_i, X_j)$. Once the

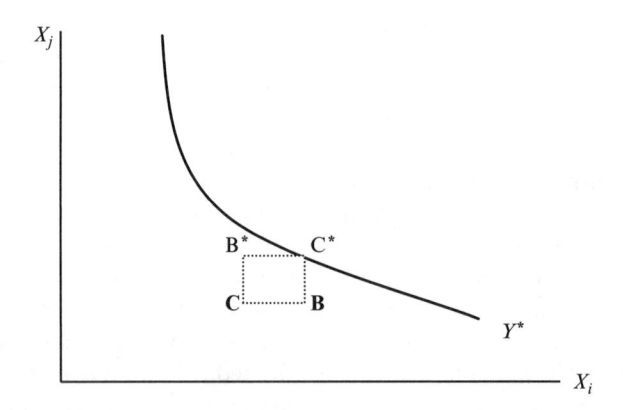

Figure 10.2: Decomposing the endowment component of poverty

function is estimated, it is straightforward to solve for X^* or ΔX. This, in general, requires information on factor prices of Xs, which may not be available in many cases, especially when human capital variables are involved. Fortunately, the popular Cobb–Douglas, CES, and homogenous translog functions, commonly used in production modelling, are homothetic. Under homotheticity, all expansion paths coincide and can be represented graphically as a straight line from the origin of the production space, implying proportionate usage of factor inputs. In this case, $X^* = r\mu_X$ for all Xs and $Y^* = f(r\mu_X) = z$, which can be solved for the only unknown scalar r. In the human capital literature, the semilog form or Mincerian function is most popular. This function is not homothetic. Under this circumstance, decomposing the total endowment effect into factor components does not seem possible unless factor prices for experience and education are known. In this case, one may rely on homotheticity as a reasonable assumption or approximation. It is noted that being unable to breakdown the overall endowment component does not affect the usefulness of other decomposition results.

Measurement of these endowment effects is informative not only because it allows ranking of various resources for poverty elimination. More importantly, it can shed light on the likely time horizon for poverty reduction. For example, if education is found to dominate the endowment component, a short-run solution may not be hoped for. On the other hand, if physical capital is dominating, aid and borrowings may suffice for significant reduction in poverty.

10.3 Accounting for Poverty Difference[6]

Accounting for poverty changes typically follows Datt and Ravallion (1992) which is similar to Jain and Tendulkar (1990) and Kakwani and Subbarao (1990). Apart from the perception issue discussed in the introduction section of this chapter, the Datt–Ravallion framework comes with a residual term which may obscure main findings from numerical analyses. Kolenikov and Shorrocks (2005) introduce the Shapley value approach, leading to the disappearance of the residual term. The latter, however, still maintains the output-based perception.

Let ΔP denote a poverty change and assuming both Y and z are measured in real terms (changes in the poverty line can also be accommodated), a change in poverty from time 0 to time T can be written as:

$$\Delta P = P(Y_T; z) - P(Y_0; z) \qquad (10)$$

By definition, the growth component is the change in poverty due to a change in the mean of Y while holding its dispersion (characterized by the Lorenz

---

[6] A parallel literature on decomposing inequality changes exists, see, for example, Mookherjee and Shorrocks (1982); Wan (1997, 2001); and Fields and Yoo (2000).

curve) constant. Meanwhile, the inequality or redistribution component is the change in poverty due to a change in the dispersion of Y while holding its mean constant. Using $Y(L,\mu)$ to represent a hypothetical distribution with Lorenz curve L and mean μ, and denoting the corresponding poverty by $P(L, \mu)$, ΔP can be expressed as:

$$P(Y_T;z) - P(Y_0;z) = P(Y_T;z) - P(L,\mu) + P(L,\mu) - P(Y_0;z) \quad (11)$$

Two ways exist for the construction of the hypothetical distribution $Y(L, \mu)$. Using the base period as the reference point, we can replace $P(L, \mu)$ by $P(L_0, \mu_T)$ which represents the poverty level when Y possesses the same dispersion as Y_0 but has the mean of Y_t or μ_T. Consequently, equation (11) becomes:

$$\begin{aligned}P(Y_T;z) - P(Y_0;z) &= [P(Y_T;z) - P(L_0,\mu_T)] + [P(L_0;\mu_T) - P(Y_0;z)] \\ &= [\text{inequality component}] + [\text{growth component}]\end{aligned} \quad (12)$$

If the terminal period is used as the reference point, we can replace $P(L,\mu)$ by $P(L_T;\mu_0)$ in (11) to produce:

$$\begin{aligned}P(Y_T;z) - P(Y_0;z) &= [P(Y_T;z) - P(L_T;\mu_0)] + [P(L_T;\mu_0) - P(Y_0;z)] \\ &= [\text{growth component}] + [\text{inequality component}]\end{aligned} \quad (13)$$

where $P(L_T;\mu_0)$ is defined analogously as $P(L_0,\mu_T)$. Adding up (12) and (13) and rearranging yield:

$$\begin{aligned}\Delta P = &\ 0.5\{[P(Y_T;z) - P(L_0,\mu_T)] + [P(L_T;\mu_0) - P(Y_0;z)]\} \\ &+ 0.5\{[P(L_0;\mu_T) - P(Y_0;z)] + [P(Y_T;z) - P(L_T;\mu_0)]\}\end{aligned} \quad (14)$$

The above is equivalent to using both periods as the reference point and taking the average. This is acceptable since using either period as the reference point is equally arbitrary or equally justified. In fact, equation (14) is identical to what Shorrocks (1999) derived using Shapley value. Thus, we can decompose poverty difference into a growth component G and an inequality component I without any residuals or parametric estimations:

$$G = 0.5\{[P(L_0;\mu_T) - P(Y_0;z)] + [P(Y_T;z) - P(L_T;\mu_0)]\} \quad (15)$$

$$I = 0.5\{[P(Y_T;z) - P(L_0,\mu_T)] + [P(L_T;\mu_0) - P(Y_0;z)]\} \quad (16)$$

How to obtain the hypothetical distributions $P(L_T;\mu_0)$ and $P(L_0;\mu_T)$? To leave the dispersion of a variable or Lorenz curve intact but with a new mean, one can simply scale the variable. That is, we can simply obtain $Y(L_T,\mu_0) = Y_T\mu_0/\mu_T$ and $Y(L_0;\mu_T) = Y_0\mu_T/\mu_0$.

Poverty Accounting

The above decomposition, while useful, does not provide sufficiently insightful details. It is more interesting to breakdown the overall growth and inequality components into those associated with individual factors. This is fairly straightforward for given $Y_t = f(X_{ti}, X_{tj})(t = 0, T)$ and changes in Xs. Let $r_i = \mu_{0i}/\mu_{ti}$ and $m_i = \mu_{ti}/\mu_{0i}$; both are scalars for scaling the X_i variable (the relevant notations corresponding to X_j can be defined in the same way). Then, a two-stage decomposition procedure can be established. In the first stage, the change from $P(Y_0; z) = P(L_0, u_0) = P(X_{0i}, X_{0j})$ to $P(Y_T; z) = P(L_T, \mu_T) = P(X_{Ti}, X_{Tj})$ can be decomposed into the inequality and growth components I and G using (15) and (16). The equivalence between (15) and (16) and those derivable using the Shapley value is demonstrated by Figure 10.3, where MC_I and MC_G denote marginal contributions to the overall inequality or growth components, respectively.

In the second stage, each of the marginal contributions can be attributed to individual Xs by the Shapley value. For example, the first round marginal contribution to poverty due to growth, corresponding to the path from $P(X_{0i}, X_{0j})$ to $P(m_i X_{0i}, m_j X_{0j})$, can be decomposed, as shown in Figure 10.4.

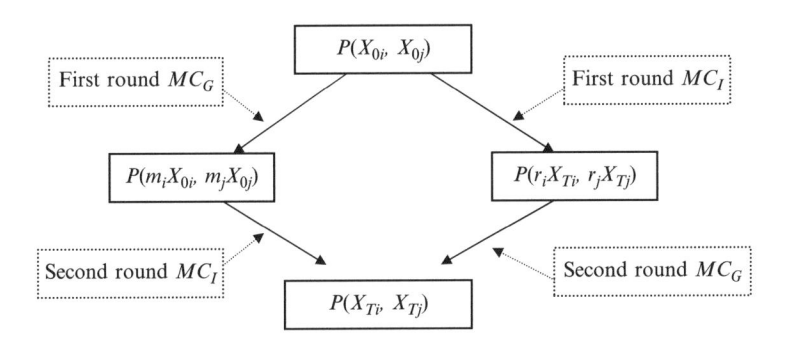

Figure 10.3: Decomposing poverty changes

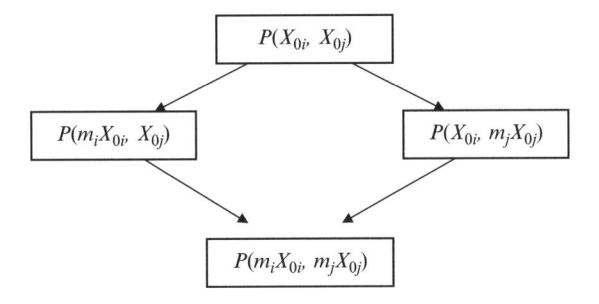

Figure 10.4: Decomposing a marginal contribution

The marginal contributions attributable to X_i and X_j are then given by:

$$MC_G(X_i) = 0.5\{[P(X_{0i}, X_{0j}) - P(m_i X_{0i}, X_{0j})] + [P(X_{0i}, m_j X_{0j}) - P(m_i X_{0i}, m_j X_{0j})]\}$$
$$MC_G(X_j) = 0.5\{[P(X_{0i}, X_{0j}) - P(X_{0i}, m_j X_{0j})] + [P(m_i X_{0i}, X_{0j}) - P(m_i X_{0i}, m_j X_{0j})]\}$$

Other marginal contributions shown in Figure 10.3 can be decomposed in a similar way. As usual, averages must be computed within each level and then across levels. Once again, the Shapley value will ensure $G = G_i + G_j$ and $I = I_i + I_j$ where I and G denote the inequality and growth effects attributable to the factors indicated by the relevant subscripts. Note that this decomposition procedure yields components of $P(X_{0i}, X_{0j}) - P(X_{Ti}, X_{Tj})$, which is positive as long as poverty decreases over time.

10.4 An Empirical Illustration: The Case of Rural China

Until recently, poverty had been basically a rural phenomenon in China. Success in poverty eradication since late 1980s is being hailed as an outstanding achievement of the Chinese government. However, despite continued efforts, reduction in poverty has slowed down considerably in the new millennium. And urban poverty has emerged after significant reforms in the labor market and urban sector. Nevertheless, a large majority of China's poor still live in the countryside. Unlike urban residents, the rural population does not have access to social welfare due to the absence of a social safety net (Chen and Wang 2001).

The purpose of this section is to illustrate the applicability of the proposed frameworks, not providing a full empirical study. This is largely due to lack of appropriate data. The data used in this chapter are from the Research Centre for Rural Economy (RCRE) of the Ministry of Agriculture of China. The RCRE survey began in 1986 and has since been conducted every year except for 1992 and 1994. All households covered by the survey are asked to keep records of incomes and expenses as well as other information. These are collected, checked, processed and reported by the survey team. The survey instruments have evolved over the years. Those used for 1986–91 were the same (with 312 variables). They were expanded for the 1993 survey (with 394 variables) and further expanded in 1995 (with 439 variables). Data between 1995 and 2002 only are used in this study to estimate the income generation function as they are consistent over time.

It is not possible to access the complete data set. For this study, we use data from three provinces, Guangdong, Hubei, and Yunnan. Guangdong, located in southeast China, is among the richest provinces. Hubei, a province in central China, is of a medium development status. Western China is represented by Yunnan, a well-known poor province. From each province, three villages are chosen, representing different development status within the county. While not claiming to be representative of China, the data do cover a variety of geo-economic conditions and are more representative than studies relying on data from a single province or single county. Morduch and Sicular (2002) use survey data of 259 rural households in Zouping county of Shandong province, covering the period of 1990–3.

Although observations for some 700 rural households over the period of 1995–2002 are used to estimate the empirical model, we only use 2000–1 data for poverty decomposition. This is done for two reasons. First, the empirical application only serves as an illustration, demonstrating the workability of the proposed framework. Use of 2000–1 data is sufficient for this purpose. Second and more importantly, implementing the proposed decomposition is rather difficult when sample sizes from different years differ. The 1995–2000 data come with different sample sizes for different years except for the years 2000 and 2001. Therefore, we only consider poverty and its change over these two years.

In specifying the needed income generation function for rural China, consideration must be given to both human capital theory and production theory. This is because farmers, unlike wage earners, must use land and physical capital in addition to labour in deriving their income. Thus, standard production inputs of land, labour, and capital should be included. The human capital theory calls for inclusion of skill variables such as education, training, and experience (often represented by age). As an accepted practice in the development literature, the education level and age of the household head will be used.

It is also necessary to consider factors which could alter income even if production inputs and human capital are the same. One such factor is the type of business activity that a household engages in, by which households are classified into ten different categories. These include cropping, forestry, animal husbandry, fishery, industry, construction, transportation, retailing, food, and other services, and finally no business activity. These indicate the main sector from which a household derives most of its income. Clearly, a set of dummy variables is needed to capture differences in income levels arising from different business activities. These dummy variables, taken together, will be referred to as a sector indicator. On the other hand, it is known that grain cropping in China is often enforced administratively due to low or negative returns (Wan 2004). Consequently, two identical households may receive different income simply because one grows grain and the other grows vegetable or other cash crops. Thus, cropping pattern is crucial, which is defined as the ratio of area sown to grain crops over total sown area. Finally, consider two rural households with the same amount of resources but one with wage earners and the other not. Wage earners are those working for the government or industries not run by the household. The number of wage earners reflects the level of urbanisation, thus its inclusion in the model enables one to make inference about the impact of urbanization on poverty in rural China. Ideally, urbanization should be defined at the town or county level. However, this is not possible given the availability of household level data only.

Geography is important in income determination as it is closely related to non-removable resources as well as to market access, infrastructure, and local culture. Data unavailability prevents direct inclusion of geographic variables. However, given the control for physical and human capital inputs and other factors, village dummies can be used to capture the effects of geography or location. It is noted that inclusion of these village dummies does not necessarily entail a fixed effects model as household level observations are to be used to estimate the income generation function. Finally, year dummies are included in the estimation to take into account technical changes and reform impacts.

The variables included in the income function are given below:

1. Dependent variable

    - Income: per capita annual net income

2. Independent variables (dummy variables not listed)

    - Capital: per capita capital stock
    - Land: per capita arable land area
    - Labour: number of labourers divided by household size
    - Wage earner: proportion of wage earners in household labour force
    - Education: number of schooling years of household head
    - Education squared
    - Training: proportion of household members who received vocational training
    - Age: age of household head
    - Age squared
    - Grain: ratio of grain sown area to total sown area

The choice of the parametric functional form is dictated by the standard Mincer model, augmented with production inputs and other variables. In other words, the income generation function takes the form of:

$$\text{Ln (Income)} = f(\text{Land, Labour, Capital}, \ldots, \text{dummy variables}),$$

where f stands for the standard linear function. The use of the semi-log specification is also prompted by the finding that the income variable can be approximated well by a log-normal distribution (Shorrocks and Wan 2005).

The panel data model can be estimated by various techniques. However, the iterative GLS method outlined in Kmenta (1986) is found to work well with Chinese data (Wan and Cheng 2001). This method allows for both

Table 10.1: Estimated income generation function (dummy variables not included)

Variable	Coefficient estimate	t-ratio	Level of significance
Capital	0.0958	15.59	0.000
Land	0.0192	2.59	0.009
Labour	0.5999	17.18	0.000
Wage earner	0.0224	3.43	0.001
Education	0.1365	3.72	0.000
Education squared	−0.0107	−1.51	0.130
Training	0.1318	2.74	0.006
Age	0.1450	4.88	0.000
Age squared	−0.0255	−5.33	0.000
Grain	−0.3164	−11.72	0.000
Constant	7.0841	84.61	0.000

Loglikelihood value = −4648.32
Sample size = 6121

Source: Author's calculations.

heteroscedasticity across households and autocorrelation over time. The model estimation results are tabulated in Table 10.1.

Leaving the dummy variables aside, all coefficient estimates are of the expected signs and most of them are statistically significant at the 1 per cent or 5 per cent level of significance. In particular, the negative estimates for the quadratic age and quadratic education variables are consistent with standard human capital theory. As expected, the cropping pattern variable, denoted by 'Grain' in Table 10.1, has a negative and significant coefficient estimate.

In what follows, we group education, training, and age to form a new term, namely 'human capital'. Similarly, the grain, wage-earner, and business-type dummies are combined to form what is termed 'structure', indicating farming structure. The village dummies, taken together, will be referred to as location. It is important to note that when data set contains matching observations, the location variable remains the same over time thus its impact on poverty changes must be nil. When observations do not match as in this chapter, the location variable captures the impact of location on poverty.

Before proceeding to poverty decomposition, two issues must be dealt with. First, poverty measure(s) must be chosen. In this chapter, the family of poverty measures developed by Foster et al. (1984) or FGT measures will be used. It is important to point out that the proposed frameworks place no restrictions on the choice of poverty measures: any measure can be used. However, since a useful feature of the devised methodology lies in its capability to disentangle the redistribution effects, the transfer axiom becomes particularly relevant. It is thus recommended not to use measures insensitive to transfers such as the headcount ratio. When redistribution is insufficient to eliminate poverty, the headcount ratio always yields a value of 1 for the overall endowment component and always $1/K$ for each of the K production factors. The poverty gap ratio satisfies the weak transfer axiom but not the strong version; it is not sensitive to transfers among the poor. The squared poverty gap ratio satisfies both. Thus, we will not place much significance on the results under the headcount or poverty gap ratio. Second, a poverty line must be determined. Following conventional practice, the absolute rather than relative poverty line will be used. Recognizing possible sensitivity of analytical results to poverty lines, three poverty lines will be used: the official poverty line set by the Chinese government (RMB 625 in 2000), US$1 and US$2 a day (PPP-adjusted) poverty lines of the World Bank (equivalent to RMB 929.03 and 1858.05 in 2000). There is little change in the price level in rural China between 2000 and 2001.

Table 10.2 presents the level decomposition results, showing contributions to poverty due to existing inequality in the relevant factors. A positive (negative) value indicates decrease (increase) in poverty when the corresponding factor is equalized. It can be seen that the total redistribution components are all equal to the actual poverty levels. This finding is significant and surprising, significant in the sense that it is true in both 2000 and 2001 and no matter what poverty line or what poverty measure is used. And it is surprising because all endowment effects are nil, implying that China possesses sufficient resources to eliminate rural poverty under complete redistribution of income generating factors. Complete redistribution is of course not possible for some factors such as location or as far as policy feasibility is concerned.

Another major finding from Table 10.2 is that land inequality is a poverty reducing factor in every case, though its effect is small. Thus, redistribution of land will lead to increases in rural poverty in China. This is consistent with the observation that poor households are usually engaged in or more engaged in farming. In other words, the poor possess more land resource in China. This finding also corroborates well with the large positive contribution of the structure variable to poverty. The structure variable reflects allocation of household resources (labour, capital, land) to different activities such as non-farming, cash crop, grain, and so on. The large and positive contribution of the structure variable reflects gaps in returns among different economic activities. In fact, structure represents the second largest contributor to poverty in rural China, next to location or geography.

Not surprisingly, location factors contribute a dominant share to poverty in rural China. Depending on the year, the poverty line and poverty measure, this share varies between 37.2 per cent (in 2001 under the Chinese government official poverty line and using the squared poverty gap index) and 99.6 per cent (in 2001 under US$1 a day and using the headcount ratio). This part of poverty cannot be eliminated in the short-run despite that infrastructure investment may help poorly located farmers to increase income in the long run.

Poverty Accounting

Table 10.2: Effects of factor inequality on poverty level

	2000			2001		
Poverty line	RMB 625	US$1	US$2	RMB 625	US$1	US$2
			Headcount ratio (%)			
Capital	0.26	0.00	1.48	0.30	0.01	1.25
Land	−0.65	−0.06	−0.42	−0.59	−0.05	−0.42
Labour	−0.04	−0.06	2.38	0.19	−0.05	1.96
Structure	3.58	0.11	13.69	3.40	0.08	13.20
Human capital	1.49	0.08	5.04	1.35	0.06	5.00
Location	6.98	12.97	14.46	6.56	12.99	15.25
Sum	11.60	13.04	36.64	11.21	13.04	36.25
Poverty level	11.60	13.04	36.64	11.21	13.04	36.25
			Poverty gap index (x100)			
Capital	0.08	0.09	0.32	0.08	0.09	0.30
Land	−0.20	−0.23	−0.15	−0.19	−0.22	−0.14
Labour	0.15	0.07	0.34	0.21	0.12	0.31
Structure	0.88	1.00	2.49	0.83	0.95	2.42
Human capital	0.47	0.55	1.21	0.46	0.55	1.18
Location	1.11	4.39	9.62	1.05	4.30	9.55
Sum	2.49	5.88	13.84	2.44	5.79	13.61
Poverty level	2.49	5.88	13.84	2.44	5.79	13.61
			Squared poverty gap index (x1000)			
Capital	0.27	0.65	1.31	0.25	0.62	1.23
Land	−0.66	−1.61	−1.64	−0.62	−1.51	−1.55
Labour	0.70	0.96	1.33	0.82	1.30	1.60
Structure	2.15	6.84	11.43	2.06	6.48	10.96
Human capital	1.44	3.85	6.26	1.40	3.81	6.16
Location	2.42	16.71	61.55	2.31	16.17	60.79
Sum	6.32	27.40	80.23	6.21	26.87	79.20
Poverty level	6.32	27.40	80.23	6.21	26.87	79.20

Source: Author's calculations.

Among all the factors considered, uneven distribution of human capital ranks third in most cases as a positive contributor to poverty. Its absolute contributions are small, possibly because inequality in human capital is low, thanks to the public education system in rural China. Moreover, unlike in the urban areas, human capital does not seem to play a major role in income generation in rural China, as dictated by the current state of technology prevailing in rural economic activities. Nevertheless, educational inequality is likely to increase and premium for better education is likely to rise in rural China as industrialization proceeds. Therefore, the small contribution of the human capital variable must be interpreted with caution as far as future policy design is concerned.

The level decomposition results are consistent for 2000 and 2001 and across different poverty measures or poverty lines, with the only exception of labour contributions under the headcount ratio. These contributions change signs across different poverty lines, even for the same year. This is because the headcount ratio violates the transfer axiom so that inequality effects cannot be captured appropriately.

Table 10.3 shows components of the poverty change from year 2000 to year 2001. A positive value means poverty enhancing effect, and vice versa. It is noted that over this period average capital, structure, and labour inputs rose while other inputs decreased. These explain all the growth effects, being positive or negative. As reported in Wan and Zhou (2005), overall inequality declined from 2000 to 2001, which explains why sums of inequality effects are all negative in Table 10.3. Note that the overall changes in poverty match those reported in Table 10.2, showing constant or decreasing poverty from 2000 to 2001 in every case. For example, the poverty gap index shows a total change of −0.023 under US$2 a day. On the other hand, the contributions from all factors sum to −0.39 percent when the headcount ratio is used with China's official poverty line.

A number of interesting findings can be discerned from Table 10.3. First, growth in labour and human capital plus improvement in farming structure help to reduce poverty. Second, declines in physical capital and land inputs lead to increases in poverty. Third, worsening location, meaning that the 2001 sample contains more farmers from location-disadvantageous villages, dominates the growth effects (more than offsetting growth effects of all other factors combined). This renders the overall growth effects a positive value, making growth a poverty increasing contributor. Fourth, factor inequalities improved so overall inequality effects are negative or poverty reducing. In fact, the sum of inequality induced effects (poverty reducing) overweighs the sum of growth related effects (poverty increasing) in every case, giving rise to small reductions in total poverty. It is important to point out that all these four findings are robust to different poverty measures and different poverty lines.

While all growth effects are consistent in terms of signs across poverty measures and poverty lines, this is not the case with respect to inequality effects. This, again, is related to the differing properties of alternative poverty measures. Also, different poverty lines imply different poor populations under consideration. Unless all factor endowments are perfectly correlated with total income, which is unlikely, the inequality effects may well differ in sign under different poverty lines.

Under US$1 a day and the headcount ratio, no change is observed in the poverty level between 2000 and 2001. However, this zero-sum result is due to a poverty increasing growth effect of 0.46 and a poverty reducing inequality effect of −0.46. Without improving factor distributions, poverty would have been increased by 0.46 per cent due to negative growth of factor inputs. Such a finding clearly demonstrates the importance of redistribution in combating poverty. In fact, factor redistribution was more powerful than factor growth in eradicating poverty as the sums of inequality effects outweigh the growth counterparts in all cases of Table 10.3.

Table 10.3: Growth and inequality effects on poverty change from 2000 to 2001, by factors

	Poverty line = RMB 625			Poverty line = US$1			Poverty line = US$2		
	Growth (1)	Inequality (2)	Total (1) + (2)	Growth (3)	Inequality (4)	Total (3) + (4)	Growth (5)	Inequality (6)	Total (5) + (6)
Headcount ratio (%)									
Capital	0.002	0.013	0.015	0.001	0.001	0.002	0.003	0.022	0.025
Land	0.038	−0.301	−0.263	0.012	−0.103	−0.091	0.026	0.075	0.101
Labour	−0.036	0.196	0.160	−0.001	0.096	0.095	−0.124	0.123	−0.001
Structure	−0.278	0.297	0.018	−0.023	0.364	0.341	−1.193	0.775	−0.418
Human capital	−0.022	0.203	0.181	−0.001	0.199	0.198	−0.066	0.168	0.102
Location	3.751	−4.254	−0.503	0.468	−1.013	−0.544	1.419	−1.619	−0.200
Sum	3.455	−3.846	−0.391	0.456	−0.456	0.000	0.065	−0.456	−0.391
Poverty gap index (%)									
Capital	0.001	0.002	0.002	0.001	0.002	0.003	0.002	0.007	0.009
Land	0.017	0.056	0.073	0.016	−0.012	0.004	0.017	−0.049	−0.033
Labour	−0.014	−0.074	−0.088	−0.014	−0.002	−0.016	−0.046	0.117	0.071
Structure	−0.150	−0.193	−0.343	−0.140	0.001	−0.139	−0.392	0.240	−0.152
Human capital	−0.006	−0.099	−0.105	−0.006	0.026	0.019	−0.023	0.124	0.101
Location	2.681	−2.276	0.405	2.287	−2.244	0.043	1.938	−2.166	−0.228
Sum	2.528	−2.583	−0.055	2.143	−2.228	−0.085	1.496	−1.727	−0.232
Squared poverty gap index (%)									
Capital	0.000	0.001	0.001	0.001	0.002	0.002	0.001	0.003	0.004
Land	0.008	0.057	0.064	0.013	0.031	0.044	0.014	−0.024	−0.009
Labour	−0.006	−0.056	−0.062	−0.011	−0.039	−0.050	−0.022	0.060	0.038
Structure	−0.071	−0.128	−0.199	−0.115	−0.106	−0.221	−0.213	0.075	−0.138
Human capital	−0.003	−0.070	−0.073	−0.005	−0.040	−0.045	−0.010	0.081	0.071
Location	1.275	−1.017	0.259	1.972	−1.756	0.216	1.972	−2.041	−0.069
Sum	1.203	−1.214	−0.011	1.854	−1.908	−0.053	1.741	−1.845	−0.104

Source: Author's calculations.

10.5 Conclusion

Given the overwhelming importance of the poverty–growth–inequality triangle (Bourguignon 2004), policymakers must face the vital and pragmatic questions: what output, or more fundamentally, what factor's growth or redistribution for poverty eradication—physical capital, human capital, or other inputs? Simply saying 'promoting growth' or 'reducing inequality' is far from being sufficient. Towards answering these questions, this chapter develops a procedure for attributing total poverty at a given point of time to components associated with income generating factors or resources. Another procedure is proposed to attribute a change in poverty to the growth and redistribution effects of individual income generating factors. These procedures are applied to a set of data from rural China, demonstrating the usefulness of the proposed frameworks. Empirical evidence, though limited, forcefully highlights the importance of redistribution more than that of growth as a policy instrument in setting poverty reduction strategies.

Theoretically speaking, redistribution can be complete in the sense that resources are evenly allocated among agents. It can also be partial in the sense that some endowments are to be taken from the rich for allocation among the poor. In this case, factor inequalities still exist after redistribution, although reduced. There is essentially an infinite number of ways to implement partial redistribution. Clearly, partial or incomplete redistribution is more feasible in reality. Nevertheless, complete redistribution is often assumed in the inequality literature when constructing counterfactuals. For example, in the classic example of inequality decomposition by population subgroups, the methodology is founded on the assumption of complete redistribution of total income within different groups. Another example is the popular Oaxaca–Blinder procedure, which assumes equal returns and complete redistribution of endowments within individual groups.

Though rare, redistribution may lead to worsening poverty, such as land redistribution in rural China. Needless to say, factor redistribution can be difficult to implement in reality. Unlike growth there is always a limit to the extent of redistribution. As far as policy instruments are concerned, however, redistributing factor inputs seem easier than redistributing outputs (such as income). Factor redistribution makes more sense in promoting sustainable growth as it gives the poor the means for income generation. Simply providing income support usually ends up with no future growth potential unless the support is invested not consumed.

References

Bourguignon, F. (2004). 'The Poverty–Growth–Inequality Triangle', mimeo, World Bank: Washington, DC.

Cancian, M., and D. Reed (1998). 'Assessing the Effects of Wives' Earning On Family Income Inequality', *Review of Economics and Statistics* 80: 73–9.

Chen, S., and Y. Wang (2001). 'China's Growth and Poverty Reduction: Recent Trends Between 1990 and 1999', paper presented at WBI–PIDS seminar Strengthening Poverty Data Collection and Analysis, Manila, 30 April–4 May.

Datt, G., and M. Ravallion (1992). 'Growth and Redistribution Components of Changes in Poverty Measures: A Decomposition with Application to Brazil and India in the 1980s', *Journal of Development Economics* 38: 275–95.

Dollar, D., and A. Kraay (2002). 'Growth *is* Good for the Poor', *Journal of Economic Growth* 7(3): 195–225.

Fields, G. S., and G. Yoo (2000). 'Falling Labor Income Inequality in Korea's Economic Growth: Patterns and Underlying Causes', *Review of Income and Wealth* 46(2): 139–59.

Foster, J., J. Greer, and E. Thorbecke (1984). 'A Class of Decomposable Poverty Measures', *Econometrica* 52: 761–5.

Jain, L. R., and S. D. Tendulkar (1990). 'Role of Growth and Distribution in the Observed Change in Headcount Ratio Measure of Poverty: A Decomposition Exercise for India', *Indian Economic Review* 25: 165–205.

Kakwani N., and K. Subbarao (1990). 'Rural Poverty and its Alleviation in India', *Economic and Political Weekly*.

Kmenta, J. (1986). *Elements of Econometrics*, Prentice-Hall: New Jersey.

Kolenikov, S., and A. Shorrocks (2005). 'A Decomposition Analysis of Regional Poverty in Russia', *Review of Development Economics* 9(1): 25–46.

Mookherjee D., and A. F. Shorrocks (1982). 'A Decomposition Analysis of the Trend in UK Income Inequality', *Economic Journal* 92(368): 886–902.

Morduch, J., and T. Sicular (2002). 'Rethinking Inequality Decomposition, With Evidence from Rural China', *The Economic Journal* 112: 93–106.

Moulin, H. (1988). *Axioms of Co-operative Decision Making*, Cambridge University Press: Cambridge.

Sastre, M., and A. Trannoy (2002). 'Shapley Inequality Decomposition by Factor Components: Some Methodological Issues', *Journal of Economics (Zeitschrift für Nationalökonomie)*, supplement 9: 51–90.

Shapley, L. (1953). 'A Value for N-Person Games', in H. W. Kuhn and A. W. Tucker (eds), *Contributions to the Theory of Games* Vol. 2, Princeton University Press: Princeton, NJ.

Shorrocks, A. F. (1980). 'The Class of Additively Decomposable Inequality Measures', *Econometrica* 48: 613–25.

—— (1982). 'Inequality Decomposition by Factor Components', *Econometrica* 50: 193–211.

—— (1984). 'Inequality Decomposition by Population Subgroups', *Econometrica* 52: 1369–85.

—— (1999). 'Decomposition Procedures For Distributional Analysis: A Unified Framework Based on the Shapley Value', unpublished manuscript, Department of Economics, University of Essex.

Shorrocks, A., and G. Wan (2005). 'Spatial Decomposition of Inequality', *Journal of Economic Geography* 5(1): 59–81.

Thorbecke, E. (2004). 'Conceptual and Measurement Issues in Poverty Analysis', WIDER Discussion Paper 2004/04, UNU-WIDER: Helsinki.

Wan, G. (1997). 'Decomposing Changes in the Gini Index By Factor Components', unpublished manuscript, Centre for China Economic Research, Peking University.

—— (2001). 'Changes in Regional Inequality in Rural China: Decomposing the Gini Index by Income Sources', *Australian Journal of Agricultural and Resource Economics* 43: 361–81.

—— (2004). 'Accounting for Income Inequality in Rural China', *Journal of Comparative Economics* 32(2): 348–63.

—— E. Cheng (2001). 'Effects of Land Fragmentation and Returns to Scale in the Chinese Farming Sector', *Applied Economics* 33: 183–94.

—— Z. Zhou (2005). 'Income Inequality in Rural China: Regression-Based Decomposition Using Household Data', *Review of Development Economics* 9(1): 107–20.

Index

Acemoglu, D. 19
agglomeration 93, 98, 126
Aghion, P. 4
agriculture 43–4, 158
Ahluwalia, M. 19
Alesina, A. 4, 11, 19
Andersen, T. B. 114
Anselin, L. 130, 131, 133
Arellano, M. 94
Arestis, P. 113
Armstrong, H. W. 127
Aroca, P. xiii, 79, 88, 125, 128, 133, 134
Ashenfelter, O. 163, 180
Atkinson, A. B. 6
Attanasio, O. P. 3
Au, C. C. 93
Audretsch, D. 146, 158
Aziz, J. 68

Banerjee, A. V. ix, 1, 6, 12
banks, state-owned 114–15
Bao, S. 127
Barro, R. J. 1, 2, 6, 7, 9, 64, 68, 69, 71, 75, 127, 130
Barsberg, B. L. 144, 146
Baumont, C. 128, 134
Beck, T. 114
Becker, G. 163, 180
Beijing 131–2, 146, 158
Benabou, R. 1, 4, 11, 127
Bencivenga, V. R. 113
Benhabib, J. 4
Benjamin, D. 39
Bera, A. K. 130
Bian, Y. 163

Bickenbach, F. 127, 128
Blau, P. M. 163, 180
Blundell, R. 119
Bode, E. 127, 128
Bodie, Z. 113
Bond, S. 119
Boudon, R. 173
Bourguignon, F. ix, 7, 19, 202
Boyreau-Debray, G. 117
Brakman, S. 93
Bramall, S. 81, 101
Brandolini, A. 6
Brandt, L. 37, 146, 153
Breen, R. 175
Brock, W. A. 13
Brooks-Gunn, J. 173
business cycles 2–3

Cai, F. 68, 69, 79
Cancian, M. 187
capital 90, 96
  see also human capital; investment
capital intensive heavy industries 58, 60, 62
Charumilind, C. 4
Chatterji, M. 128
Chen, B. 56
Chen, J. 58, 112, 126
Chen, S. 33, 37, 38, 43, 163, 194
Chen, Z. xi, 8
Cheng, Y. 69, 196
Christoph, D. 68
Clarke, G. R. G. 7, 9
Cloodt, M. 146

Index

coastal region:
  advantages of 126
  development 116
coastal-inland inequality 86, 116–17, 121
Coleman, J. S. 180
comparative advantage 58–9, 61, 75–6, 81, 82, 92
credit constraints 4
Cremin, L. 164
crime xv
Cultural Revolution 85, 96, 130, 165

data 66, 129
  average versus annual 2–3
  education 167–8
  financial development 120
  generating process (DGP) 3
  measurement errors 6
  patents 146
  population 83–4
  poverty 33–4, 37, 38–40, 44
data adjustment 84
  capital stock 103–4
  labour 104–6
  population 106
  provincial GDP 102–3
Datt, G. 34, 186, 191
Dayal-Gulati, A. 58, 68
de la Croix, D. 4
De la Fuentes, A. 130
Deininger, K. 19, 22
demand 4, 68
Demetriades, P. O. 113, 114
Démurger, S. 58, 112
Deng, Xiaoping 8, 61
Deng, Z. 163, 165
development strategies:
  comparative advantage defying (CAD) 62, 75
  comparative advantage following (CAF) 62, 65
Dewhurst, J. 128
Doepke, M. 4
Dollar, D. 184
Donnithorne, A. 81, 88

Du, Y. 68
Duflo, E. ix, 1, 6, 12
Duncan, O. D. 163, 180
Durlauf, S. N. 3, 6, 13, 127, 128

earnings:
  and education 180
  from wages 195–6
economic structure 68–9, 71, 75
  see also rural structure
economies of scale 81, 82, 92
education 101, 163–81
  compulsory 166, 169
  data 167–8
  dropouts 171, 175–6
  elementary and junior high 173–4
  endogenized 3
  expansion of 99, 100
  female 166, 171
  historical background 81, 164–7
  and innovation 153
  public 21, 26, 29
  returns to 163–4, 180
  urban bias 176–9
  see also human capital
education equation 8, 9, 10–11, 12
educational inequality 165–6
  inter-cohort 173–6
  inter-provincial 172–3, 175
  within cohort 169–73
efficiency, and equity 20
Ertur, C. 127
Esteban, J. 128
ethical judgement 90

famine 165
Fan, G. 21
Fan, P. xiii, 144, 160
Fan, S. 112
Fargerberg, J. 144
Feldman, M. 146, 158
Feng, Y. 56
Fields, G. S. 191
Figini, P. 38
financial development:
  and inequality 112–22

206

Index

the literature 113–14
model 118–20
financial reforms 114–18
Fingleton, B. 127–8
fiscal decentralization 61, 82
Fishman, A. 4, 11
Fleisher, B. M. 58, 112, 126
Forbes, K. J. 1, 2, 3
foreign direct investment (FDI) 58, 68, 92, 96–7, 158–9
Foster, J. E. 36, 86, 197
Fujian 82, 93
Fujita, M. 79, 92, 126, 134

Galor, O. 4, 11, 19
Gansu 178
Ge, Z. 127
generalized entropy 147, 154
geographic variables 196
 see also spatial effects
Giles, J. 39
Gini coefficient 18, 22–30, 147, 154
Goldthorpe, J. H. 175
Goodman, D. S. G. 79
Gottschalk, P. 180
government:
 expenditure 9
 investment funds 80–1
 investment policy 58
great leap forward 58, 62–4, 71, 83, 85, 164
Greenwood, J. 113
Greer, J. 36
Griliches, Z. 146
growth:
 and demand 68
 and economic structure 68–9, 71, 75
 input-based 185
 and inter-provincial inequality dynamics 80, 88–93
 neoclassical theory 64, 67, 68, 71
 and poverty 42–3
Guangdong 82, 93, 98, 146, 158
Guerrero, D. C. 145, 153
Guizhou 178

Guo, D. xiii
Gustafsson, B. 37

Hagedoorn, J. 146
Hannum, E. 167, 179, 180
Hasan, I. 112
Heerink, N. 3
Henderson, V. 93
Hewings, G. J. D. xiii
high-tech development 159
high-tech parks 144
Holz, C. A. 37, 79, 146, 153
Hu, A. 79
Hu, D. 79, 92, 126, 134
Huabei Area 158
human capital:
 definition 67, 197
 and inequality 5, 158
 and poverty 199–200
 see also education
human capital theory 195
human development 4
Hunan 178
Husain, A. M. 58, 68
Hussein, K. A. 114

Im, K. S. 93
income 7, 9
 grey 21–2, 27, 29
 regional disparities 56–76
 redistribution 20
income convergence 125–41
 the literature 125–9
income inequality 18–30
 the literature 18–22
industrial restructuring 96–7, 100
industrialization 19
inequality:
 changes in 129
 coastal-inland 86, 100–2, 116–17, 121
 decomposition 88–92
 distributional description 134–40
 of education 163–81
 and financial development 112–22
 and human capital 5

207

Index

inequality: (*cont.*)
  of innovation 145
  inter-provincial 83–92
  land 198
  and poverty 42–4
  provincial trends 83–8
  urban 25–6
  within-region xv, 87, 101
  see also educational inequality; income inequality; innovation inequality
inequality-growth nexus:
  empirical evidence 8–13
  models 5–8
  theories 4–5
  turning point 2
inflation 43, 83
infrastructure 21, 26–7, 29
innovation 144–61
  inequality 145
    decomposition 151–61
    measuring 147–51
  the literature 145–6
  regression analysis 153–61
institutional arrangements 21, 27, 29
investment:
  equation 10–11
  function 7
  funds 80–1
  policy 58
  spatial flows of 92
  see also capital

Jain, L. R. 34, 191
Japan 144
Jencks, C. 180
Jian, T. 68, 69, 79, 126, 130, 134
Jiang Zemin 79
Jovanovic, B. 113

Kakwani, N. 34, 191
Kanbur, R. 6, 163, 167, 176, 179
Keidel, A. 83, 84
Khan, A. R. 38, 39, 167
Kim, Y. J. 177
King, R. G. 113

Kitagawa, E. M. 177
Kmenta, J. 196
Knight, J. B. 176, 178, 180
knowledge production function 151–2
Kolenikov, S. 35, 191
Kraay, A. 184
Kroeber, A. 167
Krugman, P. 126, 127
Kuznets, S. ix, xii, 18–19, 125, 179
Kuznets curves 7–8, 9, 22–4, 30

labour 99, 104–6, 200
land 198, 200
Lardy, N. 80, 88
Le Gallo, J. 127, 128
Lee, M.-D. P. xiv, 58, 68, 112
Levine, R. 113, 114
Li, H. 1, 4
Li, S. 61, 176, 178
Liang, Z. xiii
Liaoning 98, 146
Lin, J. Y. xii, 56, 62–5, 81, 137
Lin, Y. 79
Liu, P. xii, 81, 137
location 153, 158, 198, 200
  see also spatial effects
Logan, J. 163
López-Bazo, E. 127, 135
Lu, M. xi, 8, 127
Lundberg, M. 3, 7
Lyons, T. P. 79, 83

Ma, J. 69
McKinnon, R. L. 113
Malecki, E. J. 144
Mankiw, N. G. 67
Mann, H. 164
Mansfield, E. 146
Mao 79, 165
Mare, R. D. 168
marketization index 21
Matthews, R. 180
Mayer, S. E. 12
Meng, X. 163
Merton, R. C. 113
Meyer, J. W. 164

Index

middle-class xv
migration 170
Mincer, J. 163, 180
Mitchell, D. W. 5, 9
Moav, O. 4
Moller, S. 180
Montouri, B. D. 127, 134
Mookherjee, D. 191
Morgan, S. L. 175
Morrison, C. 7
mortality rate 169–70
Mossi, M. B. 125, 127, 128
Moulin, H. 188

National Basic Sciences Initiative 144
National High-tech Research and Development Plan 144
national innovation system (NIS) 159–60
Naughton, B. 79, 80, 81, 88, 93, 94, 95
Nee, V. 163, 176, 180

oil 60
Open Door policies 115–16
openness 8

Partridge, M. D. 9
patents 145, 146
Paukert, F. 19
People's Bank of China (PBC) 114
Pepper, S. 164
Perotti, R. 12, 19
Persson, T. 4, 11
Polacheck, S. w. 180
polynomial inverse lag (PIL) 5, 13
population data 83–4
population growth 90
poverty:
   data 33–4, 37, 38–40, 44
   endowment component 186, 189–91
   and growth 42–3, 191–3
   inequality component 192–3
   measures of 197–8
   official line 198
   reduction x
   rural 39, 41, 46–9, 184–202

static and dynamic decomposition 184, 185–6
trends 34–8, 40–2, 43, 45, 51–3
unequal distribution 187–9
urban 39–40, 42, 50
poverty-growth-inequality (PGI) triangle ix–x, xi–xii
Preston, S. H. 177
private enterprises 56–8
privatization 8, 21, 27
production functions, provincial 89, 92–3
production theory 195
productivity:
   effects of agglomeration 93, 98
   total factor 90, 91–2, 94, 96, 100
Pudong New Area 158
Puga, D. 127

Quah, D. 128, 135, 136, 137

Raiser, M. 79
Ram, R. 114, 179
Ravallion, M. 33, 34, 37, 38, 41, 43, 163, 186, 191
Rawski, T. G. 79, 83
Ray, D. 128
redistribution 202
Reed, D. 187
reforms xiv, 61, 63
regional development strategy 80–2
regional protectionism 58
Rey, S. 126, 127, 128, 134, 135, 136, 138
Riskin, C. 39, 167
Robinson, J. 19
Rodrik, D. 4, 11
Roubini, N. 113
Rouse, C. 163, 180
rural structure 195, 197, 200
   see also economic structure
Rustichini, A. 4

Sabot, R. H. 180
Sachs, J. 127
Saint-Paul, G. 4, 113
Sala-i-Martin, X. 68, 69, 113, 127, 130
Sastre, M. 188

209

Index

savings index 67
Schumpeter, J. 144
Sen, A. 90
Sero, M. A. 145, 153
Sewell, W. H. 163, 180
Shandong 146
Shanghai 131-2, 158
Shapley, L. 188-9, 192
Shaw, E. S. 113
Shen, K. 69
Shorrocks, A. 35, 85-6, 187-8, 191, 192, 196
Sichuan 178
Siebert, W. S. 180
Silverman, B. W. 128, 136
Simhon, A. 4, 11
Simpson, M. 12
Smeeding, T. M. 180
Smith, B. D. 113
social security system 20-1, 26
Solow, R. M. 64
Song, L. 167, 171
Soviet Union 60
spatial effects 127-8, 137-9, 196
  see also location
spatial univariate measure 130-3
Speaker, P. J. 5, 9
special economic zones 82, 115
Squire, L. 3, 7, 19, 22
stability 4
state-owned enterprises (SOEs) 44, 64
stock markets 115
stratification 136
Strobino, D. M. 177
Studwell, J. 167
Subbarao, K. 34, 191
Sun, Y. 145, 150, 152, 153, 160

Tabellini, G. 4, 11
Tan, G. 64
Tan, K. 117
Tarp, F. 114
taxation 4, 62
technology 4
technology choice index (TCI) 65-7, 75
Tendulkar, S. D. 34, 191
Theil entropy measure 84, 85, 106-9

Thierry, V. 4
third front campaign 85
Thorbecke, E. 4, 36, 186
Tianjin 158
Todaro, M. P. 170
Torch programme 144
township and village enterprises
  (TVEs) 10
trade 158-9
Trannoy, A. 188
transfer payments 20, 26
transport and telecommunications
  26-7
Treiman, D. J. 163, 165
Tsiddon, D. 4, 11
Tsui, K.-Y. xiii, 38, 68, 69, 79, 83, 88, 112

unemployment 21, 26
university entrance 180
urban inequality 25-6
urban-rural divide x, 6, 10, 27-8
urbanization 8, 19, 20, 153
USA 144

viability problem 62-4, 75

wage earners 195-6
Wan, G. H. xi-xiv, 6, 8-10, 22, 39, 112,
  117, 121, 144-5, 154, 158, 191,
  195-6, 200
Wang, E. 127
Wang, M. 61
Wang, S. 79
Wang, X. xii, 21
Wang, Y. C. 164, 194
Wang, Z. 127
Watanabe, C. 144, 160
Weeks, M. 126
Wei, H. 69
Wei, S. 6, 117
welfare indicator 37, 43
Williamson, J. G. 125, 126
Wong, C. 20, 82
Wooldridge, J. M. 94
WTO 64, 76, 115
Wu, H. X. 83

Wu, X. 163, 167, 180
Wu, Y. 6

Xie, Y. 163, 167, 180
Xizang (Tibet) 177–8
Xu, X. 83

Yang, D. L. 63
Yang, D. T. 163, 164, 176
Yao, J. Y. 126
Yao, S. 127
Ying, L. 127
Yoo, G. 191
Yoo, K. 39
Young, A. 79, 83, 93, 102, 112

Zeira, J. 4, 11, 19
Zhang, J. 112
Zhang, K. 117
Zhang, L. 21
Zhang, X. 6, 112, 117, 163, 167, 176, 179
Zhang, Y. xii 117
Zhang, Z. 68, 127, 134
Zhao, Y. 170
Zhejiang 177–8
Zhou, M. 112
Zhou, X. 163, 164, 167, 171, 176
Zhou, Z. Y. 39, 117, 121, 158, 200
Zhu, H. 21
Zou, H.-F. 1, 4